"A must for anyone,
from novice to expert, who
is interested in birds."

—Seattle *Times*

The National Audubon Society Interactiv
CD-ROM Guide to North American Bird

With more than 700 species and 63 habits
brought to life with color photos, range ma,
songs, and text from 13 Audubon guides, s
is the multimedia reference for field and ba
yard birders, families, and classrooms.

Highest Ratings from the Detroit *Free Fre*

Ease of Use   ☆☆☆
Overall Multimedia Quality   ☆☆☆

· *both Mac and Windows systems* • ISBN 0-679-76016-4

wherever Audubon books are so
by calling 1-800-793-2665.

http://www.randomhouse.com/audubon/

National Audubon Society® Field Guide to North American Birds

A Chanticleer Press Edition

National Audubon Society®
Field Guide to
North American Birds

Western Region

Revised Edition

Miklos D. F. Udvardy
Revised by John Farrand, Jr.

Visual Key by Amanda Wilson
and Lori Hogan

Alfred A. Knopf, New York

This is a Borzoi Book.
Published by Alfred A. Knopf, Inc.

Copyright © 1994 by Chanticleer
Press, Inc. All rights reserved under
International and Pan-American
Copyright Conventions. Published in
the United States by Alfred A. Knopf,
Inc., New York, and simultaneously in
Canada by Random House of Canada,
Limited, Toronto. Distributed by
Random House, Inc., New York.

www.randomhouse.com

Knopf, Borzoi Books, and the
colophon are registered trademarks
of Random House, Inc.

Prepared and produced by
Chanticleer Press, Inc., New York.

Printed and bound by Dai Nippon
Printing Co., Ltd., Tokyo, Japan.

Published July 1977
Second edition, fully revised August
1994
Sixth printing, January 2001

Library of Congress Cataloging-in-
Publication Number: 94-7415
ISBN: 0-679-42851-8

CONTENTS

Part II Species Accounts

Part III Appendices

ACKNOWLEDGMENTS

The revisor is very grateful to Wayne R. Petersen, of the Massachusetts Audubon Society, for his critical reading of the entire text and his comments on the illustrations. His scrutiny has improved the accuracy of the book, but any remaining errors are the responsibility of the revisor.

This revision has been made possible by the creative and enthusiastic contributions of Andrew Stewart and his staff at Chanticleer Press: Edie Locke, Lori Hogan, Amanda Wilson, Deirdre Duggan Ventry, and Kelly Beekman. Paul Steiner, the founding publisher of Chanticleer Press, and Milton Rugoff, Gudrun Buettner, Susan Rayfield, Mary Suffudy, Kathy Ritchell, Helga Lose, and Carol Nehring all made highly valuable contributions to the first edition of this field guide. This revision has benefited greatly from the editorial skills of Amy Hughes. The revised edition follows the effective and workable design created by Massimo Vignelli for the first edition. The original range maps were researched by David Ewert, John Dunn, and Kimball Garrett, and were coordinated by Jill Farmer. The range maps themselves, including recent revisions, have been skillfully rendered by Paul Singer.

THE AUTHORS

Miklos D. F. Udvardy is Professor of Biological Sciences at California State University, Sacramento. He taught at the University of British Columbia from 1952 to 1966, has been a visiting professor in the German Federal Republic, in Honduras, and at the University of Hawaii, and has lectured at other universities. He is a Research Associate of the Los Angeles County Museum of Natural History and has been an officer of several North American ornithological associations as well as a member of eight international ornithological congresses. His specialties include biogeography, ecology, and animal behavior, but he is primarily a research ornithologist. He has published more than 185 scientific papers and several books, including *Dynamic Zoogeography* (1969).

The late *John Farrand, Jr.* authored several field guides, including the *National Audubon Society Handbooks* (McGraw-Hill, 1988) and several volumes in the *National Audubon Society Pocket Guide* series (Knopf). He was the general editor of the *National Audubon Society Master Guide to Birding* (Knopf, 1983). He was a past president of the Linnaean Society of New York, a Life Elective Member of the American

Ornithologists' Union, and a Life
Member of the Wilson Ornithological
Society. Before becoming a free-lance
nature writer, he served in the Division
of Birds at the Smithsonian Institution
and the Ornithology Department of the
American Museum of Natural History.
He watched birds in most parts of
North America, as well as in Central
America, South America, Europe,
Turkey, and East Africa.

INTRODUCTION

Each year thousands of people take up
the absorbing hobby of bird-watching,
or birding. Regardless of their motives,
their first goal is learning to identify the
hundreds of species in their own area.
This book has been prepared with the
intention of making that step as simple
and pleasurable as possible. The book's
pocket size and its format make it easy
to carry into the field and consult on the
spot. Take it with you. And welcome to
the hobby, or sport, or science, of birding.

Geographical
Scope
A number of American bird guides
divide North America into eastern and
western regions at the 100th meridian.
This is an arbitrary line that bears no
relationship to natural habitats. We
have chosen a line (see map) that
follows the eastern front of the Rocky
Mountains, a natural barrier in the
range of many eastern and western birds.
Of course, many birds can and do pass
over this barrier in both directions.
People who live near the dividing line
may need to own both this guide and
its eastern companion, the *National
Audubon Society Field Guide to North
American Birds (Eastern Region)*. Slowly
but surely, the number of species found
on both sides is increasing. Indeed, an
ornithologist long ago predicted that by
the year 2000 all the species in the

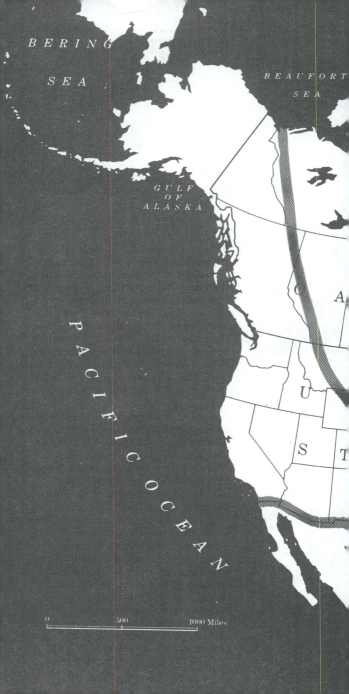

United States will have reached
California. This prophecy has not yet
been fulfilled, but the century is not
yet over.

Photographs as a   There are two major ways of illustrating
Visual Guide   bird guides, each with its advantages
and disadvantages: One is the
traditional way, by means of paintings,
and the other is a newer way, by means
of photographs. In these guides we have
chosen to use color photographs because
it has become possible in recent years
to obtain superb photographic portraits
of almost every bird seen regularly in
North America. In using the work of
America's leading bird photographers,
we believe we have added an exciting
dimension to what generally appears
in guides illustrated by an artist. Every
artist's rendering of a bird is his own
interpretation, whereas a good
photograph captures the natural color
and stance of birds as one usually sees
them. In most instances it also shows
birds in their usual habitat or in a
typical natural setting, making
identification that much easier. Finally
there is the beauty of pictures made
by outstanding photographers: This
guide is meant to be a delight to look
at as well as to use.

How the Guide   In most field guides the birds are
Works   arranged according to scientific
classification, which is based on
anatomic or even biochemical
differences. These features can be subtle
or even invisible in a living bird. What
a birder first notes when he or she
glimpses a bird is its size, shape, and
color. But if he then consults a standard
field guide, organized by families, he
must already know what family the bird
belongs to—whether it is a warbler, a
vireo, a finch—in order to locate it in
the guide. What he generally ends up
doing is thumbing laboriously through
the book until he happens on an

illustration that resembles the bird he has seen. By the time he finds what he is looking for, the bird may have disappeared. A new birder must go through this trial-and-error procedure each time he tries to identify a bird. To avoid this hit-or-miss approach, the photographs in this guide have been organized on visual principles, that is, by what you see. The 676 photographs (in the first half of the book) are arranged according to a bird's shape and, in most cases, its color or pattern. Captions under each pictured species include the plate number (which refers to the photograph), the size of the bird, and the number of the page on which the species is described in the text. If the photograph is not of a breeding male—or an adult if the sexes are alike—that is also indicated.

Since you may be afforded only a brief glimpse of a bird, you must learn to note essential details quickly. Such essentials include the following:

Field Marks When you see a new bird, make note of such points as the size and shape of the bill (whether long or short, slender or stout, curved or straight), the tail (long or short, rounded, squared, wedge-shaped, notched, or forked), and the wings (long or short, rounded or pointed). Note any distinctive features such as a crest, eye rings, or wing bars, or a flashing white patch in the wings, in the tail, or on the rump. Many species have color patterns that identify them at a glance; by studying the pictures in this book in advance, you may be able to identify many species at first sight.

Relative Size It is useful to keep in mind the sizes of a few common species like the House Sparrow, Scrub Jay or Steller's Jay, American Robin, and American Crow so that you can quickly estimate the relative size of an unfamiliar bird.

Behavior   Note what the bird is doing. Is it alone, or in a flock? Is it walking like a starling, or hopping like a sparrow? Is it foraging in foliage, like a warbler or a vireo? Is it foraging on the ground like a thrasher or a sparrow? Is it creeping about on the trunk of a tree? If so, is it hitching up the tree like a woodpecker or a creeper, or is it working its way headfirst down the trunk like a nuthatch? If the bird is in flight, is it flapping or soaring? If it is soaring, are the wings held horizontally, as with gulls and most hawks, or in a shallow V or dihedral, as with the Turkey Vulture, Rough-legged Hawk, and Northern Harrier? If the bird is in the water, is it feeding at the surface or diving? Make note also of the bird's song or calls.

What the Photographs Show   Most of the photographs show adult males, or adults when the sexes are alike, since the plumages of these are characteristic of a species, but pictures of females (♀), immatures (imm.), juveniles (juv.), color phases, and birds in winter plumage are also included when they differ significantly from the typical breeding male or adult.
The photographs are grouped according to (*a*) obvious similarities in appearance, such as "Long-legged Waders" or "Duck-like Birds," or (*b*) a visible similarity in behavior or habitat, as in "Tree-clinging Birds." Sometimes (*a*) and (*b*) coincide, as in "Chicken-like Marsh Birds," many of which not only look alike but have much the same lifestyle and live in the same habitat.

Groups   The photographs are grouped as follows:

Long-legged Waders
Gull-like Birds
Upright-perching Water Birds
Duck-like Birds
Sandpiper-like Birds
Chicken-like Marsh Birds
Upland Ground Birds

Owls
Hawk-like Birds
Pigeon-like Birds
Swallow-like Birds
Tree-clinging Birds
Hummingbirds
Perching Birds:
   Brown
   Red
   Orange
   Yellow
   Olive
   Green
   Blue
   Gray
   Black

These broad categories are of course not foolproof and are intended to serve only as a starting point.

Within each major category, the birds are grouped according to other similarities. Thus, among the "Duck-like Birds" the photographs of the Canvasback and Redhead, or of the Common Goldeneye and Barrow's Goldeneye, are shown together so that they can be compared at a glance. Similarly, among the "Tree-clinging Birds" all the woodpeckers with barred backs are placed together for easy comparison.

Silhouette and Thumbprint Guides

Preceding the photographs is a section showing silhouettes of birds typical of each group. For example, the "Long-legged Waders" are represented by a silhouette of an ibis; and each type of bird within this group, such as herons, bitterns, and cranes, is also represented by a typical silhouette. To make it easy to locate each group, a silhouette typical of the group has been inset as a "thumbprint" on the left of all the picture spreads in that section.

Perching Birds: Grouped by Color

The perching birds are by far the largest category, but that term is now technically restricted to the songbirds that make up the group known as the

passerines. We have included additional
species that we thought belonged best
in this section, such as the cuckoos and
kingfishers. Because songbirds are so
numerous, these birds are arranged
according to their most prominent color
(either an overall color or a distinctive
patch) in the following nine groups:
Brown, Red, Orange, Yellow, Olive,
Green, Blue, Gray, and Black.
This arrangement of the perching birds
by color depends, of course, on such
factors as the light in which a bird is
seen or even on individual judgment
as to color. A few birds, such as the
multicolored male Painted Bunting,
do not fit easily into any single color
category. We have placed each species
in the color category where it seemed to
fit best. Since most birds the average
birder will see are perching birds, this
color key will help you make a more
rapid initial identification.
Finally, following this Introduction,
under the title "How to Use This
Guide" are samples of how to use this
book to identify a particular bird.

Species
Accounts:
Arranged by
Family

In the species accounts, which follow
the color plates, birds have been
grouped according to their formal
classification, as given in the 1983
edition of the American Ornithologists'
Union's *Check-list of North American
Birds* and as revised in *Check-list*
supplements published through 1994.
Bird species are grouped into families.
At the beginning of each family's
section in the text, a short essay
provides general information about
the birds in the family, emphasizing
features its members share. The
scientific classification can help in the
identification process: Even if you pick
the wrong photograph you will be
referred to a species account within a
family of similar birds. Reading about
the various members of the family may
allow you to identify the bird you saw.

The number to the left of the bird's English name is that of the photograph of the bird.

English and Scientific Names
The English or "common" names of birds are those accepted in the American Ornithologists' Union's *Check-list of North American Birds,* as revised through 1994. When a bird has recently had a different but widely used English name, we have included this name in quotation marks.

Every bird has a scientific name consisting of two Greek or Latin words. The first word is the genus and the second is the species. The genus, which is always capitalized, may include a number of species. Thus, the scientific name of the Mallard, *Anas platyrhynchos,* tells us that it is a member of the genus *Anas,* which includes most of the surface-feeding or dabbling ducks in North America and elsewhere. The species name, *platyrhynchos,* refers specifically to the Mallard. The scientific name of the Green-winged Teal, *Anas crecca,* tells us at once that this is another species of dabbling duck, closely related to the Mallard. Since common names vary not only from country to country but even from region to region within North America, the scientific names identify birds everywhere and provide ornithologists with an international language.

Species Descriptions
The first paragraph of each species account describes the physical characteristics of that bird—its size, color, distinguishing marks or features—often with reference to another related or similar bird. The description of each species covers all or almost all of the following:

Size
Measurements of average overall length (from tip of bill to tip of tail) of each species are given in inches, along with the metric equivalent. Since

measurements of either living birds or museum specimens depend on the way they are measured as well as the individual bird, these measurements are only approximate and are useful mainly for comparison.

Wingspread measurement (W.) is given for many of the larger birds.

Color and Plumage

The opening paragraph of each species account covers physical characteristics and plumage. In general, the most striking or distinctive features or field marks are italicized. While species such as Steller's Jay and the American Crow look much the same throughout the year and at every age, in many birds the plumage varies with age, sex, or season. In the European Starling, for example, adults of both sexes look much alike, but juveniles, instead of being glossy black like the adults, are dull gray; adults have white spots in winter and, except in late fall and early winter, a yellow bill. The breeding plumage is usually the brightest plumage in both sexes and is generally worn in spring and summer.

The young of some species, such as the Herring Gull, pass through a number of distinct plumages before they acquire their final adult plumage. In many species the male and female differ in appearance, but the young bird looks like the female; in the Black-headed Grosbeak, for example, the adult male is clad in black and rich tawny-orange, while the female and young are duller birds, streaked with brown like sparrows. Many species show seasonal variation: Male Eared Grebes are black above in the breeding season, with a black crest and golden ear tufts, but in winter they fade to a dark gray, losing the high crest and tufts. These variations in plumage may be puzzling at first, but one soon learns to recognize the major variations in each species. For several species that resemble each other closely, we have described the features that distinguish them. Certain birds, such as some of the hawks, ducks, gulls, and swallows, are likely to be glimpsed in flight. To help in recognizing them on the wing, many drawings of birds in flight have been provided.

Voice Most species have characteristic songs and calls. A few birds, among them some of the dull-colored flycatchers, are more readily identified by their songs and calls than by appearance. The song, generally more complex than any of the calls, is given to advertise ownership of a nesting or feeding territory, and in most species is sung only by males. Calls are usually shorter and simpler, and generally express some emotion, such as alarm or anger. A brief description or a simple phonetic transcription is given for all species. Although one can now obtain recordings of voices of many species, a knowledge of calls is best gained by experience with birds in the field.

Habitat We next describe the habitat or habitats that each species prefers—beaches, lakes, mountain coniferous forests, grasslands, city parks, suburban areas— as well as the type of area preferred within the habitat. When a species has a different habitat during the winter from that occupied during the breeding season, this, too, is indicated.

Nesting The eggs and nests of each species are briefly described. The number of eggs given is the range normally found in a nest; sometimes a larger clutch may be found, perhaps due to the fact that a second female has laid eggs in a nest.

Range The geographic range in North America is given for all species, even when the bird is one whose range extends beyond this continent. The breeding range is described first, followed by detailed information on the North American portion of the winter range. Following common practice, we have generally given the range of each species from west to east and from north to south. We have tried to name enough localities for the reader to be able to draw a clear line between the various points. Thus, when we say that Virginia's Warbler breeds from southeastern California, southern Idaho, and northern Colorado south to Arizona, New Mexico, and western Texas, a line connecting the first three localities defines the northern limits of the species' breeding range, and another line, drawn through the latter three localities, gives the southern limits. The term "local" is used when birds occur at widely scattered localities, usually because of very specific habitat requirements.

Range Maps   In addition to a statement of the geographic range, a range map is provided for species of more than irregular or casual occurrence within the area covered by this book. No range maps are provided for exclusively oceanic species or for species that appear only occasionally and in unpredictable places. On these maps the following designations are used:

 Breeding range

 Winter range

Areas in which a species occurs in both winter and summer are indicated by cross-hatching:

 Permanent range

Notes   At the end of each species account are notes on such subjects as behavior and feeding habits, population status, and lore.

How to Find   Although it is almost impossible to go
Birds   outdoors without seeing at least a few

birds, some advance planning will enable you to increase the number of species you see on a field trip. Many birds tend to confine their activity to one particular habitat, so you should plan to visit as many different habitats as possible during a day of birding. A good system is to begin your field trip at dawn, going first to a freshwater marsh. Rails, bitterns, and other marsh birds are most active and vocal at that hour, and a few minutes in a marsh at sunrise can be more productive than several hours later in the day. Desert birds, too, are most active in the early hours of the morning. From the marsh or desert you can go on to woodlands, fields, or thickets. Until the middle of the morning most songbirds are busily searching for food and singing and are relatively easy to see. From mid-morning until late in the afternoon land birds are quiet, while the birds of the beaches, lakes, and other aquatic or marine habitats are active all day. The middle of the day, then, is the time to search for herons, cormorants, ducks, and sandpipers. Late in the day land birds start singing and foraging again, so you can return to woods and other inland habitats to find species you may have missed in the morning. To round out a full day of birding, make an after-dark visit to a forest or wooded swamp to listen for owls.

The greatest variety of birds can be seen during the migration seasons. It is therefore a good idea to plan several field trips during the spring and fall. In spring the best time to search is during March, April, and the first half of May, when most migrant songbirds travel through western North America. Most migrating birds fly at night, breaking their journey during the day, when they rest and feed. They tend to gather in quiet places where food is easy to find. In woods along a stream, where there are newly opened leaves and an abundance of small insects, it is possible to see dozens of migrant species on a single spring morning. Migrating songbirds also concentrate in isolated groves of trees along the coast or in prairies and deserts, and in well-planted city parks. When the land bird migration tapers off in late May, sandpipers and plovers are still flying through. Then is the time to visit beaches, lakes, and marshes. The fall migration is under way by August, when the first of the sandpipers and plovers reappear. In September and October most of the songbirds pass through. The migration of ducks, geese, and other water birds continues into November; visits to lakes and bays will pay dividends then. While many species are rather tame, others are shy or secretive. Learn to move slowly and quietly, and avoid wearing brightly colored or black clothing. Some of these elusive birds can be lured into view by an imitation of the sound of a bird in distress, or by a whistled imitation of a screech-owl or pygmy-owl. Rails and certain other secretive species can be attracted by playing tape recordings of their calls.

PARTS OF A BIRD

The generalized drawing of a bird on the following two pages shows the external parts of a bird that are mentioned frequently in the species accounts in this book. Definitions of terms that are not in everyday use (such as "gorget" or "mantle") will also be found in the Glossary on pp. 789–794.

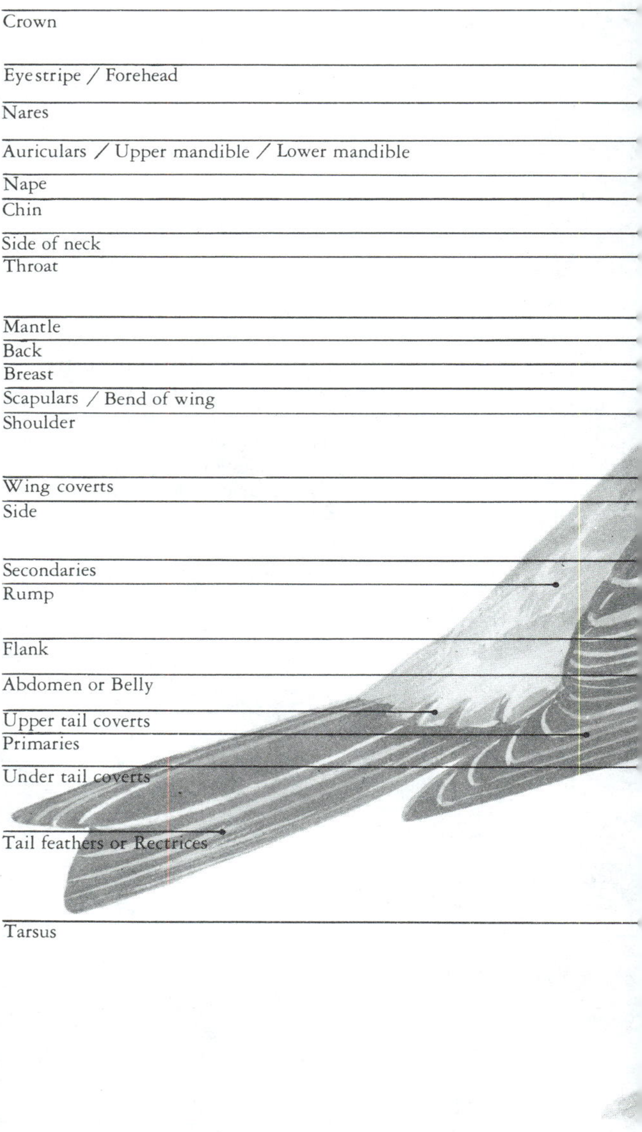

Crown

Eye stripe / Forehead

Nares

Auriculars / Upper mandible / Lower mandible

Nape

Chin

Side of neck

Throat

Mantle

Back

Breast

Scapulars / Bend of wing

Shoulder

Wing coverts

Side

Secondaries

Rump

Flank

Abdomen or Belly

Upper tail coverts

Primaries

Under tail coverts

Tail feathers or Rectrices

Tarsus

HOW TO USE THIS GUIDE

Example:
An Orange-
Capped Bird

You have seen a bird with an orange cap and underparts and a black throat, upper breast, back, and wings, perched on a tree limb in a park. It was smaller than an American Robin.

1. To make sure it was one of the Perching Birds, check the typical silhouettes preceding the entire color section.
2. Turn to the photographs in the section labeled Perching Birds.
3. Turn to the group of Perching Birds labeled Orange. Of the four photographs in this section, two resemble the bird you saw: Northern Oriole and Hooded Oriole. Of the two birds, only the Hooded Oriole has an orange cap.
4. The caption under the photograph of the Hooded Oriole will refer you to the page on which it is described. You find that the habitats listed include "city parks, and suburban areas with palm or eucalyptus trees and shrubbery," which helps confirm your identification.
5. The description further confirms the identification by describing the Hooded Oriole as having a black throat, upper breast, and wings, while the measurements indicate that this bird is smaller than an American Robin.

Example:
Birds Flying
Over a Beach

You have seen several birds flying
overhead. They had white bodies with
gray backs, white tails, yellow legs
and feet, and bills that were yellow
and black.

1. You turn to the bird silhouettes at the
   opening of the color section and find
   that your birds look most like the gulls,
   found in plates 19–45.
2. After glancing at the color plates, you
   find that the Herring Gull, Ring-billed
   Gull, and Glaucous Gull all resemble
   the birds you saw. But the Glaucous
   Gull has no black on its wing tips or
   bill, and the Herring Gull has pinkish
   feet and no black on its bill. Only the
   Ring-billed Gull seems to fit.
3. In the captions under the plates you find
   the page numbers on which these three
   birds are described. The descriptions
   confirm that the birds you saw were
   Ring-billed Gulls.

Part I
Color Key

Keys to the Color Plates

The color plates in the following pages
are divided into fourteen groups:

Long-legged Waders
Gull-like Birds
Upright-perching Water Birds
Duck-like Birds
Sandpiper-like Birds
Chicken-like Marsh Birds
Upland Ground Birds
Owls
Hawk-like Birds
Pigeon-like Birds
Swallow-like Birds
Tree-clinging Birds
Hummingbirds
Perching Birds

Thumb Prints To make it easy to locate a group, a
typical outline of a bird from that
group is inset as a thumb print at the
left edge of each double page of plates.
Thus you can find the Long-legged
Waders by flipping through the color
pages until you come to a series of
thumb prints showing the outline of a
typical wading bird.

Silhouettes of To help you recognize birds by their
the Families in general shape, the color plates are
Each Group preceded by pages that show silhouettes
of the families in each group. If the
bird you saw looks like one of these
silhouettes, you will find the bird in
that group.

Captions The caption under each photograph
gives the common name of the bird,
its size, and the page number on which
it is described. The color plate number
is repeated in front of each description
as a cross reference.
Most of the photographs show birds
in typical breeding plumage. Certain
birds, as indicated in the caption, are
also shown in distinctive immature,
juvenile, or winter plumage.

Symbol	Category
	Long-legged Waders

Family Symbols		Plate Numbers
	herons, egrets	1–8, 11–14
	bitterns	15–16
	storks	10
	ibises	18
	cranes	9, 17

Symbol	Category
	Gull-like Birds

Family Symbols		Plate Numbers
	gulls	19–45
	fulmars, shearwaters, albatross	57–66
	terns	46–55
	skuas, jaegers	56, 77–79
	tropicbirds	70
	frigatebirds	67
	boobies	68–69
	storm-petrels	71–76

Symbol	Category
	Upright-perching Water Birds
	Duck-like Birds

Family Symbols		Plate Numbers
	cormorants	80–84
	auks, murres, puffins	85–101
	diving ducks	102–104, 107, 109, 114–120, 124–125, 129–145, 148–151, 160–161
	surface-feeding ducks	105–106, 108, 110–113, 128, 146, 152–159, 162
	mergansers	122–123, 126, 164, 166–167
	coots	121
	stiff-tailed ducks	127, 147
	whistling-ducks	163, 165
	pelicans	186–187

Symbol	Category
	Duck-like Birds

Family Symbols	Plate Numbers
 swans	188–189
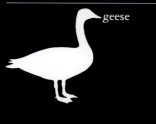 geese	190–196
loons	168–175
grebes	176–185

Symbol	Category
	Sandpiper-like Birds

Family Symbols		Plate Numbers
	plovers	215–216, 218–219, 245–246, 248–257
	sandpipers	197–214, 217, 220–235, 247, 258, 260–262
	phalaropes	239–244
	oystercatchers	259
	avocets, stilts	236–238

Symbol	Category
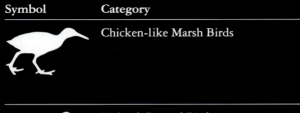	Chicken-like Marsh Birds
	Upland Ground Birds

Family Symbols		Plate Numbers
	rails	263–268
	nightjars	299–302
	grouse	269–275, 277–284
	roadrunners	285
	pheasants, quail, partridges	276, 286–290, 293–298
	turkeys	291–292

Symbol	Category
	Owls

Family Symbols		Plate Numbers
	true owls	303–315, 317–320
	barn owls	316

Symbol	Category
	Hawk-like Birds

Family Symbols		Plate Numbers
	ospreys	323
	caracaras	324
	vultures	321–322, 328
	hawks	329–342
	falcons	343–346, 351–353
	harriers	347–348
	kites	349–350
	eagles	325–327

Symbol	Category
	Pigeon-like Birds
	Swallow-like Birds

Family Symbols		Plate Numbers
	pigeons, doves	354–361
	swallows	362–369
	swifts	370–372

Symbol	Category
	Tree-clinging Birds
	Hummingbirds

Family Symbols	Plate Numbers
woodpeckers	373–396
nuthatches	398–400
creepers	397
hummingbirds	401–423

Symbol	Category
	Perching Birds

Family Symbols		Plate Numbers
	buntings, finches, sparrows	425, 427–430, 432–436, 438–455, 457–458, 463–465, 500, 502–507, 512, 515–517, 524–525, 532–533, 556–557, 562, 596–597, 602–605, 617, 619–620, 627, 635–636, 650–651, 659
	wood warblers	472, 494, 514, 519, 529, 540–555, 563–564, 628–629, 633–634, 648, 661
	flycatchers	521, 558–561, 566–581, 590–592, 631–632, 640, 655
	titmice	456, 536, 630, 638, 641, 644–647
	meadowlarks	534–535
	wagtails, pipits	460–462, 653

Symbol	Category
	Perching Birds

Family Symbols		Plate Numbers
	cardinals, grosbeaks	424, 493, 496–498, 513, 520, 539, 615–616, 618, 621
	orioles, blackbirds	459, 466–469, 508–511, 526–527, 537–538, 588, 658, 662–669
	tanagers	522–523, 530–531, 565, 589
	thrushes	426, 470–471, 473, 491–492, 499, 528, 606–609, 625
	trogons	518
	jays, magpies	610–614, 652, 654, 657, 660

Symbol	Category
	Perching Birds

Family Symbols		Plate Numbers
	shrikes	642, 643
	mockingbirds, thrashers	474–479, 623, 626
	wrentits	639
	silky flycatchers	671–672
	dippers	624
	becards	595

Symbol	Category
	Perching Birds

Family Symbols		Plate Numbers
	gnatcatchers, kinglets	593–594, 637, 649
	parrots	598–599
	kingfishers	600–601
	vireos	582–587
	wrens	484–490
	starlings	622, 656, 670

Symbol	Category
	Perching Birds

Family Symbols		Plate Numbers
	cuckoos	480–481
	waxwings	482–483
	larks	495, 501
	weaver finches	431, 437
	crows, ravens	673–676

The color plates on the following pages are numbered to correspond with the number preceding each species description in the text. Most of the birds shown are adults or adult males, but also shown are some distinctive females, immatures, and juveniles, as well as a few instances of seasonal changes in plumage.

Long-legged Waders

These are medium to large-sized water birds with long legs adapted for wading in fresh or salt water. Most of these species, such as herons, egrets, cranes, and ibises are conspicuously patterned, and many are entirely white.

1   **Snowy Egret nonbreeding plumage, 20–27″, p. 383**

2   **Snowy Egret, 20–27″, p. 383**

4   Great Egret nonbreeding plumage, 35–41″, p. 382

5   Great Egret, 35–41″, p. 382

6   Black-crowned Night-Heron, 23–28″, p. 387

7   **Cattle Egret**, 20″, p. 386

9 Whooping Crane, 45–50″, p. 470

10 Wood Stork, 40–44″, p. 390

11   Little Blue Heron, 25–30", p. 384

12   Tricolored Heron, 25–30", p. 385

13   **Black-crowned Night-Heron imm., 23–28″, p. 387**

14   **Green Heron, 16–22″, p. 386**

15   American Bittern, 23–34″, p. 380

16   Least Bittern, 11–14″, p. 381

17   Sandhill Crane, 34–48″, p. 469

Gull-like Birds

These water birds spend much of their time in flight. All have long, pointed wings. Gulls, terns, and boobies are predominantly white, while frigatebirds are black. Most of these birds occur along seacoasts or on the ocean, but some of the gulls and terns are found on inland waters.

19   Laughing Gull, 15–17″, p. 511

20   Franklin's Gull, 13–15″, p. 512

21   Common Black-headed Gull, 15″, p. 512

22 Bonaparte's Gull, 12–14", p. 513

23 Sabine's Gull, 13–14", p. 524

24 Ross' Gull, 12–14", p. 523

25   Yellow-footed Gull, 21–23″, p. 519

26   Western Gull, 24–27″, p. 519

27   Heermann's Gull, 18–21″, p. 514

28 Ring-billed Gull, 18–20″, p. 515

29 Herring Gull, 23–26″, p. 517

30 Mew Gull, 16–18″, p. 515

31   California Gull, 20–23″, p. 516

32   Thayer's Gull, 24″, p. 518

33   Bonaparte's Gull, winter plumage, 12–14″, p. 513

34   Glaucous-winged Gull, 24–27″, p. 520

35   Glaucous Gull, 28″, p. 521

37   California Gull first winter, 20–23″, p. 516

38   Glaucous-winged Gull juv., 24–27″, p. 520

39   Herring Gull juv., 23–26″, p. 517

40　Glaucous Gull first winter, 28″, p. 521

41　Mew Gull juv., 16–18″, p. 515

42　Western Gull imm., 24–27″, p. 519

43   **Black-legged Kittiwake, 16–18″, p. 522**

44   **Black-legged Kittiwake imm., 16–18″, p. 522**

46 Aleutian Tern, 13½–15″, p. 530

47 Gull-billed Tern, 13–15″, p. 525

Tern, 8–10″, p.

49   Caspian Tern, 19–23″, p. 526

50   Arctic Tern, 14–17″, p. 529

51   Elegant Tern, 16–17″, p. 528

52 **Common Tern,** 13–16″, p. 528

53 **Forster's Tern,** 14–15″, p. 530

55   Black Tern, 9–10″, p. 532

56   South Polar Skua, 21″, p. 510

57   Northern Fulmar, 18″, p. 358

58   Northern Fulmar, dark phase, 18″, p. 358

59   Black-vented Shearwater, 12½–15″, p. 363

60   Buller's Shearwater, 16½–18″, p. 361

61   Pink-footed Shearwater, 20″, p. 360

62 Sooty Shearwater, 16–18″, p. 362

63 Flesh-footed Shearwater, 19½″, p. 360

64 Short-tailed Shearwater, 13–14″, p. 363

65   Black-footed Albatross, 28–36″, p. 357

66   Laysan Albatross, 32″, p. 356

67   Magnificent Frigatebird, 38–40″, p. 378

68 Blue-footed Booby, 32–34″, p. 370

69 Brown Booby, 30″, p. 371

71　Black Storm-Petrel, 9″, p. 368

72　Ashy Storm-Petrel, 7½″, p. 367

73　Leach's Storm-Petrel, 8–9″, p. 366

74 Fork-tailed Storm-Petrel, 8–9″, p. 365

75 Wilson's Storm-Petrel, 7″, p. 365

77   **Pomarine Jaeger, 22″, p. 508**

78   **Parasitic Jaeger, 21″, p. 509**

Upright-perching Water Birds

These birds are usually seen perching on rocks or trees at the edge of the water. In most cases, their feet are located far back on the body, which gives the birds a distinctive upright posture when perching. The auklets, murres, and puffins are patterned in black and white, while the cormorants are largely or entirely black.

82 Double-crested Cormorant, 30–35″, p. 374

83 Neotropic Cormorant, 25″, p. 375

84   **Brandt's Cormorant** adult and imm., 33–35″, p. 376

86   Pigeon Guillemot, 12–14", p. 535

88   Common Murre, 17″, p. 533

89   Thick-billed Murre, 18″, p. 534

94   Horned Puffin, 14½", p. 544

95   Tufted Puffin, 14½–15½", p. 543

97 Parakeet Auklet, 10″, p. 540

98 Crested Auklet, 9½–10½″, p. 542

100   Cassin's Auklet, 8–9″, p. 539

Duck-like Birds

Included here are the many ducks, geese, and swans, as well as other birds that, like the ducks, are usually seen swimming. Many of the male ducks, and breeding-plumaged loons and grebes, are boldly patterned, while female ducks and winter-plumaged loons and grebes are clad in modest browns and grays.

102   **Eurasian Wigeon, 18–20″, p. 406**

103   **Canvasback, 19–24″, p. 407**

105   Cinnamon Teal, 14–17", p. 403

106   Northern Pintail, 25–29", p. 402

107   Common Goldeneye ♀, 16–20", p. 419

108   Green-winged Teal, 12–16″, p. 400

109   Bufflehead, 13–15″, p. 420

111 American Wigeon, 18–23″, p. 406

112 Northern Shoveler, 17–20″, p. 404

114   Lesser Scaup, 15–18″, p. 411

116   Tufted Duck, 17″, p. 409

117   Ring-necked Duck, 14–18″, p. 408

118　White-winged Scoter, 19–24″, p. 418

120   Surf Scoter, 17–21", p. 417

122   Common Merganser, 22–27″, p. 422

124   **Barrow's Goldeneye, 16½–20″, p. 419**

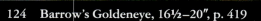

125   **Common Goldeneye, 16–20″, p. 419**

126   Hooded Merganser, 16–19″, p. 421

127   Ruddy Duck, 14–16″, p. 423

128 Blue-winged Teal, 14–16″, p. 403

129 Harlequin Duck, 14–20″, p. 415

130   King Eider, 18–25″, p. 412

131   Common Eider, 23–27″, p. 412

133 Spectacled Eider, 20½–22″, p. 413

134 Steller's Eider, 17–18½″, p. 414

135 Oldsquaw breeding plumage, 19–22″, p. 416

136   Greater Scaup ♀, 15–20″, p. 410

137   Lesser Scaup ♀, 15–18″, p. 411

138   Barrow's Goldeneye ♀, 16½–20″, p. 419

139   Tufted Duck ♀, 17″, p. 409

140   **Bufflehead** ♀, 13–15″, p. 420

142 **Black Scoter** ♀, 17–21″, p. 416

143 **White-winged Scoter** ♀, 19–24″, p. 418

144 Ring-necked Duck ♀, 14–18″, p. 408

145 Harlequin Duck ♀, 14–20″, p. 415

146   Wood Duck ♀, 17–20″, p. 399

148　　**King Eider** ♀, 18–25″, p. 412

150 Common Eider ♀, 23–27″, p. 412

151 Oldsquaw ♀, 15–17″, p. 416

152 Gadwall, 18–21″, p. 405

154   Mallard ♀, 18–27″, p. 401

155   Northern Shoveler ♀, 17–20″, p. 404

156   Green-winged Teal ♀, 12–16″, p. 400

157   Blue-winged Teal ♀, 14–16″, p. 403

160   Redhead ♀, 18–22″, p. 408

162 Northern Pintail ♀, 21–23″, p. 402

163 Fulvous Whistling-Duck, 18–21″, p. 391

164　Hooded Merganser ♀, 16–19″, p. 421

166 Red-breasted Merganser ♀, 19–26″, p. 423

mon Mergans

168   Red-throated Loon, 24–27″, p. 347

169   Common Loon, 28–36″, p. 349

171   Yellow-billed Loon winter plumage, 33–38″, p. 350

172   Pacific Loon winter plumage, 24″, p. 348

174   Red-throated Loon winter plumage, 24–27″, p. 347

175   Common Loon winter plumage, 28–36″, p. 349

177   Horned Grebe winter plumage, 12–15″, p. 352

178   Pied-billed Grebe winter plumage, 12–15″, p. 351

179   Eared Grebe winter plumage, 12–14″, p. 353

180   Western Grebe, 22–29″, p. 354

181   Clark's Grebe, 22–29″, p. 355

183　Red-necked Grebe, 18–20″, p. 352

184　Pied-billed Grebe, 12–15″, p. 351

d Grebe, 12–

186   **Brown Pelican, 45–54″, p. 373**

188   Tundra Swan, 48–55″, p. 393

189   Trumpeter Swan, 60–72″, p. 393

190   **Snow Goose, 25–31″, p. 395**

191   **Ross' Goose, 24″, p. 396**

193   **Brant, 22–30″, p. 398**

194   **Canada Goose, 22–45″, p. 398**

195   **Greater White-fronted Goose, 27–30″, p. 394**

Sandpiper-like Birds

This is a large group of small to medium-sized birds that have long legs and slender bills and are usually seen foraging on the beach or along the margins of lakes, ponds, marshes, or streams. Although these birds are collectively called "shorebirds," a few, such as the Killdeer, are often found on bare ground, far from water. Many of these birds are cryptically colored, but some, like the avocets and stilts, are boldly patterned in black and white.

197   Semipalmated Sandpiper, 5½–6¾″, p. 494

198   Least Sandpiper, 6″, p. 496

199   Western Sandpiper, 6½″, p. 494

200   Buff-breasted Sandpiper, 8″, p. 502

201   Pectoral Sandpiper, 9″, p. 497

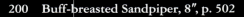

202   Spotted Sandpiper, 7½″, p. 485

203   Solitary Sandpiper, 8½″, p. 482

204   Baird's Sandpiper, 7½″, p. 497

206 Upland Sandpiper, 11–12½″, p. 485

207 Spotted Sandpiper winter plumage, 7½″, p. 485

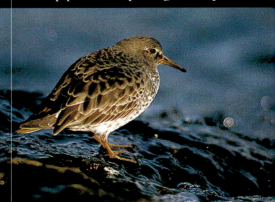

208 Rock Sandpiper winter plumage, 8–9″, p. 499

209 Semipalmated Sandpiper winter plumage, p. 494

210 Least Sandpiper winter plumage, 6″, p. 496

212   Greater Yellowlegs, 14″, p. 481

213   Lesser Yellowlegs, 10½″, p. 482

215 Ruddy Turnstone, 8–10″, p. 490

216 Black Turnstone, 9″, p. 491

218   Ruddy Turnstone winter plumage, 8–10″, p. 490

219   Black Turnstone winter plumage, 9″, p. 491

220   Sanderling winter plumage, 8″, p. 493

221   Red Knot winter plumage, 10½″, p. 492

222   Willet winter plumage, 15″, p. 483

224   Red Knot, 10½″, p. 492

225   Willet, 15″, p. 483

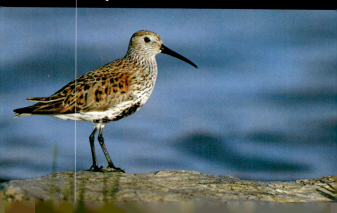

227 Short-billed Dowitcher, 12″, p. 503

228 Long-billed Dowitcher, 12″, p. 504

230   Whimbrel, 17″, p. 486

231   Long-billed Curlew, 23″, p. 487

232   Bristle-thighed Curlew, 17″, p. 487

233 Marbled Godwit, 18″, p. 489

234 Hudsonian Godwit, 15″, p. 488

236 American Avocet, 16–20″, p. 480

237 American Avocet winter plumage, 16–20″, p. 480

238 Black-necked Stilt, 13–16″, p. 479

239 Red Phalarope ♀ breeding plumage, 8″, p. 507

240 Red-necked Phalarope ♀ breeding plumage, p. 506

242   Red Phalarope winter plumage, 8″, p. 507

243   Red-necked Phalarope winter plumage, 7″, p. 506

244   Wilson's Phalarope winter plumage, 9″, p. 505

245   Surfbird breeding plumage, 10″, p. 492

246   Surfbird winter plumage, 10″, p. 492

248   Killdeer, 9–11″, p. 476

249   Semipalmated Plover, 6–8″, p. 475

251   American Golden-Plover, 9–11″, p. 472

252   Black-bellied Plover, 10–13″, p. 471

254 **American Golden-Plover winter plumage, p. 472**

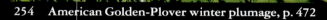

255 **Pacific Golden-Plover winter plumage, p. 474**

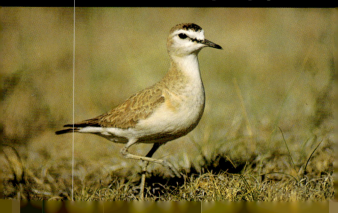

257   **Eurasian Dotterel, 8–9″, p. 477**

258   **Common Snipe, 10½″, p. 505**

259   **Black Oystercatcher, 17–17¼″, p. '78**

260   Stilt Sandpiper winter plumage, 8½″, p. 501

261   Ruff winter plumage, 11″, p. 502

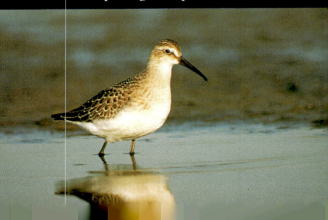

Chicken-like Marsh Birds

These are small to medium-sized marsh birds, most of which keep themselves well concealed in the reeds or marsh grasses. The bill may be long and slender, as in the Clapper Rail or Virginia Rail, or stubby and chicken-like, as in the Sora. The Common Moorhen, allied to the modestly plumaged rails that make up the rest of this group, is more often seen in the open and is more brightly colored.

263 Yellow Rail, 6–8″, p. 464

264 Clapper Rail, 14–16″, p. 465

266   Black Rail, 5–6″, p. 464

267   Virginia Rail, 9–11″, p. 466

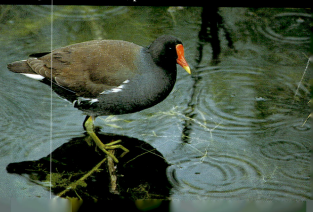

Upland Ground Birds

This group contains the familiar game birds—grouse, quail, and pheasants—as well as certain other cryptically colored birds of woodlands, such as the nightjars. Many of these birds are difficult to detect against a background of dead leaves or grass until they flush unexpectedly into the air.

269   Spruce Grouse, 15–17″, p. 451

270   Sharp-tailed Grouse, 15–20″, p. 457

271   **Blue Grouse, 15½–21″, p. 452**

d Grouse, 16–

273   Sage Grouse, 26–30″, p. 456

274   Blue Grouse, displaying male, 15½–21″, p. 452

275   Sage Grouse ♀, 22–23″, p. 456

277   White-tailed Ptarmigan, 12–13″, p. 454

278   Rock Ptarmigan, 13–14″, p. 454

280　White-tailed Ptarmigan winter plumage, p. 454

281　Rock Ptarmigan winter plumage, 13–14″, p. 454

282　Willow Ptarmigan winter plumage, 15–17″, p. 453

283 Lesser Prairie-Chicken displaying male, 16″, p. 457

284 Lesser Prairie-Chicken, 16″, p. 457

285 Greater Roadrunner, 24″, p. 554

286   Northern Bobwhite, 8–11″, p. 460

287   Northern Bobwhite ♀, 8–11″, p. 460

289 **Ring-necked Pheasant** ♀, 30–36″, p. 450

291　Wild Turkey ♀, 36″, p. 458

293   Gambel's Quail, 10–11½″, p. 461

294   Gambel's Quail ♀, 10–11½″, p. 461

296   California Quail ♀, ♂, 9–11″, p. 462

297   Montezuma Quail, 8–9½″, p. 459

299   Common Nighthawk, 10″, p. 569

301   Common Poor-will, 7–8½″, p. 570

302   Whip-poor-will, 10″, p. 571

Owls

This well-known group of birds scarcely needs a description. They are small to large birds with large round heads, loose, fluffy plumage, and disk-like faces. Many are nocturnal and are usually seen roosting quietly in trees during the day, but a few, such as the all-white Snowy Owl or the Short-eared Owl, often hunt by day and may be seen in open country.

303   Great Horned Owl, 25″, p. 558

304   Long-eared Owl, 15″, p. 565

305   Great Gray Owl, 24–33″, p. 564

307   Elf Owl, 5½", p. 562

309   Northern Saw-whet Owl, 7″, p. 567

310   Burrowing Owl, 9″, p. 562

311   Spotted Owl, 16½–19″, p. 563

312   Flammulated Owl, 6–7″, p. 556

313   Barred Owl, 20″, p. 564

314   Snowy Owl, 24″, p. 559

315 Short-eared Owl, 16″, p. 566

317　Northern Pygmy-Owl, 7–7½″, p. 560

318　Ferruginous Pygmy-Owl, 6½–7″, p. 561

319   Western Screech-Owl, 7–10″, p. 557

320   Whiskered Screech-Owl, 6½–8″, p. 558

Hawk-like Birds

The hawks and their allies range in size from the American Kestrel, scarcely larger than a Blue Jay, to the huge eagles and vultures. All have sharply hooked bills for tearing their prey, and many are often seen soaring high in the air. The wings may be rounded, as in the Red-tailed and Sharp-shinned hawks, or pointed, as in the falcons and some of the kites.

321   **Turkey Vulture, 25–32″, p. 425**

323 Osprey, 21–24″, p. 427

325   Bald Eagle imm., 30–31″, p. 430

327 Bald Eagle, 30–31″, p. 430

328 California Condor, 45–55″, p. 426

329 Zone-tailed Hawk, 18½–21½″, p. 438

330 Common Black-Hawk, 20–23″, p. 434

331 Gray Hawk, 16–18″, p. 435

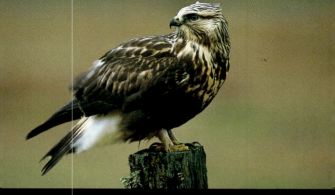

332   Rough-legged Hawk, 19–24″, p. 440

333   Red-tailed Hawk light phase, 18–25″, p. 439

334   Swainson's Hawk dark phase, 18–22″, p. 437

335   Cooper's Hawk, 14–20″, p. 432

336   Sharp-shinned Hawk, 10–14″, p. 431

338   Red-tailed Hawk dark phase, 18–25″, p. 439

339   Swainson's Hawk light phase, 18–22″, p. 437

340   Harris' Hawk, 18–23″, p. 435

341   Ferruginous Hawk, 22½–25", p. 440

342   Red-shouldered Hawk, 16–24", p. 436

343   Gyrfalcon, 22", p. 447

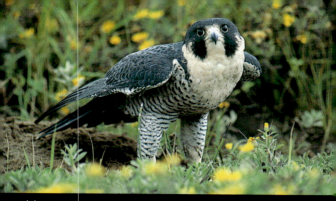

344   Peregrine Falcon, 15–21″, p. 446

345   Prairie Falcon, 17–20″, p. 446

347   Northern Harrier, 16–24″, p. 431

349   Mississippi Kite, 12–14″, p. 429

350   White-tailed Kite, 15–16″, p. 428

351   American Kestrel, 9–12″, p. 443

352   American Kestrel ♀, 9–12″, p. 443

Pigeon-like Birds

This group includes the familiar Rock Dove, or city pigeon, and its allies. These are small to medium-sized birds, small-headed, and clad in soft browns and grays. On the ground they walk with a characteristic mincing gait.

354   Inca Dove, 8″, p. 550

355   Mourning Dove, 12″, p. 549

357　Ringed Turtle-Dove, 12″, p. 547

358　Band-tailed Pigeon, 14–15½″, p. 546

360   Rock Dove, 13½″, p. 545

Swallow-like Birds

Included here are the swallows and martins and the similar but unrelated swifts. These are small birds that spend most of their time in the air, flying gracefully about in pursuit of their insect prey. They have pointed wings and often gather in large flocks.

362   Purple Martin ♂, ♀, 7–8½″, p. 622

363   Violet-green Swallow ♂, ♀, 5–5¼″, p. 624

364   Barn Swallow, 5¾–7¾″, p. 627

368　Cliff Swallow, 5–6″, p. 626

370   Black Swift, 7–7½″, p. 572

371   White-throated Swift, 6–7″, p. 574

Tree-clinging Birds

The woodpeckers, nuthatches, and creepers are usually seen climbing about on the trunks of trees, in search of insects hidden in the bark. Most of the woodpeckers are clad in black and white, although a few, like the Northern Flicker, are mainly brown. The nuthatches are soft gray above and whitish or rusty below, and the creepers are brown and streaked.

373 Downy Woodpecker, 6", p. 594

374 Ladder-backed Woodpecker, 7", p. 593

376   Red-naped Sapsucker, 8–9″, p. 591

377   Acorn Woodpecker, 8–9½″, p. 589

379 **Yellow-bellied Sapsucker, 8½″, p. 590**

381 Red-breasted Sapsucker, 8–9", p. 592

383   Lewis' Woodpecker, 10½–11½″, p. 588

385 Williamson's Sapsucker, 9½″, p. 592

386 Williamson's Sapsucker ♀ 9½″, p. 592

387 Black-backed Woodpecker, 9″, p. 597

389   Black-backed Woodpecker ♀, 9″, p. 597

390   Three-toed Woodpecker ♀, 8¼″, p. 597

391   Northern "Gilded" Flicker, 12″, p. 598

393 Northern "Yellow-shafted" Flicker, 12", p. 598

395   Downy Woodpecker ♀, 6″, p. 594

396   Ladder-backed Woodpecker ♀, 7″, p. 593

398   White-breasted Nuthatch, 5–6″, p. 648

399   Red-breasted Nuthatch, 4½–4¾″, p. 647

Hummingbirds

These tiny to small perching birds have rather short tails and long, thin bills. Metallic, flashy colors are displayed especially on head and throat (gorget) of male. Their display flights are often spectacular. Flying with a hum of fast-beating wings, they move forward or backward with equal ease. They hover over flowers, sucking nectar and taking insects from the flower, and they defend food sources with noisy calls and much chasing about.

401 Anna's Hummingbird, 3½–4″, p. 580

402 Lucifer Hummingbird, 3¾″, p. 579

403 White-eared Hummingbird, 3½″, p. 576

404 Anna's Hummingbird ♀, 3½–4″, p. 580

405 Costa's Hummingbird, 3–3½″, p. 581

406 Black-chinned Hummingbird, 3¼–3¾″, p. 579

407 Blue-throated Hummingbird, 4½–5″, p. 577

408 Blue-throated Hummingbird, ♀, 4½–5″, p. 577

409   Black-chinned Hummingbird ♀, 3¼–3¾″, p. 579

410   Allen's Hummingbird ♀, 3–3¼″, p. 584

411   Rufous Hummingbird, 3½–4″, p. 583

412   Allen's Hummingbird, 3–3½″, p. 584

414　Rufous Hummingbird ♀, 3½–4", p. 583

415　Broad-tailed Hummingbird ♀, 4–4½", p. 582

416　Costa's Hummingbird ♀, 3–3¼", p. 581

417   Broad-billed Hummingbird, 3¼–4″, p. 575

418   Magnificent Hummingbird, 4½–5½″, p. 578

419 Broad-billed Hummingbird ♀, 3¼–4″, p. 575

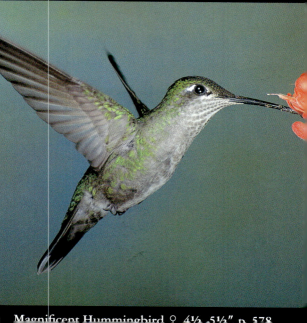

420 Magnificent Hummingbird ♀, 4½–5½″, p. 578

421 Violet-crowned Hummingbird, 3¾–4½″, p. 577

422 Calliope Hummingbird, 2¾–3¼″, p. 582

423 Broad-tailed Hummingbird, 4–4½″, p. 582

Perching Birds

This very large group includes nearly
all of the songbirds, as well as cuckoos
and kingfishers, which, while unrelated,
resemble songbirds rather closely.
They range in size from the four-inch
kinglets to the large crows and ravens.
They occur in a great variety of habitats
and show an even greater variety of
patterns and colors.

424   **Black-headed Grosbeak,** 7½″, p. 715

425   **Rufous-sided Towhee,** 7–8½″, p. 720

427　Lapland Longspur, 6–7″, p. 745

428　Dark-eyed "Oregon" Junco, 5–6¼″, p. 742

430   White-throated Sparrow, 6–7″, p. 739

431   House Sparrow, 5–6½″, p. 775

433   Black-throated Sparrow, 5¼″, p. 732

434   Chestnut-collared Longspur, 5½–6½″, p. 747

435   Lark Sparrow, 5½–6½″, p. 731

436　Golden-crowned Sparrow, 6–7″, p. 740

437　House Sparrow ♀, 5–6½″, p. 775

439 Fox Sparrow, 6–7½", p. 737

440 Clay-colored Sparrow, 5–5½", p. 728

Sparrow

442   Song Sparrow, 5–7″, p. 737

443   Lincoln's Sparrow, 5–6″, p. 738

445　**Baird's Sparrow,** 5–5½″, p. 735

446　**Grasshopper Sparrow,** 4½–5″, p. 736

447　**Cassin's Sparrow,** 5¼–5¾″, p. 733

448 Sage Sparrow, 5–6″, p. 733

449 Rufous-winged Sparrow, 5–5½″, p. 724

451   Black-chinned Sparrow, 5–5½″, p. 730

452   American Tree Sparrow, 5½–6½″, p. 726

453   Chipping Sparrow, 5–5½″, p. 727

454　Rufous-crowned Sparrow, 5–6″, p. 725

455　Five-striped Sparrow, 5½″, p. 734

456　Chestnut-backed Chickadee, 4½–5″, p. 642

457 McCown's Longspur, 5¾–6", p. 744

458 Smith's Longspur, 5¾–6½", p. 746

459 Bobolink ♀, 6–8", p. 749

460   American Pipit, 6–7″, p. 679

461   Red-throated Pipit, 6″, p. 679

ague's Pipit, 6

463   Lark Bunting ♀, 6–7½″, p. 734

464   Snow Bunting winter plumage, 6–7¼″, p. 747

465   Lazuli Bunting ♀, 5–5½″, p. 716

466   Red-winged Blackbird ♀, 7–9½″, p. 750

468   Rusty Blackbird ♀, 9″, p. 754

469   Yellow-headed Blackbird ♀, 8–11″, p. 753

470   Gray-cheeked Thrush, 6½–8″, p. 666

471   Swainson's Thrush, 6½–7¾″, p. 667

472　Northern Waterthrush, 6″, p. 705

473　Hermit Thrush, 6½–7½″, p. 668

474   California Thrasher, 11–13″, p. 675

475   Curve-billed Thrasher, 9½–11½″, p. 674

476   Bendire's Thrasher, 9–11″, p. 674

477   Sage Thrasher, 8½″, p. 673

478   Crissal Thrasher, 10½–12½″, p. 675

479   Le Conte's Thrasher, 10–11″, p. 676

480   Yellow-billed Cuckoo, 10½–12½″, p. 553

481   Black-billed Cuckoo, 12″, p. 552

482   Bohemian Waxwing, 7½–8½″, p. 681

484   Cactus Wren, 7–8¼″, p. 650

485   Bewick's Wren, 5½″, p. 652

486   Rock Wren, 5–6½″, p. 651

487   Canyon Wren, 5½–6″, p. 652

488   Winter Wren, 4–4½″, p. 654

490   Marsh Wren, 4–5½″, p. 655

491   Northern Wheatear, 5½–6″, p. 662

492   Veery, 6½–7¼″, p. 666

493   Pine Grosbeak ♀, 8–10″, p. 763

494   Yellow-rumped Warbler ♀, 5–6″, p. 699

496 **Blue Grosbeak** ♀, 6–7½″, p. 716

497 **Black-headed Grosbeak** ♀, 7½″, p. 715

498 **Evening Grosbeak,** ♀, 7½–8½″, p. 773

499   Mountain Bluebird ♀, 7″, p. 664

500   Pine Siskin, 4½–5″, p. 770

an Skylark, 7-   p. 621

502   Cassin's Finch ♀, 6–6½″, p. 765

503   House Finch ♀, 5–6″, p. 766

504   Purple Finch ♀, 5½–6½″, p. 764

505   Gray-crowned Rosy-Finch, 5¾–6¾", p. 761

506   Brown-capped Rosy-Finch, 5¾–6½", p. 763

508   Brown-headed Cowbird ♀, 6–8″, p. 757

509   Brown-headed Cowbird, 6–8″, p. 757

510   Common Grackle juv., 12", p. 756

512 Common Redpoll, 5–5½″, p. 768

513 Pine Grosbeak, 8–10″, p. 763

514 Painted Redstart, 5″, p. 708

515   Purple Finch, 5½–6½″, p. 764

516   Cassin's Finch, 6–6½″, p. 765

518　**Elegant Trogon,** 11–12″, p. 585

519　**Red-faced Warbler,** 5¼″, p. 707

521   Vermilion Flycatcher, 6″, p. 612

522   Hepatic Tanager, 7–8″, p. 710

524   White-winged Crossbill, 6–6½", p. 767

526   Hooded Oriole, 7–7¾″, p. 758

527   Northern "Bullock's" Oriole, 7–8¼″, p. 759

528   **Varied Thrush, 9–10″, p. 669**

529   **Olive Warbler, 4½–5″, p. 709**

534 Western Meadowlark, 8½–11″, p. 752

535 Eastern Meadowlark, 9–11″, p. 751

537   Yellow-headed Blackbird, 8–11″, p. 753

538   Scott's Oriole, 7½–8¼″, p. 760

ng Grosbeak   ½″, p. 773

540   Yellow-breasted Chat, 6½–7½", p. 709

541   American Redstart ♀, 4½–5½", p. 704

543   Wilson's Warbler, 4½–5", p. 707

544   Townsend's Warbler, 4¼–5", p. 701

545   Yellow-rumped "Audubon's" Warbler, p. 699

546   **Black-throated Gray Warbler, 4½–5″, p. 700**

547   **Magnolia Warbler, 5″, p. 698**

549   **Northern Parula,** 4½", p. 697

550   **MacGillivray's Warbler,** 4¾–5½", p. 705

551   **Nashville Warbler,** 4–5", p. 694

552   Grace's Warbler, 4½–5″, p. 702

553   Blackpoll Warbler imm., 5½″, p. 703

555   Tennessee Warbler, 5″, p. 693

556   Lesser Goldfinch, 3½–4″, p. 771

558   Tropical Kingbird, 8–9½″, p. 616

559   Cassin's Kingbird, 8–9″, p. 616

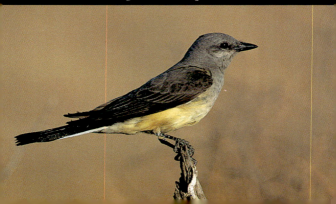

561 Thick-billed Kingbird, 9″, p. 617

562 Northern "Bullock's" Oriole ♀, 7–8½″, p. 759

563 Common Yellowthroat ♂, 4¼–5″, p. 706

564   Common Yellowthroat ♀, 4½–6″, p. 706

565   Western Tanager ♀, 6–7½″, p. 712

567   Sulphur-bellied Flycatcher, 7½–8½″, p. 615

568   Pacific-slope Flycatcher, 5½–6″, p. 608

570   Vermilion Flycatcher ♀, 6″, p. 612

571   Gray Flycatcher, 5½″, p. 607

573   Alder Flycatcher, 5–6″, p. 603

574   Buff-breasted Flycatcher, 4½–5″, p. 609

576   Brown-crested Flycatcher, 9½″, p. 614

578   Ash-throated Flycatcher, 8″, p. 613

6″, p. 602

580   Least Flycatcher, 5¼", p. 605

582   Red-eyed Vireo, 5½–6½″, p. 691

584   Solitary Vireo, 5–6″, p. 689

585   Solitary "Plumbeus" Vireo, 5–6″, p. 689

587   Hutton's Vireo, 4¼–4¾″, p. 690

588   Scott's Oriole ♀, 7½–8¼″, p. 760

590   Say's Phoebe, 7–8″, p. 611

591   Black Phoebe, 6–7″, p. 610

593   **Ruby-crowned Kinglet,** 3¾–4½″, p. 658

594   **Golden-crowned Kinglet,** 3½–4″, p. 657

595   **Rose-throated Becard,** 6½″, p. 620

596 Green-tailed Towhee, 6¼–7″, p. 719

598 Rose-ringed Parakeet, 15–17″, p. 551

600   Green Kingfisher, 8″, p. 587

601   Belted Kingfisher, 13″, p. 586

603   Painted Bunting, 5½″, p. 718

604   Varied Bunting, 4½–5½″, p. 718

606   **Mountain Bluebird, 7″, p. 664**

608   Eastern Bluebird, 7″, p. 663

609   Bluethroat, 4¾″, p. 661

610   Blue Jay, 12″, p. 630

611   Scrub Jay, 11–13″, p. 631

612   Pinyon Jay, 9–11¾″, p. 632

613   Steller's Jay, 12–13½″, p. 629

614   Gray-breasted Jay, 11½–13″, p. 632

615   Blue Grosbeak, 6–7½″, p. 716

616   **Northern Cardinal** ♀, 8–9″, p. 713

617   **Canyon Towhee**, 8–10″, p. 722

619   Abert's Towhee, 8–9″, p. 722

620   California Towhee, 8–10″, p. 721

uloxia ♀, 7½-

622 European Starling juv., 7½–8½″, p. 686

623 Northern Mockingbird, 9–11″, p. 672

625 Townsend's Solitaire, 8–9½″, p. 665

626 Gray Catbird, 8–9¼″, p. 671

628   Arctic Warbler, 4¾″, p. 656

630 Plain Titmouse, 5–5½", p. 644

631 Northern Beardless-Tyrannulet, 4", p. 600

632   Eastern Kingbird, 8–9″, p. 618

633   Virginia's Warbler, 4–4¼″, p. 695

635   Yellow-eyed Junco, 5½–6½″, p. 743

636   Dark-eyed "Gray-headed" Junco, 5–6¼″, p. 742

637   Blue-gray Gnatcatcher, 4½–5″, p. 650

638 Bushtit, 3¾–4″, p. 646

639 Wrentit, 6–6½″, p. 670

641   Bridled Titmouse, 4½–5″, p. 643

642   Loggerhead Shrike, 8–10″, p. 685

643   Northern Shrike, 9–10½″, p. 684

644   Black-capped Chickadee, 4¾–5¾″, p. 639

645   Boreal Chickadee, 5–5½″, p. 642

646   Mountain Chickadee, 5–5¾″, p. 640

647   **Mexican Chickadee, 5″, p. 639**

648   **Blackpoll Warbler, 5½″, p. 703**

649   **Black-tailed Gnatcatcher, 4½–5″, p. 659**

650   McKay's Bunting, 7″, p. 748

651   Snow Bunting, 6–7¼″, p. 747

653   White Wagtail, 7″, p. 678

654   Gray Jay, 10–13″, p. 629

656   Crested Myna, 10½″, p. 687

657   Black-billed Magpie, 17½–22″, p. 634

659   Lark Bunting, 6–7½″, p. 734

660   Yellow-billed Magpie, 16–18″, p. 634

661   American Redstart, 4½–5½″, p. 794

662   Red-winged Blackbird, 7–9½″, p. 750

663   Tricolored Blackbird, 7½–9″, p. 751

665   **Brewer's Blackbird,** 8–10″, p. 754

666   **Bronzed Cowbird,** 8½″, p. 757

667   Bronzed Cowbird ♀, 8½″, p. 757

668   Common Grackle, 12″, p. 756

669   Great-tailed Grackle, 16–17″, p. 755

670   European Starling, 7½–8½″, p. 686

671   Phainopepla, 7–7¾", p. 683

672   Phainopepla ♀, 7–7¾", p. 683

673   American Crow, 17–21", p. 635

674   Northwestern Crow, 16–17″, p. 636

675   Chihuahuan Raven, 19–21″, p. 637

676   Common Raven, 21–27″ , p. 637

Part II
Species Accounts

The number preceding each species
description in the following pages
corresponds to the number of the
illustration in the color plates section.
If the description has no number,
there is no color plate.

FAMILY GAVIIDAE
Loons

5 species: Northern Hemisphere. All
five species breed or have bred in North
America. These birds are excellent
swimmers and divers that prey mainly
on fish. They have long bodies with
webbed feet set far back, and long
pointed bills. When swimming they
ride low in the water. On the wing
loons hold both their heads and feet
below the level of the body, which gives
them a distinctive humpbacked flight
silhouette. Loons nest on lakes and
along rivers and spend the winter mostly
in coastal waters.

168, 174 Red-throated Loon
Gavia stellata

Description: 24–27″ (61–69 cm). A small loon
seldom seen far from salt water. In
breeding plumage, has *gray head and
neck, rusty throat,* black back spotted
with white. In winter, similar to
Common Loon but smaller, paler, with
bill thinner and seemingly upturned.

Voice: Call, rarely sounded away from breeding
grounds, is a series of high-pitched wails
and shrieks.

Habitat: Coastal and tundra ponds during
summer; large lakes, bays, estuaries, and
ocean in migration and winter.

Nesting: 2 brownish-olive, usually spotted eggs
in nest of aquatic vegetation floating in
or beside water.

Range: Breeds in Aleutian Islands, Alaska, and
Canadian Arctic south to British
Columbia, northern Manitoba, and
Newfoundland. Winters south along
Pacific Coast to southern California and
along Gulf Coast and both coasts of
Florida. Also in northern Eurasia.

While not as social as Pacific Loons,
wintering Red-throated Loons may

gather in large numbers where food is abundant. They are common on salt water of all depths but frequently forage in shallow bays and estuaries rather than far out at sea. Most loons must paddle furiously across the surface of the water before becoming airborne, but the small Red-throated can practically spring directly into the air from land, a useful ability on its tundra breeding grounds.

170, 172 Pacific Loon
Gavia pacifica

Description: 24" (61 cm). A *small* loon with *straight, slender bill.* In breeding plumage, head pale gray; neck and back black with white stripes; throat black with purple reflections. In winter plumage, blackish above, white below; often shows thin "chin strap." Red-throated Loon in winter is paler, with less contrast between dark crown and hindneck and white throat, and a seemingly upturned bill. Common Loon is larger, with stouter bill.

Voice: A harsh *kok-kok-kok-kok;* wailing notes on breeding grounds.

Habitat: Breeds on lakes and ponds in tundra and northern forests; winters on coastal bays and inlets and on the ocean.

Nesting: 2 spotted olive-brown eggs, usually in a slight depression lined with aquatic vegetation (sometimes on bare ground) at edge of water.

Range: Breeds from Alaska east to Hudson Bay, and south to northern British Columbia, Manitoba, and Ontario. Winters chiefly along Pacific Coast; very rare in northeastern United States.

Until recently thought to be a form of the Old World's Arctic Loon (*Gavia arctica*), the Pacific Loon is well named, for nearly all of these birds winter along the Pacific Coast. More social than other loons, this species frequently gathers in large flocks. On the northern breeding grounds adults often fly many miles between their nesting ponds and suitable feeding areas.

169, 175   Common Loon
Gavia immer

Description: 28–36" (71–91 cm). A large, heavy-bodied loon with a *thick, pointed, usually black or dark gray bill held horizontally.* In breeding plumage, head and neck black with white bands on neck; back black with white spots. In winter, crown, hindneck, and upperparts dark grayish; throat and underparts white.

Voice: Best-known call a loud, wailing laugh, also a mournful yodeled *oo-AH-ho* with middle note higher, and a loud ringing *kee-a-ree, kee-a-ree* with middle note lower. Often calls at night and sometimes on migration.

Habitat: Nests on forested lakes and rivers; winters mainly on coastal bays and ocean.

Nesting: 2 olive-brown or greenish, lightly spotted eggs in a bulky mass of vegetation near water's edge, usually on an island.

Range: Breeds from Aleutian Islands, Alaska, and northern Canada south to California, Montana, and Massachusetts. Winters along Great Lakes, Gulf Coast, Atlantic and Pacific coasts. Also breeds in Greenland and Iceland.

The naturalist John Muir, who knew the Common Loon during his early years in Wisconsin, described its call as "one of the wildest and most striking of all the wilderness sounds, a strange, sad, mournful, unearthly cry, half laughing, half wailing." Expert divers, loons have eyes that can focus both in air and under water and nearly solid bones that make them heavier than many other birds; they are able to concentrate oxygen in their leg muscles to sustain them during the strenuous paddling that can take them as far as 200 feet (60 meters) below the surface.

171, 173 Yellow-billed Loon
Gavia adamsii

Description: 33–38″ (84–97 cm). Breeding and winter plumages similar to those of Common Loon, but *bill ivory-yellow and seemingly upturned.* In winter plumage, has more white on face; typically shows dark spot behind eyes.

Voice: Calls similar to those of Common Loon.

Habitat: Tundra lakes and ponds in summer; inshore coastal waters in winter.

Nesting: 2 brownish eggs placed in a grass-lined depression, usually on an island at the water's edge.

Range: Breeds from northern Alaska and northern Canada east nearly to Hudson Bay. Winters along coast from Alaska south to British Columbia, and occasionally to California. Also in northern Eurasia.

This large loon, closely related to the Common Loon, nests in a relatively small part of the Arctic, and is probably the least abundant of the five loons that nest regularly in North America. A winter visitor to the West Coast, it is rare enough to attract crowds of birders whenever it appears.

FAMILY PODICIPEDIDAE
Grebes

21 species: Worldwide. Seven species breed in North America. Grebes are similar to loons, but smaller, and have lobed, rather than webbed, feet. Like loons, grebes dive expertly; they can also sink gradually out of sight, leaving

only their bills and nostrils above the surface. They eat fish but also take crayfish and other small aquatic animals. Grebes breed on lakes, ponds, and marshes, and build floating nests. They winter mainly on the coast.

178, 184 Pied-billed Grebe
Podilymbus podiceps

Description: 12–15″ (30–38 cm). Pigeon-sized. A stocky, uniformly brownish water bird, with *stout whitish* bill that has black ring around it during breeding season.

Voice: A series of hollow cuckoo-like notes, *cow-cow-cow-cow, cow, cow, cowp, cowp, cowp,* that slows down at the end; various clucking sounds.

Habitat: Marshes, ponds; salt water in winter if freshwater habitats freeze.

Nesting: 5–7 whitish eggs, stained brown, in a well-hidden floating mass of dead marsh vegetation anchored to adjacent plants.

Range: Breeds from British Columbia, southern Mackenzie, and Nova Scotia southward. Winters in southern states or wherever water remains open.

On ponds and marshes where it breeds, the Pied-billed Grebe advertises its presence with loud, barking calls. It eats small fish, crustaceans, and aquatic insects but is especially fond of crayfish, which it crushes easily with its stout bill. When alarmed, this grebe often sinks slowly into the water, resurfacing out of sight among the reeds. But it can also dive with amazing speed, a habit that has earned it the nickname "Hell-diver." It is also called the "Dabchick" in some areas.

177, 185 Horned Grebe
Podiceps auritus

Description: 12–15″ (30–38 cm). Small, slender-
necked, with short, sharply pointed bill.
In breeding plumage, body dark, with
rufous neck and flanks; head blackish,
with *conspicuous buff ear tufts.* In winter,
upperparts dark; chin and foreneck
white. The most common saltwater
grebe in the East.

Voice: Usually silent. On breeding grounds a
variety of croaks, shrieks, and chatters.

Habitat: Breeds on marshes and lakes; winters
mainly on salt water, but also on lakes
and rivers where the water does not
freeze.

Nesting: 4–7 bluish-white eggs, stained buff, on
nest of floating vegetation anchored to
marsh plants.

Range: Breeds from Alaska and northern
Canada south to Washington and
Oregon, Dakotas, and rarely to
Wisconsin. Winters in Aleutians and
south along Pacific Coast to southern
California, and along Atlantic and Gulf
coasts to Texas. Also in Eurasia.

Like other grebes, the Horned Grebe
swallows large numbers of its own
feathers, which lodge in the stomach
and prevent fish bones from passing into
the intestines. Even newly hatched
young eat feathers, taking those of their
parents. Birds of fresh water during
the nesting season, Horned Grebes
migrate to salt water for the winter,
but some can be found on open water in
the interior of California and other
western states.

176, 183 Red-necked Grebe
Podiceps grisegena

Description: 18–20″ (46–51 cm). A slender bird.
In breeding plumage, has rufous neck,
black cap, *whitish cheeks,* and *long, pointed*

yellowish bill. In winter, mainly gray, with paler cheeks, pale (not necessarily yellow) bill. In flight, distinguished from loons by its smaller size and white wing patches.

Voice: Usually silent. On breeding grounds, a variety of squeaks, growls, and wailing calls.

Habitat: Ponds and lakes in summer; coastal bays and estuaries in winter.

Nesting: 4 or 5 bluish-white eggs, stained brown, on a floating mass of dead reeds and grass in reedy lakes. Rarely nests in colonies.

Range: Breeds from Alaska and northern Canada south to Oregon, Idaho, Ontario, and southern Minnesota; rarely east to southern Quebec. Winters south along coasts to southern California and Georgia, rarely to Florida. Also in Eurasia.

Highly aquatic, grebes can swim with only their heads above water, concealing themselves in low pond vegetation. The young, handsomely striped in black and white, are often seen riding on the parents' backs. Like loons, grebes are expert divers, propelling themselves with their lobed toes as they pursue fish, crustaceans, and aquatic insects.

179, 182 Eared Grebe
Podiceps nigricollis

Description: 12–14″ (30–36 cm). A small, slender-necked, slender-billed grebe. In breeding plumage, black head and back; *golden ear tufts; black crest.* In winter plumage, dark gray above, white below; neck dusky. Similar in winter to Horned Grebe, but chunkier, and *bill appears slightly upturned,* sides of face smudged with gray, whitish patch behind ear.

Voice: On breeding grounds, frog-like cheeping notes.

Habitat: Marshy lakes and ponds; open bays and ocean in winter.

Nesting: 3–5 bluish-white eggs, stained brown, laid on a floating mass of vegetation in a marsh. Usually nests in dense colonies.

Range: Breeds from British Columbia, southern Manitoba, and Dakotas south to California and New Mexico. Winters on Pacific, Gulf, and Atlantic (rare) coasts, occasionally on open water in interior Southwest and Texas. Also in Eurasia.

In the fall most Eared Grebes migrate southwestward to the Pacific, but the species also winters on open water in the Southwest and as far east as Texas. Unlike the Horned Grebe, which supplements its diet with small fish, the Eared Grebe feeds almost exclusively on aquatic insects and small crustaceans. These birds are highly gregarious, not only nesting in large, dense, and noisy colonies but also assembling in large flocks in winter.

180 Western Grebe
Aechmophorus occidentalis

Description: 22–29" (56–74 cm). A large slender grebe with a *long neck*. Blackish above with *black of cap extending below eyes;* white below and on front of neck. *Bill long, slender, and greenish yellow.* Long white wing stripe shows in flight. See Clark's Grebe.

Voice: A rolling *kr-r-rick, kr-r-rick!* sounded most often on breeding grounds but sometimes heard in winter.

Habitat: Breeds on large lakes with tules or rushes; winters mainly on shallow coastal bays and estuaries.

Nesting: 3 or 4 bluish-white eggs, stained brown or buff, on a floating nest anchored to reeds. Nests in dense, noisy colonies.

Range: Breeds from British Columbia, Saskatchewan, and Minnesota south to southern California; sparsely in Arizona, New Mexico, and Colorado. Winters along Pacific Coast from southeastern

Alaska to California, on Gulf Coast of Louisiana and Texas, and on large river systems in West.

The mating display of the Western Grebe is spectacular, with both members of a pair paddling vigorously and churning across the surface of the water in an upright posture. Sometimes many pairs in a colony display simultaneously. During migration Western Grebes fly in loose flocks but spread out to feed during the day. On their coastal wintering grounds these birds often fall victim to oil spills and to insecticides that accumulate in their food, build up in their bodies, and reduce their breeding success.

181 Clark's Grebe
Aechmophorus clarkii

Description: 22–29" (56–74 cm). Very similar to Western Grebe, but black of cap does not reach eyes, so *face is largely white; bill bright yellow or orange-yellow.*

Voice: A loud *kr-r-rick,* not doubled as in Western Grebe; heard most often on breeding grounds.

Habitat: Breeds on large lakes with tules or rushes; winters mainly on shallow coastal bays and estuaries.

Nesting: 3 or 4 bluish-white eggs, stained brown or buff, on a floating nest anchored to reeds. Nests in dense, noisy colonies.

Range: Breeding range broadly overlaps that of Western Grebe, from British Columbia, Saskatchewan, and Minnesota south to southern California, and sparsely to Arizona, New Mexico, and Colorado. Winters along coast from southeastern Alaska to California, and on large river systems in West.

First described in 1858, at the same time as the Western Grebe, Clark's Grebe was originally regarded as a distinct species and then as a color phase of the Western Grebe. These two birds are once again considered separate species because they nest side by side with very little interbreeding. In most respects the two are alike. Clark's Grebe is more common in the southern portions of the combined range of the two species, and relatively rare in the northern part.

FAMILY DIOMEDEIDAE
Albatross

14 species: Mostly in the oceans of the Southern Hemisphere, all distinctly migratory. Three visit North America when not breeding. These seabirds are goose-sized or larger, with a powerful bill, hooked at the tip; tube-like nostrils; and very long, narrow wings that allow them to glide effortlessly over the waves, picking live squid or floating edibles from the ocean. They lay one egg in a scrape or mound on the beach, mainly on islands but also on remote coasts.

66 Laysan Albatross
Diomedea immutabilis

Description: 32″ (81 cm). W. 6′6″ (2 m). A *large, black and white seabird with very long wings and short tail.* Back, wings, and tail dark gray or blackish; head, neck, and underparts white; underwing white with black edging and irregular black patches; bill thick, hooked, and either yellow with gray tip or solid gray. Conspicuous dark patch around eye visible at close range.

Voice: Silent at sea, except for grunting calls when squabbling over food.

Habitat: Open ocean, usually well offshore.

Nesting: 1 buff-white egg in a shallow sandy depression on an offshore island. Nests in colonies.

Range: Breeds on mid-Pacific islands, chiefly in
Hawaiian chain. Rare visitor to offshore
waters of North Pacific and Gulf of
Alaska.

Although the Laysan Albatross occurs
off the West Coast less frequently than
the Black-footed Albatross, the Laysan
is regularly observed from Alaska
to northern California. Unlike the
Black-footed Albatross, it pays little
attention to refuse from ships, but
feeds mainly on squid. Sailors and
Pacific islanders know albatross as
"Gooney Birds."

65 Black-footed Albatross
Diomedea nigripes

Description: 28–36" (71–91 cm). W. 6'6"–7'
(1.9–2.1 m). A large, very long-winged
seabird. *Mainly blackish brown,* with
white on face and a dark bill. Amount of
white increases as birds age.
Conspicuous white primary shafts show
in flight. Some adults have white
undertail coverts. Glides like a
shearwater, with stiff wingbeats.

Voice: Shrieks and squeals during fights over
food; on nesting grounds, makes a
variety of bill-clapping sounds, quacks,
and whistles.

Habitat: Open ocean, rarely seen from shore.

Nesting: 1 dull-white egg, spotted with reddish
brown, in a shallow depression on the
ground. Nests on islands in loose
colonies.

Range: Breeds on islands in mid-Pacific Ocean.
Nonbreeding visitor along entire Pacific
Coast of North America.

The only albatross that regularly visits
the West Coast, the Black-footed is
most common during the summer, when
it can be found following shrimp or
fishing boats to feed on refuse. Its
primary diet consists of fish and squid,

which it catches mainly at night. Once they leave their nesting islands young albatross do not return for six or seven years. Aside from humans they have few enemies and may live for many years. Marked birds recaptured on Midway have reached 25 years of age or more.

FAMILY PROCELLARIIDAE
Shearwaters and Petrels

80 species: Worldwide. Only three species breed in North America, but many winter here. Members of this family, mainly oceanic in the nonbreeding season, nest in burrows on islands and along coasts, where they are chiefly nocturnal. These birds have tubular nostrils, webbed feet, and long pointed wings that are held stiffly during prolonged effortless glides low over the waves. As in the closely related storm-petrels, the nostrils are enclosed in horny tubes on top of the bill. Most species feed on fish, squid, crustaceans, or plankton. Among North American species shearwaters tend to be larger than petrels.

57, 58 Northern Fulmar
Fulmarus glacialis

Description: 18" (46 cm). A stocky gull-like seabird, seldom seen from shore. 2 color phases are common in the West: pale gray on back and wings, white elsewhere; and uniformly dark gray. Intermediates, as well as nearly all-white birds, also occur. *Bill yellow.* Easily distinguished from a gull by its flight: several fast wingbeats followed by a stiff-winged glide.

Voice: Chuckling and grunting notes when feeding; various guttural calls during breeding season.

Habitat: Open ocean; nests on cliffs and rocky

islands, often in colonies of many thousands of birds.

Nesting: 1 white egg placed on a bare rock or in a shallow depression or hollow lined with fresh vegetation.

Range: Breeds in Aleutians and on coasts and islands of Alaska and Canadian Arctic. Winters at sea, in Pacific Ocean south to California and in Atlantic south to North Carolina. Also in northern Eurasia.

The Northern Fulmar feeds on fish, squid, shrimp, and the refuse cast overboard by fishing boats. The expansion of commercial fishing in this century caused a great increase in the population of this species, especially in the North Atlantic, but new mechanized methods of processing fish at sea have reduced the amount of refuse, and numbers of these birds have begun to decline again.

Mottled Petrel
Pterodroma inexpectata

Description: 14" (36 cm). A small petrel with a distinctively short, heavy bill. Gray above, with *dark bars on upper surfaces of wings forming a flattened M shape;* darker gray on breast and belly. The undersides of the wings show broad, sharply defined black bands.

Voice: Usually silent at sea.

Habitat: Open ocean.

Nesting: 1 white egg placed in a burrow in a cliff or in a rock crevice.

Range: Breeds on islands off New Zealand. Spring and summer visitor to Bering Sea and cool northeastern Pacific; rarely south to Oregon and California.

At sea the Mottled Petrel flies rapidly, darting and gliding up and down over the waves more quickly than a shearwater, searching for fish and squid.

This petrel does not follow ships and
usually remains far from land.

61 Pink-footed Shearwater
Puffinus creatopus

Description: 20″ (51 cm). A gull-sized shearwater,
dark gray-brown above and whitish below;
undersides of wings are white with dark
borders. Bill pinkish with dark tip; feet
pale pink.

Voice: Silent at sea.

Habitat: Open ocean; seldom seen from shore.

Nesting: 1 white egg placed in a burrow on
an island.

Range: Breeds on islands off coast of Chile.
Nonbreeding visitor in summer to
waters off California and Oregon, rarely
as far north as southeastern Alaska.

This pale-bellied shearwater usually stays
far offshore, but when it comes within
sight of land it is often seen foraging
with flocks of smaller Sooty Shearwaters.
At such times thousands may gather at
places such as Monterey Bay or just
outside San Francisco's Golden Gate
strait. The Sooties often dive for food,
but the Pink-footed Shearwater seldom
does. A broad-winged species, it soars
more frequently and for longer periods
than other shearwaters.

63 Flesh-footed Shearwater
Puffinus carneipes

Description: 19½″ (50 cm). W. 3′3″ (1 m). Largest
and heaviest of the dark-bodied
shearwaters in the North Pacific. *Sooty
black above, below, and on wing linings;*
heavy pinkish or yellowish bill with
dark tip; pale pink feet. Wingbeats
slower than those of other shearwaters.
Sooty Shearwater has whitish wing
linings, dark bill and feet.

Voice: Usually silent at sea.
Habitat: Open ocean.
Nesting: 1 white egg laid in a burrow. Nests in colonies.
Range: Breeds on islands off western Australia, on Lord Howe Island east of Australia, and in New Zealand. Summer visitor to North Pacific south to British Columbia and more rarely to California.

This dark shearwater is most often found in feeding flocks of Sooty Shearwaters, where its larger size attracts attention. Its normal diet consists of fish and squid, but it has recently developed a habit of taking bait from fishing lines. Near its nesting grounds in the Southern Hemisphere it is often seen to dive, but seldom does so in northern waters.

60 Buller's Shearwater
"New Zealand Shearwater"
Puffinus bulleri

Description: 16½–18″ (42–46 cm). A small shearwater with a *blackish, wedge-shaped tail.* Gray above, with distinct *blackish cap; pure white underparts and wing linings.* In flight, dark bar on upper surface of wings and lower back forms an M-shaped pattern. Similar Mottled Petrel lacks black cap.
Voice: Silent at sea.
Habitat: Open ocean.
Nesting: 1 white egg laid in a burrow; nests in colonies.
Range: Breeds on islands near New Zealand. A summer visitor to North Pacific, appearing off West Coast from Aleutian Islands south to California.

This distinctive shearwater doesn't follow ships but searches for squid and crustaceans on its own. Its flight, more languid and graceful than that of most other shearwaters, is characterized by less frequent wing flapping and longer glides with wings arched. Buller's Shearwater is not a common bird in our waters, but is likely to be seen in pure flocks where its food is plentiful.

62   Sooty Shearwater
Puffinus griseus

Description: 16–18″ (41–46 cm). A large shearwater, uniformly dark sooty brown above and below, with whitish wing linings. Bill and feet dark.

Voice: Silent at sea; a variety of cooing and croaking notes on breeding grounds.

Habitat: Open ocean.

Nesting: 1 white egg laid in a burrow. Nests in colonies.

Range: Breeds on islands in cold southern oceans. Spends Northern Hemisphere summer in North Pacific and North Atlantic.

Sooty Shearwaters seen off our West Coast breed mainly on islands in the cool southwestern part of the Pacific Ocean. They raise their single chicks there and then migrate northward to spend the Southern Hemisphere winter on the warm seas of the North. The Sooty is the most abundant shearwater off our Pacific Coast, both near shore and at the edge of the continental shelf, where flocks of hundreds of thousands may be found at good feeding places. These flocks are worth inspecting closely because they often contain other, less common shearwaters.

64 Short-tailed Shearwater
"Slender-billed Shearwater"
Puffinus tenuirostris

Description: 13–14″ (33–36 cm). A dark shearwater,
with dark bill and feet. Distinguished
from Sooty Shearwater by slightly
smaller size, dull gray (rather than
whitish) wing linings, shorter tail and
bill, and slightly faster wingbeat.

Voice: Silent at sea.

Habitat: Open ocean.

Nesting: 1 white egg laid in a burrow in a
nesting colony.

Range: Breeds on coasts and islands of
southeastern Australia. Summer visitor
to Pacific Coast of North America,
from Bering Sea and Aleutian Islands
south to California; rare south of
British Columbia.

This species, abundant near its breeding
grounds, is called the "Mutton Bird" in
Tasmania and Australia, where the
young are taken for food. In the Bass
Strait, which separates Tasmania from
mainland Australia, an observer once
saw a flock he estimated to contain
150 million birds. After the breeding
season this species migrates in a great
figure eight: first northward toward
Japan, then on into the waters around
Alaska, then southward along the
Pacific Coast of the United States, and
then southwestward across its earlier
flight path to Australia.

59 Black-vented Shearwater
Puffinus opisthomelas

Description: 12½–15″ (32–38 cm). The smallest
shearwater that regularly visits the
West Coast. Blackish-brown above,
contrasting white underparts and wing
linings. Bill black, feet pink. Flight
rapid, with much flapping and little
gliding. The form that visits California

waters has dark undertail coverts and was formerly considered a race of the Manx Shearwater (*Puffinus puffinus*), a resident of the North Atlantic.

Voice: Usually silent at sea.

Habitat: Open ocean; often seen from shore.

Nesting: 1 white egg placed in a burrow or a crevice. Nests in colonies.

Range: Breeds on islands off Baja California. A year-round visitor to waters off southern California, most common in late fall and winter.

This bird flies close to the waves, its flight more fluttery than that of other shearwaters. It rarely follows ships, but feeds by snatching food from the water's surface and sometimes by diving. This shearwater even swims beneath the surface, aided by its wings. Its diet includes small fish and crustaceans.

FAMILY HYDROBATIDAE
Storm-Petrels

21 species: Worldwide in tropical and temperate oceans. Four species breed in North America. These small birds flutter over the surface of the water, where they feed on small crustaceans, fish, and plankton. Like the shearwaters, they have tubular nostrils on top of the bill. Most species are black, and some have white on the rump, but a few are gray. Because they are small and usually seen from the deck of a pitching boat, they can be difficult to identify; flight characteristics, rather than color and pattern, are often the best clues. Storm-petrels nest in burrows on offshore islands and isolated coasts, which they visit only at night.

75 Wilson's Storm-Petrel
Oceanites oceanicus

Description: 7″ (18 cm). A small seabird that darts
and skims over the waves like a swallow.
Black with *white rump, square-tipped or
rounded tail.* Has longer legs than other
western storm-petrels, with yellow webs
between toes.

Voice: A soft peeping, heard at close range
when birds are feeding.

Habitat: Open ocean.

Nesting: 1 white egg placed in a crevice among
rocks or in a burrow in soft earth.

Range: Breeds on islands in Antarctic and
subantarctic seas; in nonbreeding season
ranges northward over Atlantic, Pacific,
and Indian oceans; in eastern Pacific very
rarely north to Monterey Bay.

Wilson's Storm-Petrel, named after
the pioneer American ornithologist
Alexander Wilson (1766–1813), is
much rarer in the North Pacific than
it is in the North Atlantic. It has a
more fluttery flight style than other
black storm-petrels found on the West
Coast, and often hovers, dangling its
feet in the water, as it searches for food.
Nesting in immense colonies in the
Southern Hemisphere, it is a good
candidate for the world's most
numerous wild bird.

74 Fork-tailed Storm-Petrel
Oceanodroma furcata

Description: 8–9″ (20–23 cm). A *gray* storm-petrel,
somewhat darker above than below,
with forked tail but without white
rump. All other Pacific storm-petrels are
blackish. Flies with deep, regular
wingbeats.

Voice: Twittering and squeaking notes given
near nest.

Habitat: Open ocean; nests in colonies on rocky
islands.

Nesting: 1 white egg, with a ring of black or purplish spots around large end, placed in a burrow or crevice. Nests in colonies.

Range: Breeds on islands from southern Alaska south to northern California. Also on Pacific coast of Asia.

Fork-tailed Storm-Petrels use their nesting burrows year after year, the male and female often spending many days in the burrow together before the single egg is laid. Once they have an egg they incubate it irregularly, often leaving it for several days at a time. The chick inside thus grows slowly, taking as long as 68 days to hatch. These storm-petrels spend the day feeding at sea and approach their nesting islands at dusk. Birds still on the sea at night are attracted by lights and often gather near vessels.

73 Leach's Storm-Petrel
Oceanodroma leucorhoa

Description: 8–9″ (20–23 cm). A black storm-petrel with a *shallowly forked tail.* Birds nesting in the North Pacific south to central California have a *white rump with a dark center;* farther south, birds lack the white rump. Flies like a nighthawk, with much bounding and veering. This species seldom follows boats.

Voice: A variety of trills, screams, and cooing notes.

Habitat: Open ocean; nests on spruce-covered islands and rocky coasts.

Nesting: 1 white egg placed in a shallow burrow in the ground or hidden under a log. Nests in colonies.

Range: Breeds on coasts and offshore islands from Aleutians south to Baja California. Also breeds in western Pacific and North Atlantic south to New England. Winters mainly in tropical seas.

Visiting their nesting islands only at night, and preferring moonlit nights, Leach's Storm-Petrels locate their burrows partly by detecting the musky odor. Both female and male incubate the egg, changing places roughly every three days. The egg hatches in about six weeks, and the young bird leaves its burrow after about ten weeks.

72 Ashy Storm-Petrel
Oceanodroma homochroa

Description: 7½" (19 cm). An *all-black* storm-petrel with shallowly forked tail and somewhat rounded wings. Ashy color of head and neck and light mottling on undersides of wings may be visible at close range. Flies with very shallow wingbeats. Similar Black Storm-Petrel larger, with longer wings and more leisurely flight style. Dark- or white-rumped Leach's Storm-Petrel has pointier wings and flies like a nighthawk.

Voice: Twittering and squeaking notes given near nest burrow.

Habitat: Open ocean; nests on rocky islands.

Nesting: 1 white egg, sometimes with a ring of fine red speckling, laid in a crevice in a rock slide or in a burrow.

Range: Breeds on islands from northern California south to northern Baja California.

This little-known bird nests on only a few islands off the West Coast, usually in colonies of several hundred or a few thousand pairs. Such a limited range places the Ashy Storm-Petrel at risk, and indeed in the late 1960s and early 1970s researchers found evidence of thinning of eggshells caused by pesticides. Like other storm-petrels, the Ashy ejects a musky orange oil when disturbed. Its favorite food, at least in southern California, is the larvae of one of the spiny lobsters; it is also known to feed on plankton and algae.

71 Black Storm-Petrel
Oceanodroma melania

Description: 9″ (23 cm). A *large all-dark storm-petrel* with long pointed wings and a forked tail. Flight smoother and more languid, with deeper and more graceful wingbeats, than that of other storm-petrels. Other all-dark storm-petrels are smaller, with different flight styles.

Voice: A loud *tuck-a-roo,* given at nesting colonies.

Habitat: Open ocean; nests on rocky islands.

Nesting: 1 white egg placed in a crevice or in the abandoned burrow of another seabird. Nests in colonies.

Range: Breeds on islands off both coasts of Baja California. Ranges from coast of northern California to South America.

This is the largest and most commonly seen of the all-dark storm-petrels in California. It is also the species most likely to enter bays and estuaries in search of its food, which consists of the larvae of spiny lobsters and other small marine animals. The Black Storm-Petrel often gathers in feeding flocks and follows ships.

76 Least Storm-Petrel
Oceanodroma microsoma

Description: 6″ (15 cm). The smallest storm-petrel on the West Coast. An *all-dark* bird with short wings; *tail short and wedge-shaped* rather than forked. Often appears tailless at a distance. Flight swift and low, with very rapid wingbeats.

Voice: Twittering and squeaking notes at nesting colonies.

Habitat: Open ocean.

Nesting: 1 white egg placed in a crevice among rocks. Nests in colonies.

Range: Breeds on islands off both coasts of Baja California. In summer and fall ranges northward to San Diego County, California.

The world's smallest storm-petrel, this species is probably the least-known member of its family in North America. But its dark color, small size, and tailless look make it the easiest West Coast storm-petrel to identify.

FAMILY PHAETHONTIDAE
Tropicbirds

3 species: Tropical and subtropical oceans of the world. Tropicbirds look like huge terns with long tail streamers. They are numerous and easy to see near their nesting colonies on oceanic islands, but outside the breeding season they roam widely over the ocean and are usually solitary. They feed on squid and small fish.

70 Red-billed Tropicbird
Phaethon aethereus

Description: 40″ (1 m), including tail feathers. W. 3′8″ (1.1 m). Adult is a large white seabird with *very long central tail feathers,* fine black bars on back and upper surface of wings, and *red bill.* Young birds similar, but lack long tail streamers.

Voice: A loud rattling call given in flight.

Habitat: Open ocean.

Nesting: 1 reddish or buff egg, spotted or blotched with brown, placed in a burrow or in a cavity on a cliff.

Range: Breeds on rocky islands in tropical seas. A rare visitor in summer and fall to

Pacific Coast, irregularly north to
Washington.

With their mainly white plumage and
long central tail feathers, tropicbirds are
unmistakable in flight. Near breeding
colonies they habitually display in the
air with tail and feet spread, soaring
and circling up and down. They have
very short legs and are rarely seen at
rest on land except on cliffs and at
burrow entrances.

FAMILY SULIDAE
Boobies and Gannets

9 species: Nearly worldwide on islands
and coasts. Boobies and gannets are
large seabirds with long pointed bills,
webbed feet, and pointed wings adapted
for plunge diving from great heights
into the ocean for fish. They nest on
steep sea cliffs and rocky islands and
sometimes in trees.

68 Blue-footed Booby
Sula nebouxii

Description: 32–34" (81–86 cm). Large seabird with
long pointed bill, wings, and tail. Head
and neck pale, streaked brown. Wings,
back, and tail dark brown; white
patches on nape and rump; underparts
white. *Legs and feet bright blue.* Back and
rump of immatures slightly mottled.
Brown Booby lacks white patches on
nape and rump; its feet are yellow or
greenish yellow.

Voice: Usually silent; trumpeting and
whistling noises on breeding grounds.

Habitat: Open sea.

Nesting: 2 or 3 chalky pale blue or green eggs
laid on the ground. Usually nests in
colonies on islands or isolated cliffs.

Range: Breeds from Gulf of California south to

Peru. In summer, a few stray to Salton
Sea in southeastern California or,
infrequently, to southern California
coast.

Boobies fly fairly high over the ocean
with steady, rapid, even strokes,
followed by a short glide. When fishing,
Blue-footed Boobies plunge headlong
into the water with wings partly folded;
they sometimes snatch flying fish out of
the air.

69 Brown Booby
Sula leucogaster

Description: 30" (76 cm). Adult has dark brown
head, upperparts, and breast, with
sharply contrasting white belly and white
underwing coverts. Immature is gray-
brown above and below; darker on head,
wings, and tail.

Voice: Usually silent, but gives a variety of
quacking, grunting, and screeching calls
on the breeding grounds.

Habitat: Tropical and subtropical seas; breeds on
coastal islands.

Nesting: 1–3 pale blue or green eggs on bare
ground in a slight mound of broken
shells and scattered vegetation, usually
at the edge of a cliff.

Range: Worldwide in tropical seas. Summer
visitor to Gulf Coast; occasionally seen
in southern California's Salton Sea;
accidental along Pacific Coast.

Frigatebirds often harass boobies,
chasing them and forcing them to
disgorge their prey, which the agile
frigatebird then catches in midair.
When on the wing, but not fishing,
boobies often flap and glide in lines
close to the surface of the waves and may
resemble shearwaters.

FAMILY PELECANIDAE
Pelicans

8 species: Nearly worldwide. Two species breed in North America. Pelicans are huge birds with webbed feet, very long bills, and enormous bill pouches. The American White Pelican inhabits inland waters and coastal lagoons, catching fish at the surface, while the Brown Pelican is exclusively coastal and plunge dives from the air to catch its prey. Flocks of both species fly in long lines, alternately flapping and gliding, or occasionally soaring high in the sky.

187   **American White Pelican**
Pelecanus erythrorhynchos

Description: 55–70″ (1.4–1.8 m). W. 8′(2.4 m). A *huge white bird* with a *long flat bill* and black wing tips. In breeding season, has short yellowish crest on back of head and horny plate on upper mandible. Young birds duskier than adults.

Voice: Usually silent; grunts or croaks on nesting grounds.

Habitat: Shallow lakes and coastal lagoons.

Nesting: 1–6 whitish eggs on a low mound of earth and debris on a marshy island; occasionally on rocky islands in desert lakes. Nests in colonies.

Range: Breeds from British Columbia and Mackenzie south to northern California, Utah, and Manitoba; also along Texas Gulf Coast. Winters from central California, Gulf Coast, and Florida south to Panama.

American White Pelicans are gregarious birds, usually traveling in flocks and nesting in colonies, often associated with Double-crested Cormorants. With their broad wings they soar easily and can frequently be seen wheeling in wide circles high in the air. These birds are

more buoyant than Brown Pelicans
and do not dive for their food. They
cooperate to surround fish in shallow
water, scooping them into their
pouches. Because of pesticides, human
disturbance, and the draining of
wetlands, this species is in decline.
The number of active colonies has
dropped sharply in recent decades.

186 Brown Pelican
Pelecanus occidentalis

Description: 45–54" (1.1–1.4 m). W. 7'6" (2.3 m).
A *very large,* stocky bird with a *dark
brown body* and a *long flat bill.* Head
whitish in adults, with dark brown
on hindneck during breeding season.
Young birds have dark brown heads
and whitish bellies.

Voice: Usually silent, but utters low grunts
on nesting grounds.

Habitat: Sandy coastal beaches and lagoons,
waterfronts and pilings, and rocky cliffs.

Nesting: 2 or 3 chalky white eggs in a nest of
sticks, straw, or other debris, usually
on a rocky island near the coast. Nests
in colonies.

Range: Resident of Pacific coast from southern
California south to Chile, dispersing
northward as far as southern British
Columbia after nesting season. Also on
Atlantic coast from North Carolina
south to Venezuela.

These social colonial birds fly in single
file low over the water; on sighting prey
they plunge from heights of up to 50
feet (15 meters), surfacing to swallow
fish. Unlike its larger white relative, the
Brown Pelican seldom soars. Around
waterfronts and marinas individual
birds become quite tame, taking fish
offered them by humans. Both species
are sensitive to chemical pollutants
absorbed from the fish they eat. The
pollutants affect calcium metabolism,

resulting in thin-shelled eggs that break when moved by the incubating bird. Because of its more limited, exclusively coastal range, the Brown Pelican has suffered more acutely than its relative, but after the banning of many pesticides, these familiar birds are staging a comeback.

FAMILY PHALACROCORACIDAE
Cormorants

38 species: Worldwide. Six species breed in North America. These are large birds, usually black, with long necks, long hooked bills, and webbed feet. The feet of these expert divers are located far back on the body to give them forward thrust under water. On land cormorants stand upright, often with their wings partly extended to dry. In the air, they fly in long lines or wedge-shaped formations.

82   Double-crested Cormorant
Phalacrocorax auritus

Description: 30–35" (76–89 cm). A solidly built black cormorant with *orange throat pouch* and long neck. Long hooked bill tilted upward when bird swims. Adults have short tuft of feathers over each eye during breeding season. Young birds are browner, whitish or buffy on breast, upper belly, and neck. In flight, the neck shows a slight crook, not seen in the similar Brandt's Cormorant.

Voice: Deep guttural grunts.

Habitat: Lakes, rivers, swamps, and coasts.

Nesting: 3–5 chalky, pale blue-green eggs in a well-made platform of sticks, or of seaweed on the coast, placed in a tree or on a cliff or rocky island. Nests in colonies.

Range: Breeds locally in interior from Alaska,

Manitoba, and Newfoundland south to Mexico and Bahamas. Winters mainly on coasts, north to Alaska and southern New England.

The Double-crested is the only cormorant that nests commonly in the interior in the West. Along the coast, where it nests on cliffs, it is usually outnumbered by Brandt's Cormorant. It takes some practice to pick out the crook in the neck of a Double-crested, but once this field mark is spotted, distinguishing the two is easy. Double-crested Cormorants often take shortcuts over land, whereas both Brandt's and the smaller Pelagic nearly always fly over water.

83 Neotropic Cormorant
"Olivaceous Cormorant"
Phalacrocorax brasilianus

Description: 25" (64 cm). A small, delicate-looking cormorant of southern lagoons and marshes; black glossed with olive, with *orange throat pouch narrowly bordered with white.* Double-crested Cormorant is larger, lacks white border on throat pouch, has shorter tail, and flies with crook in neck.

Voice: Soft grunts.

Habitat: Brackish and fresh water.

Nesting: 2–6 chalky blue eggs, often stained with brown, in a shallow nest of sticks lined with grass. Nests in trees or bushes in small colonies.

Range: Resident along Gulf Coast of Louisiana and Texas, in southern New Mexico, and south to southern South America.

Primarily a tropical species, the Neotropic Cormorant is most likely to be seen along the Gulf Coast, but a few individuals live near Elephant Butte, on the Rio Grande in New Mexico, and the species has turned up more rarely elsewhere in the Southwest. The only other cormorant found here is the Double-crested.

84   Brandt's Cormorant
Phalacrocorax penicillatus

Description: 33–35" (84–89 cm). A solidly built cormorant, *thick-necked and large-headed,* black with little gloss. Breeding birds have *bright cobalt-blue throat pouch* bordered with yellow, and slender white plumes on face and back. Young birds are duller, buff colored on breast. Double-crested Cormorant similar, but flies with more of a crook in its neck and has conspicuous orange throat pouch. Pelagic is smaller and more slender, with smaller head; adult has white flank patches.

Voice: Croaks and grunts.

Habitat: Coastal or offshore rocks and waters near shore.

Nesting: 3–6 chalky bluish eggs in a large nest of seaweed or other debris. Nests in colonies on cliffs and rocky islands.

Range: Resident along Pacific Coast from southeastern Alaska south to Baja California.

Brandt's Cormorants often gather in flocks of several hundred and fly to feeding grounds in long straggling lines. This species and the Pelagic Cormorant frequently nest on the same cliffs, with Brandt's forming colonies on level ground at the top of the cliff and the Pelagic choosing inaccessible ledges. Nest robbing by Western Gulls is such a serious problem that nests are rarely left unguarded.

80 Pelagic Cormorant
Phalacrocorax pelagicus

Description:
25–30″ (64–76 cm). The smallest and most delicate of the Pacific cormorants. Glossy black, with dark bill, *long, slender neck held out straight in flight,* head no wider than neck, and *red throat pouch.* Breeding birds have *bold white spot on each flank.* At close range 2 crests, fore and aft, are visible. Immature birds dark brown, with same proportions as adults. Other coastal cormorants are bulkier, with slower wingbeats.

Voice:
Groaning and hissing calls around breeding colonies.

Habitat:
Offshore and inshore waters. Nests on sea cliffs and rocky islands.

Nesting:
3–7 chalky bluish eggs in a nest of seaweed, feathers, and other debris. Nests are used year after year and may grow quite large.

Range:
Breeds from Bering Sea south to northern Baja California. Winters south from southern Alaska. Also in northeastern Asia.

The Pelagic Cormorant feeds mainly on fish, which it pursues both close to shore and far out at sea. It also takes crabs and other crustaceans. To catch this prey it dives deeply; birds have been taken in fishing nets at depths of 180 feet (55 meters). This species' small size enables it to spring directly from the water, rather than paddling along the surface as other cormorants do.

81 Red-faced Cormorant
Phalacrocorax urile

Description:
28–30″ (71–76 cm). Similar to Pelagic Cormorant but larger, with *brighter red of throat pouch extending onto face,* and pale bill. Young birds are dull brown but still have red face and pale bill.

Voice: A low *korr.* Hoarse croaking notes at breeding colonies.

Habitat: Open ocean; nests on sea cliffs.

Nesting: 3 or 4 chalky bluish eggs in a large nest of seaweed or grass. Nests in colonies.

Range: Resident in Alaska, from Aleutian and Pribilof islands east and south to Kodiak Island and Prince William Sound. Also in northeastern Asia.

The Red-faced Cormorant is one of several seabirds confined to the northernmost parts of the Pacific Ocean. Based on its appearance and its courtship displays, it seems most closely related to the Pelagic Cormorant. But the Red-faced is more social than the Pelagic and nests on the open tops of cliffs, areas the Pelagic normally avoids.

FAMILY FREGATIDAE
Frigatebirds

5 species: Tropical oceans of the world. In North America one species breeds in extreme southern Florida on the Marquesas Keys off Key West. Frigatebirds are large, extremely long-winged birds with long, deeply forked tails, hooked bills, and webbed feet. Males have inflatable throat pouches. Nesting chiefly on oceanic islands, they commit piracy on other seabirds, forcing their victims to disgorge the fish they have caught.

67 **Magnificent Frigatebird**
Fregata magnificens

Description: 38–40″ (97–102 cm). W. 7′6″ (2.3 m). Black with very long, narrow, pointed wings, deeply forked tail, and long hooked bill. Male has brilliant red throat pouch in breeding season, which it inflates to huge size during courtship.

Female has white breast. Young have white heads and underparts.

Voice: Usually silent at sea; harsh guttural calls during courtship.

Habitat: Open ocean and inshore waters.

Nesting: 1 white egg placed in a flimsy nest of sticks in bushes or trees or on rocks.

Range: In United States breeds locally on mangrove islands in Florida Bay; also in tropical Atlantic, Gulf of Mexico, and eastern Pacific. A rare but regular visitor to West Coast, wandering to northern California, Salton Sea, and lower Colorado River in summer.

Magnificent Frigatebirds do not nest on the Pacific Coast of the United States, but those that wander northward to California (and casually to southern Alaska), probably come from colonies on islands off the western coast of Mexico. Although they are exclusively marine, these birds rarely venture far offshore. They cannot take off from the surface of the water and so must return to land to perch and rest.

FAMILY ARDEIDAE
Bitterns and Herons

64 species: Worldwide. Twelve species breed in North America. This family is made up of large to medium-sized long-legged wading birds, some of which have long necks that they fold over their backs in flight. Bitterns and herons have long bills for catching prey, and their toes are unwebbed. Some species have elaborate plumes during the breeding season. Many of these birds nest colonially in trees and bushes.

15 American Bittern
Botaurus lentiginosus

Description: 23–34" (58–86 cm). A secretive,
medium-sized, streaked brown heron.
Outer wing appears blackish brown in flight,
contrasting with lighter brown of inner
wing and body. At close range adults
show long black stripe down side of
throat. Young night-herons are similar
but stockier, with shorter necks and
more rounded wings without dark tips;
they lack the secretive habits of bitterns.

Voice: On breeding grounds, a loud pumping
sound, *oong-KA-chunk!* repeated a few
times and often audible for half a mile.
Flight call a low *kok-kok-kok.*

Habitat: Freshwater and brackish marshes and
marshy lakeshores; regular in salt
marshes during migration and winter.

Nesting: 2–6 buff or olive-buff eggs placed on a
platform of reeds concealed in a marsh.
Does not nest in colonies.

Range: Breeds from southeastern Alaska,
Manitoba, and Newfoundland south to
California, New Mexico, Arkansas, and
Carolinas. Winters from coastal British
Columbia, Southwest, Illinois, and
along Atlantic Coast to Long Island
(occasionally farther north), and south to
Costa Rica (rarely) and Greater Antilles.

The American Bittern has a remarkable,
though rarely seen, courtship display.
The male arches his back, exposing
whitish plumes, shortens his neck, dips
his breast forward, and "booms" at the
female. Both members of the pair
engage in a complicated aerial display
flight. Bitterns spend most of their lives
in concealment, stepping slowly and
methodically through the reeds in search
of food. When one is approached it will
point its neck and bill skyward and sway
back and forth, thus resembling the
shifting reeds of its surroundings.

16 Least Bittern
Ixobrychus exilis

Description: 11–14″ (28–36 cm). A tiny, secretive
heron with blackish back and *conspicuous
buff wing patches* and underparts. Female
and young are similar but duller,
more buffy.

Voice: A soft *coo-coo-coo,* easily overlooked.

Habitat: Freshwater marshes where cattails and
reeds predominate.

Nesting: 2–7 pale blue or green eggs placed on a
flimsy platform of dead cattails or reeds,
usually about a foot above the water.

Range: Breeds locally in Oregon, California,
and Southwest, and from Manitoba and
Texas east to Atlantic Coast. Winters
from southern California, lower
Colorado River, and Gulf Coast
southward. Also in South America.

Except in the few places where the Least
Bittern is very abundant, it takes luck or
patience to see one. Even more furtive
than the American Bittern, this species
seldom flies, and then does so only for a
few seconds before it drops out of sight.
It spends most of its time picking its
way quietly through the densest
marshes, looking for frogs, crayfish, and
other small aquatic creatures. It is a
skilled climber and can be found several
feet above the water, holding onto the
swaying reeds with its long toes.

3 Great Blue Heron
Ardea herodias

Description: 39–52″ (99–132 cm). W. 5′10″ (1.8 m).
A common *large, mainly grayish* heron
with a pale or yellowish bill. Often
mistaken for a Sandhill Crane, but flies
with its neck folded, not extended like
that of a crane.

Voice: A harsh squawk.

Habitat: Lakes, ponds, rivers, and marshes.

Nesting: 3–7 pale greenish-blue eggs placed on a

shallow platform of sticks lined with finer material, usually in a tree but sometimes on the ground or concealed in a reedbed. Nests in colonies.

Range: Breeds locally from coastal Alaska, south-central Canada, and Nova Scotia south to Mexico and West Indies. Winters as far north as southern Alaska, central United States, and southern New England. Also in Galápagos Islands.

An adaptable bird whose large size enables it to feed on a variety of prey—from large fish to mice, small birds, and insects—the Great Blue has one of the widest ranges of any North American heron. This wide choice of food enables it to remain farther north during the winter than other species, wherever there is open water. Most Great Blues nest in colonies in tall trees; their presence is often unsuspected until the leaves fall and the groups of saucer-shaped nests are exposed to view. In late summer young herons disperse widely and may be encountered at small ponds, in mountain waters, or even in backyard pools—wherever fish are plentiful.

4, 5 Great Egret
Casmerodius albus

Description: 35–41" (89–104 cm). W. 4'7" (1.4 m). A large, all-white heron with a *yellow bill and black legs.* In breeding plumage, has long lacy plumes on back. Much smaller Snowy Egret has black bill and legs and yellow feet.

Voice: A guttural croak. Also loud squawks at nesting colonies.

Habitat: Fresh and salt marshes, marshy ponds, and tidal flats.

Nesting: 3–5 pale blue-green eggs placed on a platform of sticks in a tree or bush. Nests in colonies, often with other species of herons.

Range: Breeds locally from Oregon south to western Mexico, and from Minnesota to Mississippi Valley and Southeast, and along Atlantic Coast north to southern New England. Winters regularly from Oregon south through Southwest, Texas, and Gulf Coast states to Mexico, and on Atlantic Coast north to New Jersey. Also in tropical America and warmer parts of Old World.

At the turn of the century the Great Egret was close to extinction, its numbers reduced by hunters who took the long lacy plumes of the breeding plumage and sold them to milliners. The first great success of the National Audubon Society was the banning of this trade in bird plumes. Today the Great Egret, emblem of the society, has reclaimed nearly all of its original range. But it is still not out of danger: The destruction of wetlands, especially in the West where colonies are few and widely scattered, poses a current threat to these majestic birds.

1, 2 Snowy Egret
Egretta thula

Description: 20–27" (51–69 cm). W. 3'2" (97 cm). A small, delicate white heron with a *slender black bill, black legs, and yellow feet.* In breeding season, it has long lacy plumes on its back. Immature bird similar to adult, but has yellow stripe up back of leg. Adult Cattle Egret has pale bill, legs, and feet; immature has dark bill, legs, and feet. Much larger Great Egret has yellow bill and black legs and feet. Similar to immature of rare Little Blue Heron, but that species has a stouter, bluish-gray bill, greenish-yellow legs and feet, no yellow skin between eyes and base of bill. Snowy Egrets often forage by sprinting rapidly through water.

Voice: A harsh squawk.

Habitat: Marshes, ponds, swamps, and mudflats.

Nesting: 3–5 pale blue-green eggs placed on a platform of sticks in a bush or reedbed or on the ground. Nests in colonies, often with other species of herons.

Range: Breeds locally from Oregon and California east to New England, mainly along coasts but also at scattered localities inland. Winters regularly from California, Arizona, and Virginia south to West Indies and South America. Also resident in tropical America.

There is evidence that members of a pair of Snowy Egrets, like other large waders, cannot recognize one another except at the nest. Even there, a bird arriving to relieve its mate must perform an elaborate greeting ceremony in order to avoid being attacked as an intruder. During this display the plumes on the head are raised and the incoming bird bows to the one that is sitting. Appeased by this display, the sitting bird leaves and the other takes over.

11   Little Blue Heron
Egretta caerulea

Description: 25–30" (64–76 cm). W. 3'5" (1 m). Adult slate blue with maroon neck. Bill grayish with black tip; legs greenish. Immature is white, usually with dusky tips on primaries. Young birds acquiring adult plumage usually have a piebald appearance. Snowy Egret somewhat smaller, all white, with black bill and legs, yellow lores and feet.

Voice: Usually silent; squawks when alarmed. Various croaks and screams at nesting colonies.

Habitat: Freshwater swamps and lagoons in the South; coastal thickets on islands in the North.

Nesting: 3–5 pale blue-green eggs placed in a nest of sticks in a small tree or bush. Nests in colonies.

Range: Breeds from southern California (rare),
southern New Mexico, Texas, and
Oklahoma east to southern Missouri and
southern New England, and south to
Gulf Coast; more common along coast.
Winters along Gulf Coast, in Florida,
and on Atlantic Coast north to New
Jersey. Also in tropical America.

The Little Blue Heron is a new arrival
in southern California, where it began
nesting in 1979. Adults usually forage
alone, stalking the marshes for prey, but
immatures tend to feed in groups, their
white plumage serving as a signal,
drawing distant birds together at good
foraging places.

12 Tricolored Heron
"Louisiana Heron"
Egretta tricolor

Description: 25–30" (64–76 cm). W. 3'2" (97 cm).
A *slender* gray-blue heron with rufous
neck and *white belly.*

Voice: Guttural croaks and squawks.

Habitat: Swamps, bayous, coastal ponds, salt
marshes, mangrove islands, mudflats,
and lagoons.

Nesting: 3 or 4 blue-green eggs in a nest of
sticks placed in a tree or reedbed, or on
the ground.

Range: Breeds in southeastern New Mexico
and Texas, on Gulf Coast, and along
Atlantic Coast north to southern Maine
(rare). Winters along coast from Texas
and New Jersey south to northern South
America and West Indies. Also resident
in tropical America.

After the nesting season most herons
disperse northward, appearing in areas
where they are seldom seen during the
rest of the year. The Tricolored Heron is
no exception. Although in the West it
nests only in southern New Mexico, it is
liable to turn up in late summer as far

away as Arizona, California, Oregon, Colorado, and even Manitoba.

7, 8 Cattle Egret
Bubulcus ibis

Description: 20″ (51 cm). A small, stocky white heron, with buff on crown, breast, and back during breeding season. Legs pale yellow or orange in adults, blackish in some immatures. *Bill short and yellow or orange;* dark in juveniles. No other small white heron has a yellow bill.

Voice: Hoarse croaks.

Habitat: Forages mainly alongside livestock in open fields and pastures, but breeds near water with other herons.

Nesting: 3–5 pale blue eggs placed in a nest of sticks in a bush or tree. Usually nests in colonies with other herons in a marsh.

Range: Breeds locally from California and most western states east to Great Lakes and Maine, and southward to Gulf Coast. Also in American tropics and Old World.

As in the Old World, Cattle Egrets in North America follow large grazing animals to feed on the insects they disturb and can often be seen perched on the backs of livestock. At some airports, especially those near salt marshes, these small herons wait at the edge of runways for passing airplanes to blow insects out of the grass. Unlike other egrets, this species rarely takes fish, although it is known to capture an occasional frog or toad.

14 Green Heron
"Green-backed Heron"
Butorides virescens

Description: 16–22″ (41–56 cm). A *dark, crow-sized* heron. Crown black, *back and wings dark gray-green or gray-blue* (depending on lighting); *neck chestnut colored.* Bill dark; legs bright orange. Immatures have streaks on neck, breast, and sides.

Voice: Call is a sharp *kyowk!* or *skyow!*

Habitat: Breeds mainly in freshwater or brackish marshes with clumps of trees. Feeds along margin of any body of water.

Nesting: 3–6 pale green or pale blue eggs in a loose nest of sticks built in a tree or dense thicket.

Range: Breeds in West from Fraser River delta of British Columbia south to California and Arizona and throughout Mexico. Widespread eastern population breeds from Dakotas east to New Brunswick, south to Texas and Florida; also in Central America and West Indies. Winters from central southern Arizona and southern Texas to Gulf Coast and north on Atlantic Coast to Carolinas. Also in tropical America.

The Green Heron is rather solitary, feeding alone or in pairs. A wary bird, it erects its short crest, straightens its neck, and nervously flicks its short tail when alarmed. Our smallest heron except for the diminutive Least Bittern, the Green Heron preys on a wide variety of insects, frogs, and small fish; its broad diet enables it to breed on small inland ponds and marshes that won't support other herons.

6, 13 Black-crowned Night-Heron
Nycticorax nycticorax

Description: 23–28″ (58–71 cm). W. 3′8″ (1.1 m). A medium-sized, stocky, rather short-necked heron with *black crown and back,* gray wings, and *white underparts.* Bill short and black, legs pinkish or yellowish. In breeding season it has 2 or more long white plumes on back of head. Young birds are dull gray-brown lightly spotted with white.

Voice: Loud, barking *kwok!* or *quawk!* often heard at night or at dusk. Utters a variety of croaks, barks, and other harsh calls in nesting colonies.

Habitat: Marshes, swamps, and wooded streams.

Nesting: 3–5 pale blue-green eggs in a shallow saucer of sticks or reeds in a thicket or reedbed; occasionally in tall trees. Nests in colonies, sometimes with other species of herons.

Range: Breeds from Washington, Saskatchewan, Minnesota, and New Brunswick south to southern South America; absent from Rocky Mountains. Winters in southern half of United States. Also in Old World.

These birds are sluggish hunters, standing quietly for long periods of time waiting for a frog or fish to pass by. They also plunder the nests of other herons and make regular nighttime visits to colonies of terns or Franklin's Gulls, where they sometimes take large numbers of chicks. Night-herons also stalk in grasslands in places where meadow voles are abundant, preying on these small rodents.

FAMILY THRESKIORNITHIDAE
Ibises and Spoonbills

33 species: Chiefly tropical regions of the world. Four species breed in North America, including the colorful Roseate Spoonbill (*Ajaia ajaja*) of the Southeast. The bills of ibises are long and curved downward; those of spoonbills are straight and spatulate. They are aquatic birds that feed on fish, frogs, insects, and other small animals in the water. They nest in colonies in trees and bushes, often with herons.

18 White-faced Ibis
Plegadis chihi

Description: 22–25″ (56–64 cm). W. 3′1″ (94 cm).
A large, chestnut-bronze marsh bird
with a long, down-curved bill. Very
similar to the Glossy Ibis (*Plegadis
falcinellus*) of the East, but with band of
white feathers around bare face, and red
eyes and legs. Glossy Ibis has narrow
band of white skin around edge of bare
face, brown eyes, and gray legs. In
winter, White-faced Ibis has streaks on
head and neck, and brown eyes; it is
then virtually impossible to distinguish
the two species.

Voice: Low croaks and grunts.

Habitat: Salt and fresh marshes in the West, and
coastal marshes and islands in Louisiana
and Texas.

Nesting: 3 or 4 pale blue-green eggs in a shallow
cup of reeds lined with grass in low
bushes in a marsh.

Range: Breeds from Oregon sporadically east to
Minnesota and south to southeastern
New Mexico and Texas, and east to
coastal Louisiana. Winters from
southern California and Gulf Coast of
Texas and Louisiana to El Salvador.

The only ibis in the West, the White-
faced overlaps with other ibises only in
coastal Texas and Louisiana, outside the
range of this book. Formerly much
depleted because of pesticides, this
marsh bird is now making a modest
comeback in much of its range. Its diet
is diverse, consisting of insects,
salamanders, crustaceans, and small fish
and shellfish.

FAMILY CICONIIDAE
Storks

17 species: Chiefly tropical regions of
the world. Only one species breeds in
North America. Storks are large, long-
legged, long-necked, and long-billed
birds that live chiefly in open marshy
country. They nest either singly or
colonially in trees and bushes, often
with herons and ibises. They feed on all
sorts of animal matter, and a few species
eat carrion.

10   Wood Stork
Mycteria americana

Description: 40–44" (1–1.1 m). W. 5'6" (1.7 m).
White with black flight feathers and
tail. Head and neck bare, dark gray.
Bill long, stout, and slightly curved;
black in adults and dull yellow in
immatures. Unlike herons, storks fly
with neck extended.

Voice: Dull croak. Usually silent except around
nest. Young make clattering noises with
their bills.

Habitat: On or near the coast, breeding chiefly in
cypress swamps; also in mangroves.

Nesting: 2 or 3 white eggs on a huge stick
platform in a tree. Nests in colonies.

Range: Breeds in Florida and Georgia; very
rarely elsewhere along coast from South
Carolina to Texas. Outside breeding
season wanders as far as California and
Massachusetts (very rarely). Also breeds
in tropical America.

This tall wader is only a nonbreeding
visitor to the West, where it is most
often seen at the Salton Sea in inland
southern California. It is easily
distinguished from white herons by its
large size, upright posture, dark, naked
head and neck, and heavy bill with a
downward curve at the tip. It obtains
its food—mainly fish and snakes—by

probing the water with its bill, locating its prey by its sense of touch.

FAMILY ANATIDAE
Swans, Geese, and Ducks

150 species: Worldwide. At least 40 species breed in North America. In the swans and geese the sexes are alike, but many species of ducks have marked sexual dimorphism, with the males the brighter in coloration. All members of the family have webbed feet, and most are aquatic, although the geese are primarily terrestrial. As might be expected from such a diverse family, food habits are extremely varied; some forms are vegetarians, others eat fish, snails, and insects. This successful family has been able to colonize very remote oceanic islands in all parts of the globe.

163 Fulvous Whistling-Duck
Dendrocygna bicolor

Description: 18–21″ (46–53 cm). A long-legged, long-necked, goose-like duck. Body mainly *tawny, with white stripe on side;* wings dark; rump and undertail coverts white.

Voice: A hoarse whistle, *ka-wheee.*

Habitat: Rice fields, freshwater marshes, wet meadows, and lagoons.

Nesting: 12–15 buff-white eggs in a shallow cup of grass or a well-woven basket of reeds in a marsh. Sometimes several females lay in the same nest.

Range: Resident in southern California, coastal Texas and Louisiana, and southern Florida. Also in American tropics and Old World.

Although Fulvous Whistling-Ducks in North America breed only in California,

Texas, Louisiana, and Florida, they sometimes wander. Small flocks have turned up as far away as British Columbia and Nova Scotia. These long-legged ducks do most of their feeding on land, eating green grass, seeds, and acorns. This species was formerly known as the "Fulvous Tree Duck." The name "fulvous" refers to its tawny color.

165   Black-bellied Whistling-Duck
Dendrocygna autumnalis

Description: 20–22″ (51–56 cm). A tall, long-necked, long-legged duck. Body of adult mainly chestnut and black; bill red; legs pink. Large white wing patch visible in flight. Immature similar but much duller.

Voice: Mellow whistles.

Habitat: Wooded or tree-lined streams and ponds.

Nesting: 12–16 white eggs placed in a tree cavity or man-made nest box without a nest lining, occasionally on the ground among reeds.

Range: Breeds in extreme southern Texas and Arizona; introduced birds have bred in southern Florida. Also in American tropics.

These handsome, conspicuous birds often rest on large tree branches, stakes, or poles in the water or, less commonly, on the ground. They are easily domesticated and are quite tame even in the wild. Almost entirely herbivorous, they feed in shallow water on tubers and other aquatic vegetation, as well as in grain fields. Unlike many ducks, this species is largely nocturnal, migrating at night and resting and feeding during the day. It was formerly known as the "Black-bellied Tree Duck."

188 Tundra Swan
"Whistling Swan"
Cygnus columbianus

Description: 48–55" (1.2–1.4 m). The most common swan in the West. Large, all white; bill black, usually with small yellow spot in front of eye. Rare Trumpeter Swan is larger and lacks yellow on bill.

Voice: Mellow bugling call, *hoo-ho-hoo,* usually heard from a flock of migrating birds.

Habitat: Arctic tundra; winters on marshy lakes and bays.

Nesting: 4–6 creamy-white eggs placed on a large mound of grass and moss on an island or beside a marshy tundra lake.

Range: Breeds in Alaska and far northern Canada east to Baffin Island. Winters from southern Alaska south to Nevada, Utah, and Baja California and on mid-Atlantic Coast; rare on Gulf Coast of Texas; occasional on Great Lakes.

In one study, Tundra Swans were marked with colored neck bands at Chesapeake Bay in Maryland, and their migration was followed to their Alaska breeding grounds. One bird, banded on the Atlantic Coast the previous winter, was sighted in the Central Valley of California in the following March. This Arctic breeder alternately visited the Atlantic and Pacific coasts of the huge North American continent, surely something of a record for birds.

189 Trumpeter Swan
Cygnus buccinator

Description: 60–72" (1.5–1.8 m). One of North America's largest birds. Adult similar to Tundra Swan but larger, with all-black bill. Young birds dusky gray-brown; bill pink with black base and tip. Mute Swan (*Cygnus olor*), an introduced species and a tame pond bird, is smaller, with black knob at base of orange bill; holds neck in graceful curve.

Voice: A bugling *ko-hoh,* lower-pitched than Tundra Swan's call.

Habitat: Marshes, lakes, or rivers with dense vegetation.

Nesting: 4–6 whitish eggs in a huge nest on a bulrush-covered island or a beaver lodge.

Range: Breeds in southern Alaska, northern British Columbia, western Alberta, Oregon, Idaho, Montana, and Wyoming. Winters in southeastern Alaska, western British Columbia, and on open water in United States breeding range.

Draining of marshes, hunting, and other disturbances, along with a low rate of reproduction, brought the Trumpeter Swan close to extinction by the beginning of this century. Conservation measures, including reintroductions, have allowed it to increase from a very small number in the 1930s to more than 6,000 today, with 4,500 of these in Alaska.

---

195 Greater White-fronted Goose
"White-fronted Goose"
Anser albifrons

Description: 27–30" (69–76 cm). A dusky-brown goose with conspicuous white belly and undertail coverts; *white patch on front of face;* underparts barred and flecked with black. Bill usually pink; legs orange. Young birds lack white face and black bars on underparts.

Voice: A distinctive bark: *kla-ha!* or *kla-hah-luk!*

Habitat: Breeds on marshy tundra; winters on marshes and bays.

Nesting: 5 or 6 cream-colored eggs in a down-lined grassy depression on the tundra.

Range: Breeds in Alaska, far-northern Canada, and Greenland. Winters from coastal British Columbia to California, in New Mexico, and along Gulf Coast in Texas

and Louisiana; more rarely on East Coast and in interior. Also breeds in northern Eurasia.

The winter headquarters of this Arctic goose is California's Sacramento Valley. These geese often migrate in large flocks at night, when they can be identified by their distinctive call. Like other geese they often leave the marshes to feed in nearby stubble fields, where they are frequently concealed from view until the observer is very close, when they explode noisily into the air. The "Tule Goose" of the West Coast is a large race of the Greater White-fronted; its breeding grounds were unknown until 1979, when birds were found nesting near Anchorage, Alaska.

190, 196 Snow Goose
including "Blue Goose"
Chen caerulescens

Description: 25–31" (64–79 cm). Smaller than the domestic goose. *Pure white with black wing tips; bill pink with black "lips"; legs pink.* Young birds have dark bill and are mottled with brownish gray above. A dark phase, once considered a separate species called the "Blue Goose," has bluish-gray upperparts, brownish underparts, and *white head and neck.* Blue-phase birds have spread westward in recent decades and are now found among the thousands of white Snow Geese wintering in California.

Voice: A high-pitched, barking *bow-wow!* or *howk-howk!*

Habitat: Breeds on the tundra and winters in salt marshes and marshy coastal bays; less commonly in freshwater marshes and adjacent grainfields.

Nesting: 4–8 white eggs in a nest sparsely lined with down on the tundra. Nests in colonies.

Range: Breeds in Arctic regions of North

America and extreme eastern Siberia.
Winters on Pacific Coast from southern
British Columbia south to Baja
California; also mid-Atlantic Coast and
Gulf Coast from Mississippi to Texas. In
smaller numbers in interior.

In the Far North fresh plant shoots are
scarce in early spring, but the geese
arrive with good fat reserves, built up
from plants consumed on prairie
marshes where they pause during their
long spring migration. Snow Geese
graze fields and marshes of Pacific
coastal areas and the Southwest all
winter. The largest concentrations are
in California's Central Valley and
along the Gulf Coast of Texas and
Louisiana. As they do elsewhere, these
birds spend the night resting on
open water.

---

191 **Ross' Goose**
Chen rossii

Description: 24″ (61 cm). A Mallard-sized edition of

the Snow Goose. White wings, black
wing tips, pink bill, and pink legs.
Differs from Snow Goose in its smaller
size, *very stubby bill,* and rounder head.
The rare blue phase looks like a
miniature "Blue Goose" (see Snow
Goose).

Voice: Soft cackling and grunting notes.

Habitat: Arctic tundra in the breeding season,
salt or fresh marshes in the winter.

Nesting: 4 or 5 creamy-white eggs in a down-
lined grass nest placed on a small island
in a lake or river. Nests in loose colonies.

Range: Breeds in northeastern Mackenzie and
on Southampton Island in Hudson Bay;
winters mainly in California, but now
occurs in increasing numbers in lower
Mississippi Valley and on East Coast.

This relatively rare bird is carefully
monitored by both Canadian and

United States game biologists, but some hunting is allowed on its winter grounds. The population has increased in recent years, and there are now estimated to be more than 80,000 Ross' Geese, the great majority of which winter in California's Sacramento Valley. Although it shares these wintering grounds with the larger Snow Goose, the two species tend to stay in separate flocks.

192 Emperor Goose
Chen canagica

Description: 26–28" (66–71 cm). As large as Snow Goose or Greater White-fronted Goose. Body and wings *silvery gray;* black and white feather margins give a scaled bluish appearance. *Head, hindneck, and tail white; throat black;* bill pinkish; legs and feet bright orange. Juveniles are gray overall.

Voice: Loud musical notes, *kla-ha, kla-ha, kla-ha.*

Habitat: Seacoasts, mudflats, and coastal tundra.

Nesting: 3–8 creamy-white eggs in a down-lined nest placed on the ground on islets of marshy tundra or among driftwood on the coast.

Range: Breeds on islands and marshy coasts of western Alaska. Winters mainly in Aleutian Islands east to Kodiak Island.

As in other tundra-dwelling birds, the head and neck of these geese take on a deep rust stain from the iron in stagnating waters, for they feed with head and neck submerged, plucking vegetation from the bottom. The black pattern on the throat distinguishes this species from the "Blue Goose," which is relatively rare in Alaska.

193 Brant
including "Black Brant"
Branta bernicla

Description: 22–30" (56–76 cm). Similar to Canada Goose but smaller, shorter-necked, darker, and lacking conspicuous white cheek patch. Dark brown above with black head and neck; white collar on neck. Atlantic birds have whitish bellies; West Coast birds have dark bellies and were formerly considered a separate species, the "Black Brant."

Voice: A low guttural *ruk-ruk.*

Habitat: Tundra and coastal islands in the Arctic; salt marshes and estuaries in winter.

Nesting: 3–5 dull-white eggs in a large mass of moss and down, placed on the tundra. Often nests in loose colonies.

Range: Breeds in coastal Alaska and Canadian Arctic. Winters along coasts south to California and Carolinas. Also in Eurasia.

Because their food consists mainly of eelgrass and other marine plants, Brant rarely stray far from salt water. These geese usually spend the winter in very large flocks, feeding on mudflats, constantly uttering their low, muttering calls. They usually migrate in irregular bunches rather than in lines like other geese. Many are shot by hunters each year, but a greater danger to the species is the steady loss of winter habitats to encroaching civilization.

194 Canada Goose
Branta canadensis

Description: Small races, 22–26" (56–66 cm); large races, 35–45" (89–114 cm). Brownish body with *black head, long black neck, conspicuous white cheek patch.* The smaller Brant has a shorter neck and lacks white cheek patch.

Voice: Rich musical honking in larger races; high-pitched cackling in smaller races.

Habitat: Lakes, bays, rivers, and marshes. Often feeds in open grasslands and stubble fields.

Nesting: 4–8 whitish eggs in a large mass of grass and moss lined with down; usually on the ground near water or on a muskrat lodge, but sometimes in a tree in an abandoned Osprey or Bald Eagle nest.

Range: Breeds from Alaska east to Baffin Island and south to California, Illinois, and Massachusetts. Winters south to northern Mexico and Gulf Coast. Widespread as a semidomesticated bird in city parks and on reservoirs.

Well known for their V-shaped migrating flocks and rich, sonorous honking, Canada Geese are among the most familiar of North America's waterfowl. There are 11 geographical races, ranging in size from the "Giant Canada Goose" of the northern prairies to the diminutive "Cackling Goose," which nests in the Yukon and winters mainly in California. The most abundant race is the one that nests south of Hudson Bay, which numbers well over a million, while the rarest is the Aleutian Islands form, which nests on only two small islands and numbers barely over a thousand. Like other geese, these birds are chiefly grazers, feeding on stubble fields and eating marsh vegetation.

110, 146 **Wood Duck**
Aix sponsa

Description: 17–20″ (43–51 cm). A beautiful, crested, multicolored duck. Male patterned in iridescent greens, purples, and blues with distinctive white chin patch and face stripes; bill mainly red; tail long. Female grayish with broad white eye ring.

Voice: Female, loud *wooo-eeek!;* male, softer *jeee?* or *ter-weeeee?*

Habitat: Wooded rivers and ponds; wooded swamps. Visits freshwater marshes in late summer and fall.

Nesting: 9–12 whitish or tan eggs in a nest made of down in a natural tree cavity or a man-made nest box, sometimes up to 50′ (15 m) off the ground.

Range: Breeds from British Columbia south to California, and from Montana east to Nova Scotia and south to Texas and Florida; absent from Rocky Mountains and Great Plains. Winters near Pacific Coast north to Washington, and to New Jersey in East, rarely farther north.

One of the most beautiful of American waterfowl, the Wood Duck was hunted nearly to extinction during the late 19th and early 20th centuries. In 1918 the hunting season was closed, and for the next two decades numbers rose steadily. There are now well over a million Wood Ducks in North America.

108, 156   Green-winged Teal
including "Common Teal"
Anas crecca

Description: 12–16″ (30–41 cm). A small *dark* duck. Male has chestnut head, green ear patch, flashing *green speculum,* pale gray sides, and pinkish breast with a vertical white stripe down the side. Female is dark brown without distinctive markings. "Common Teal," race in Old World, has horizontal white stripe above flanks and no vertical white stripes on sides.

Voice: Clear repeated whistle. Females quack.

Habitat: Marshes, ponds, and marshy lakes.

Nesting: 10–12 whitish or pale buff eggs in a down-lined cup in tall grass, often several hundred yards from water.

Range: Breeds in northern Alaska, Manitoba, and Quebec south to California, Colorado, Nebraska, and New York. Winters in southern states and along coasts. Also in Eurasia.

Flocks of Green-winged Teal fly swiftly, executing sharp turns in unison like flocks of shorebirds. When the flock settles on water, the birds often separate into small groups consisting of one female courted by several males. Eventually the female chooses a mate and the chosen male wards off other suitors. In spring the pair returns to the previous breeding place of the female, not that of the male.

113, 154 Mallard
including "Mexican Duck"
Anas platyrhynchos

Description: 18–27" (46–69 cm). Male has a *green head, white neck ring,* chestnut breast, and grayish body; inner feathers of wing (speculum) are metallic purplish blue, bordered in front and back with white. Female mottled brown with *white tail* and purplish-blue speculum; mottled orange and brown bill. Form in Southwest ("Mexican Duck") similar to typical female Mallard but darker; speculum blue; bill of male yellow-green; bill of female dusky orange; *no white in tail.*

Voice: Male utters soft, reedy notes; female, a loud quack.

Habitat: From large marshes to small river bends, bays, and even ditches and city ponds.

Nesting: 8–10 light olive-green eggs in a down-lined nest often placed some distance from water, occasionally even in a tree.

Range: Breeds from Alaska and Quebec south to southern California, Virginia, Texas, and northern Mexico. Winters throughout United States and south to Central America and West Indies. Also in Eurasia.

Mallard courtship starts in the fall, and by midwinter pairs have formed. Mated pairs migrate northward together, heading for the female's place of origin.

The male stays with the female until incubation is well underway, then leaves to join a flock of other males to begin the annual molt. Normally shy, Mallards become tame in city parks and on reservoirs, where they can be fed by hand; they often interbreed with domestic ducks and produce a variety of odd-looking hybrids.

106, 162 Northern Pintail
Anas acuta

Description: Male, 25–29" (64–74 cm); female, 21–23" (53–58 cm). Long-necked slender duck. Male has *brown head, white neck* and underparts, grayish back and sides, and *long, black, pointed central tail feathers.* Speculum metallic brown and green with white rear border that shows in flight. Feet gray. Female has brownish head, gray bill, and somewhat pointed tail.

Voice: Distinctive 2-tone whistle; females quack.

Habitat: Marshes, prairie ponds, and tundra; sometimes salt marshes in winter.

Nesting: 6–9 pale greenish-buff eggs in a shallow bowl of grass lined with down, often some distance from water.

Range: Breeds from Alaska and Labrador south to California, Nebraska, and Maine. Locally in East and occasionally elsewhere. Winters south to Central America and West Indies. Also in Eurasia.

Although not as numerous as the Mallard, this graceful game bird is still a widespread and common duck, especially in the West, where about half of North America's six million are found. Winter flocks can be very large, numbering in the thousands. Male Northern Pintails are aggressive, often forcing their attentions on females of other species.

128, 157 Blue-winged Teal
Anas discors

Description: 14–16″ (36–41 cm). A small brown
duck with *pale blue shoulder patches*. Male
has gray head and *white crescent in front of
eye*. Female mottled brown, similar to
female Cinnamon Teal but with obscure
patterning on face.

Voice: Soft lisping or peeping note. Female
utters a soft quack.

Habitat: Marshes, shallow ponds, and lakes.

Nesting: 9–12 dull white eggs in a down-lined
hollow concealed in grass near water.

Range: Breeds from southeastern Alaska and
western Canada to Canadian Maritimes
and south to northeastern California,
New Mexico, and New York. Winters
from southern California, southern
Texas, and Carolinas southward through
tropical America.

Fast and wary, Blue-winged Teal fly in
small groups or flocks, turning in unison
and flashing the blue area of the wing.
They arrive latest of all ducks at their
breeding grounds and leave early in the
fall. In the past, when large numbers of
these ducks left the prairies on
migration, they were heavily hunted,
and their population drastically
declined. They are in less danger today
because the hunting season opens later,
after most of the birds have already
migrated.

105, 158 Cinnamon Teal
Anas cyanoptera

Description: 14–17″ (36–43 cm). Male bright rufous
with pale blue shoulder patches. Female
mottled sandy brown, dusky, with pale
blue shoulder patches; face plainer than
female Blue-wing's, but the two are
often not distinguishable in the field.

Voice: A soft quack; various chattering and
clucking notes.

Habitat: Marshes, ponds, and streams bordered with reeds.

Nesting: 9–12 pale buff or whitish eggs in a down-lined nest of grass concealed in vegetation, usually near water.

Range: Breeds in western North America from southern British Columbia and Montana south to Texas. Winters in southern part of breeding range south to tropical America. Rare in East, usually found in flocks of Blue-winged Teal. Also in South America.

A western relative of the more widespread Blue-winged Teal, this is a sociable species that travels in small, fast flocks. Males of the two species look very different, but their close relationship is revealed by the females, which are very similar and distinguishable only at close range and in good light.

112, 155   Northern Shoveler
Anas clypeata

Description: 17–20″ (43–51 cm). *Large shovel-shaped bill.* Male has green head, white body, and *chestnut flanks.* Female streaked brown with pale blue shoulder patches; similar to female Blue-winged Teal, but bill much larger.

Voice: Low croak, cluck, or quack.

Habitat: Marshes and prairie potholes. Sometimes on salt or brackish marshes.

Nesting: 8–12 pale buff or greenish eggs in a down-lined cup of grass concealed in vegetation, often some distance from water.

Range: Breeds from Alaska and northern Manitoba south to California, Nebraska, and Wisconsin; local and uncommon in Great Lakes area and Northeast. Winters from Oregon across southern half of United States to Gulf Coast and South Carolina, south to Central America. Also in Eurasia.

The Northern Shoveler, related to the Blue-winged and Cinnamon teal, favors broad, shallow marshes where it can use its large bill to strain small animals and seeds from the water. Like the two teal, male shovelers wear eclipse plumage until February, much later than ducks whose courtship begins in the fall. Though less numerous than in ancient times, the Northern Shoveler and other marsh ducks have lately become relatively abundant because game departments and private organizations in Canada, the United States, and Mexico have purchased wetland habitat to ensure their survival.

152, 153 Gadwall
Anas strepera

Description: 18–21" (46–53 cm). Male is a medium-sized grayish duck with *white patch on hind edge of wing,* black rump, and sandy brown head. Female mottled brown, with white patch on hind edge of wing.

Voice: Duck-like quack; also chatters and whistles.

Habitat: Freshwater marshes, ponds, and rivers; locally in salt marshes.

Nesting: 9–11 cream-white eggs in a down-lined nest of grass, usually hidden near water but sometimes in upland fields.

Range: Breeds from southern Alaska, British Columbia, and Minnesota south to California and western Texas; occasionally in East. Winters in much of United States. Also in Old World.

Often considered drab, the male Gadwall is a handsome duck clad in soft pastel grays and tans. This species is one of the dabbling ducks; it feeds by tipping forward so that the tail sticks up as it reaches for plants on the bottom.

102 Eurasian Wigeon
"European Wigeon"
Anas penelope

Description: 18–20" (46–51 cm). Male has *rusty head, buff crown,* pinkish-buff breast, and gray body. Female is streaked gray-brown or rust-brown. Both sexes have *large white shoulder patches* and dull blue bills. Female American Wigeon is very similar to gray female Eurasian, but usually has grayer head.

Voice: Piping 2-note whistle, seldom heard in America.

Habitat: Marshes, ponds, and lakes; tidal flats in nonbreeding season.

Nesting: 7 or 8 cream-white eggs in a down-lined nest of grass, hidden in vegetation, often some distance from water.

Range: Breeds in Eurasia; an uncommon but regular visitor to North America, mainly along Atlantic and Pacific coasts.

The Eurasian Wigeon is usually found associating with flocks of its American counterpart. Like the American Wigeon, this species is unorthodox in its feeding habits: It spends much of its time grazing on land like a goose and also loiters around feeding flocks of diving ducks, snatching food from them when they bob back to the surface.

111, 159 American Wigeon
Anas americana

Description: 18–23" (46–58 cm). Male is brownish with *white crown,* green ear patch, and bold *white shoulder* patches easily visible in flight. Female is mottled brown with grayish head and whitish shoulder patches. Bill pale blue in both sexes.

Voice: Distinctive whistled *whew-whee-whew;* also quacks.

Habitat: Marshes, ponds, and shallow lakes.

Nesting: 9–11 whitish or cream-colored eggs in a

down-lined nest of grass, often several hundred yards from water.

Range: Breeds from Alaska, northern Manitoba, and southern Quebec south to Nevada, Dakotas, and Great Lakes region; rarely farther east. Winters mainly along Pacific, Atlantic, and Gulf coasts.

The American Wigeon, or "Baldpate," is a wary bird, taking flight the instant it is disturbed. Flocks rise straight up from the surface of the water, uttering their whistling calls. Unlike many dabbling ducks, these birds often spend the night on large open bays, sleeping in rafts well out from shore.

103, 161 Canvasback
Aythya valisineria

Description: 19–24" (48–61 cm). Male has a *whitish body,* black chest, and reddish head with low forehead. *Long bill gives head a distinctive sloping profile.* Female grayish, with sandy-brown head. At a distance male Canvasbacks can be distinguished from similar Redheads by their white bodies, the male Redhead's body being largely gray.

Voice: Males grunt or croak; females quack.

Habitat: Nests on marshes; winters on lakes, bays, and estuaries.

Nesting: 7–10 greenish eggs in a floating mass of reeds and grass anchored to stems of marsh plants.

Range: Breeds from Alaska south and east to Nebraska and Minnesota. Winters in coastal and interior West from British Columbia south and in East from Massachusetts south to Gulf Coast and in Mississippi Valley.

Inhabitants of large prairie marshes during the summer, these wary birds usually spend the winter on large lakes, bays, and estuaries. A major item in their diet is wild celery, which gives their flesh a rich taste; they are generally regarded as the best-tasting of North American waterfowl.

104, 160 Redhead
Aythya americana

Description: 18–22" (46–56 cm). Male *gray, with brick-red head and black breast.* Female duller and browner, with light area around base of bill; has rounder head than female Ring-necked Duck. Both sexes have pale gray wing stripe and pale blue-gray bill. Similar Canvasback has whiter body and sloping forehead and bill.

Voice: Like the meow of a cat; also quacks.

Habitat: Nests in marshes but at other times is found on open lakes and bays; often on salt water in winter.

Nesting: 10–16 buff eggs in a woven cup of reeds lined with white down and attached to marsh vegetation.

Range: Breeds from Alaska and British Columbia east to Minnesota and south to California and Colorado. Winters in southern half of United States, Mississippi Valley, and Great Lakes region.

Throughout its western breeding range, the Redhead is a local bird, common on some marshes and rare or absent on others. Formerly more abundant, this diving duck has declined because of the twin pressures of hunting and habitat destruction; there are now said to be about 600,000 Redheads left in North America.

117, 144 Ring-necked Duck
Aythya collaris

Description: 14–18" (36–46 cm). Male has black back and breast; purple-glossed, black-appearing head; pale gray flanks; vertical white mark on side of breast. Female brownish, paler around base of bill, with narrow white eye ring. Bill pale gray with white ring. The high angular shape of the head and white ring on bill distinguish this bird from the scaup.

Voice: Soft purring notes, but usually silent.

Habitat: Wooded lakes, ponds, and rivers; seldom on salt water except in the southern states.

Nesting: 8–12 buff or olive eggs in a down-lined cup concealed in vegetation near the edge of a pond.

Range: Breeds from Alaska, Manitoba, and Newfoundland south to California, Arizona, Great Lakes, and Maine. Winters from Washington south along Pacific Coast, east through Southwest and Gulf Coast states, and north to New England.

This duck of woodland ponds and streams is a vegetarian, so its flesh is tasty, but because it never gathers in large flocks it has not been hunted extensively like some of its relatives. A fast flier, the Ring-neck undertakes longer migrations than most other diving ducks.

116, 139 Tufted Duck
Aythya fuligula

Description: 17″ (43 cm). Male a stocky blackish duck with flashing *white flanks and wispy crest.* Female warm brown, paler on flanks, with small white patch at base of bill; little or no crest.

Voice: Various soft growling notes; low whistles.

Habitat: Wooded lakes, streams, and marshes; in winter often in estuaries and shallow coastal bays.

Nesting: 8–10 pale buff or greenish eggs in a down-lined bowl of grass concealed under a bush or tussock, usually near water.

Range: Breeds in northern Eurasia; casual in North America, chiefly along coasts in Alaska, California, and northeastern states. Most often seen near urban areas.

Tufted Ducks that appear in North America may arrive with other waterfowl that have migrated to the Pacific Coast from Siberia. Fast-flying diving ducks, they may be found in the company of Ring-necked Ducks, Oldsquaws, scaup, and goldeneyes, or by themselves on urban reservoirs. Some North American Tufted Ducks undoubtedly represent escaped captive birds.

115, 136 Greater Scaup
Aythya marila

Description: 15–20″ (38–51 cm). Male has very light gray body, blackish chest, and *black-appearing, green-glossed head.* Female is a uniform dark brown with white patch at base of bill. Both sexes have long whitish wing stripe. See Lesser Scaup.

Voice: Usually silent; discordant croaking calls on breeding grounds.

Habitat: Lakes, bays, and ponds; often on salt water in winter.

Nesting: 8–12 olive-buff eggs in a down-lined cup of grass concealed in a clump of grass on land or in marsh vegetation well out from shore.

Range: Breeds in Alaska and northern Canada east to Hudson Bay and occasionally in Maritime Provinces. Winters mainly along Pacific, Gulf, and Atlantic coasts. Also in Eurasia.

For most birders the Greater Scaup is either a winter duck or a rarity. It is found in flocks, or rafts, often mixed with other diving ducks. It feeds on oysters, small clams, and rock crabs in sheltered bays, inshore waters, and the mouths of large rivers, but in summer it also consumes quantities of buds and seeds of submerged plants.

114, 137 **Lesser Scaup**
Aythya affinis

Description: 15–18" (38–46 cm). Similar to the Greater Scaup, but crown is higher and forehead steeper, giving the head a more angular appearance. Head of male glossed with purple, not green. Female dark brown with a small white face patch; not easily distinguishable from female Greater Scaup. In flight, white stripe is shorter than that of the Greater Scaup, which extends three-fourths of the wing's length.

Voice: Seldom heard; sharp whistles and guttural scolding notes.

Habitat: Ponds and marshes; during migration and in winter it occurs on lakes, rivers, and ponds, and in the southern states on salt water.

Nesting: Usually 9–12 dark olive-buff eggs in a down-lined cup of grass hidden in vegetation, often located some distance from the edge of the water.

Range: Breeds from interior Alaska and northern Canada south to Colorado and Iowa; occasionally farther east. Winters regularly along coasts south from British Columbia and Massachusetts to Gulf of Mexico; also inland south of Colorado and Great Lakes.

Both the Lesser and Greater scaup are popularly called "Bluebills." This is one of the most abundant ducks in North America; of an estimated seven million scaup, the great majority are Lessers.

131, 150 Common Eider
Somateria mollissima

Description: 23–27″ (58–69 cm). Our largest duck. Male has *black underparts; white back;* white head and breast; dark crown; greenish tinge on back of head. Female is mottled brown with barred flanks. Long sloping bill gives bird a distinctive profile. Usually holds bill pointing slightly down toward surface of water. See King Eider.

Voice: During courtship the male gives a hollow moan and various cooing notes. Female quacks.

Habitat: Rocky coasts and coastal tundra.

Nesting: 4–7 olive or buff eggs in a substantial mass of grass thickly lined with down. Often several pairs form a loose colony.

Range: Breeds on Arctic coasts of Alaska and Canada and south from Maritimes to Massachusetts. Winters south along Pacific Coast from Alaska to Washington and along Atlantic Coast to Long Island, occasionally farther. Also northern Eurasia.

Down from the female Common Eider's breast, harvested from the birds' nests, is used for expensive parkas and sleeping bags. Most eiderdown comes from Iceland, where artificial nesting sites attract the females and allow easy access to the down. Once her first lining of down has been harvested, the female produces a second. This too is taken after the eggs have hatched and the young have left the nest.

130, 148 King Eider
Somateria spectabilis

Description: 18–25″ (46–64 cm). A large duck. Similar to the Common Eider, but male has *black back,* conspicuous orange-yellow bill, and "shield" on forehead. Female similar to female Common

Eider, but bill is shorter, not extending as far back toward eye, and lacks the distinctive sloping profile; flanks marked with black crescents, not bars. Usually holds bill horizontal to surface of water.

Voice: A guttural croaking.

Habitat: Rocky coasts and islands.

Nesting: 4–7 buff-olive eggs in a down-lined depression on rocky tundra, often some distance from the edge of the water.

Range: Breeds in freshwater ponds and lakes in Alaska and Arctic islands of Canada, south locally to Hudson Bay. Winters along coasts south to southern Alaska and from Labrador to New Jersey; rarely farther south and on Great Lakes. Also in Eurasia.

Although few western birders have seen a King Eider, this species is one of our most abundant ducks, with a North American population of about two million. These birds nest in remote regions of the Arctic, where until recently they have suffered little disturbance. The migrations of the King Eider are spectacular, with huge flocks, often consisting entirely of males or of females, traveling in long lines along the coast, heading to or from their breeding or wintering grounds.

133, 149 **Spectacled Eider**
Somateria fischeri

Description: 20½–22″ (52–56 cm). Breeding male has white neck, back, and shoulders, black breast and belly. Head light olive green with *large, white, black-rimmed "spectacles."* Female is mottled buff, with *pale buff "spectacles"* and *large bill feathered at base.*

Voice: Usually silent; a soft *ah-hoo!*

Habitat: Coastal tundra during breeding season; inshore waters during most of year.

Nesting: 4–9 greenish or olive-buff eggs in a

down-lined depression in the tundra
near fresh or brackish water.

Range: Breeds along northern and western
coasts of Alaska. Winters off Alaska
Peninsula and eastern Aleutians, but
main wintering grounds not known.

During the winter the Spectacled Eider's
diet consists largely of mussels and
other mollusks, which it captures in
deep dives over submerged ledges and
reefs, but on its tundra breeding
grounds this duck feeds mainly on
aquatic insects, crustaceans, and the
seeds of water plants. The largest
breeding concentration is on the
Yukon-Kuskokwim delta, where some
70,000 of the world's 200,000 pairs of
Spectacled Eiders nest. The population
is declining rapidly, probably due to
persecution and disturbances in Siberia.

134 Steller's Eider
Polysticta stelleri

Description: 17–18½″ (43–47 cm). A very small
eider, the size of a goldeneye. Male is
*pale chestnut below, boldly black and white
above;* head white with black ring around
eye and small black and green crest on
nape. Female is rich mottled brown
like other eiders, but with smaller head.
Both sexes have speculum like that of
Mallard—purple, bordered in front and
back with white.

Voice: Male has a weak moan similar to
Common Eider's; female makes low
growling notes.

Habitat: Tundra pools and adjacent coastal waters.

Nesting: 6–10 yellowish or greenish eggs in a
down-lined depression in moss on tundra.

Range: Breeds on northern and western coasts
of Alaska. Winters on southern coast of
Alaska and Aleutians.

This fast-flying, beautiful duck dives for
crustaceans, insect larvae, and even

aquatic plants and their seeds. It has been observed to feed on crowberries, a staple tundra fruit preferred by several kinds of waterfowl. Birds resting on the water often hold the tail at an angle above the surface.

129, 145 Harlequin Duck
Histrionicus histrionicus

Description: 14–20″ (36–51 cm). A small dark duck. Male is blue-gray (appearing black at a distance), with chestnut flanks and distinctive white patches on head and body. Female is dusky brown with 2 or 3 whitish patches on sides of face. In flight, this species lacks large white patches on wings.

Voice: A mouse-like squeak and various low whistles.

Habitat: Swift-moving streams in summer; rocky, wave-lashed coasts and jetties in winter.

Nesting: 6–8 pale buff or cream-colored eggs in a mass of down concealed in a crevice in rocks along a stream.

Range: Breeds from Alaska and Yukon south to Wyoming and Sierra Nevada of California, and from southern Baffin Island south to Labrador and Gaspé Peninsula. Winters along coasts south to central California and Long Island. Also in Eurasia.

High in the Rockies and the Sierra Nevada the Harlequin Duck is a bird of swift mountain streams, where it catches the nymphs of stone flies, caddis flies, and other aquatic insects. In the fall the birds move down to the coast, where they thrive in rough water of a different kind, riding the surf in toward rocky cliffs, and wrenching mussels, chitons, barnacles, and other attached animals from the surface and diving for crabs and other crustaceans.

132, 135, 151   Oldsquaw
Clangula hyemalis

Description: Male, 19–22″ (48–56 cm); female,
15–17″ (38–43 cm). Male boldly
patterned in black and white (mainly
white in winter, mainly black in
summer), with very long, slender central
tail feathers. Females are duller and lack
the long tail feathers. Males and females
show *all-dark unpatterned wings in flight.*

Voice: Various clucking and growling notes;
male's courtship call a musical *ow-owdle-
ow, ow-owdle-ow,* frequently repeated.

Habitat: Breeds on tundra; winters on open bays
and inshore waters.

Nesting: 5–11 yellowish or cream-colored eggs in
a down-lined cup of grass concealed on
tundra near water.

Range: Breeds in Alaska and Arctic Canada.
Winters along coasts from Bering Sea
south to California, from Labrador south
to Carolinas, along portions of Gulf Coast,
and on Great Lakes. Also in Eurasia.

In midwinter Oldsquaws begin their
courtship displays. Several males gather
around a single female and give their
far-carrying call. Although courtship
lasts until after the birds have returned
to their nesting grounds, most birds
are paired when they arrive in the
North. In winter these diving ducks
feed mainly on mollusks, shrimps, and
crabs, but when nesting they switch to
roots, buds, and seeds; the ducklings
feed mainly on insect larvae.

119, 142   Black Scoter
"Common Scoter"
Melanitta nigra

Description: 17–21″ (43–53 cm). Male black; bill
black with *large yellow knob at base.*
Female duller, with pale cheeks and all-
dark bill. Both sexes show silvery wing
linings in flight.

Voice: In spring a musical whistled *cour-loo.*
Habitat: Breeds on ponds in boreal forests;
winters on oceans and in large saltwater
bays.
Nesting: 5–8 pale buff eggs in a down-lined cup
of grass hidden in a rock crevice or
clump of grass near edge of water.
Range: Breeds in western Alaska, Labrador, and
Newfoundland. Winters along coasts
from Alaska south to California, from
Newfoundland south to Carolinas, along
portions of Gulf Coast, and on Great
Lakes. Also in Eurasia.

Scoters are gregarious, and the three
species often feed together, gathering
over submerged reefs where mollusks
abound. The Black Scoter is the least
common of the three in North America,
numbering about 500,000; it is more
numerous and deserving of its former
name, "Common Scoter," in parts
of Eurasia.

120, 141 **Surf Scoter**
Melanitta perspicillata

Description: 17–21″ (43–53 cm). Male black with
white patches on crown and nape. Bill
colorful, swollen at base, bearing large
black spot. Female brownish black,
with 2 whitish patches on cheek. Both
sexes lack white wing patch.
Voice: A low guttural croaking.
Habitat: Breeds on northern lakes; winters
almost entirely on the ocean and in large
coastal bays.
Nesting: 5–8 pinkish-buff eggs in a down-lined
depression hidden under bushes or
in marsh vegetation, not necessarily
near water.
Range: Breeds in Alaska and across northern
Canada to Labrador. Winters mainly
along coasts, from Alaska south to
California and from Newfoundland
south to Florida and rarely to Texas.

The most common scoter on the Pacific Coast in winter, the Surf Scoter sometimes feeds quite close to rocky headlands and in shallow inlets. The bold white patches on the male's head are used in displays; a bird may threaten a rival simply by turning its head and presenting its white nape. These scoters depart for breeding grounds in early spring, but a few, usually young males, may spend their second summer on wintering grounds.

118, 143 White-winged Scoter
Melanitta fusca

Description: 19–24" (48–61 cm). Male black with *bold white wing patches,* white crescents around eyes, and yellow bill with black knob at base. Females are dull brown, with 2 whitish facial spots and white wing patches.

Voice: Soft whistles and guttural croaks.

Habitat: Breeds on large lakes; winters mainly on the ocean and on large coastal bays, but a few remain on lakes in the interior.

Nesting: 5–17 buff or pink eggs in a hollow lined with sticks and down, under a bush, or in a crevice near water, often on an island in a lake.

Range: Breeds in Alaska and much of western and central Canada. Winters along coasts, from Alaska south to California and from Newfoundland south to Carolinas, rarely to Florida and Texas. Also in Eurasia.

Scoters dive for shellfish, flying in long lines to and from their favorite feeding areas. Sociable birds, they gather in large flocks or rafts, both to feed and to sleep at night. Like all birds that dive and rest on the sea, they are vulnerable to oil spills.

107, 125 Common Goldeneye
Bucephala clangula

Description: 16–20" (41–51 cm). Male has white
body; black back; black-appearing
(actually glossy *greenish*) head; and *large,
round white spot in front of eye.* Eye bright
yellow. Female grayish, with warm
brown head, white neck ring, and *dark
bill.* Both sexes have a distinctive puffy
head shape and a large white wing
patch, conspicuous in flight. See
Barrow's Goldeneye.

Voice: Courtship call of male a high-pitched
jeee-ep! Females utter a low quack.

Habitat: Breeds on wooded lakes and ponds;
winters mainly on coastal bays and
estuaries.

Nesting: 8–12 pale green eggs in a mass of down
in a natural tree cavity, up to 60' (18 m)
above the ground.

Range: Breeds in Alaska and across Canada to
Newfoundland and Maritime Provinces,
south to mountains of Montana and
Great Lakes. Winters in much of
United States, wherever water is open.
Also in Eurasia.

Among goldeneyes pair formation
begins in midwinter, and until then the
two sexes often form separate flocks.
Indeed, male Common Goldeneyes
winter farther north than do the females.
Goldeneyes can dive to depths of 20 feet
(6 meters) or more, but generally limit
themselves to about 10 feet (3 meters).
Their preferred winter foods are
mollusks and mud crabs; the crop of
one bird on the Pacific Coast contained
the remains of 26 mud crabs.

124, 138 Barrow's Goldeneye
Bucephala islandica

Description: 16½–20" (42–51 cm). Male has white
body, black back, and black-appearing
(actually glossed with *purple*) head.

Similar to male Common Goldeneye, but has more black on sides, stubbier bill, and *crescent-shaped, rather than round, white spot in front of eye.* Female gray with brown head, white collar, and (usually) *orange-yellow bill.* Both sexes differ from Common Goldeneye in having steeper forehead and smaller white wing patches.

Voice: Soft grunts and croaks during courtship; otherwise usually silent.

Habitat: Breeds on forested lakes and rivers; winters mainly on open bays and estuaries along coast.

Nesting: 5–15 pale green eggs on a bed of down in a hollow tree or, in treeless areas, in a crevice among rocks.

Range: Breeds in mountains from Alaska south to central California and Wyoming, and in northern Quebec and Labrador. Winters along Pacific Coast from Alaska south to California and in smaller numbers along Atlantic from Maritime Provinces south to Long Island. Also breeds in western Greenland and Iceland.

Barrow's Goldeneye is usually found in smaller flocks than the Common Goldeneye. It feeds almost entirely on mollusks obtained by diving, but also takes an occasional snail, sea urchin, or marine worm. While there are well over a million Common Goldeneyes in North America, the population of Barrow's Goldeneyes is less than 200,000.

109, 140   Bufflehead
Bucephala albeola

Description: 13–15″ (33–38 cm). A small, chubby duck. Male largely white, with black back, black head with greenish and purplish gloss, and *large white patch from behind eye to top and back of head.* Female all dark, with single whitish patch on cheek. A fast flier, with a rapid wingbeat.

Voice: Male has a squeaky whistle; female, a
soft, hoarse quack.

Habitat: Breeds on wooded lakes and ponds;
winters mainly on saltwater bays and
estuaries.

Nesting: 6–12 pale buff or ivory eggs in a mass of
down placed in a woodpecker hole up to
20′ (6 m) off the ground.

Range: Breeds in Alaska and in Canada east to
western Quebec, and south in mountains
to Washington and Montana. Winters
along Atlantic to northern Florida and
across southern United States, south to
Mexico and Gulf Coast.

These beautiful ducks, relatives of the
goldeneyes, fly fast and usually close to
the water. They tend to travel in smaller
flocks than goldeneyes and often feed
closer to shore. While a flock is diving
for food there is almost always least one
bird on the surface watching for danger.

126, 164 **Hooded Merganser**
Lophodytes cucullatus

Description: 16–19″ (41–48 cm). A small duck with
a slender pointed bill. Male has *white,
fan-shaped, black-bordered crest,* blackish
body with dull rusty flanks, and white
breast with 2 black stripes down side.
Female is dull gray-brown, with warmer
brown head and crest. Both sexes show
white wing patch in flight.

Voice: Hoarse grunts and chatters.

Habitat: Breeds on wooded ponds, lakes, and
rivers; winters in coastal marshes
and inlets.

Nesting: 8–12 white eggs in a down-lined cup
in a natural tree cavity or sometimes
in a fallen hollow log.

Range: Breeds from southern Alaska south
to Oregon and Montana, and from
Manitoba and Nova Scotia south to
Arkansas and northern Alabama.
Winters near coast from British
Columbia south to California and

from New England south to Florida and Texas.

Small wintering flocks can be found on fresh water throughout the West. Males perform a beautiful courtship display and, once mated, swim energetically around the female in further ritual displays. This duck's diet includes aquatic invertebrates, small frogs, newts, and tadpoles.

122, 167   Common Merganser
Mergus merganser

Description: 22–27″ (56–69 cm). Male has *flashing white sides, green head,* white breast, and long, thin red bill. Female has gray body and sides; reddish-brown crested head sharply set off from white throat. Red-breasted Merganser is similar, but male has gray sides, white neck ring, and rust-colored breast; female has reddish-brown head that blends into gray of neck.

Voice: Low rasping croaks.

Habitat: Breeds on wooded rivers and ponds; winters mainly on lakes and rivers, occasionally on salt water.

Nesting: 9–12 pale buff or ivory eggs in a down-lined tree cavity or sometimes on the ground or in an abandoned hawk's nest.

Range: Breeds across Canada from eastern Alaska, Manitoba, and Newfoundland south in mountains to California, northern New Mexico, Great Lakes, and northern New England. Winters south to northern Mexico, Gulf Coast states, and Georgia (rarely farther). Also in Eurasia.

This large, streamlined duck dives and pursues its aquatic prey in rivers and lakes. The narrow bill, with a hooked upper mandible and saw-like teeth along the edges, is specialized to catch slippery fish.

123, 166 Red-breasted Merganser
Mergus serrator

Description: 19–26" (48–66 cm). Male has green
head with wispy crest, *gray sides, white
neck ring, and rusty breast.* Female
grayish, with reddish-brown head
shading gradually into gray of neck.
Both sexes are crested and have red bills.

Voice: Usually silent; various croaking and
grunting notes during courtship.

Habitat: Breeds on wooded lakes and tundra
ponds; winters mainly on salt water.

Nesting: 8–10 olive-buff eggs in a down-lined
depression concealed under a bush or in
a brush pile.

Range: Breeds in Alaska and across northern
Canada to Newfoundland and south
to Great Lakes. Winters chiefly along
coasts from Alaska south to California,
from Maritime Provinces south to
Florida, and along Gulf Coast. Also
in Eurasia.

The Red-breasted Merganser breeds
farther north than its relatives and is
also the most common winter merganser
on salt water, especially where rocky
coves provide good fishing. Often found
searching for food alone, these birds
also gather in large flocks where fish
are abundant.

127, 147 Ruddy Duck
Oxyura jamaicensis

Description: 14–16" (36–41 cm). A small, chunky
duck with a long tail that is often held
straight up. Male in breeding plumage
has chestnut body, black crown, and *white
cheeks.* Female and winter male are dusky
brown, with whitish cheeks of female
crossed by a dark stripe. Male's bill is blue
in breeding season, black at other times.

Voice: Usually silent. Courting male produces
ticking and clapping sounds by pressing
its bill against its breast.

Habitat: Breeds on freshwater marshes, marshy
           lakes, and ponds; winters on marshes
           and in shallow coastal bays.

Nesting: 6–20 white or cream-colored eggs in a
           floating nest of dry stems lined with
           down, concealed among reeds or
           bulrushes in a marsh.

Range: Breeds from British Columbia,
           Mackenzie, and Quebec south to
           California, southern New Mexico, and
           southern Texas, with occasional breeding
           farther east. Winters on coasts north to
           British Columbia and Massachusetts
           and as far inland as Missouri.

This duck is one of the most aquatic
members of the family and like a grebe
can sink slowly out of sight. Although it
can avoid danger by diving or by hiding
in marsh vegetation, it is a strong flier
and undertakes long migrations to and
from its nesting places. Largely
vegetarian, it favors pondweed and the
seeds of other aquatic plants, but also
consumes large numbers of midge
larvae during the breeding season.

FAMILY CATHARTIDAE
American Vultures

7 species: Tropical and temperate
America. Three species, including the
nearly extinct California Condor, breed
in North America. These scavengers
feed on carrion and refuse. They possess
weak feet and stubby claws instead of
sharp talons like those of hawks.
Vultures are large, mostly blackish birds
with broad wings and bare heads; their
naked heads prevent their feathers from
becoming fouled when feeding on
carrion. They nest in tree cavities, on
rock ledges, or on the ground.

322 Black Vulture
Coragyps atratus

Description: 22–24″ (56–61 cm). W. 4′6″ (1.4 m).
Black, with white patch near each wing
tip, conspicuous in flight; head bare,
grayish; feet extend beyond the short
tail. Flaps its shorter and rounder wings
more often and more rapidly than
Turkey Vulture.

Voice: Hisses or grunts; seldom heard.

Habitat: Open country, but breeds in light
woodlands and thickets.

Nesting: 2 white or gray-green eggs, blotched
with brown, laid under a bush, in a
hollow log, under large rocks, or in
a cave.

Range: Resident from western Texas and
Arkansas north and east to New Jersey
(rarely to Massachusetts and Maine)
and south to Florida. Also in American
tropics.

Black Vultures soar in a group,
alternately flapping and gliding,
until one of them discovers carrion,
whereupon all the others converge on the
find. This species, with its shorter wings,
is adapted to foraging in towns, where it
can maneuver among buildings. In parts
of its range, this enables it to feed in
places that are inaccessible to the larger
Turkey Vulture.

321 Turkey Vulture
Cathartes aura

Description: 25–32″ (64–81 cm). W. 6′ (1.8 m).
Eagle-sized blackish bird, usually seen
soaring over the countryside. In flight,
the long wings are held upward in a
wide, shallow V; flight feathers silvery
below. Tail long; head small, bare, and
reddish; gray in immatures. Similar to
Black Vulture, but wings narrower;
flaps wings less frequently and rolls and
sways from side to side.

Voice: Usually silent; hisses or grunts when feeding or at nest.

Habitat: Mainly deciduous forests and woodlands; often seen over adjacent farmlands.

Nesting: 2 whitish eggs, heavily marked with dark brown, placed without nest or lining in a crevice in rocks, in a hollow tree, or in a fallen hollow log.

Range: Breeds from southern British Columbia, central Saskatchewan, Great Lakes, and New Hampshire southward. Winters in Southwest, and in East northward to southern New England.

The familiar "buzzard" of open country and woodlands in the West, the Turkey Vulture can coast for hours, swaying from side to side, as it searches for a carcass. As they soar, vultures ride on rising columns of warm air called thermals to save energy as they cover miles of territory. The importance of this energy saving is clear from the fact that we seldom see a Turkey Vulture on a windless day, when thermals do not form.

328 California Condor
Gymnogyps californianus

Description: 45–55" (1.1–1.4 m). W. 8'6"–9'6" (2.6–2.9 m). Largest bird of prey in North America. Black with bare head (reddish orange in adults, blackish in young), black ruff, *conspicuous white wing linings,* and pale feet.

Voice: Usually silent.

Habitat: Mountains and surrounding open, sparsely covered brush country where it can easily detect and safely approach carrion.

Nesting: 1 white egg placed in an inaccessible cave or cavity on a cliff.

Range: Mountains north of Los Angeles, California.

The California Condor has been declining since prehistoric times, probably because herds of large mammals became scarce. By the 20th century its range had shrunk to a small area in the mountains north of Los Angeles. In the 1980s researchers discovered that some of the few surviving birds were dying of lead poisoning, and so all the remaining wild birds—five in number—were trapped and placed in zoos. Young birds have been reared in captivity, but it remains to be seen whether the effort to save the species from extinction will succeed.

FAMILY ACCIPITRIDAE
Hawks and Eagles

240 species: Worldwide. Twenty-four species breed in North America. This varied group of birds ranges from the very large eagles to small hawks not much bigger than an American Robin. All are predators, with hooked bills and sharply pointed talons. Some, the buteos (eagles, the Red-tailed Hawk, and similar birds), have short broad tails and wide rounded wings adapted for soaring as they search for prey. Others, the accipiters, have short rounded wings and long narrow tails well suited for darting and twisting among dense branches in pursuit of prey. Some of the kites have narrow pointed wings and are expert gliders, while the Osprey, a fish eater, has long talons and sharp spines on the soles of its feet for grasping slippery prey.

323 **Osprey**
Pandion haliaetus

Description: 21–24" (53–61 cm). W. 4'6"–6' (1.4–1.8 m). A large, long-winged "fish hawk." Brown above and white below;

head white with dark line through eye and on side of face. Wing shows distinctive bend at "wrist." At a distance, can resemble a gull.

Voice: Loud musical chirping.

Habitat: Lakes, rivers, and seacoasts.

Nesting: 2–4 white, pink, or buff eggs, blotched with brown, in a bulky mass of sticks and debris placed in a tree, on a telephone pole, on rocks, or on flat ground.

Range: Breeds from Alaska, north-central Canada, and Newfoundland south to Arizona and New Mexico; also along Gulf Coast and on Atlantic Coast south to Florida. Winters regularly in North America north to Gulf Coast and California. Also in South America and Old World.

Ospreys search for fish by flying and hovering over the water, watching the surface below. When prey is sighted, an Osprey dives steeply, its talons outspread, and splashes into the water. It quickly resurfaces and, if it has made a catch, flies off, adjusting the fish in its claws so that the head is pointed forward. Ospreys declined drastically because of pesticides during the 1950s and 1960s, but since then they have made a comeback and are nesting again in areas from which they had disappeared.

---

350 White-tailed Kite
"Black-shouldered Kite"
Elanus leucurus

Description: 15–16" (38–41 cm). W. 3'4" (1 m). A delicate, graceful, gull-like bird of prey. *Largely white,* with gray back, black patch on shoulder and undersurface of the pointed wing, and *white tail.* The back and breast of young birds are streaked with warm brown. Often dangles its feet in flight.

Voice: A whistled *keep-keep-keep;* also a longer, plaintive *kreep.*

Habitat: Open country and farmlands with
scattered trees or fencerows; mesquite
grasslands.

Nesting: 4 or 5 white eggs, heavily spotted with
brown, in a nest of sticks and twigs
lined with grass and placed in a tall
tree, usually near water.

Range: Resident in coastal and interior
California, Arizona, and southern Texas.
Also in American tropics.

Almost extinct in the 1930s and 1940s,
White-tailed Kites have since made a
spectacular comeback in California and
are now common in suitable lowland
habitats. Like other kites, they are
sociable outside the breeding season,
congregating at roosts in groups of a
dozen or more. They feed mainly on
small rodents and insects, which they
locate by hovering kestrel-like high in
the air. These kites prefer to rest on
treetops or other high lookouts.

349 Mississippi Kite
Ictinia mississippiensis

Description: 12–14" (30–36 cm). W. 3' (91 cm). A
small bird of prey with narrow pointed
wings. Adult gray, paler below and on
head; tail and outer flight feathers in
wings blackish, inner flight feathers
whitish. Young bird streaked below,
with banded tail.

Voice: 2 or 3 high clear whistles, seldom
heard.

Habitat: Open woodlands and thickets, usually
near water.

Nesting: 2 or 3 white eggs in a stick nest placed
in a tree.

Range: Breeds from Arizona and southern
Great Plains east to Carolinas and
south to Gulf Coast. Its range has
expanded somewhat in recent years;
increasingly wanders north to southern
New England in spring. Winters
in tropics.

This graceful, buoyant kite is a marvelous flier and spends hours in the air. It is quite gregarious, often seen in flocks and even nesting in loose colonies. Although chiefly insectivorous, feeding largely on grasshoppers and dragonflies, it occasionally takes small snakes and frogs.

325, 327 Bald Eagle
Haliaeetus leucocephalus

Description: 30–31″ (76–79 cm). W. 6–7′6″ (1.8–2.3 m). A large blackish eagle with *white head and tail* and heavy yellow bill. Young birds lack the white head and tail, and resemble adult Golden Eagles, but are variably marked with white and have a black, more massive bill.

Voice: Squeaky cackling and thin squeals.

Habitat: Lakes, rivers, marshes, and seacoasts.

Nesting: 2 or 3 white eggs in a massive nest of sticks in a tall tree or, less frequently, on top of a cliff.

Range: Breeds from Alaska east to Newfoundland and south locally to California, Great Lakes, and Virginia; also in Arizona, along Gulf Coast, and in Florida. Formerly more widespread. Winters along coasts and large rivers in much of United States.

Although the Bald Eagle eats carrion and sometimes catches crippled waterfowl, it is primarily a fish eater. Its beachcombing habit was its downfall, for it accumulated pesticides from contaminated fish and wildlife. Hunting, poaching, and the encroachment of civilization reduced its populations drastically except on the rain-forest coasts of Alaska and northern and central British Columbia. Now that the damaging pesticides have been banned, however, our national bird is staging a comeback.

347, 348 Northern Harrier
"Marsh Hawk"
Circus cyaneus

Description: 16–24" (41–61 cm). W. 3′6″ (1.1 m).
A long-winged, long-tailed hawk
with a *white rump,* usually seen gliding
unsteadily over marshes with its wings
held in a shallow V. Male has pale gray
back, head, and breast; wing tips black.
Female and young are brown above,
streaked below, young birds with a
rusty tone.

Voice: At the nest it utters a *kee-kee-kee-kee* or a
sharp whistle, but usually silent.

Habitat: Marshes and open grasslands.

Nesting: 4 or 5 pale blue or white eggs,
unmarked or with light brown spots, on
a mound of dead reeds and grass in a
marsh or shrubby meadow.

Range: Breeds from Alaska, northern Canada,
and Maritime Provinces south to
southern California, Arizona, Kansas,
and Virginia. Winters from South
America north to British Columbia,
Great Lakes, and New Brunswick. Also
in Eurasia.

This is the only North American
member of a group of hawks known as
harriers. All hunt by flying close to the
ground and taking small animals by
surprise. They seldom pursue their prey
in the air or watch quietly from an
exposed perch, as do other birds of prey.
Harriers have keener hearing than
other hawks; their disk-shaped faces, not
unlike those of owls, enable them to
amplify sound.

336 Sharp-shinned Hawk
Accipiter striatus

Description: 10–14" (25–36 cm). W. 21" (53 cm).
A jay-sized, fast-flying hawk with a
*long, narrow, square-tipped tail and short
rounded wings.* Adult slate-gray above,

pale below, with fine rust-colored barring. Immature birds brown above with whitish spots, creamy white below with streaks on breast, barring on flanks. Cooper's Hawk bigger, with proportionately larger head and more rounded tail tip; flies with slower wingbeats.

Voice: Sharp *kik-kik-kik-kik;* also a shrill squeal.

Habitat: Breeds in dense coniferous forests, less often in deciduous forests. During migration and in winter, may be seen in almost any habitat.

Nesting: 4 or 5 whitish eggs, marked with brown, on a shallow, well-made platform of twigs concealed in a dense conifer.

Range: Breeds from Alaska through Mackenzie to Newfoundland, and south to California, New Mexico, northern Gulf Coast states, and Carolinas. Winters across United States north to British Columbia and Canadian Maritimes.

The smallest and most numerous of the accipiters, the Sharp-shinned Hawk feeds mainly on birds, which it catches in sudden and swift attacks. Its rounded wings and long narrow tail enable it to pursue birds through the woods, making sharp turns to avoid branches. In the East this species seems to be undergoing a decrease in number, perhaps because some of its prey species are also declining. Nonetheless, it is still one of the most common species at hawk migration lookouts in both the East and the West.

335 Cooper's Hawk
Accipiter cooperii

Description: 14–20″ (36–51 cm). W. 28″ (71 cm). A crow-sized hawk, with long tail and short rounded wings. Adult slate-gray above, with dark cap, and finely rust-barred below. Immature brown above, whitish below with fine streaks. Tail tip rounded, not squared-off. See Sharp-shinned Hawk.

Voice: Loud *cack-cack-cack-cack.*

Habitat: Deciduous and, less often, coniferous forests, especially those interrupted by meadows and clearings.

Nesting: 4 or 5 dull-white eggs, spotted with brown, on a bulky platform of sticks and twigs, usually more than 20′ (6 m) above the ground.

Range: Breeds from British Columbia east to Manitoba and Canadian Maritimes, and south to Mexico, Gulf Coast, and northern Florida; absent or local throughout much of Great Plains. Winters from Central America north to British Columbia and southern New England.

Like its smaller look-alike the Sharp-shinned Hawk, Cooper's feeds mainly on birds, which it chases relentlessly through the woods. It also takes small mammals and, in the West, lizards and snakes. During incubation and the early stages of brooding the young, the male bird does all the hunting, bringing food to both his mate and the nestlings. Cooper's Hawks mature rapidly for birds their size; a full 25 percent of young birds breed the year after they are hatched, and the rest the year after that.

---

337 Northern Goshawk
Accipiter gentilis

Description: 20–26″ (51–66 cm). W. 3′6″ (1.1 m). A robust hawk with a long narrow tail, short rounded wings, and *bold white eyebrow.* Adults blue-gray above with a black crown; pale underparts finely barred with gray. Young bird similar in size and shape, but brown above, streaked below.

Voice: Loud *kak-kak-kak-kak-kak* when disturbed.

Habitat: Breeds in coniferous forests; winters in farmlands, woodland edges, and open country.

Nesting: 3 or 4 white or pale bluish eggs in a large mass of sticks lined with fresh sprigs of evergreen and placed in a tree.

Range: Breeds from Alaska east through Mackenzie and northern Quebec to Newfoundland, and south to New Mexico, Great Lakes, and New England; also southward to northern Appalachians. Winters south to Virginia and Southwest.

This big raptor is mainly a resident of mountainside coniferous forests. It is fearless in defense of its nest and will boldly attack anyone who ventures too close. It has recently begun extending its range to the South and now breeds in small numbers in deciduous forests.

330   Common Black-Hawk
Buteogallus anthracinus

Description: 20–23″ (51–58 cm). A stocky *black* bird of prey with broad wings and a *broad white band across the tail; cere and legs yellow,* latter visible in flight. When soaring, holds its wings flat and somewhat resembles Black Vulture; light spot visible on underwing at base of primaries. Immatures similar in size and shape but dark brown with tawny barring above, pale buff with streaks below, tail dark with several pale bands.

Voice: Shrill whistled screams.

Habitat: Wooded canyons and riverside woodlands.

Nesting: 1 or 2 white eggs, lightly spotted with brown, in a bulky nest of sticks lined with green leaves and grass.

Range: Breeds from southernmost Utah south through Arizona and southwestern New Mexico, and in southwestern Texas. Most winter south of United States. Also in American tropics.

These sluggish birds feed mainly on aquatic creatures such as frogs, small fish, crabs, and crayfish. They often perch for long periods on a branch over water, waiting for their prey to appear. This species is vulnerable to disturbance near its nesting sites and seems to be declining in the United States.

340 Harris' Hawk
Parabuteo unicinctus

Description: 18–23" (46–76 cm). W. 3'7" (1.1 m). A black, crow-sized hawk with chestnut shoulders and thighs, white on rump and base of tail, and white tail tip. Immatures similar but more streaked.

Voice: A low, harsh hissing sound.

Habitat: Semiarid regions in scrub with mesquite, cacti, and yucca.

Nesting: 2–4 dull-white eggs, faintly spotted with brown, in a stick nest lined with grass, usually placed low in scrubby brush, cacti, or small trees.

Range: Resident in southern Arizona, southeastern New Mexico, and southern Texas. Also in American tropics.

This strikingly marked hawk, normally tame and fearless, is often seen perched on a telephone or power pole along the highways of southern Texas, or flying slowly along searching for rabbits, quail, lizards, or snakes. Members of a pair or family group hunt cooperatively and share food. Harris' Hawk is occasionally observed on the ground feeding on carrion with vultures.

331 Gray Hawk
Buteo nitidus

Description: 16–18" (41–46 cm). W. 3' (91 cm). A small compact hawk with a yellow cere; *pale gray above with white underparts finely barred with gray, and bold white bands on tail.* Immatures have streaked brown upperparts, pale underparts blotched with dark brown, narrowly banded tail.

Voice: A clear whistle, *who-fleeer.*

Habitat: Riverside woodlands of cottonwoods, willows, and sycamores.

Nesting: Usually 2 whitish eggs in a small nest of sticks lined with fresh green sprigs placed in a tall tree.

Range: Breeds in southeastern Arizona and southwestern New Mexico. Most migrate south in winter. Also in American tropics.

Like many birds of prey living in deciduous woods, these hawks often line their nests with fresh leafy branches. These are plucked from the vicinity of the nest at first, but the male brings in fresh branches even after the nest is finished and incubation is underway. Gray Hawks feed mainly on lizards, dropping on them from a perch.

342 Red-shouldered Hawk
Buteo lineatus

Description: 16–24″ (41–61 cm). W. 3′4″ (1 m). A large, long-winged hawk with white barring on dark wings, *rusty shoulders,* pale underparts barred with rust, and *narrowly banded tail.* In flight shows translucent area near tip of wing, visible from below. Young birds streaked below; best distinguished from young Red-tailed Hawks by somewhat smaller size, narrower tail, longer, narrower wings, and absence of white chest.

Voice: Shrill scream, *kee-yeeear,* with a downward inflection.

Habitat: Deciduous woodlands, especially where there is standing water.

Nesting: 2 or 3 white eggs, spotted with brown, in a large mass of leaves and twigs placed 20–60′ (6–18 m) up in a forest tree.

Range: Breeds from Minnesota east to New
Brunswick and south to Gulf Coast
and Florida, and on Pacific Coast in
California. Winters in breeding range
north to southern New England.

The Red-shouldered Hawk prefers
lowlands, especially swampy woods
and bogs. There it hunts by watching
quietly from a low perch, dropping
down to capture snakes and frogs. It
also eats insects and small mammals.
Normally shy, these birds become tame
if they are not persecuted and in some
places may nest in suburban areas.
During courtship a pair can be quite
noisy, wheeling in the sky above their
nesting territory and uttering their
distinctive whistled scream.

334, 339 Swainson's Hawk
Buteo swainsoni

Description: 18–22″ (46–56 cm). W. 4′1″ (1.2 m).
A large hawk, uniform brown above,
white below with warm-brown breast;
tail dark brown and indistinctly banded.
Longer, more pointed wings than Red-
tailed Hawk. Young bird similar to
immature Red-tail, but tends to have
darker markings on the breast, whereas
young Red-tails are more heavily
marked on flanks and belly. A rare all-
dark form also occurs. Soars with wings
held in shallow V.
Voice: Long, plaintive, whistled *kreee.*
Habitat: Open plains, grasslands, and prairies.
Nesting: 2–4 white eggs, unmarked or lightly
spotted with brown or black, in a
large nest of sticks, often placed
conspicuously in an isolated tree.
Range: Breeds across much of western United
States south to northern Mexico
and Texas; locally in Alaska, Yukon,
and Mackenzie. Winters chiefly in
tropics, but small numbers winter
in Florida.

Named after the English naturalist William Swainson (1789–1855), this species is highly gregarious, often migrating in great soaring flocks of thousands of birds. Its migrations are longer than those of other species; most individuals go all the way to Argentina to spend the winter, making a round trip of as much as 17,000 miles (27,000 kilometers). On its breeding grounds on the Great Plains, this hawk preys mainly on rodents and huge numbers of grasshoppers.

---

329   Zone-tailed Hawk
Buteo albonotatus

Description: 18½–21½″ (47–55 cm). W. 4′ (1.2 m). A mainly *black* hawk with long narrow wings held in a shallow V like those of a Turkey Vulture. Adults have 3 or 4 pale bands in tail. Immatures have several light narrow tail bands, wide dark terminal tail band, and fine white spotting on black breast.

Voice: A loud scream falling in pitch at the end.

Habitat: Forested canyons and riverside woodlands.

Nesting: 2 or 3 white eggs, often lightly marked with brown, in a large nest of sticks and green branches in a tall tree or cliff.

Range: Breeds in southern Arizona, southern New Mexico, and western Texas. Winters south of United States.

Except for its tail bands, this long-winged black hawk bears a superficial resemblance to the larger, nonpredatory Turkey Vulture. This resemblance is thought to deceive small birds and other prey, who allow it to approach. Then, without warning, this supposed vulture makes its catch.

333, 338 **Red-tailed Hawk**
including "Harlan's Hawk"
Buteo jamaicensis

Description: 18–25″ (46–64 cm). W. 4′ (1.2 m). A large stocky hawk. Typical light-phase birds have whitish breast and *rust-colored tail.* Young birds duller, more streaked, lacking rust-colored tail of adult; they are distinguished from Red-shouldered and Swainson's hawks by their stocky build, broader, more rounded wings, and white chest. This species quite variable in color, especially in West, where blackish individuals occur; these usually retain rusty tail.

Voice: High-pitched descending scream with a hoarse quality, *keeeeer.*

Habitat: Deciduous forests and open country of various kinds, including tundra, plains, and farmlands.

Nesting: 2 or 3 white eggs, spotted with brown, in a bulky nest of sticks lined with shreds of bark and bits of fresh green vegetation, placed in a tall tree or on a rock ledge.

Range: Breeds throughout North America, from Alaska east to Nova Scotia and southward. Winters across United States north to southern British Columbia and Maritime Provinces.

The Red-tail is the most common and widespread American member of the genus *Buteo,* which also includes the Red-shouldered, Swainson's, and Gray hawks, among others. Like other hawks of this group, it soars over open country in search of its prey but just as often perches in a tree at the edge of a meadow, watching for the slightest movement in the grass below. The Red-tail rarely takes poultry, feeding mainly on small rodents. Certain western birds with grayish, faintly streaked or mottled tails were formerly considered a separate species called "Harlan's Hawk."

341 Ferruginous Hawk
Buteo regalis

Description: 22½–25" (57–64 cm). W. 4'8" (1.4 m).
A large hawk. Light-phase adult *rufous above, mainly whitish below,* with rufous "wrist" patch and leg feathers, and black primary tips. In rare dark phase, deep rufous above and below, tail whitish. Legs and feet feathered down to talons. Immatures resemble light-phase adults but with few or no rufous markings.

Voice: A loud descending *kree-e-ah.*

Habitat: Prairies, brushy open country, badlands.

Nesting: 3–5 white eggs, blotched or spotted with brown, in a nest of roots, sticks, sagebrush, cow dung, or even old cattle bones, placed in a tree or bush, or on a rocky hillside.

Range: Breeds from Canadian prairie provinces south to eastern Oregon, Nevada, Arizona, New Mexico, and western Oklahoma. Winters in southern half of breeding range and southwestern states from central California to southwestern Texas into Mexico.

The clutch of three to five eggs is large for a *Buteo* hawk and may result from a fluctuating food supply. Ferruginous Hawks, which feed mainly on prairie dogs and ground squirrels, lay more eggs when prey abounds, fewer eggs in years when rodent populations decrease. They also take grasshoppers, birds, and lizards.

332 Rough-legged Hawk
Buteo lagopus

Description: 19–24" (48–61 cm). W. 4'4" (1.3 m).
A large, long-winged hawk that often hovers. Tail white at base with a dark terminal band. Light-phase adult has sandy-brown head and neck, blackish belly, and dark "wrist" marks on underside of wing. All-dark forms can

usually be identified by underwing and
tail pattern.

Voice: Loud or soft whistles, often in a
descending scale.

Habitat: Tundra; winters on open plains,
agricultural areas, and marshes.

Nesting: 2–7 white eggs, speckled with brown
and black, in a nest of moss and sticks
placed on a cliff or rocky outcropping
on the tundra.

Range: Breeds in Aleutians and northern Alaska
east to Baffin Island, and south to
northern Manitoba and Newfoundland.
Winters from southern Canada and
across United States irregularly south
to California, Texas, and Virginia. Also
in Eurasia.

This large hawk often hovers above its
prey like a kestrel. Lemmings, other
rodents, and birds are its main sources of
food during the breeding season. On the
wintering grounds, where it takes larger
rodents and upland birds, it can be
strikingly tame, probably because it
encounters few humans in the Far North.

326 Golden Eagle
Aquila chrysaetos

Description: 30–41" (76–104 cm). W. 6'6" (2 m).
A large, all-dark eagle with a pale
golden nape. Bill smaller and darker
than that of Bald Eagle. In young birds,
tail white at base, black at tip; white
patches on undersides of wings.

Voice: A high-pitched *kee-kee-kee;* also a high
scream or squeal, but usually silent.

Habitat: Mountain forests and open grasslands;
found in any habitat during migration.

Nesting: 1–4 whitish eggs, unmarked or lightly
speckled with dark brown, in a large
mass of sticks placed on a rocky ledge or
in a tall tree.

Range: Breeds from Alaska east across northern
Canada south to Mexico, Canadian
prairie provinces, and Labrador. Winters

in southern part of breeding range and in much of United States, except Southeast. Also in Eurasia.

Common in much of the West, these majestic eagles prey mainly on jackrabbits and large rodents but will also feed on carrion. In some parts of their range Golden Eagles are not migratory but remain in their territories all year.

FAMILY FALCONIDAE
Caracaras and Falcons

63 species: Worldwide. Seven species breed in North America. This family includes the true falcons (genus *Falco*) and also the caracaras, which are larger and often feed on carrion, as vultures do. True falcons have long pointed wings and long tails and are among the fastest-flying birds in the world. They mainly inhabit open country, and many pursue birds on the wing. Unlike other birds of prey, true falcons do not build nests of their own but utilize other birds' nests or lay eggs in hollow trees, on cliffs, or on the ground. Caracaras do build nests like other birds of prey.

324 Crested Caracara
Caracara plancus

Description: 20–22" (51–56 cm). W. 4' (1.2 m). A large, long-legged, hawk-like bird with rounded wings. Dark brown with black cap and bare red face; throat, neck, and base of tail white; tip of tail has black band. In flight, shows large white patches near wing tips. Often seen on the ground.

Voice: High, harsh cackle.

Habitat: Prairies, savannas, desert scrub, and seashores.

Nesting: 2 or 3 white eggs, with heavy brown spots and blotches, in a nest of twigs, grasses, weeds, and briars lined with leaves and moss; usually in palmettos or live oaks, rarely on the ground.

Range: Resident in southern Arizona, southern Texas, southwestern Louisiana (rare), and central and southern Florida. Also in American tropics.

The national bird of Mexico, this scavenger has probably the most varied diet of any bird of prey. It often accompanies and dominates vultures at fresh kills or carrion and also eats small animals. It is primarily a ground-inhabiting falcon of open prairies, with long legs that enable it to walk and run with ease.

351, 352 **American Kestrel**
"Sparrow Hawk"
Falco sparverius

Description: 9–12" (23–30 cm). W. 21" (53 cm). A jay-sized falcon, often seen hovering. Recognizable in all plumages by *rusty tail and back.* Adult male has slate-blue wings. Female has rusty wings and back, narrow bands on tail. Both sexes have 2 black stripes on face.

Voice: Shrill *killy-killy-killy.*

Habitat: Towns and cities, parks, farmlands, and open country.

Nesting: 4 or 5 white or pinkish eggs, blotched with brown, placed without nest or lining in a natural or man-made cavity.

Range: Breeds from Alaska and Northwest Territories east through Maritime Provinces and south throughout continent. Winters north to British Columbia, Great Lakes, and New England. Also in American tropics.

Unlike larger falcons, the "Sparrow Hawk" has adapted to humans and nests even in our largest cities, where it preys chiefly on House Sparrows. In the countryside it takes insects, small birds, and rodents, capturing its prey on the ground rather than in midair like other falcons. The female does most of the incubating and is fed by the male. The male calls as he nears the nest with food; the female flies to him, receives the food, and returns to the nest. After the eggs hatch, the male continues to bring most of the food. The young stay with the adults for a time after fledging, and it is not uncommon to see family parties in late summer.

353 Merlin
"Pigeon Hawk"
Falco columbarius

Description: 10–14" (25–36 cm). W. 23" (58 cm). A jay-sized falcon, stockier than American Kestrel. Slate colored (males) or brownish (females) above; light and streaked below. Long tail boldly banded. Lacks facial stripes of most other falcons.

Voice: High, loud cackle, also *klee-klee-klee* like an American Kestrel, but usually silent.

Habitat: Coniferous forests; more widespread in winter.

Nesting: 5 or 6 buff eggs, stippled with purple and brown, placed in a tree cavity without a nest or lining, on a rocky ledge, or in an abandoned crow's nest.

Range: Breeds from Alaska east through Mackenzie to Newfoundland and south to Wyoming, Montana, and northeastern Maine. Winters mainly in southern United States north along West Coast to British Columbia and on East Coast to southern New England; locally elsewhere north to southern Canada. Also in tropical America and Eurasia.

The so-called "Pigeon Hawk" is most abundant during the migrations of smaller birds, on which it feeds. It is

swift and aggressive, regularly harassing
larger hawks and gulls and attacking
intruders at its nest. As with other
falcons, the female begins incubating as
soon as the first egg is laid so the young
hatch at intervals; when food is scarce,
the larger young are fed first, the smaller
ones sometimes dying of starvation.
This seemingly heartless procedure
ensures that some young will be raised
successfully even in hard times.

346 Aplomado Falcon
Falco femoralis

Description: 15–18″ (38–46 cm). Like a small, long-
tailed, boldly patterned Peregrine
Falcon. Adult *blue-gray above, with bold
"mustache" on face, white eyebrow, and
black stripe through eye.* Nape rusty;
throat white; upper breast buff with
heavy streaks; lower breast and flanks
black; thighs and belly cinnamon.
Young birds brown above, streaked on
breast, plain brown on flanks.

Voice: A rapid *kak-kak-kak-kak.*

Habitat: Open arid country, grasslands, deserts,
and savannas.

Nesting: 3 or 4 white or pinkish eggs, spotted
with brown, in a deserted nest of a raven
or other large bird.

Range: Formerly ranged from southeastern
Arizona to southern Texas southward
to Argentina. Now reported only
occasionally in border states, where
recently reintroduced.

This beautiful falcon is usually found
perched on a tall cactus or telephone
pole. When it flies off in alarm, or in
pursuit of prey, it often dips down and
courses low over the ground. Most of its
diet consists of small birds, but it also
takes reptiles and large insects. It is
most active at dawn and dusk.

345 Prairie Falcon
Falco mexicanus

Description: 17–20″ (43–51 cm). W. 3′6″ (1.1 m). A
large falcon, sandy brown above, whitish
or pale buff below with fine spots and
streaks, narrow brown "mustache"
stripe, and *dark wing linings.*

Voice: A loud *kree-kree-kree,* most often heard
near nest.

Habitat: Barren mountains, dry plains, and
prairies.

Nesting: 4 or 5 white or pinkish eggs, blotched
with brown, placed without a nest on a
cliff ledge or in the abandoned nest of
some other large bird.

Range: Breeds from British Columbia and
Canadian prairie provinces south to
Mexico and northern Texas. Winters in
breeding range.

The Prairie Falcon is usually found
in places far from water, while the
Peregrine is nearly always found near
a river or a lake. The Prairie Falcon's
diet consists mainly of birds, which
it pursues on the wing but usually
captures on the ground. Its numbers
are declining, due to rodent-poisoning
programs and other factors.

---

344 Peregrine Falcon
Falco peregrinus

Description: 15–21″ (38–53 cm). W. 3′4″ (1 m). A
large robust falcon with a black hood
and wide black "mustaches." Adults
slate-gray above and pale below, with
fine black bars and spots. Young birds
brown or brownish slate above, heavily
streaked below.

Voice: Rasping *kack-kack-kack-kack,* usually
heard at nest; otherwise generally silent.

Habitat: Open country, especially along rivers;
also near lakes, along coasts, and in
cities. Migrates chiefly along coasts.

Nesting: 2–4 cream or buff eggs, spotted with

reddish brown, placed in a scrape with little lining on a cliff or building ledge or in an abandoned bird's nest.

Range: Breeds from Alaska and Canadian Arctic south locally through mountainous West, and sparingly in East. Winters coastally, north to British Columbia and Massachusetts. Also in southern South America and Old World.

Following an alarming decline during the 1950s and 1960s, this spectacular falcon, also called the "Duck Hawk," is on the increase again, now that pesticides that caused thinning of eggshells have been banned. After an intensive program of rearing birds in captivity and releasing them in the wild (a process called "hacking"), this large falcon is reclaiming nesting grounds from which it disappeared a few decades ago. A favorite nesting site nowadays is a tall building or bridge in a city; these urban Peregrines subsist mainly on pigeons.

343 Gyrfalcon
Falco rusticolus

Description: 22" (56 cm). W. 4' (1.2 m). The largest of the true falcons. 3 color phases occur: blackish, white, and gray-brown. All phases are more uniformly colored than Peregrine Falcon, which has bold dark "mustaches" and hood and a proportionately larger head.

Voice: A chattering scream, *kak-kak-kak-kak.*

Habitat: Arctic tundra and rocky cliffs, usually near water. Each winter a few move south to coastal beaches and marshes.

Nesting: Usually 4 whitish or buff eggs, finely spotted with reddish brown, on a rock ledge or in the abandoned nest of a Rough-legged Hawk or Common Raven.

Range: Breeds on tundra of northern Alaska and northern Canada. Winters in breeding

range and also rarely but regularly south to northern tier of states, especially along coasts.

It is a memorable occasion when a Gyrfalcon is sighted on a coastal salt marsh or over open country inland. In the Far North it feeds mainly on ptarmigans, but during the summer months it also takes shorebirds, eiders, and gulls, and makes frequent raids on the great colonies of murres and Dovekies.

FAMILY PHASIANIDAE
Partridges, Grouse, Turkeys, and Quail

189 species: Worldwide except Australian region. This large and varied family contains almost all the birds that resemble chickens. They have stocky bodies; short thick legs; large toes that are adapted for walking and scratching; and short, blunt bills that are well suited for crushing seeds and feeding on a variety of insects and other small creatures. In North America these birds can be divided into four groups: the introduced pheasants and partridges; the grouse, which have feathered legs and feet; the turkeys; and the native quail, of which the Northern Bobwhite is the most widespread.

276 Gray Partridge
Perdix perdix

Description: 12–14″ (30–36 cm). A small, stocky, chicken-like bird, largely gray, with black U-shaped mark on underparts and *bright rust-colored tail,* most evident when it flies.

Voice: Hoarse *kee-ah;* when flushed, a rapid cackle.

Habitat: Grainfields, agricultural grasslands.

Nesting: 10–20 unmarked olive eggs in a shallow depression lined with grass and concealed in vegetation.

Range: Introduced and locally established in Nova Scotia, New Brunswick, northern New York, Ontario, Ohio, Indiana, southern Michigan, Iowa, Minnesota, and across northern part of western United States to British Columbia. Introduction in West has been much more successful than in East. Native to Eurasia.

Also called the "Hungarian Partridge," this bird is well adapted to areas of intensive agriculture, a habitat claimed by no native game bird. It forms coveys outside the breeding season, like the Northern Bobwhite, but does not defend a territory. In spring the flocks break up into pairs. While the male takes no part in incubating the eggs, he does help care for the young, which leave the nest soon after hatching. The Gray Partridge's high reproductive rate enables it to withstand hunting, predators, and cold, snowy northern winters, all of which take a heavy toll.

288 Chukar
Alectoris chukar

Description: 13–15½" (33–39 cm). Similar in size and shape to Gray Partridge. Light brown back and wings; creamy-white belly; gray-tinged cap, breast, and rump. *White cheek and throat framed by broad black band.* Bold chestnut and black diagonal striping on flanks; bright rufous outer tail feathers. Bill and legs orange-red.

Voice: A loud fast *chuck-chuck-chuck;* various cackling calls.

Habitat: Rocky arid hillsides and canyons.

Nesting: 8–15 whitish eggs, spotted with brown, in a nest lined with grass and feathers in the shelter of rocks or brush.

Range: Resident from British Columbia and Alberta south to California and Colorado. Native to Eurasia.

Best known for its loud call, the Chukar has been successfully introduced to the West from the dry Mediterranean area of southern Europe. It is a hardy bird, able to outrun a hunter. Outside the breeding season, it moves about in coveys of up to 40 birds.

289, 290 Ring-necked Pheasant
Phasianus colchicus

Description: 30–36″ (76–91 cm). Larger than a chicken, with a long pointed tail. Male has red eye patch, brilliant green head, and (usually) white neck ring; body patterned in soft brown and iridescent russet. Female mottled sandy brown, with shorter tail.

Voice: Loud crowing *caw-cawk!* followed by a resonant beating of the wings. When alarmed flies off with a loud cackle.

Habitat: Farmlands, pastures, and grassy woodland edges.

Nesting: 6–15 buff-olive eggs in a grass-lined depression concealed in dense grass or weeds.

Range: Introduced from British Columbia, Alberta, Minnesota, Ontario, and Maritime Provinces south to central California, Oklahoma, and Maryland. Native to Asia.

The North American birds of this species are descended from stock brought from several different parts of the Old World and thus are somewhat variable. They are very tolerant of humans and can get by with a minimum of cover; they often nest on the outskirts of large cities. Although successful in most grassland habitats, this species has its North American headquarters in the central plains. After the breakup of

winter flocks, males establish large
territories and mate with several
females. At first the chicks feed largely
on insects but soon shift to the adult
diet of berries, seeds, buds, and leaves.

269 Spruce Grouse
Dendragapus canadensis

Description: 15–17″ (38–43 cm). A dark, chicken-
like bird with a fan-shaped tail. Male
dusky gray-brown, with red comb over
eye, black throat and upper breast,
white-spotted sides, chestnut-tipped
tail. Birds in northern Rockies and
Cascades (known as "Franklin's Grouse")
have white tips on upper tail coverts
and lack chestnut tail tip. Females of
both forms browner; underparts barred
with brown.

Voice: Males give a low *krrrrk, krrrk, krrk,
krrk, krrk,* said to be the lowest-pitched
vocal sound of any North American
bird. Females produce low clucking
notes.

Habitat: Coniferous forests, edges of deep forests.

Nesting: 8–11 buff eggs, plain or spotted with
brown, in a hollow lined with grass and
leaves concealed on the ground under
low branches of a young spruce.

Range: Resident from Alaska, northern
Manitoba, Quebec, and Nova Scotia
south to Washington, Wyoming, central
Manitoba, Michigan, and northern
New England.

This northern grouse is extraordinarily
tame and can occasionally be approached
and caught; hence its local name, "Fool
Hen." It is generally a quiet bird, thinly
distributed in its habitat and therefore
difficult to find. Its principal foods are
the needles and buds of evergreens,
although young birds consume large
quantities of insects. Spruce Grouse
are generally found singly or in small
family groups, quietly picking their

way over the forest floor or sitting in dense conifers.

271, 274 Blue Grouse
Dendragapus obscurus

Description: 15½–21″ (39–53 cm). A large grouse. Male dusky gray or bluish gray, with orange-yellow or red comb over eye, patch of yellow skin on neck surrounded by rosette of white feathers, some mottling on wings, and blackish tail with pale gray terminal band. Birds in Rockies lack terminal tail band and have red skin in center of rosette on neck. Females and immatures mottled brown with dark tail.

Voice: Male gives a series of deep hoots, *whoop, whoop, whoop, whoop, whoop,* increasing in tempo and volume.

Habitat: Burned areas, brush in coastal rain forest; montane forests, slashes, and subalpine forest clearings.

Nesting: 5–10 cream-colored eggs, lightly spotted with brown, in a scrape lined with pine needles and grass, usually sheltered by a stump or rock.

Range: Resident from southeastern Alaska and Northwest Territories south to California, Arizona, Colorado, and New Mexico.

The deep booming hoots of a courting male Blue Grouse are audible for many yards but because they are so low in pitch, the bird itself can be extremely difficult to find. It is worth the effort, however, because as he hoots the male fans his tail over his back, spreads the feathers on his neck to reveal the patch of brightly colored skin, and erects the combs over the eyes, producing a striking display. In winter this grouse feeds exclusively on conifer needles; its summer diet consists of insects, seeds, and berries.

279, 282 Willow Ptarmigan
Lagopus lagopus

Description: 15–17″ (38–43 cm). A small tundra grouse with red comb over each eye. In winter, *entirely white except for black tail.* In summer, male rusty red with white wings and belly; female mottled and barred with brown except for white wings. Spring and fall molting plumages show a variety of checkered patterns. Summer males of other ptarmigan species more grayish. Winter Rock Ptarmigan has black stripe through eye. White-tailed Ptarmigan has entirely white tail.

Voice: In flight, courting males have a loud, staccato *go-back, go-back, go-back,* and other guttural calls.

Habitat: Tundra; also thickets in valleys and foothills; muskeg.

Nesting: 7–10 yellowish eggs, blotched with brown, in a scrape lined with grass and feathers, often sheltered by vegetation, rocks, or logs.

Range: Breeds from Alaska east to Labrador, and south to central British Columbia, northern Ontario, and central Quebec. Winters south to forested regions of central Canada. Also in Eurasia.

The most widespread ptarmigan of the Far North, this species increases in number in some years but in others is very scarce. While the female incubates, the male guards the territory. When the chicks grow up, several families gather in large flocks and often migrate southward together when winter arrives. In summer ptarmigans feed on green shoots, buds, flowers, and insects; in winter they take mainly twigs and buds of willows and alders.

278, 281   **Rock Ptarmigan**
Lagopus mutus

Description: 13–14" (33–36 cm). In winter, *entirely white except for black tail* and, in males and most females, *black line through eye.* In summer, male is flecked with dark gray-brown, wings and belly white. Female paler, with gray, yellowish, and brown on most feathers. Smaller than Willow Ptarmigan, with smaller bill. See White-tailed Ptarmigan.

Voice: Courting male gives a snoring *kurr-kurr.* Female has clucking and purring notes.

Habitat: Upland tundra with thickets of willows and heaths.

Nesting: 6–9 buff eggs, spotted with dark brown, in a sheltered hollow lined with grass and moss.

Range: Breeds in Alaska and northern Canada. Winters south to tree line.

Pairs of Rock Ptarmigans remain together until midway through incubation, when the male deserts his mate. The female raises the chicks, which move about on the tundra in search of insects, buds, and berries, becoming independent at about three months old. The white winter plumage of ptarmigans provides both good camouflage and protection against the cold, because white feathers have empty cells filled with air that help in insulation, whereas colored feathers contain pigment.

277, 280   **White-tailed Ptarmigan**
Lagopus leucurus

Description: 12–13" (30–33 cm). The smallest of the ptarmigans, the only one with an all-white tail, and the only one found in alpine tundra of the western United States. In winter, *pure white except for black bill and eyes.* In summer, mottled and barred with brown on head, breast, and back, with white wings, belly, and tail. Red comb above eye (larger in spring males).

Voice: High-pitched "creaking" notes and soft low clucks.

Habitat: Alpine meadows and open rocky areas above timberline.

Nesting: 6–8 buff eggs, faintly spotted with brown, in a hollow sparsely lined with grass, leaves, and feathers.

Range: Resident in Rocky Mountains from Alaska south to New Mexico, and coastal ranges south to Washington; introduced in Sierra Nevada of California.

This mountain-dwelling ptarmigan engages in short migrations, moving down to the edge of the forest in the fall and back onto the alpine tundra in spring. The two sexes often winter separately, with females gathering in larger flocks than males.

272 Ruffed Grouse
Bonasa umbellus

Description: 16–19" (41–48 cm). A brown or gray-brown, chicken-like bird with slight crest, *fan-shaped, black-banded tail,* barred flanks, and black "ruffs" on sides of neck.

Voice: Female gives soft hen-like clucks. In spring displaying male sits on a log and beats the air with his wings, creating a drumming sound that increases rapidly in tempo.

Habitat: Deciduous and mixed forests, especially those with scattered clearings and dense undergrowth; overgrown pastures.

Nesting: 9–12 pinkish-buff eggs, plain or spotted with dull brown, in a shallow depression lined with leaves and concealed under a bush.

Range: Resident from tree line in Alaska and northern Canada south to California, Wyoming, Minnesota, Missouri, and

Carolinas, and in Appalachians to
Georgia.

This secretive grouse is easy to find in
winter, when snow covers the ground
and the birds fly up into the treetops to
feed on buds and catkins. The summer
diet, much more varied, consists of
insects, seeds, fruits, and even an
occasional small snake or frog.

273, 275 Sage Grouse
Centrocercus urophasianus

Description: Male, 26–30″ (66–76 cm); female,
22–23″ (56–58 cm). *Both sexes mottled
gray-brown above with black belly.* Male
has long pointed tail, black throat,
white breast, with elongated neck
plumes flanking breast. Female's head,
back, and breast uniformly barred.
Displaying male fans tail and tilts
it forward; inflates pair of naked
yellowish-green air sacs in neck
and breast.

Voice: When flushed, a chicken-like cackling
call. Males make bubbling sound
during courtship.

Habitat: Open country and sagebrush plains.

Nesting: 6–9 olive-green eggs, lightly spotted
with brown, in a well-concealed grass-
lined depression.

Range: Resident from southern Alberta and
Saskatchewan south to eastern
California, Nevada, Colorado, and
South Dakota.

The Sage Grouse is well named, for it is
quite dependent on sagebrush. In the
fall and winter the leathery leaves of
sagebrush are one of its only foods, and
during the rest of the year sagebrush
provides it with cover. Each spring the
males gather on a traditional display
ground, called a lek, to court the
females. Once a female has mated, she
goes off and raises her family by herself.

283, 284 Lesser Prairie-Chicken
Tympanuchus pallidicinctus

Description: 16" (41 cm). A chicken-like bird, *barred* above and below with grayish brown, with *short black tail.* Courting male has long black feathers on sides of neck that form erect "horns"; inflates reddish-purple air sacs during courtship display. Horns of female shorter. Greater Prairie-Chicken (*Tympanuchus cupido*) of plains farther east is similar but larger and more strongly barred, with yellow-orange air sacs.

Voice: Various cackling and clucking notes; male "booms" during courtship.

Habitat: Dry grasslands with shrubs and short trees.

Nesting: 11–13 creamy or buff-colored eggs in a grass-lined depression, usually under a low bush or shrub.

Range: Resident in southern Colorado and Kansas, south locally in western Oklahoma, Texas, and eastern New Mexico.

The Lesser Prairie-Chicken likes short-grass prairies where stands of scrub oaks are common. Here males gather and engage in communal courtship displays in which the birds dance about with the colorful air sacs on their necks inflated, uttering low cooing or "booming" notes. This species replaces the Greater Prairie-Chicken in higher, drier grasslands.

270 Sharp-tailed Grouse
Tympanuchus phasianellus

Description: 15–20" (38–51 cm). Resembles, but slightly smaller than, female pheasant. Mottled with buff, slightly paler below. Tail short and *pointed, with white outer tail feathers.* Male has purple neck patch and yellow comb over eye; tail longer than that of female. Similar prairie-chickens are barred, not mottled, and show no white in tail.

Voice: During courtship, a low single or double cooing note.

Habitat: Grasslands, scrub forest, and arid sagebrush.

Nesting: 10–13 buff-brown eggs in a grass-lined depression in tall grass or brush.

Range: Resident from Alaska east to Hudson Bay and south to Utah, northeastern New Mexico, and Michigan.

Sharp-tails, like prairie-chickens and Sage Grouse, perform elaborate displays on communal mating grounds called leks, to which they return faithfully every year. In one case a homestead was built over a lek, and the grouse displayed on the farmhouse roof the following spring.

291, 292 Wild Turkey
Meleagris gallopavo

Description: Male, 48″ (1.2 m); female, 36″ (91 cm). Unmistakable. Dusky brown, barred with black, with iridescent bronze sheen; head and neck naked, with bluish and reddish wattles; tail fan-shaped, with chestnut, buff, or white tail tips. Male has spurs and long "beard" on breast. Female smaller, lacks spurs and usually "beard." Domestic turkeys similar, but usually tamer and stockier.

Voice: Gobbling calls similar to those of domestic turkey.

Habitat: Oak woodlands, pine-oak forests.

Nesting: 8–15 buff-colored eggs, spotted with brown, in a shallow depression lined with grass and leaves.

Range: Resident in much of southern United States from Arizona east, as far north as New England. Introduced to many western states, including California.

Although the Wild Turkey was well known to American Indians and widely

used by them as food, certain tribes considered these birds stupid and cowardly and did not eat them for fear of acquiring these characteristics. Turkeys are swift runners and quite wary. They often roost over water because of the added protection that this location offers. They are polygamous, and the male gobbles and struts with tail fanned to attract and hold his harem.

297 Montezuma Quail
"Harlequin Quail"
Cyrtonyx montezumae

Description: 8–9½″ (20–24 cm). A stocky quail with a complex face pattern. Male has striking black-and-white face markings, rounded *buff* crest, and bold white spots on sides and flanks. Female duller, face markings less obvious.

Voice: A soft whinnying call.

Habitat: Grassy and brush-covered ground in pine-oak woodlands.

Nesting: 8–14 white eggs in a grass-lined depression concealed in dense grass.

Range: Resident from southern Arizona to western Texas and southward into Mexico.

At the approach of danger, the Montezuma Quail often crouches and freezes rather than flying off. It may sometimes be seen creeping stealthily away, looking more like a rodent than a bird. This bird relishes berries and acorns as well as its winter staples, tubers and bulbs, which it scratches out with its sturdy feet. By the time it breeds in summer the rains have come and insect food is abundant.

286, 287 Northern Bobwhite
Colinus virginianus

Description: 8–11″ (20–28 cm). A small, chunky, brown bird; underparts pale and streaked; *face patterned in black and white in males, buff and white in females.* Usually seen in groups called coveys.

Voice: Clear, whistled *bob-WHITE* or *poor-bob-WHITE.*

Habitat: Brushy pastures, grassy roadsides, farmlands, and open woodlands.

Nesting: 10–15 white eggs in a grass-lined hollow concealed in weeds or grass.

Range: Permanent resident from Kansas, Iowa, Pennsylvania, and Cape Cod southward. Fluctuating populations farther north and west. Introduced locally elsewhere.

The Northern Bobwhite is mainly an eastern and Mexican bird but is also found in the foothills of the southern Rocky Mountains. After the breeding period these birds live together in a covey, huddling together at night and in cold weather. When danger threatens they fly out in every direction, startling the would-be predator, who often catches none of the birds.

298 Scaled Quail
Callipepla squamata

Description: 10–12″ (25–30 cm). A small stocky quail, gray-brown above, with *buff-white crest.* Bluish-gray feathers on breast and mantle have black semicircular edges, creating *scaled effect;* belly also has brown "scales." Sexes alike.

Voice: Call is a low nasal *pe-cos.* Also harsh clucking calls.

Habitat: Dry grasslands and brushy deserts.

Nesting: 12–14 pale buff eggs, evenly spotted with reddish brown, in a grass-lined hollow.

Range: Resident in Arizona, Colorado, western

Kansas, and western Oklahoma south to central Mexico.

These modestly plumaged quail, often called "Cotton Tops" by hunters and also known as "Blue Quail," are characteristic birds of the drier desert areas of the Southwest. They seldom fly, preferring to run from intruders. Though birds of arid habitat, Scaled Quail must visit water holes regularly. They nest in the rainy season, when moisture produces some vegetation, and do not breed during extremely dry summers. Their numbers fluctuate markedly from year to year, because the birds are sensitive to both drought and heavy rains. They spend most of the year in small flocks, breaking up into pairs at the beginning of the breeding season.

293, 294 Gambel's Quail
Callipepla gambelii

Description: 10–11½" (25–29 cm). A stocky, mainly gray quail with a *curved black head plume.* Male has bold black face and throat, chestnut crown, rusty sides with diagonal stripes, and unscaled buff-white belly with *black patch in center.* See California Quail.

Voice: A ringing *puk-kwaw-cah,* with second syllable highest in pitch.

Habitat: Desert thickets; arid country.

Nesting: 10–20 buff-colored eggs, spotted with brown, in a depression lined with grass and twigs at base of tall shrub or mesquite.

Range: Resident in southwestern deserts from California east to Texas. Introduced in Idaho and western New Mexico.

These desert-dwelling quail are attracted to water and gather in large numbers, often representing several coveys, to drink at stock tanks maintained for cattle. The ringing call of the male, heard even in the heat of day, is one of the characteristic sounds of the desert Southwest.

296 California Quail
Callipepla californica

Description: 9–11″ (23–28 cm). Similar to Gambel's Quail, but crown brown, not chestnut; forehead buff, not black; and belly scaled, lacking black patch in center. Female less boldly marked than male.

Voice: A loud distinctive *ka-kah-ko* or *Chi-ca-go,* the second note highest.

Habitat: Brushy chaparral foothills and live-oak canyons; also adjacent desert and suburbs.

Nesting: 12–16 cream- or buff-colored eggs, blotched and dotted with brown, in a shallow depression lined with grass.

Range: Originally resident from southern Oregon south to Baja California. Introduced to Pacific Northwest, Idaho, and other inland states.

Perched on a tree or a fence post, the male California Quail claims his territory by cackling and posturing. The entire family takes to trees for roosting as well as for safety. After the breeding season, these birds become gregarious, gathering in large coveys and often visiting city parks, gardens, and yards. This is the quail with the "topknot" featured in the animated films of Walt Disney.

295 Mountain Quail
Oreortyx pictus

Description: 10½–11½″ (27–29 cm). A large quail with a long *straight head plume.* Brown above, with gray head, neck, and breast; chestnut throat; chestnut flanks with bold white bars. Female similar, but duller.

Voice:	Its frequent call is a loud echoing *kyork* or *woook*. Other notes include soft whistles.
Habitat:	Dry mountains, brushy wooded areas, and chaparral.
Nesting:	8–12 light reddish eggs in a depression lined with dry grass and leaves, hidden among protective rocks, logs, or thick vegetation.
Range:	Resident in Washington, Idaho, Oregon, and California. Introduced to southern Vancouver Island, British Columbia.

This quail migrates on foot from its high-elevation breeding territory to protected valleys, where it winters in coveys of 6 to 12 birds. Mountain Quail are difficult to flush since they persistently run through the thickest cover.

FAMILY RALLIDAE
Rails, Gallinules, and Coots

130 species: Worldwide. Nine species breed in North America. Rails are mainly marsh-dwelling birds, with short rounded wings, large feet, and long toes. Their bodies are laterally compressed to enable them to slip between reeds and cattails. This family also contains the moorhens, gallinules, and coots. The coots have lobed feet adapted for swimming in open water. Gallinules are brightly colored, but most other members of this family are cryptically colored, their grays, browns, and buffs blending in with the reeds. Their nests are well hidden among the dense rushes and other aquatic growth of marshes.

263   Yellow Rail
Coturnicops noveboracensis

Description: 6–8″ (15–20 cm). A sparrow-sized rail.
Brownish buff, with a short yellow bill
and yellow feet. *White wing patch* shows
in flight.

Voice: 2 or 3 clicks, sounding like pebbles
being tapped together, repeated over
and over in a long series. Usually heard
at night.

Habitat: Grassy marshes and wet meadows.

Nesting: 7–10 buff eggs, with a ring of dark spots
around larger end, in a firm cup of grass
well concealed in a grassy marsh.

Range: Breeds from northern Alberta east to
Quebec and New Brunswick, and south
to North Dakota, northern Michigan,
and Maine. Winters from Carolinas
south to Florida and along Gulf Coast;
rarely in southern California.

Most rails live in dense marsh
vegetation and are difficult to observe
or even flush, but this tiny rail is
especially secretive. It is seldom seen
even by active and experienced bird-
watchers. Little is known about its
behavior, but it is known that
incubation is done by the female alone,
and that the female continues to add
material to the nest until the eggs are
hatched. The young—clad in black
down like young of other rails—leave
the nest and follow the female about
in search of food.

266   Black Rail
Laterallus jamaicensis

Description: 5–6″ (13–15 cm). A sparrow-sized rail.
Black, with rusty nape, white flecks on
back, black bill, and greenish legs and
feet. Can be confused with downy black
young of larger rails.

Voice: A piping *ki-ki-doo,* the last note lower
in pitch.

Habitat: Coastal salt marshes; more rarely, inland freshwater marshes.

Nesting: 6–8 pale buff eggs, lightly spotted with brown, in a loose cup of grass, usually concealed under a mat of dead marsh vegetation.

Range: Breeds along Pacific and Atlantic coasts from San Francisco Bay and Long Island southward, and locally in midwestern interior and along lower Colorado River. Winters north to Gulf Coast and Florida and in its breeding range in West.

The Black Rail is a little-known and secretive species. In California, where suitable nesting areas are few, the bird is rare. Its numbers are dwindling further because of destruction of its habitat. The birds spend much of their time creeping about under mats of dead marsh grass or through thick stands of such marsh plants as salicornia.

---

264 Clapper Rail
Rallus longirostris

Description: 14–16″ (36–41 cm). A long-billed, chicken-sized rail of salt marshes. Grayish brown with *tawny breast and barred flanks.*

Voice: Harsh clattering *kek-kek-kek-kek-kek.*

Habitat: Salt marshes and some freshwater marshes.

Nesting: 9–12 buff eggs, spotted or blotched with brown, in a shallow saucer or deep bowl of dead marsh grasses, often domed.

Range: Breeds along coasts from central California and Massachusetts southward. Also inland on Salton Sea and lower Colorado River. Winters north to central California and New Jersey, rarely farther north.

Although it is still common in the East, the Clapper Rail has become endangered in the western United States because of the gradual destruction of its habitat.

Its stronghold is San Francisco Bay, where a few thousand birds remain. A freshwater population, containing only several hundred birds, lives along the lower Colorado River of California, Arizona, and Mexico.

---

267 **Virginia Rail**
Rallus limicola

Description: 9–11″ (23–28 cm). A small rail with a long *reddish bill*, rusty underparts, barred flanks, and *gray cheeks*.

Voice: A far-carrying *ticket, ticket, ticket, ticket;* various grunting notes.

Habitat: Freshwater and brackish marshes; may visit salt marshes in winter.

Nesting: 5–12 pale buff eggs, spotted with brown, in a shallow and loosely constructed saucer often woven into surrounding marsh vegetation.

Range: Breeds from British Columbia east to Maritime Provinces and south to southern California, Oklahoma, and Virginia. Winters regularly on coasts north to Washington and Virginia, occasionally farther north.

Like other rails, the Virginia Rail prefers to escape intruders by running through protective marsh vegetation rather than by flying. When it does take wing, it often flies only a few yards before slipping back out of sight into the marsh. Despite its apparently weak flight, it migrates long distances each year and has even been recorded as far out of its normal range as Bermuda and Greenland.

---

265 **Sora**
Porzana carolina

Description: 8–10″ (20–25 cm). A quail-sized rail with *short yellow bill, gray breast, and black face.* Upperparts mottled brown; lower abdomen banded with black and white. Young birds in fall lack black face and have buff breast.

Voice: Most familiar call is a musical series of piping notes rapidly descending the scale; also a repeated *ker-wee,* with rising inflection. Near the nest, birds utter an explosive *keek!*

Habitat: Freshwater marshes and marshy ponds; rice fields and salt marshes in winter.

Nesting: 6–15 pale yellow-buff eggs, spotted with brown, in a cup of cattails and dead leaves, usually placed in a clump of reeds in an open part of the marsh.

Range: Breeds from British Columbia east through Mackenzie to Maritime Provinces and south to Pennsylvania, Oklahoma, Arizona, and central California; winters mainly along coasts north to California and Virginia.

The Sora is a common rail throughout its nesting area, its whinnying call familiar to anyone who has watched birds in a marsh. But it is seldom seen except by birders who wait patiently beside an opening in the reeds or who wade quietly through the cattails. It is a noisy bird and especially at dawn it fills the air with its sharp calls and whinnying notes.

---

268 Common Moorhen
"Common Gallinule"
Gallinula chloropus

Description: 13″ (33 cm). A duck-like swimming bird that constantly bobs its head while moving. Adult slate-gray, with conspicuous *red frontal shield and red bill with yellow tip.* White stripe on side; white undertail coverts. Young birds similar but duller, without colorful bill.

Voice: Squawking and croaking notes similar to those of coots.

Habitat: Freshwater marshes and ponds with
cattails and other aquatic vegetation.

Nesting: 7–14 cinnamon or buff eggs, lightly
spotted with brown, on a shallow
platform of dead cattails, rushes, and
other marsh plants, usually a few inches
above water level.

Range: Breeds in California, Nevada, Arizona,
and New Mexico, and from Minnesota
east to New Brunswick and south to
Gulf Coast and Florida. Winters in
California, Arizona, and along Atlantic
and Gulf coasts from Virginia to Texas.
Also in American tropics and in
Old World.

This bird owes its wide distribution to
its choice of a common habitat and a
varied diet. Almost any open water
fringed by marsh plants will do, and
these birds eat mosquitoes, spiders,
tadpoles, insect larvae, fruits, and seeds.
Their long toes enable them to swim in
water or walk on floating vegetation
with equal ease.

---

121 American Coot
Fulica americana

Description: 15″ (38 cm). A gray, duck-like bird
with *white bill and frontal shield,* white
undertail coverts, and lobed toes.
Frontal shield has red swelling at upper
edge, visible at close range. Immatures
similar but paler, with duller bill.

Voice: A variety of clucks, cackles, grunts, and
other harsh notes.

Habitat: Open ponds and marshes; in winter, also
on coastal bays and inlets.

Nesting: 8–10 pinkish eggs, spotted with brown,
on a shallow platform of dead leaves and
stems, usually on water but anchored
to a clump of reeds.

Range: Breeds from British Columbia, western
Canada, and New York locally southward.
Winters north to British Columbia,

Kansas, Illinois, and Massachusetts.
Also in American tropics.

Coots feed in many ways: by diving to
the bottom, dabbling at the surface,
grazing on land near shore, and stealing
food from other diving birds. They are
expert swimmers, propelled by wide
lobes on their toes.

FAMILY GRUIDAE
Cranes

15 species: Fairly widespread, but
absent in South America. Two species
breed in North America. One, the
nearly extinct Whooping Crane, is
strictly protected; the other, the Sandhill
Crane, is more numerous and has a
fairly wide range. Cranes superficially
resemble herons but are not related to
them. Unlike herons, cranes fly with
the neck outstretched and with the
upstroke of the wingbeat faster than the
downstroke. Among the tallest birds in
the world, they inhabit open country,
where they nest on the ground and lay
only two eggs. Their colors run to black,
white, and gray; most cranes have a bare
patch on the head.

17 Sandhill Crane
Grus canadensis

Description: 34–48" (86–122 cm). W. 6'8" (2 m).
Very tall, with long neck and legs.
Largely gray, with red forehead;
immature browner, no red on head.
Plumage often appears rusty because of
iron stains from water of tundra ponds.
Voice: A loud rattling *kar-r-r-r-o-o-o*.
Habitat: Large freshwater marshes, prairie ponds,
and marshy tundra; also on prairies and
grainfields during migration and in
winter.

Nesting: 2 buff eggs, spotted with brown, in a large mound of grass and aquatic plants in an undisturbed marsh.

Range: Breeds from Siberia and Alaska east across Arctic Canada to Hudson Bay and south to western Ontario, with isolated populations in Rocky Mountains, northern prairies, and Great Lakes region, and in Mississippi, Georgia, and Florida. Winters in California's Central Valley, and across southern states from Arizona to Florida. Also in Cuba.

Apparently the Sandhill Crane was always more numerous than the larger Whooping Crane, and the fact that it breeds mostly in the remote Arctic has saved it from the fate of its relative. But it is sensitive to human disturbance, and the draining of marshes has reduced nesting populations in the United States. These cranes migrate in great flocks and assemble in vast numbers at places like the Platte River in Nebraska. Here it is possible to see what must have been a common sight when the species bred over most of the interior United States.

9 Whooping Crane
Grus americana

Description: 45–50″ (1.1–1.3 m). W. 7′6″ (2.3 m). A very large crane, *pure white with black wing tips,* red on forehead and cheeks. Young birds similar, but strongly tinged with brown.

Voice: A trumpet-like call that can be heard for several miles.

Habitat: Breeds in northern freshwater bogs; winters on coastal prairies.

Nesting: 2 buff eggs, blotched with brown, on a mound of marsh vegetation.

Range: Breeds in Wood Buffalo National Park on Alberta-Mackenzie border. Winters on Gulf Coast of Texas at Aransas National Wildlife Refuge. A second

flock, recently introduced but not yet fully established, breeds at Grays Lake National Wildlife Refuge in Idaho and winters at Bosque del Apache National Wildlife Refuge in New Mexico.

One of our most spectacular birds, the Whooping Crane was reduced by hunting and habitat destruction to about 15 birds in 1937. Strictly protected and monitored since then, the population wintering at Aransas has grown to about 130 birds. In recent decades an attempt has been made to augment this number by placing eggs of this species in the nests of Sandhill Cranes at Grays Lake National Wildlife Refuge in Idaho. This effort has not yet been declared a complete success, but including captives there are now more than 170 Whooping Cranes in existence.

FAMILY CHARADRIIDAE
Plovers

60 species: Worldwide. Nine species breed in North America. Plovers are small to medium-sized shorebirds with short bills slightly swollen at the tip. These birds run along the sand or mud for a way, suddenly stop, and probe in the soft ooze, snatching worms, snails, small crustaceans, and insects from the ground. Most species have characteristic black or brown breast bands on a white background.

252, 253   **Black-bellied Plover**
Pluvialis squatarola

Description: 10–13" (25–33 cm). A quail-sized plover. Breeding adults gray, with flecks of light and dark above, black on face and breast, and white on belly. Winter adults similar, but face and breast are white like belly. Young birds have upperparts flecked with yellow, breast and belly finely streaked. In all plumages, bold white wing stripe, *white rump,* and *black patch under wing.* See American Golden-Plover.

Voice: A clear whistled *pee-a-wee.*

Habitat: Breeds on tundra; winters on beaches, mudflats, and coastal marshes, less commonly on inland marshes, lakeshores, and plowed fields.

Nesting: 3 or 4 buff eggs, spotted with brown, in a shallow depression lined with moss, lichens, and grass.

Range: Breeds in northwestern Alaska and Arctic Canada. Winters mainly along coasts from British Columbia and Massachusetts southward. Also in Eurasia.

Most of us see the Black-bellied Plover during the winter or in migration, when it may lack its bold black underparts but is nonetheless conspicuous among the smaller shorebirds that frequently accompany it. It is one of the shyer species, usually the first to take flight when a flock of shorebirds is approached. Its plaintive call is a characteristic winter sound on mudflats and beaches.

251, 254 **American Golden-Plover**
"Lesser Golden-Plover"
Pluvialis dominica

Description: 9–11″ (23–28 cm). A quail-sized plover. In breeding plumage, dull golden-brown above, with black throat, breast, flanks, belly, and undertail coverts; bold white stripe runs from forehead, over eye, and down side of neck and breast. In winter, has bold whitish eyebrow, grayish-white underparts. Lacks white wing stripe, white rump, and black patch under wing of larger and paler

Black-bellied Plover. See Pacific
Golden-Plover.

Voice: A mellow *quee-lee-la.*

Habitat: Breeds on tundra; during migration
found on coastal beaches and mudflats
and inland on prairies and plowed fields.

Nesting: 3 or 4 buff eggs, spotted with brown, in
a shallow depression lined with reindeer
moss, usually on a ridge or other
elevated spot in the tundra.

Range: Breeds from Alaska east to Baffin
Island. In migration, most birds
travel south over Atlantic Ocean
from Canadian Maritimes to South
America, but some winter on islands in
Pacific and appear along West Coast
during migration.

The American Golden-Plover annually
performs one of the longest migrations
of any American bird. In late summer
birds from the eastern Arctic gather in
eastern Canada, where they fatten on
crowberries and other small fruits before
beginning their nonstop flight over the
ocean to the northern coast of South
America, a journey of some 2,500 miles
(4,000 kilometers). Smaller numbers
move southward in the fall across the
Great Plains. Relatively few American
Golden-Plovers are found along the East
Coast of the United States. Once in
South America they make another long
flight across the vast Amazon Basin,
finally arriving at their principal
wintering grounds on the pampas of
central Argentina and in Patagonia and
Tierra del Fuego. In former times they
gathered here in enormous numbers,
but heavy shooting in both North and
South America took a serious toll, from
which the species has not fully
recovered. In spring the birds return to
the Arctic but at that time they move
north by way of the Great Plains.

255　**Pacific Golden-Plover**
Pluvialis fulva

Description:　9–11" (23–28 cm). A quail-sized
plover. Similar to American Golden-
Plover but more slender. In breeding
plumage, has narrow white stripe along
flanks and mottled black and white
undertail coverts (American usually
has all-black flanks and mainly black
undertail coverts). In winter plumage,
has buff (not white) eyebrow, warmer
brown upperparts, buff (not grayish)
underparts. Juvenile similar to
American but buffier, with buff
eyebrow.

Voice:　A mellow *quee-lee-lee.*

Habitat:　Breeds on tundra; on migration, found
on coastal beaches and mudflats.

Nesting:　3 or 4 buff eggs, spotted with brown,
in a shallow depression lined with
reindeer moss, usually on a ridge or
other elevated spot in the tundra.

Range:　Breeds along coast of Bering Sea in
Alaska. Winters locally along Pacific
Coast of California. Also in Asia.

The Pacific Golden-Plover is a long-
distance migrant like the American
Golden-Plover. Although some winter
along the California coast, most migrate
to islands in the South Pacific. The two
birds were until recently considered
races of a single species, but their
breeding ranges overlap in western
Alaska, and they do not interbreed.

250　**Snowy Plover**
Charadrius alexandrinus

Description:　5–7" (13–18 cm). A small whitish plover
with pale brown upperparts, black legs,
slender black bill, and small black mark
on each side of breast. The similar
Piping Plover (*Charadrius melodus*) has
stubbier yellow bill and yellow legs.

Voice:　A plaintive *chu-we* or *o-wee-ah.*

Habitat: Flat sandy beaches, salt flats, and sandy areas with little vegetation.

Nesting: 2 or 3 buff eggs, spotted with black, in a sandy depression lined with a few shell fragments or bits of grass.

Range: Resident along Pacific Coast from British Columbia to Mexico, and along Gulf Coast from Texas to Florida Panhandle. Also breeds locally in interior from California and Nevada east to Oklahoma and Texas. Also in Old World.

This small, sand-colored plover has the perfect camouflage on sandy shores. As soon as it stops running it seems to disappear, blending into its surroundings. The eggs also blend with dry sand or salty barren soil and are almost impossible to find once the incubating bird slips off them. Inland, these birds feed mainly on insects but along the coast they also take crustaceans, worms, and other small marine creatures.

249 Semipalmated Plover
Charadrius semipalmatus

Description: 6–8″ (15–20 cm). A brown-backed plover with white underparts and *1 black breast band.* Bill stubby, yellow-orange, with dark tip. Immature has all-black bill and brownish breast band. Piping Plover similar but much paler above. Larger Killdeer has 2 black breast bands.

Voice: A plaintive 2-note whistle, *tu-wee.* Also a soft, rather musical rattle.

Habitat: Breeds on sandy or mossy tundra; during migration found on beaches, mudflats, shallow pools in salt marshes, and lakeshores.

Nesting: 4 buff eggs, spotted with dark brown and black, placed in a shallow depression sparsely lined with shell

fragments, pebbles, and bits of
vegetation on the tundra.

Range: Breeds from Alaska east to
Newfoundland and Nova Scotia.
Winters regularly from California and
Carolinas south and along Gulf Coast;
rarely farther north.

Like other plovers, the Semipalmated
forages in short bursts—a quick run
followed by a stop—during which it
scans the sand or mud in front of it for
any sign of life before running on. It
does not probe like its usual associates,
the longer-billed sandpipers. Taking
most of their food right from the surface,
Semipalmated Plovers prey mainly on
small crustaceans and mollusks.

248 Killdeer
Charadrius vociferus

Description: 9–11″ (23–28 cm). Our largest "ringed"
plover. Brown above and white below,
with *2 black bands across breast*, long legs,
and relatively long tail. In flight, shows
rusty uppertail coverts and rump.

Voice: A shrill *kill-deee, fill-deee* or *killdeer,
killdeer*. Also *dee-dee-dee*.

Habitat: Open country generally: plowed fields,
golf courses, and short-grass prairies.

Nesting: 4 pale buff eggs, spotted with blackish
brown, in a shallow depression lined
with grass on bare ground.

Range: Breeds from Alaska east across continent
to Newfoundland and southward.
Winters north to British Columbia,
Utah, Ohio Valley, and Massachusetts.
Also in South America.

If a predator approaches, a nesting
Killdeer performs a conspicuous
distraction display, dragging itself as if
mortally wounded, often on one foot, its
wings seemingly broken and its rusty
tail fanned toward the intruder. This
feigning of injury is effective in luring

the predator away from the eggs or young, at which point the adult flies safely away.

256 Mountain Plover
Charadrius montanus

Description: 8–9½" (20–24 cm). A long-legged, sandy-brown plover. Breeding adult has black forecrown, white forehead, and thin black eye line. In winter adults and young birds, face plain, dark eye conspicuous. In all plumages, whitish wing stripe, whitish wing linings, black band near tail tip.

Voice: A harsh single note, *krrrp.*

Habitat: Arid plains, short-grass prairies, and fields.

Nesting: 3 dark olive eggs, heavily spotted with brown, in a shallow depression on the ground, sometimes lined with bits of cow dung, twigs, or grass.

Range: Breeds in Montana, Wyoming, Colorado, New Mexico, and Texas Panhandle east to Nebraska. Winters from central California and southern Arizona southward into Mexico.

With its range centered on the short-grass prairie, a region subject to heavy grazing and cultivation, the Mountain Plover has been drastically reduced in number. It feeds singly or in small flocks, mostly on insects. In winter larger concentrations can be seen.

257 Eurasian Dotterel
Charadrius morinellus

Description: 8–9" (20–23 cm). A chunky Arctic plover. Breeding adult brown above, with *bold white eyebrow, white band across breast, and russet breast.* Winter adult and young are duller, with buff eyebrows and vague breast band.

Voice: A soft *pip-pip* or *pip-pip-pip*.
Habitat: Alpine tundra.
Nesting: 2 or 3 buff, yellowish, or greenish eggs, spotted with blackish-brown, in a shallow depression in tundra vegetation.
Range: Breeds in northwestern Alaska on Seward Peninsula and on nearby Saint Lawrence Island. Winters in Old World. Also in Eurasia.

The Eurasian Dotterel, a familiar bird in northern Europe, is only a rarity in Alaska. This tundra-dwelling bird is quite tame and can be approached easily.

FAMILY HAEMATOPODIDAE
Oystercatchers

7 species: Widespread in warm regions. Two species breed in North America. Both are large birds, boldly patterned in black or in black and white, with reddish bills and legs. They inhabit seacoasts and, less often, inland rivers, where they feed on shellfish, crustaceans, and sandworms. They are conspicuous birds whether feeding on mud banks or nesting on the sand, where they lay from two to five eggs.

259   Black Oystercatcher
Haematopus bachmani

Description: 17–17½″ (43–44 cm). A large stocky shorebird, black with a *long, stout, red bill.* American Oystercatcher (*Haematopus palliatus*), boldly patterned in black and white, breeds in Baja California and is a casual visitor to California.
Voice: A whistled *wheeee-whee-whee-whee.*
Habitat: Rocky seacoasts.
Nesting: 2 or 3 olive-buff eggs, with brownish-black blotches, among pebbles in a shallow rocky depression or in a hollow on a beach.

Range: Resident from Aleutian Islands southward along Pacific Coast to Baja California.

The Black Oystercatcher is only rarely found on sandy beaches—the normal habitat of the American Oystercatcher—but favors rocky coasts. It can be hard to see against a background of wet, seaweed-encrusted rocks and usually forages alone or in small groups. It feeds on a variety of marine life, specializing in creatures that cling to rocks below the high-tide line.

FAMILY RECURVIROSTRIDAE
Stilts and Avocets

7 species: Fairly widespread in warmer regions. Two species breed in North America. Avocets and stilts are flashy shorebirds with vivid patterns of black, white, tan, and pink. Both are long-legged; the long bills are upturned in avocets, straight in stilts. The avocets have partially webbed feet, presumably as an aid in swimming in deeper water than most waders attempt.

238 Black-necked Stilt
Himantopus mexicanus

Description: 13–16" (33–41 cm). A slender, long-legged shorebird. Black above, white below; head patterned in black and white; neck long; bill long and thin; legs very long, red, and slender.

Voice: A sharp *kip-kip-kip-kip*.

Habitat: Salt marshes, shallow coastal bays, and freshwater marshes.

Nesting: 3 or 4 buff eggs, spotted with brown, in a shallow depression lined with grass or shell fragments in a marsh. Nests in loose colonies.

Range: Breeds along coasts from Oregon and

Delaware southward, and locally in western interior states east to Idaho, Kansas, and Texas. Winters along Pacific Coast north to central California; also in Florida and other Gulf Coast states.

Noisy and conspicuous, Black-necked Stilts have declined due to hunting and habitat destruction. In the nesting season they are particularly aggressive and will often fly low over an intruder—their long red legs trailing behind them—uttering a sharp alarm call.

236, 237   American Avocet
Recurvirostra americana

Description: 16–20″ (41–51 cm). A large, long-legged shorebird with a *slender, upturned bill.* Upperparts and wings patterned in black and white; underparts white. Head and neck rust-colored in summer, white in winter.

Voice: A loud repeated *wheep.*

Habitat: Freshwater marshes and shallow marshy lakes; breeds locally in salt or brackish marshes. Many move to the coasts in winter.

Nesting: 4 olive-buff eggs, spotted with brown and black, in a shallow depression sparsely lined with grass on a beach or mudflat. Often nests in loose colonies.

Range: Breeds from interior Washington, Saskatchewan, and Minnesota south to California and Texas. Winters on West Coast north to California, on Gulf Coast, and in Florida. Rare but regular visitor on Atlantic Coast in fall.

Avocets feed much like spoonbills, sweeping their bills from side to side along the surface of the water to pick up crustaceans, aquatic insects, and floating seeds. They often feed in flocks, a line of birds advancing abreast, sometimes entirely submerging their heads as they sweep the water for food.

FAMILY SCOLOPACIDAE
Sandpipers, Phalaropes, and Allies

90 species: Worldwide. Thirty-six
species breed in North America. The
members of this family that frequent
our waters range in size from the large
Long-billed Curlew to one of the
smallest, the Least Sandpiper. They are
wading birds found on seacoasts and
along inland lakes and rivers, and most
of them nest on the Arctic tundra. Many
perform tremendous migrations to the
Southern Hemisphere in autumn and
back north again in spring. This family
includes the curlews, godwits, snipes,
woodcocks, turnstones, phalaropes,
dowitchers, yellowlegs, and the
"peeps"—the smallest sandpipers
of the genus *Calidris.*

212 Greater Yellowlegs
Tringa melanoleuca

Description: 14″ (36 cm). A slender, gray-streaked
wader with conspicuous white rump and
long *yellow legs.* Lesser Yellowlegs is
similar but smaller, with a shorter,
straighter, and more slender bill and a
different call.

Voice: A series of musical whistled notes:
whew-whew-whew.

Habitat: Breeds on tundra and marshy ground;
frequents pools, lakeshores, and tidal
mudflats on migration.

Nesting: 4 tawny eggs, heavily marked with
brown, in a slight depression on the
ground in a damp open spot.

Range: Breeds from south-central Alaska east
across central Canada to Maritime
Provinces and Newfoundland. Winters
mainly along coasts from Washington
State and Virginia southward, and along
Gulf Coast.

The Greater Yellowlegs is a common
shorebird throughout the West. With

its long legs, it is adapted for foraging in deep pools. The bill, slightly upturned, is used to skim small animals from the surface of the water as the bird swings it from side to side. This behavior, seldom seen in the Lesser Yellowlegs, makes a Greater Yellowlegs recognizable at a long distance.

213 Lesser Yellowlegs
Tringa flavipes

Description: 10½" (27 cm). A smaller, more slender edition of the Greater Yellowlegs, with a proportionately shorter, straighter, more slender bill. Looks longer-legged than Greater Yellowlegs.

Voice: A flat *tu-tu,* less musical than call of Greater Yellowlegs.

Habitat: Breeds in northern bogs; frequents marshy ponds, lake and river shores, and mudflats during migration.

Nesting: 4 buff eggs, blotched with brown, in a slight depression on the open ground near water.

Range: Breeds from Alaska to Hudson Bay. Winters on coasts from southern California and Virginia southward, and along Gulf Coast.

The Lesser Yellowlegs is tamer than its larger relative and often allows close approach. It was formerly a favorite game bird—not because shooting it was good sport but because the birds were good eating—but is now fully protected.

203 Solitary Sandpiper
Tringa solitaria

Description: 8½" (22 cm). A small dark sandpiper with dark olive legs, speckled upperparts, white tail barred with black, and *prominent eye ring.* Flight is swallow-like. No white wing stripe, as seen in Spotted Sandpiper.

Voice: A high-pitched *peet-weet* or *peet-weet-weet,* more shrill than call of Spotted Sandpiper.

Habitat: Ponds, bogs, wet swampy places, and woodland streams.

Nesting: 4 pale green or buff eggs, thickly spotted with gray and brown, in deserted tree nests of thrushes, jays, or blackbirds.

Range: Breeds in Alaska and across Canada to Labrador, south to northeastern Minnesota. Winters in American tropics.

The well-named Solitary Sandpiper usually migrates alone rather than in flocks. It feeds along the edges of irrigation canals and small ponds, especially where cattle are watered. When disturbed, it bobs its head and flies up, calling loudly. Its habit of nesting in the abandoned nests of other birds is unique among North American shorebirds, which generally nest on the ground.

222, 225 Willet
Catoptrophorus semipalmatus

Description: 15″ (38 cm). A large shorebird, gray-brown, with a long straight bill. Best identified in flight by its flashy *black and white wing pattern.* Gray legs and thicker bill distinguish it from Greater Yellowlegs.

Voice: A loud ringing *pill-will-willet* and a quieter *kuk-kuk-kuk-kuk-kuk.*

Habitat: Coastal beaches, freshwater and salt marshes, lakeshores, and wet prairies.

Nesting: 4 olive-buff eggs, spotted with brown, in a nest lined with weeds or bits of shell placed in a depression on open ground or in a grass clump.

Range: Breeds from central Canada to northeastern California and Nevada; also along Atlantic and Gulf coasts south from Nova Scotia. Winters along

coasts from Oregon and Carolinas
southward.

Willets are conspicuous, noisy birds with
several distinctive calls. They separate
when feeding but remain in loose
contact. If one bird takes flight, all the
others will join it; the birds usually fly
together, calling back and forth, before
dropping down farther along the beach.

---

247 Wandering Tattler
Heteroscelus incanus

Description: 11″ (28 cm). A medium-sized sandpiper,
uniform gray above, with whitish
eyebrow, dark rump and tail, and
greenish-yellow legs. Breeding birds
have heavily barred underparts. Winter
birds whitish below, with a gray wash
on sides and flanks.

Voice: A series of 3 or 4 clear whistles, given
in flight.

Habitat: Mountain streams in summer; coastal
rocks, shell beaches, and rocky coves in
fall and winter.

Nesting: 4 greenish eggs, marked with dark
brown, in a finely built nest of roots,
twigs, and dry leaves on a gravel bar in a
mountain stream above the timberline.

Range: Breeds in mountain areas of south-
central Alaska and northwestern British
Columbia. Winters on Pacific Coast
from central California southward.

The Wandering Tattler breeds above
the timberline in Alaska's rugged
mountains, and its nest was not
discovered until 1922. Despite its
tameness, little is known about its
breeding behavior; it is not even known
how long the eggs have to be incubated
or how long the young are dependent
on their parents. These birds are better
known on their coastal wintering
grounds, where they were discovered
more than two centuries ago.

202, 207 Spotted Sandpiper
Actitis macularia

Description:	7½″ (19 cm). A starling-sized shorebird that bobs its tail almost constantly. Breeding adults are brown above, with bold white wing stripe, white below with bold black spots on breast and belly. Fall birds lack black spots below, have brownish smudge at sides of breast.
Voice:	A clear *peet-weet;* also a soft trill.
Habitat:	Ponds, streams, and other waterways, both inland and along the shore.
Nesting:	4 buff eggs, spotted with brown, in a nest lined with grass or moss in a slight depression on the ground.
Range:	Breeds from northern Alaska and Canada across most of continent to southern United States. Winters along Pacific Coast south from British Columbia and across southern states south to South America.

As one walks along a stream or the edge of a pond, a small brown shorebird is likely to jump up and fly off with its wings stiffly vibrating and held in a downward curve. When it lands it "teeters" its tail up and down nervously. These behavioral clues are all one needs to identify the Spotted Sandpiper, one of the few members of its family that nests in the United States rather than far away in the Arctic.

206 Upland Sandpiper
Bartramia longicauda

Description:	11–12½″ (28–32 cm). A sandpiper of open meadows with *long yellowish legs,* slender neck and small head, and short bill. Upperparts brown and scaly, underparts streaked and barred. Ends of wings are dark in flight; tail long and wedge-shaped. Often holds wings upward briefly on alighting, exposing black and white barring on underwing.

Voice: Alarm call a mellow *quip-ip-ip-ip.* On breeding grounds and at night during migration, a long, mournful, rolling whistle.

Habitat: Breeds in open grasslands, prairies, and hayfields; generally frequents open country during migration.

Nesting: 4 pinkish-buff eggs, with brown spots, in a grass-lined nest in a hollow on the ground.

Range: Breeds from Alaska east to New Brunswick and south to northeastern Oregon, Oklahoma, and Virginia. Winters in southern South America.

Until recently known as the "Upland Plover," this species was once very common on the prairies, but indiscriminate hunting in the 19th century and the destruction of its native habitat have reduced its numbers.

230 Whimbrel
Numenius phaeopus

Description: 17″ (43 cm). A large shorebird with a *down-curved bill.* Uniform brown or gray-brown above, with bold head stripes and long legs. Eskimo Curlew (*Numenius borealis*), now near extinction, is much smaller and more of a buff color, with a shorter, very slender, down-curved bill, cinnamon wing linings, and no bold head pattern.

Voice: A series of 5–7 loud, clear, whistled notes: *pip-pip-pip-pip-pip.*

Habitat: Breeds on Arctic tundra, especially near coast; coastal salt meadows, mudflats, and grassy shoreline slopes during migration.

Nesting: 4 olive eggs, heavily marked with brown, in a depression in moss or in a sedge clump on the ground.

Range: Breeds in Arctic Alaska and Canada. Winters in southern California, Gulf Coast, and Atlantic Coast north to Virginia. Also in Eurasia.

The Whimbrel is found along both coasts, as well as in the interior of the continent. It is still numerous because of its wary behavior and the remoteness of its nesting grounds on the Arctic tundra. Like many other tundra breeders, those in the East fly offshore over the Atlantic during their autumn migration to South America, returning in spring mainly along an interior route.

232 Bristle-thighed Curlew
Numenius tahitiensis

Description: 17″ (43 cm). Similar to Whimbrel but tinged buff, especially on breast, with pale rufous tail; base of bill pale.

Voice: A plaintive drawn-out whistle, *too-lee.*

Habitat: Mountain tundra in summer; island beaches in winter.

Nesting: 4 greenish eggs, spotted with brown, in a depression lined with tundra mosses.

Range: Breeds in small area of western Alaska; winters in Hawaii and other Pacific island groups.

The first nest of this little-known bird was found by Cornell ornithologist Arthur A. Allen in June 1948 on the lower Yukon River. Its population is small, and although it is not yet threatened on its breeding grounds, its Pacific island winter habitats are becoming increasingly settled.

231 Long-billed Curlew
Numenius americanus

Description: 23″ (58 cm). A large curlew, warm brown and buff below, with cinnamon wing linings, no head pattern, and *very long, sickle-shaped bill.*

Voice: A clear *curleee;* a sharp *whit-whit, whit, whit, whit, whit.*

Habitat: Breeds on plains and prairies; on

migration frequents lake and river
shores, mudflats, salt marshes, and
sandy beaches.

Nesting: 4 olive-buff eggs, spotted with brown,
in a grass-lined nest in a hollow on
the ground.

Range: Breeds from southern Canada to
northern California, Utah, northern
New Mexico, and Texas. Winters from
California, Texas, Louisiana, South
Carolina, and Florida southward.

Curlews are sociable birds when feeding,
roosting, and migrating. The bill of this
species looks almost as long as the body,
whereas in the smaller Whimbrel the
bill is only about the length of the head
and neck. Formerly hunted for their
delectable flesh, Long-bills are now
fully protected.

234 Hudsonian Godwit
Limosa haemastica

Description: 15″ (38 cm). A large slender shorebird
with a long, slightly upturned bill.
Breeding adult has *barred chestnut
underparts,* mottled brown upperparts.
Fall birds grayish above, whitish below.
All plumages have *black and white tail,*
broad white wing stripe, and *black
wing linings.*

Voice: Similar to call of Marbled Godwit but
higher pitched. Usually silent.

Habitat: Breeds on tundra; mainly mudflats
during migration.

Nesting: 4 olive-buff eggs, spotted with brown
and black, in a shallow grass-lined
hollow on the ground.

Range: Breeds in Alaska, Mackenzie,
northwestern British Columbia, and
around Hudson Bay. Winters in
southern South America.

Never common, the Hudsonian Godwit
was for many years hunted for food and
became scarce. Now completely

protected, it has increased in number considerably. It is still considered a rarity, however, because during migration to and from the Southern Hemisphere the Hudsonian Godwit engages in long flights, traveling nonstop between James Bay, Canada, and the Gulf Coast, and thus bypassing most birders.

235 Bar-tailed Godwit
Limosa lapponica

Description: 15–18″ (38–46 cm). Similar to Hudsonian Godwit but larger, with barred tail, no white wing stripe, and brown wing linings with white barring.

Voice: A loud *kew-wew* and various other notes.

Habitat: Tundra marshes in summer; estuarine mudflats and lake edges in winter and during migration.

Nesting: 4 greenish eggs, with small brownish spots, in a shallow depression lined with lichens, moss, or grass.

Range: Breeds in northwestern Alaska. Winters largely in Old World. A casual visitor to Pacific and Atlantic coasts.

This Eurasian godwit wades in open water and probes deeply for worms and crustaceans. A rare visitor to North America, it is the most common godwit in much of the Old World.

233 Marbled Godwit
Limosa fedoa

Description: 18″ (46 cm). A crow-sized shorebird, dark and mottled above, cinnamon-buff below, with cinnamon wing linings and *long, pinkish, upturned bill.*

Voice: A loud *kerreck* or *god-wit,* usually heard on breeding grounds.

Habitat: Breeds on grassy plains; visits salt marshes, tidal creeks, mudflats, and sea beaches on migration.

Nesting: 4 olive-buff eggs, blotched with brown, in a slight depression lined with grass on the ground.

Range: Breeds on the central plains from Saskatchewan to Minnesota. Winters on coasts from California and Virginia southward and along Gulf Coast.

In spring on the Great Plains, the aerial displays and noisy calls of Marbled Godwits are conspicuous. Males chase one another and perform figure-eight flights. The birds nest in loose colonies, and while the eggs are incubated by the female alone, both parents guard the young birds as they feed.

215, 218 Ruddy Turnstone
Arenaria interpres

Description: 8–10″ (20–25 cm). A stocky shorebird with orange legs. Upperparts mainly rusty red in summer, brown in winter; underparts white. Face and breast have conspicuous black markings, duller but still visible in winter. Bold pattern of black and white visible in flight.

Voice: A metallic but musical *netticut* or *kek-kek.*

Habitat: Breeds on coastal tundra; winters on rocky, pebbly, and sandy coasts and beaches.

Nesting: 4 buff-olive eggs, spotted with brown, in a hollow sparsely lined with grass and dead leaves and concealed under a low bush.

Range: Breeds in northwestern Alaska and islands of Canadian Arctic. Winters on coasts from Oregon and Connecticut southward and along Gulf. Also in Eurasia.

In their nesting territories neighboring turnstones display head to head, the

harlequin pattern of the face and black and white fanned tail serving as colorful banners. This sandpiper—once classified as a plover—is found most commonly on beaches, where it uses its bill to overturn stones, seaweed, and other debris in search of food.

216, 219 Black Turnstone
Arenaria melanocephala

Description: 9″ (23 cm). Resembles Ruddy Turnstone in general patterns. In breeding plumage, *black upperparts, head, and breast;* large white spot in front of eye and white line above eye; fine white spotting from nape across side of breast; white belly. In winter plumage, dusky black with unstreaked white belly. Legs dark. Bill short and slightly upturned. In flight, shows a *black and white pattern.*

Voice: A grating rattle similar to that of Ruddy Turnstone.

Habitat: Breeds in marshy coastal tundra; seaweed-covered rocky shores in fall and winter.

Nesting: 4 yellowish-olive eggs, with darker olive and brown markings, in an unlined depression on an open, pebbly ridge or a gravel bar in wet tundra.

Range: Breeds on western and southern coasts of Alaska. Winters all along West Coast from Alaska south to Baja California and Sonora, Mexico.

Unlike the Ruddy Turnstone, a more widespread species, the Black Turnstone is partial to rocky coasts. Turnstones are aggressive; a wintering bird that has found a good foraging spot will hotly defend it against other turnstones.

245, 246 Surfbird
Aphriza virgata

Description: 10″ (25 cm). A stocky, rock-dwelling shorebird, slightly larger than Black Turnstone. Breeding adults have blackish upperparts spotted with white and chestnut, whitish underparts barred with black. Winter birds dark gray above and on breast. All plumages have bold white wing stripe, white rump.

Voice: A shrill *kee-wee* in flight.

Habitat: Breeds above timberline in Arctic mountains; winters on rocky shores, headlands, and islets.

Nesting: 4 buff eggs, spotted with various colors, on bare ground among rocks.

Range: Breeds on mountain tundra of Alaska. Winters along Pacific Coast from southern Alaska southward to Baja California.

That two such distantly related shorebirds as the Surfbird and Black Turnstone have similar plumage is · attributed to a similar need for camouflage in the same environment. The bright wing stripe is a signal, perhaps helping to keep the flying flock in formation.

221, 224 Red Knot
Calidris canutus

Description: 10½″ (27 cm). A robin-sized shorebird. Breeding adults have *pinkish-rufous face and underparts,* dark brown upperparts with pale feather edgings. Fall birds gray above, whitish below. Rump dark; wing stripe faint; bill straight and slightly tapered.

Voice: A soft *quer-wer;* also a soft *knut.*

Habitat: Breeds on tundra; on migration found on tidal flats, rocky shores, and beaches.

Nesting: 4 olive-buff eggs, spotted with brown, in a slight depression lined with lichens, often among rocks.

Range: Breeds on islands in high Arctic of Canada. Winters on coasts from California and Massachusetts southward to southern South America. Also in Eurasia.

Red Knots in breeding plumage, with their rich rufous underparts set off by marbled gray backs, are among the handsomest of shorebirds. Those that winter in southern South America may make a round trip of nearly 20,000 miles (32,000 kilometers) each year.

217, 220 Sanderling
Calidris alba

Description: 8" (20 cm). A starling-sized shorebird with *conspicuous white wing stripe.* Summer adults have rufous head and breast, white belly. In winter, rufous areas replaced by pale gray, and birds look almost white. *Bill and legs black.*

Voice: A sharp *kip.* Conversational chatter while feeding.

Habitat: Breeds on tundra; winters on ocean beaches, sandbars, mudflats, and lake and river shores.

Nesting: 4 olive eggs, spotted with brown, placed in a hollow on the ground lined with grasses and lichens.

Range: Breeds in high Arctic tundra from Alaska eastward to Baffin Island. Winters along coasts from British Columbia and Massachusetts southward to southern South America. Also in Eurasia.

One of the most widespread of all shorebirds, the Sanderling turns up on almost every beach in the world. As a wave comes roaring in, the birds run up on the beach just ahead of the breaker, then sprint after the retreating water to feed on the tiny crustaceans and mollusks left exposed.

197, 209   **Semipalmated Sandpiper**
            Calidris pusilla

Description: 5½–6¾" (14–17 cm). Slightly larger
               than a Least Sandpiper. In all plumages,
               grayer above with less-streaked breast
               than other "peeps." *Feet black. Bill
               black and short,* drooping slightly at
               tip; noticeably stouter than bill of
               Least Sandpiper.

      Voice: A sharp *cheh* or *churk,* not as drawn out
               as the notes of the Least and Western
               sandpipers.

    Habitat: Breeds on tundra; winters on and
               migrates along coastal beaches, lake
               and river shores, mudflats, and pools in
               salt marshes.

    Nesting: 4 buff eggs, marked with brown, in a
               depression on the ground.

      Range: Breeds in northern Alaska and Canada
               south to Hudson Bay. Migrates
               commonly through eastern and central
               states, rarely but regularly in West.
               Winters in South America.

The word "semipalmated" means "half-
webbed," and refers to small webs
between the front toes, which help
support these birds on soft mud. These
sandpipers are abundant but in the
West are always outnumbered by the
very similar Western Sandpiper.

199, 211   **Western Sandpiper**
            Calidris mauri

Description: 6½" (17 cm). Similar to Semipalmated
               Sandpiper and not always easy to
               distinguish, but *bill tends to be longer,
               with more evident droop at tip.* In summer,
               crown and upper back rusty; in winter,
               crown and upper back dull gray.

      Voice: A soft *cheep* or *kreep,* higher and thinner
               than that of Semipalmated.

    Habitat: Shores, mudflats, grassy pools, and
               wet meadows.

    Nesting: 4 creamy eggs, with red-brown spots,

in a grass-lined depression on either wet or dry tundra.

Range: Breeds in northern and western Alaska. Winters mainly along coast from California and Virginia southward to South America.

This is the western counterpart of the Semipalmated Sandpiper, the common "peep" (a general nickname for small sandpipers) of the Atlantic and Gulf coasts. The flocks of these "peeps" that spread out on mudflats during fall and winter take to flight readily when an intruder nears. When the tide covers their shallow feeding grounds, the flocks move to higher ground; there they preen themselves, rest, and wait for the next low tide, when they can resume feeding.

---

214 Rufous-necked Stint
"Rufous-necked Sandpiper"
Calidris ruficollis

Description: 6½" (17 cm). A small sandpiper. In breeding plumage, *face, neck, and upper breast rufous,* with white chin spot, and rest of underparts white; upperparts rufous and brown with black blotches. Fall birds lack rufous tone; closely resemble Semipalmated Sandpipers but have thinner bills. Rump dark, bill and feet black, white wing stripe.

Voice: A thin *chit-chit.*

Habitat: Breeds on marshy tundra; frequents mudflats and ponds in winter and on migration.

Nesting: 4 cream-colored eggs, marked with brown, on dry willow leaves in a depression on the tundra.

Range: Breeds in Siberian Asia and northwestern Alaska. A rare migrant outside of Alaska. Winters chiefly in Old World.

With the recent increase in the number of skilled birders, we have learned that

this Eurasian species is more numerous in North America than was previously thought. Once considered a rarity confined to Alaska, it is now known to turn up occasionally in British Columbia, California, and even New England. Since the young bird scarcely differs from the young Semipalmated Sandpiper, it is likely that the Rufous-necked Stint is more numerous than records would indicate.

198, 210 Least Sandpiper
Calidris minutilla

Description: 6″ (15 cm). The smallest of American shorebirds. Brownish above, with *yellowish or greenish legs,* short thin bill, and streaked breast. Grayer in winter plumage. Bill shorter, thinner, and more pointed than in Semipalmated or Western sandpipers.

Voice: A clear *treep;* when feeding, a soft chuckle.

Habitat: Grassy pools, bogs, and marshes with open areas; also flooded fields and mudflats.

Nesting: 4 pinkish-buff eggs, spotted with brown, in a nest lined with moss and grass placed on a dry hummock in a depression on boggy tundra.

Range: Breeds from Alaska east across northern Canada to Newfoundland and Nova Scotia. Winters along coasts from northern California and North Carolina southward; also in Southwest and Southeast.

Our smallest "peep," the Least Sandpiper is a common and relatively tame bird on inland mudflats and wet grassy areas. As might be expected of an inland bird it feeds heavily on insects, but when it feeds along the coast its diet is like that of the other "peeps"—the Western, Semipalmated, White-rumped (*Calidris fuscicollis*), and Baird's sandpipers—and includes crustaceans, mollusks, and marine worms.

204 Baird's Sandpiper
Calidris bairdii

Description: 7½" (19 cm). A slender "peep" with a short straight bill; larger than Least, Semipalmated, and Western sandpipers. Wing tips extend beyond end of tail, giving bird a "pointed" look behind. Breeding adults have buff tinge on face, splotchy pattern on upperparts. Juveniles have buff face and breast, bold white scaling on upperparts. White-rumped Sandpiper (*Calidris fuscicollis*), an Alaska breeder that migrates east of the Rockies, is similar but lacks scaly pattern above and has bold white rump.

Voice: A soft *krrrt;* also a loud trill similar to that of other "peeps."

Habitat: Breeds on tundra; frequents grassy pools, wet meadows, and lake and river shores on migration.

Nesting: 4 tawny eggs, spotted with brown, in a dry depression on the ground, often among rocks.

Range: Breeds in northern Alaska and Canadian Arctic. Migrates mainly through Great Plains and along Pacific Coast in fall, through Great Plains in spring. Regular in small numbers on East Coast in fall. Winters in South America.

Research shows that in the fall adult Baird's Sandpipers fly rapidly along a narrow route through the Great Plains of North America, while young birds migrate over a broad front, and regularly appear on both Pacific and Atlantic coasts. It is suspected that they may cover up to 4,000 miles (6,400 kilometers) nonstop.

201 Pectoral Sandpiper
Calidris melanotos

Description: 9" (23 cm). A chunky, somewhat short-legged wader with *heavily streaked breast sharply delineated from unmarked white belly.* Legs yellow. In flight, wings dark with no prominent stripe.

Voice: A dull *krrrrp.*

Habitat: Breeds on tundra; during migration visits moist grassy places, grass-lined pools, golf courses and airports after heavy rains, and salt creeks and meadows.

Nesting: 4 buff-white eggs, marked with brown, in a slight depression in boggy tundra.

Range: Breeds on Arctic coasts from Alaska east to Hudson Bay. Migrates along Atlantic and Pacific coasts and through interior. Winters in southern South America.

During the short Arctic breeding season food is at a premium. To ensure an adequate supply for the young, male Pectoral Sandpipers depart for the south before the eggs hatch, so they don't compete for food with the mothers and their chicks. Then the adult females leave, too, and in the last few weeks the young have the tundra to themselves.

---

205 Sharp-tailed Sandpiper
Calidris acuminata

Description: 8½″ (22 cm). Similar to Pectoral Sandpiper in size and behavior. *Brownish overall* but more rusty than Pectoral, *cap redder,* eyebrow broader. Breast paler, more of a buff color, with faint streaking limited to sides in immatures; breast pattern less sharply contrasted with white belly than in Pectoral.

Voice: A sharp *whit-whit.*

Habitat: Grassy areas of coastal marshes and tidal flats.

Nesting: 4 buff eggs, spotted with brown, in a nest of grass on the ground.

Range: Breeds in Siberia. Appears in small numbers along West Coast in fall, less often inland and on East Coast.

A Eurasian species, the Sharp-tailed Sandpiper appears in North America

mainly after the end of the nesting season. Most of the birds recorded in North America are young of the year.

208 Rock Sandpiper
Calidris ptilocnemis

Description: 8–9″ (20–23 cm). A small, rock-dwelling sandpiper. Winter birds *plain slate-gray on head, breast, and upperparts;* dark bill has pale base. Breeding birds rusty above, with pale head and dark ear patch, black patch on lower breast (not on belly as in Dunlin). Legs greenish yellow.

Voice: Usually silent; low whistled notes sometimes heard in winter.

Habitat: Breeds on upland tundra; rocky shores in winter.

Nesting: 4 buff-olive eggs, spotted with brown, in a mossy depression on the tundra.

Range: Breeds along coast of western Alaska. Winters from Aleutians south to Washington, rarely farther south.

Along rocky coastlines, dark gray birds feeding in loose flocks at the waterline or on exposed, seaweed-covered rocks may be Rock Sandpipers, Black Turnstones, or Surfbirds. All are similarly camouflaged to match wet dark rocks. In flight, the three are easily distinguished: The Rock Sandpiper has a dark tail, the Surfbird has a white tail terminating in a black triangle, and the Black Turnstone has a checkered black and white pattern on the back.

223, 226 Dunlin
Calidris alpina

Description: 8½″ (22 cm). A starling-sized shorebird. Bill fairly long, with *distinct droop at tip.* Breeding adults have reddish back, whitish underparts, with *black patch* in center of belly. Winter birds are dull gray, paler below.

Voice: A soft *cheerp* or *chit-lit*.

Habitat: Nests on tundra; winters on beaches, mudflats, sand flats, and inland lake and river shores.

Nesting: 4 olive eggs, blotched with brown, in a grass clump on a dry hummock on the open tundra.

Range: Breeds from western and northern Alaska east to Hudson Bay. Winters along coasts from southern Alaska and Massachusetts southward. Also in Eurasia.

These handsome birds, formerly known as "Red-backed Sandpipers," are very tame and thus easy to approach and study. They are among the hardiest of shorebirds. Thousands sometimes spend the winter months on sandbars or inlets along the coast as far north as southeastern Alaska, where they feed on mollusks, crustaceans, and marine worms.

---

262 Curlew Sandpiper
Calidris ferruginea

Description: 8″ (20 cm). Similar in size and shape to Dunlin, but entire bill noticeably curved. Summer adults are rich cinnamon or chestnut. Winter birds gray above and white below. Immatures have buff breast, upperparts marked with buff scaling. *White rump* visible in flight.

Voice: A soft dry *chirrip*.

Habitat: Breeds on tundra; chiefly coastal mudflats on migration.

Nesting: 4 yellow-buff eggs, with dark brown spots, in a depression on the ground in tundra.

Range: Breeds in Eurasia and very rarely in northern Alaska. A rare but regular migrant to East Coast, less common on West Coast. Winters mainly in Old World.

Except for a small area on the Arctic coast of Alaska, where it is a rarity, this Old World species breeds solely in northern Siberia. During spring migration the adults are in their bright chestnut breeding plumage and, with their curved bills and white rumps, are easily distinguished in the field from their usual associates, the Red Knots and Dunlins. However, on fall migration in their dull winter plumage they are much more difficult to spot among the hordes of other shorebirds.

260 Stilt Sandpiper
Calidris himantopus

Description: 8½″ (22 cm). A starling-sized sandpiper with long greenish legs and long bill, slightly down-curved at tip. Wings lack stripe. Breeding adult has chestnut head stripes and barring below. Nonbreeding birds have much paler plumage and a white line over the eye.

Voice: Simple *tu-tu,* similar to call of Lesser Yellowlegs.

Habitat: Grassy pools and shores of ponds and lakes.

Nesting: 4 pale buff eggs, marked with brown, on open ground in a grass tussock near water.

Range: Breeds in northern Alaska and northern Canada east to Hudson Bay. Winters in small numbers in southern California's Salton Sea, Gulf Coast, and Florida.

Often associated with dowitchers and yellowlegs, Stilt Sandpipers resemble both species and appear to be intermediate between the two. Yellowlegs move about continually in nervous, jerky motions, and dowitchers feed slowly, probing deep into the mud. Stilt Sandpipers move like yellowlegs but cover more ground, while feeding deliberately like dowitchers.

200 Buff-breasted Sandpiper
Tryngites subruficollis

Description: 8″ (20 cm). A starling-sized sandpiper
with a small head. *Underparts and face
buff, legs dull orange-yellow.* Bill short
and straight.

Voice: A low *tik-tik-tik.*

Habitat: Breeds on dry tundra; visits short-
grass prairies, fields, and meadows
on migration.

Nesting: 4 pale buff, brown-blotched eggs in a
grass-lined nest on the Arctic tundra.

Range: Breeds in northernmost Alaska and
Canada. Migrates mainly through Great
Plains, but small numbers appear on
East Coast and smaller numbers on
West Coast. Winters in South America.

This species looks like a small, buffy
edition of the Upland Sandpiper, at
times its grassland associate. It is very
tame and when approached merely runs
through the short grass instead of flying
off. Like the American Golden-Plover,
it undertakes an amazing migration in
both spring and fall. After the nesting
season in the far Northwest, it migrates
southward on a broad front, eventually
ending up on the Argentine pampas,
where it spends the winter. On the
return passage in spring its movements
are much more confined, carrying it
chiefly up the Mississippi Valley and to
the West, but ultimately back to the
Arctic shores of Alaska and Canada.

261 Ruff
Philomachus pugnax

Description: 11″ (28 cm). A stocky shorebird with
a short tapered bill. Breeding males
have extraordinarily variable plumage,
showing ear tufts, ruffs, and gorgets
in any combination of black, white,
chestnut, gray, buff, etc. Females (called
"Reeves") and winter males are much

duller—gray or brown above with pale spot at base of bill, white below; leg color varies from yellow to green, brown, and red. In flight, 2 oval white patches are visible at sides of rump. In all seasons male noticeably larger than female.

Voice: Usually silent, but occasionally a soft *tu-whit* when flushed.

Habitat: Short grassy meadows and marshy ponds.

Nesting: 4 gray, green, or buff eggs, heavily marked with deep brown blotches, in a grass-lined depression in a meadow or marsh.

Range: Breeds in northern Eurasia. A rare migrant along Pacific and Atlantic coasts and on Great Lakes.

The Ruff is one of the most remarkable of all shorebirds. It is one of the few waders in which the two sexes are dramatically different in color, pattern, and size during the breeding season. The males also form leks or display grounds and engage in courting. After mating, the females build their nests away from the courtship area.

227 Short-billed Dowitcher
Limnodromus griseus

Description: 12″ (31 cm). Similar to Long-billed Dowitcher but breast and sides spotted rather than barred, belly often whitish. Best distinguished by call.

Voice: A soft *tu-tu-tu*, quite unlike call of Long-billed Dowitcher.

Habitat: Breeds on moist tundra or beside forest pools; visits mudflats, creeks, salt marshes, and tidal estuaries during migration and in winter.

Nesting: 4 greenish eggs, spotted with brown, in a nest lined with grass and moss in a depression on the ground.

Range: Breeds in southern Alaska, central interior Canada, and northern Quebec.

Winters along coast from California and Virginia southward.

These are among the first shorebirds to migrate south, with adult Short-billed Dowitchers leaving as early as July and the young following in August. In fall and winter this species is found mainly on coastal mudflats, whereas the Long-billed Dowitcher prefers freshwater ponds.

228, 229 Long-billed Dowitcher
Limnodromus scolopaceus

Description: 12" (30 cm). A snipe-like, *long-billed* shorebird with *white lower back and rump,* black and white checkered tail, dark bill, green legs. Summer adults have reddish underparts (including belly), with barring on breast, sides, and flanks, and reddish edges on feathers of upperparts. Winter birds gray overall, with pale eyebrow and white lower back and rump. See Short-billed Dowitcher.

Voice: A high sharp *keek,* quite unlike call of Short-billed Dowitcher.

Habitat: Breeds in muskeg; found on mudflats, marshy pools, and margins of freshwater ponds during migration and in winter.

Nesting: 4 olive eggs, spotted with brown, in a grass and moss-lined nest on the ground.

Range: Breeds in western Alaska and extreme northwestern Mackenzie. Winters mainly along coasts from Washington and Virginia southward.

Dowitchers are most often seen during migration. This species favors freshwater habitats, while the Short-billed Dowitcher is more partial to salt water. The main fall migration of Long-bills takes place in September and October, when most of the Short-bills have already departed.

258 Common Snipe
Gallinago gallinago

Description: 10½" (27 cm). A long-billed, brownish shorebird with striped head and back, white belly, and rust in tail. Usually seen when flushed from edge of a marsh or a pond. Flight fast and erratic.

Voice: A sharp rasping *scaip!* when flushed.

Habitat: Freshwater marshes, ponds, flooded meadows, and fields; more rarely in salt marshes.

Nesting: 4 pale olive-brown eggs, spotted with black, concealed in a grass-lined depression in a grass tussock in a marsh.

Range: Breeds from northern Alaska and Canada south to California, southwestern states, and New Jersey. Winters north from tropical America to British Columbia, northern Gulf Coast states, and Virginia. Also in Old World.

This species, an upland bird, is one of the few shorebirds that can still be hunted legally. It stays well hidden in ground cover, flushes abruptly, and zigzags sharply in flight, all habits that make it difficult to shoot and therefore a favorite among hunters. It uses its long bill to probe deeply in the mud to find small animals.

241, 244 Wilson's Phalarope
Phalaropus tricolor

Description: 9" (23 cm). A strikingly patterned shorebird with a needle-like bill, pearl-gray head and back, white underparts, *black stripe through eye and down neck, and chestnut markings on breast and back.* In fall plumage, pale gray above, white below; in this plumage, pale color, more terrestrial habits, and slender bill distinguish it from other phalaropes. Females more boldly patterned than males.

Voice: A soft *quoit-quoit-quoit.*

Habitat: Prairie pools and marshes, lake and river shores, marshy pools along the coast.

Nesting: 4 pale buff eggs, spotted with brown, in a grass-lined nest placed in a slight depression on the ground near water.

Range: Breeds from southern Yukon and Minnesota south to California and Kansas; also in Great Lakes region and in Massachusetts. Winters mainly in American tropics; a few birds winter in California and Texas.

Wilson's is larger than the Red and Red-necked phalaropes and has a much longer, thinner bill. Unlike the others, this species does not have fully lobed toes and so rarely swims, spending no time at sea. When it does feed in water, however, it spins in circles more rapidly than the other two. It is limited to the Western Hemisphere and breeds much farther south than the other phalaropes.

240, 243 Red-necked Phalarope
"Northern Phalarope"
Phalaropus lobatus

Description: 7" (18 cm). A sparrow-sized swimming shorebird with a conspicuous wing stripe. Breeding adults have dark head and back, white chin and belly separated by *chestnut upper breast and sides of neck*. Females more boldly patterned than males. In winter, darker above, with dark line through eye and usually with dark crown, and entirely white below. Bill thin.

Voice: A sharp *twit* or *whit*.

Habitat: Breeds on tundra pools; visits open ocean, beaches, flats, and lake and river shores during migration.

Nesting: 4 olive eggs, spotted with brown, in a slight hollow on the ground in marshy tundra.

Range: Breeds in Alaska and across northern Canada. Migrates along both coasts,

more rarely in interior, and winters mainly at sea in Southern Hemisphere. Also in Old World.

Red-necked Phalaropes, like Red Phalaropes but unlike other shorebirds, prefer to swim rather than wade, a habit that enables them to spend the winter on the high seas. They float buoyantly, picking small creatures from the surface of the water, often while swimming in circles or spinning around to stir up the water.

239, 242 Red Phalarope
Phalaropus fulicaria

Description: 8" (20 cm). A starling-sized swimming shorebird with a conspicuous wing stripe and a *short yellow bill with black tip.* Breeding adults *rich chestnut,* with dark crown, white face. Females more boldly patterned than males. In winter, gray above and white below, with pale crown, dark line through eye, and dark bill.

Voice: Sharp metallic *kreeep.*

Habitat: Breeds on tundra; found on open ocean, bays, inlets, lakes, shores, and coasts during migration.

Nesting: 4 olive eggs, speckled with brown, placed in a grass-lined depression on an elevated spot in low marshy tundra.

Range: Breeds in Alaska and northern Canada. Migrates off both coasts, very rarely in interior. Winters mainly at sea in Southern Hemisphere; irregular along Pacific Coast. Also in Old World.

Hundreds of these shorebirds may be seen from fishing boats far at sea; bobbing like corks, they look like miniature gulls riding the waves. While they are at sea the greater part of their diet is made up of tiny marine animals known as plankton. On land they forage around tundra pools for the aquatic larvae of mosquitoes, midges, and beetles. After egg-laying the male takes over the duties of incubating the eggs and rearing the young.

FAMILY LARIDAE
Jaegers, Gulls, and Terns

129 species: Worldwide. Thirty-four species breed in North America. Jaegers and many gulls occur in colder latitudes, while most of the terns are found in warmer climates. All species have webbed feet. The predatory jaegers have strongly hooked bills and elongated central tail feathers; gulls have less-hooked bills and are mainly clad in gray or black and white; terns have straight pointed bills used chiefly for catching fish and often have black caps. These birds are primarily colonial nesters, breeding on sea islands and coastal beaches and on inland marshes, lakes, and rivers. Sizes range from the large Great Black-backed Gull to the diminutive Least Tern.

77 Pomarine Jaeger
Stercorarius pomarinus

Description: 22" (56 cm). Larger and stockier than the Parasitic Jaeger, with a more extensive white flash on outer wing. Central tail feathers twisted and blunt or spoon-shaped, not pointed; breast band often darker and wider; bill heavier; wings broader at base. Flight more direct. Dark-phase and light-phase individuals occur.

Voice: Harsh chattering calls; a harsh *which-yew.*

Habitat: Breeds on swampy tundra; migrates and winters over ocean.

Nesting: 2 olive-brown eggs, with darker brown spots, in a grass-lined depression on the ground.

Range: Breeds above Arctic Circle in Alaska

and across northern Canada. Winters at sea as far north as California and North Carolina. Very rare in migration on Great Lakes. Also in Eurasia.

The largest of our jaegers, the Pomarine preys on birds up to the size of terns and small gulls, as well as on lemmings, carrion, and the eggs and young of colonial seabirds. Like the Parasitic Jaeger, at sea it also pursues gulls and terns, forcing them to disgorge their food, which it snatches up in midair. Although it can be spotted from land at times, it is much more often seen far offshore.

78 Parasitic Jaeger
Stercorarius parasiticus

Description: 21″ (53 cm). A fast-flying, gull-like seabird. Typical adults are brown above, white or light dusky below, with an incomplete gray-brown band across the breast; a dark, almost black, crown; and short (up to 3–4″) pointed central tail feathers. Dark-phase birds are uniform dusky brown with a darker cap; intermediates between the two color phases occur. Often seen harrying gulls and terns.

Voice: Usually silent; a variety of mewing and wailing notes on breeding grounds.

Habitat: Breeds on grassy tundra and stony ground near inland lakes; at other times on the ocean.

Nesting: 2 olive-brown eggs, with darker brown spots, in a grass-lined depression on the ground or among rocks.

Range: Breeds in Alaska and northern Canada. Winters in warm waters in Southern Hemisphere. Also in northern Eurasia.

This is the most familiar of our jaegers since it comes more readily into bays and estuaries and often feeds closer to shore. Like the other jaegers, it usually

obtains food by pursuing gulls and terns
and forcing them to drop food.

79 Long-tailed Jaeger
Stercorarius longicaudus

Description: 21" (53 cm). Adult similar to light-
phase Parasitic Jaeger but smaller, more
graceful, and with *very long central tail
feathers* (up to 6"). Upperparts paler
than in other jaegers, and blackish
cap smaller and more sharply defined.
Flight more buoyant.

Voice: A harsh *kreeah;* other yelping and
rattling notes on breeding grounds.

Habitat: Breeds on tundra and stony hillsides; at
other times ranges over open ocean.

Nesting: 2 olive-brown eggs, with brown spots,
in a grass-lined nest placed either on
bare ground or among rocks.

Range: Breeds in Alaska and Canada north of
Arctic Circle; winters far offshore in
both Atlantic and Pacific oceans.

Smallest of the three jaegers, the
Long-tailed is rarely seen, presumably
because it migrates chiefly in mid-
ocean. Although occasionally, like other
jaegers, it harries terns and gulls, it
feeds mainly by catching its own fish,
taking flying insects in the air, and
sometimes preying on small birds. On
the breeding grounds lemmings are
its staple food.

56 South Polar Skua
Catharacta maccormicki

Description: 21" (53 cm). A large, dark, heavy-
bodied, gull-like bird, most often
uniform gray with conspicuous white
patches on the outer wing. Tail short
and blunt. Immatures of larger gulls
similar, but lack white wing patches.

Voice: Usually silent in American waters.

Habitat: Open ocean.

Nesting: 1 or 2 olive-brown eggs, with dark brown spots, in a depression on the ground. Often nests in colonies.

Range: Breeds in Southern Hemisphere; rare summer visitor off Pacific and Atlantic coasts.

This Antarctic seabird is a rare spring and fall visitor to the offshore waters of southern California; it can be found in much smaller numbers in summer. Like its relatives the jaegers, it is a predator and scavenger. In the North Pacific these birds gather around fishing fleets to feed on refuse thrown overboard.

19 Laughing Gull
Larus atricilla

Description: 15–17″ (38–43 cm). Similar to Franklin's Gull but larger, darker, with *black wing tip not separated from gray by white band.* Breeding adults have black hood. Winter adults and young birds lack hood; winter and young Franklin's Gulls have sooty half-hood.

Voice: Loud, high-pitched *ha-ha-ha-ha-haah-haah-haah-haah-haah.*

Habitat: Mainly salt marshes and lagoons in West.

Nesting: 3 olive-brown eggs, with dark blotches, in a ground nest lined with grass and weed stems placed on sand or in a salt marsh. Nests in colonies.

Range: Breeds from Nova Scotia to Caribbean; in summer and fall regularly visits Salton Sea in southern California.

The Laughing Gull is an eastern species that is only a visitor to the West. It feeds chiefly on small fish and sometimes steals the eggs of nesting terns.

20 Franklin's Gull
Larus pipixcan

Description: 13–15″ (33–38 cm). A slender gull with a *black hood* in breeding plumage. In summer, adult has dark gray back and wings; trailing edge of wing is white, *wing tip is black, separated from gray by white spots.* Smudgy half-hood in winter. Young bird is dark brown with *contrasting white rump and broad black tail band.* See Laughing Gull.

Voice: A strident *ha-ha-ha-ha-ha-ha*, similar to Laughing Gull's but higher pitched.

Habitat: Prairie marshes and sloughs. Often feeds in plowed fields.

Nesting: 3 buff-brown eggs, spotted with brown, on a loose platform in a marsh. Nests in large, noisy colonies.

Range: Breeds on prairie marshes from southern Canada to South Dakota and Iowa; also in scattered marshes in West. Migrates to southeast and winters mainly along west coast of South America.

Franklin's Gull will breed only in large colonies and so is sensitive to habitat destruction. When agriculture encroaches on a nesting marsh and it becomes too small for a large colony, the birds move elsewhere. During migration these birds often gather over the same agricultural fields to feed on insects.

21 Common Black-headed Gull
Larus ridibundus

Description: 15″ (38 cm). A small gull with gray back and inner wings and *flashing white primaries.* In breeding plumage, has dark brown hood; in winter, head becomes white. Red bill and legs. Immature is darker above, but shows some white in primaries and has narrow black tip to tail. *In all plumages, undersurface of primaries is blackish.*

Smaller Bonaparte's Gull has black bill; primaries lack dark undersurface.

Voice: A harsh *kwup;* various squealing notes.

Habitat: Bays and estuaries.

Nesting: 3 buff-brown eggs, with black blotches, in a nest lined with grass, sticks, and seaweed placed in trees, bushes, on rocks, or on the ground. Nesting colonies located on sand dunes, beaches, marshes, and in open fields.

Range: Breeds in northern portions of Europe and Asia south to their southern parts; winters from the southern portions of the breeding range south to Africa and southern Asia. Uncommon but regular winter visitor to North American Pacific Coast, also East and Great Lakes (rare).

Like that of Bonaparte's Gull, the flight of this bird is light and buoyant, resembling that of a tern more than a gull. In California it is usually seen with Bonaparte's Gulls.

22, 33 Bonaparte's Gull
Larus philadelphia

Description: 12–14" (30–36 cm). A small delicate gull, silvery gray above, with conspicuous white, wedge-shaped patches on leading edge of outer wing. Head black in breeding adults, white in winter with dark spot behind eye. Bill black. Young birds have dark markings on upper surface of wing and black tail band. Common Black-headed Gull similar but larger, with red bill and dark wing linings.

Voice: Rasping *tee-ar;* soft, nasal snarling note.

Habitat: Forested lakes and rivers; winters along coasts, in estuaries, and at mouths of large rivers.

Nesting: 2–4 olive or buff, spotted eggs in a well-made cup of grass, moss, and twigs placed in a spruce or fir tree near a lake or river.

Range: Breeds in Alaska and interior

northwestern Canada east to James Bay. Winters along both coasts, on Pacific from Washington southward, on Atlantic from southern New England southward.

Because they breed in the Far North, these beautiful gulls are most often seen on lakes and rivers during migration or along the coast in winter. They keep to themselves, seldom joining the larger gulls at dumps. They feed in tidal inlets and at sewage outlets, picking scraps of food from the water. The species is named after a nephew of Napoleon, Charles Lucien Bonaparte, who was a leading ornithologist in the 1800s in America and Europe.

27 Heermann's Gull
Larus heermanni

Description: 18–21″ (46–53 cm). *Predominantly dark. Bill red; snow-white head* blends into gray on neck, back, and rump; slate-black wings and tail, with white terminal band on tail and secondaries. Juveniles dusky, throat lighter, tail trimmed white, bill dark.

Voice: A high *see-whee.* Also a low-pitched *kuk-kuk-kuk.*

Habitat: Coastal waters, islands, and beaches.

Nesting: 2 or 3 eggs in a scrape; nests in large colonies on offshore islands.

Range: Breeds on islands in Gulf of California and on San Benito Islands off west coast of Baja California. Some migrate northward from July to October, spending winter on Pacific Coast north to Vancouver Island; others migrate southward as far as Panama. Nonbreeders found year-round on coast of California; adults leave by January.

This gull demonstrates that all migration in the Northern Hemisphere is not necessarily southward in fall and

northward in spring. On its breeding
grounds, Heermann's Gull commonly
follows fishing boats and steals fish
from Brown Pelicans. Farther north it
scavenges along beaches and feeds on
herring eggs.

30, 41 Mew Gull
Larus canus

Description: 16–18″ (41–46 cm). White with gray
mantle, black wing tips, and greenish-
yellow legs. *Bill small compared to those
of larger gulls* and in adults *unmarked*
greenish-yellow. Juvenile similar to
young Ring-billed Gull, but generally
darker with less crisply marked
tail band.

Voice: A high mewing *kee-yer.*

Habitat: Nests along rivers and lakeshores as well
as seacoasts.

Nesting: 2 or 3 olive eggs, with brown or black
blotches and scrawls, in a grass nest
placed on a beach or riverbank, or in
a treetop, on a stump, or on pilings.
Almost always nests in colonies, often
among other gulls.

Range: Breeds from Alaska east to central
Mackenzie and south to northern
Saskatchewan and along coast to
southern British Columbia. Winters
on Pacific Coast. Also along boreal
forest belt of Eurasia.

This small gull is as versatile a feeder
as the larger species of gulls, but its
egg-stealing in seabird colonies is less
destructive. It often catches insects,
sometimes from swarms in the air.

28 Ring-billed Gull
Larus delawarensis

Description: 18–20″ (46–51 cm). Adult silvery gray
on back, white on head, tail, and

underparts. Similar to Herring Gull but smaller, with *greenish-yellow feet* and narrow black ring around bill. Young birds mottled brown, paler than young Herring Gulls, with blackish tail band and flesh-colored legs. Acquires adult plumage in 3 years. See Mew Gull.

Voice: Loud, raucous mewing cry, like that of Herring Gull but higher pitched.

Habitat: Lakes and rivers; many move to salt water in winter.

Nesting: 2–4 spotted buff or olive eggs in a hollow in the ground, sometimes lined with grass or debris. In the North they sometimes nest in low trees. Nests in colonies, often with other gulls or terns, usually on islands in lakes.

Range: Breeds in Northwest (locally south to California), northern Great Plains, and southern prairie provinces of Canada; also in Great Lakes region, Canadian Maritimes, and northern New England. Winters on coasts, rivers, and lakes from southern New England south to Cuba, from Great Lakes to Gulf Coast, and from British Columbia to southern Mexico.

In most of the northern part of the United States the Ring-billed Gull is a winter visitor, less common than the Herring Gull. Mischaracterized as a seagull, this bird readily follows farm plows or scatters over meadows after heavy rains to feast on drowning earthworms.

31, 37 California Gull
Larus californicus

Description: 20–23" (51–58 cm). Similar to Herring Gull but smaller, with *darker gray mantle, dark eye, reddish eye ring, and greenish legs.* Bill of breeding adult has red spot overlapped by black. Winter and immature birds have black subterminal bar on bill and lack red eye ring of adults. A common *inland* gull.

Voice: A repetitive *kee-yah.*
Habitat: In breeding season, on interior lakes and marshes; in winter, mostly on seacoast.
Nesting: 2 or 3 heavily blotched, buff-olive eggs in a nest made of grass, dead weeds, and sticks. Large colonies are found on islands in shallow inland lakes, often together with Ring-billed Gulls, though each species remains with its own kind.
Range: Breeds in northern prairie provinces east to North Dakota, south to northwestern Wyoming and Utah, west to northeastern California. Winters mainly on coast from Oregon southward, in lesser numbers inland.

The California Gull attained fame when it arrived in great numbers at the Mormon colony near Great Salt Lake and devoured a locust swarm that threatened the settlers' first crop. A statue in Salt Lake City commemorates the event.

29, 39 Herring Gull
Larus argentatus

Description: 23–26″ (58–66 cm). Adult white with light gray back and wings; wing tip black with white spots; bill yellow with red spot on lower mandible; *feet pink or flesh colored.* First-year birds brownish. Acquires adult plumage in 4 years. See California Gull.
Voice: Loud rollicking call, *kuk-kuk-kuk, yucca-yucca-yucca,* and other raucous cries.
Habitat: Lakes, rivers, estuaries, and beaches; common in all aquatic habitats.
Nesting: 2–4 heavily spotted, olive-brown eggs in a mass of seaweed or dead grass on the ground or a cliff; most often on islands. Nests in colonies.
Range: Breeds from Alaska east across northern Canada to Maritime Provinces, south to British Columbia, north-central Canada, and Great Lakes, and along Atlantic Coast to North Carolina. Winters in all

but northernmost breeding areas; also along coasts, rivers, and lakes both in Southeast and in West from southern Alaska south to Baja California. Also in Eurasia.

This is the common "seagull" inland and along the coast. In recent decades it has become abundant, probably due to the amount of food available at garbage dumps, and has extended its range southward along the Atlantic Coast, often to the detriment of colonial birds such as terns and Laughing Gulls. Although a scavenger, it also eats large numbers of aquatic and marine animals and feeds on berries. It often drops clams and other shellfish on exposed rocks or parking lots in order to break the shells and get at the soft interior.

32 Thayer's Gull
Larus thayeri

Description: 24" (61 cm). In all plumages, very similar to the Herring Gull, gray above, white below, but *eye of adult dark* instead of yellow. Adults have less white on underside of wing tips than do Herring Gulls.

Voice: Mewing and squealing notes.

Habitat: Arctic coasts and islands, usually on rocky cliffs.

Nesting: 3 bluish or greenish eggs, spotted with brown, in a nest lined with grass, moss, or lichens placed on a high rocky cliff.

Range: Breeds in Canadian high Arctic. Winters chiefly on Pacific Coast south to Baja California. Very rare winter visitor to Maritime Canada and northeastern United States.

This bird has variously been considered a species of its own, a subspecies of the Herring Gull, a subspecies of the Iceland Gull, and even a hybrid of the two. At the moment, it is treated

as a species. Distinguishing young
Thayer's Gulls from young Herrings
is very difficult.

25 Yellow-footed Gull
Larus livens

Description: 21–23" (53–58 cm). Similar to Western
Gull, but *legs yellow.* First-winter birds
have pink legs like Westerns but are
paler, with contrasting white belly.
Voice: Similar to calls of Western Gull, but
deeper.
Habitat: Beaches, harbors, dumps; open ocean.
Nesting: 3 light buff, blotched eggs in a grass or
seaweed nest placed in a depression, on
rocky headlands or islands.
Range: Resident in Gulf of California; visits
Salton Sea and San Diego area mainly in
summer and fall.

Formerly considered a subspecies of the
more widespread Western Gull, the
Yellow-footed is only a wanderer within
the area covered by this guide. A strictly
coastal bird, it favors the immediate
shoreline at the Salton Sea.

26, 42 Western Gull
Larus occidentalis

Description: 24–27" (61–69 cm). *Snow white, with
dark slate-colored back and wings.* Yellow
eye and bill; breeding adult has a red
dot near tip of lower mandible. *Pinkish
or flesh-colored feet.* In winter, head and
nape faintly dusky. First-year birds dark
gray-brown with dark, almost black
primaries, contrasting with lighter
areas on nape and rump; dark bill.
See Yellow-footed Gull.
Voice: Squeals and raucous notes.
Habitat: Coastal waterways, beaches, harbors,
dumps; open ocean.
Nesting: 3 light buff, blotched eggs in a grass or

seaweed nest in a depression, protected
and slightly isolated by broken terrain.
Nests in colonies on rocky headlands,
islands, or dikes.

Range: Breeds on Pacific Coast from Washington
to Baja California. In winter regularly
occurs north to British Columbia.

The large gulls of the Pacific Coast have a
common ancestor but evolved separately
in isolation. The Glaucous-winged Gull
resembles the Western Gull in size and
habits, but its coloration is extremely
light. The two species regularly
hybridize in the Pacific Northwest.

34, 38 Glaucous-winged Gull
Larus glaucescens

Description: 24–27" (61–69 cm). A large *white gull
with pearly gray mantle and wings.* Gray
primaries show a white "window" near
tip of each feather; bill yellow with red
spot on lower mandible; eyes light
brown or silvery; feet pink. In winter,
red spot on bill becomes a diffuse black;
head and nape look dusky. Juvenile
similar to Western Gull juvenile, but
much paler. First-year birds gray-brown
overall, with wing tips same color as
mantle. Black bill; dark eyes and feet.
Second-year birds acquire more gray and
are generally paler.

Voice: A raucous series of similar notes on one
pitch; also soft *ga-ga* notes when an
intruder approaches.

Habitat: Rocky or sandy beaches, harbors,
dumps; open ocean.

Nesting: 2 or 3 light olive-brown eggs, with dark
speckles, in a grass or seaweed nest
placed in a depression on remote islets
or headlands. Nests in colonies.

Range: Resident from Aleutians and western
and southern coasts of Alaska south to
northwestern Washington. Winters
south along coast to southern California.
Very rare away from salt water.

Like other large gulls, this species feeds mainly along the shore. Over water it picks up edibles such as dead or dying fish and squid; on the beach it feeds on dead seabirds, seals, whales, starfish, clams, and mussels. In harbors and towns it scavenges garbage. One banded female was observed to make daily trips from her nest to a garbage dump about 40 miles (65 kilometers) away.

35, 40 Glaucous Gull
Larus hyperboreus

Description: 28″ (71 cm). A large gull. Adults pearl-gray above, *with no black in wing tips;* white on head and underparts. Bill yellowish; feet pinkish. Immatures creamy buff, with pinkish, dark-tipped bill. See Glaucous-winged Gull.

Voice: Hoarse croaks and screams.

Habitat: Shores of lakes, rivers, seacoast; also refuse dumps and sewage outflows.

Nesting: 3 light brown eggs, with dark chocolate blotches, placed in a cliff nest lined with moss and grass.

Range: Breeds in Alaska and northern Canada. Winters along coast south to California (rarely) and Virginia; rare in Great Lakes and on Gulf Coast. Also in Eurasia.

The Glaucous Gull is uncommon south of Canada; it is usually found with flocks of other gulls when it visits the United States. This is one of the most predatory of gulls, capturing and eating auks, plovers, small ducks, ptarmigans, and songbirds as well as lemmings and fish. It is also a scavenger, feeding on garbage, dead animal matter, and even bird droppings.

43, 44   Black-legged Kittiwake
Rissa tridactyla

Description:
16–18″ (41–46 cm). A small seagoing gull. Adult white with pale gray back and wings; *sharply defined black wing tip,* as if dipped in black ink. Feet black; bill yellow; tail slightly forked. Winter adult has dusky gray patch on nape. Young bird has dusky band on nape, dark diagonal wing band, and black-tipped tail. See Red-legged Kittiwake.

Voice:
Variety of loud harsh notes. Very noisy on breeding grounds. With a little imagination, its common call can seem to resemble its name: *kittiwake.*

Habitat:
Cliffs and seacoasts in the Arctic; winters at sea.

Nesting:
2 pinkish-buff spotted eggs in a well-made cup of mosses and seaweed at the top of a cliff or on a ledge. Nests in colonies.

Range:
Breeds in North Pacific, Arctic Ocean, and Atlantic south to Gulf of Saint Lawrence. Winters from edge of sea ice southward, rarely to Gulf of Mexico. Also in Eurasia.

This abundant gull is not commonly seen from shore, for it generally spends the entire winter on the open ocean, where it feeds on small fish and plankton. Most young gulls flee from the nest if disturbed, but the young of this cliff-nesting species stay put no matter how close a human observer gets—leaving a nest on a high narrow ledge could result in a fatal plunge to the rocks below. This is the only gull that dives and swims underwater to capture food.

45   Red-legged Kittiwake
Rissa brevirostris

Description:
14–15½″ (36–39 cm). Similar to Black-legged Kittiwake but smaller, darker

above, with more extensive black at wing tips, and red legs and feet.

Voice: Similar to that of Black-legged Kittiwake.

Habitat: Open ocean; nests on ledges of sea cliffs.

Nesting: 2 buff or creamy eggs, marked with brown, in a grass and mud nest placed on a ledge.

Range: Breeds in Alaska in the Aleutian Islands, the Commander Islands, and the Pribilof Islands. Winters in North Pacific Ocean.

This bird has one of the most limited distributions of any species in the West, but the Pribilof Islands colony is perhaps the most spectacular seabird colony in the world; every ledge is packed with tens of thousands of kittiwakes, murres, fulmars, and other seabirds.

24 Ross' Gull
Rhodostethia rosea

Description: 12–14″ (30–36 cm). A very rare visitor from the Arctic. Breeding adults have narrow black collar; pale gray back and wings, including underwings; pinkish tinge on underparts; and *wedge-shaped tail.* Winter adults lack collar and pinkish tinge. Flight graceful and tern-like.

Voice: A harsh *miaw;* usually silent in winter.

Habitat: Breeds on swampy tundra; winters near pack ice. Rarely visits river mouths and coastal beaches.

Nesting: 2 or 3 deep olive eggs, spotted with brown, in a grass-lined depression.

Range: Breeds mainly in Old World Arctic, but a few nest in Canada. Appears as migrant off northern Alaska. Winters very rarely south to British Columbia and mid-Atlantic Coast. Also in Eurasia.

This beautiful Siberian gull winters mainly above the Arctic Circle, only rarely visiting places where it can be seen by most birders. The appearance of a Ross' Gull in settled areas attracts hundreds of observers and often makes headlines in newspapers.

23   Sabine's Gull
Xema sabini

Description: 13–14″ (33–36 cm). A small, *fork-tailed* gull, with black primaries and *triangular white patch on rear edge of wing.* Hood dark in breeding plumage. Bill black with yellow tip. Immature lacks dark hood but can be distinguished by forked tail and striking wing pattern.

Voice: High-pitched grating or squeaking notes.

Habitat: Tundra ponds in summer; open ocean on migration and in winter.

Nesting: 3 or 4 olive-brown eggs, spotted with darker brown, placed in a grass-lined depression on the ground. Nests in small colonies.

Range: Breeds on coastal tundra around shores of Arctic Ocean, farther inland in Alaska. Migrates mainly at sea. Winter range not fully known; some birds winter off Pacific coast of northern South America.

This delicate gull is seldom seen outside the breeding season as it is almost exclusively oceanic. On the tundra coastline it gracefully plucks small crustaceans and insects from the surface of the water like a tern. It also takes eggs from nesting colonies of Arctic Terns. The best way to see this oceanic species is to take a boat trip out of Monterey, California, or some other Pacific Coast city.

36 Ivory Gull
Pagophila eburnea

Description: 17" (43 cm). A rather small, *short-legged* gull; adults are pure white with yellowish bill and legs; immatures (more often seen in southern latitudes) similar, but with *black bars and spots* in varying quantities.

Voice: A harsh *eeeer.*

Habitat: Breeds on rocky cliffs or stony ground; winters at edge of the pack ice in Arctic seas.

Nesting: 2 buff-olive eggs, marked with dark blotches, in a nest lined with moss, lichens, and seaweed, placed on bare ground among rocks or on gravel-covered polar ice.

Range: Known to breed in New World only on Somerset and Ellesmere islands in Canadian Arctic; more common in Eurasia. Winters in Arctic Ocean, appearing rarely farther south.

The Ivory Gull shares the realm of the Inuit and the polar bear. Indeed, it follows these hunters in quest of food, for it is largely a scavenger, feeding on the remains of their kills—mainly seals. It also eats wolf and fox dung, whale blubber, lemmings, crustaceans, and insects.

47 Gull-billed Tern
Sterna nilotica

Description: 13–15" (33–38 cm). A pigeon-sized tern. Very pale with almost white back and wings, black cap, and *stout black bill;* tail not as deeply forked as in other terns. Winter birds lack black cap.

Voice: Rasping *katy-did,* similar to sound made by that insect.

Habitat: Coastal marshes and sandy beaches.

Nesting: 2 or 3 spotted buff eggs in a shell-lined shallow depression (occasionally a well-made cup of dead marsh grasses) on a sandy island in a salt marsh. Nests in colonies and often breeds with other species of terns.

Range: Breeds from Long Island south to Gulf of Mexico and West Indies; also locally at Salton Sea, California. Winters north to Gulf Coast. Also in Eurasia, Africa, and Australia.

In addition to the usual tern diet of fish and crustaceans, this bird catches insects in flight and pursues them on the ground in plowed fields or croplands. Although not numerous, it is widespread, breeding in scattered colonies. In America it was one of the species hardest hit by the millinery trade and has never recovered its former numbers, although recently it has slowly extended its range northward.

49 Caspian Tern
Sterna caspia

Description: 19–23" (48–58 cm). The largest tern. Largely white, with black cap, slight crest, pale gray back and wings, heavy *bright red bill, dusky underwing.* Royal Tern similar, but has orange-red bill, more obvious crest, paler underwing; almost never seen away from coast.

Voice: Low harsh *kraa.* Also a shorter *kow.*

Habitat: Sandy or pebbly shores of lakes and large rivers and along seacoasts.

Nesting: 2 or 3 spotted buff eggs in a shallow depression or a well-made cup of dead grass, most often on a sandy or rocky island. Solitary or in small colonies.

Range: Breeds in scattered colonies from Mackenzie, Great Lakes, and Newfoundland south to Gulf Coast and Baja California. Winters north to California and North Carolina. Also breeds in Eurasia, Africa, and Australia.

Much less gregarious than other terns, Caspians usually feed singly. Pairs breed

by themselves or in small colonies or may attach themselves to colonies of other birds such as the Ring-billed Gull. Caspians are more predatory than most other terns, readily taking small birds or the eggs and young of other terns.

54 Royal Tern
Sterna maxima

Description: 18–21″ (46–53 cm). Crow-sized. A *large* tern with a long, heavy, *yellow-orange to orange-red bill.* Black cap, wispy crest, pale gray back and wings, white forehead. Tail moderately forked. Similar Caspian Tern has blood-red bill, darker forehead and underwing, and shorter tail.

Voice: Harsh *kee-rare,* like Caspian Tern but higher pitched.

Habitat: Sandy beaches.

Nesting: Usually 1 buff spotted egg in a sand scrape on an island or a sheltered peninsula.

Range: Breeds along coast from Maryland to Texas, wandering regularly farther north in summer. Winters from North Carolina, Gulf Coast, and southern California southward. Also in West Africa.

The Royal Tern breeds in large, dense colonies. Nests are sometimes washed away by storm tides, but the birds usually make a second attempt, often at a new location. This bird has fewer young than other terns but maintains its numbers wherever it has protection from disturbance. It feeds almost entirely on small fish, rather than the crustaceans and insects taken by most other terns.

51 **Elegant Tern**
Sterna elegans

Description: 16–17" (41–43 cm). A large tern with
a *long orange or yellow bill.* White with
gray mantle and wings; black cap
ending in shaggy crest; deeply forked
tail. In nonbreeding plumage, forehead
becomes white but crown, crest, and
region around eye remain black.

Voice: A loud grating *kar-eek.*

Habitat: Lagoons and beaches.

Nesting: 1 egg, often buff-colored (but the color
is variable), placed in a depression on a
sandy beach, usually on an island. Nests
in colonies.

Range: Breeds in Gulf of California and at
San Diego. Winters to south and north;
some to South America, others regularly
visiting northern California coast.

The nesting of the Elegant Tern is
restricted mostly to Isla Raza, a small
flat island in the northern part of the
Gulf of California, where it has several
colonies of hundreds of nests. Since
colonies are crowded, with each female
just out of bill range of her neighbors,
and coastal winds obliterate landmarks
that help adults find their nests, the
individual color and markings of the
single egg help parents recognize their
own. When the eggs hatch, the color
pattern of the hatchling serves the
same purpose.

52 **Common Tern**
Sterna hirundo

Description: 13–16" (33–41 cm). White with black
cap and pale gray back and wings. Bill
red with black tip; tail deeply forked.
Similar to Forster's Tern, but lacks frosty
wing tip. See also Arctic Tern.

Voice: *Kip-kip-kip;* also *tee-aar.*

Habitat: Lakes, ponds, rivers, coastal beaches,
and islands.

Nesting: 2 or 3 spotted olive-buff eggs laid in a depression in sand or in a shallow cup of dead grass, located on sandy or pebbly beaches or open rocky places. Nests in colonies, most often on islands or isolated peninsulas.

Range: Breeds in scattered colonies from Alberta and Labrador south to Montana, Great Lakes, and Caribbean. A common migrant along Pacific Coast. Winters from Florida to southern South America. Also in Eurasia.

This bird flies over the water with deliberate wingbeats, head turned down at a right angle to the body. When it sights a fish or tadpole, it dives much like a booby to catch its aquatic prey.

50 Arctic Tern
Sterna paradisaea

Description: 14–17" (36–43 cm). Deeply forked tail. Similar to Common Tern but *underparts grayer, bill blood-red,* legs shorter, tail longer.

Voice: Harsh *tee-ar* or *kip-kip-kip-tee-ar,* higher pitched than call of Common Tern.

Habitat: Coastal islands and beaches; also on tundra in summer.

Nesting: 2 spotted olive-buff eggs in a shallow depression in the ground, sometimes lined with grass or shells. Nests in colonies, usually on islands or protected sand spits.

Range: Breeds from Aleutians, northern Alaska, and northern Canada east to Ellesmere Island and Newfoundland, and south to northern British Columbia, Quebec, and Massachusetts. Winters at sea in Southern Hemisphere. Also breeds in northern Eurasia.

The Arctic Tern's harsh, rasping, high-pitched cry makes a colony a noisy place. All members assemble to mob an intruder. The nests and eggs left unattended during an attack are so well camouflaged that a predator is not likely to find them. These terns attack so fiercely that human observers have to protect their heads when walking in a colony.

---

46 Aleutian Tern
Sterna aleutica

Description: 13½–15″ (34–38 cm). Mantle and wings dark gray, *cap black but forehead white;* underparts grayish; forked tail white.

Voice: A musical *whee-hee-hee;* chirping notes like those of House Sparrow.

Habitat: Open beaches, marshes, neighboring shallow bays, and oceans.

Nesting: 2 olive or buff eggs placed in a depression above high-tide line on small offshore islands and in coastal meadows. Nests in colonies.

Range: Breeds in coastal Alaska. Winters in neighboring North Pacific.

The little-known Aleutian Tern usually nests among Arctic Terns, which are notoriously aggressive in defense of their nests. The Aleutians seem to take advantage of their neighbors' behavior, making no attempt to defend their own nests.

---

53 Forster's Tern
Sterna forsteri

Description: 14–15″ (36–38 cm). White with pale gray back and wings, black cap, and deeply forked tail. Bill orange with black tip. Similar to Common Tern, but *wing tips frosty white, bill more orange.* In winter, lacks black cap but has distinctive black mark behind eye.

Voice: Harsh nasal *beep.*

Habitat: Freshwater marshes in West; salt marshes in East.

Nesting: 3 or 4 buff, spotted eggs on a large platform of dead grass lined with finer grasses, usually placed on masses of dead marsh vegetation. Nests in colonies.

Range: Breeds along Atlantic Coast from Massachusetts to Texas and in interior from Alberta and California east to Great Lakes. Winters along coasts from California and Virginia southward.

Terns have forked tails and longer, more slender wings than gulls. They feed almost entirely by plunge diving for fish, pointing the bill downward, whereas gulls do not dive but usually feed from the surface of the water. This species was named after Johann Reinhold Forster (1729–1798), a German pastor-naturalist who accompanied Captain Cook around the world in 1772.

48 Least Tern
Sterna antillarum

Description: 8–10" (20–25 cm). A *very small* tern with a black-tipped *yellow bill* and a fast, shallow wingbeat. White with black cap, pale gray back and wings, and forked tail; *white forehead.*

Voice: Sharp *killick* or *kip-kip-kip-kiddeek.*

Habitat: Sandy and pebbly beaches along the coast; sandbars in large rivers. Often on landfill.

Nesting: 2 or 3 buff, lightly spotted eggs in an unlined scrape on a sand spit or gravel beach. Nests in colonies.

Range: Breeds along California coast, along rivers in Mississippi Valley, and coastally from Maine south to Florida. Winters from Baja California south to southern Mexico; also along coasts of South America.

Because of the Least Tern's habit of nesting on low sandbars, whole colonies are sometimes destroyed by very high tides. It is also vulnerable to human disturbance when bathers and beach strollers enter its nesting colonies. Due to the destruction of its habitat by human activities, it is an endangered species in California. Most often seen hovering over the water, it peers downward in search of small minnows and other marine or freshwater organisms.

55   Black Tern
Chlidonias niger

Description: 9–10" (23–25 cm). A medium-sized tern with *solid black head and underparts;* gray wings and moderately forked gray tail. In fall and winter, head and underparts white, with dusky smudging around eyes and back of neck.

Voice: Sharp *kick;* when disturbed, a shrill *kreek.*

Habitat: Freshwater marshes and marshy lakes in summer; sandy coasts on migration and in winter.

Nesting: 2 spotted, olive-buff eggs placed in a hollow on a mass of floating marsh vegetation or in a well-made cup of dead grass. Nests in colonies.

Range: Breeds from British Columbia east to New Brunswick and south to central California and New York. Winters south of U.S.–Mexico border, rarely in California. Also in Eurasia.

This tern usually nests in small groups and in shallow water. The nests are sometimes conspicuous; perhaps this is why the young often leave the nest at the first sign of an intruder, swimming quietly away to hide in the surrounding marsh vegetation. It is not unusual to visit an active colony and find all the nests empty. Unlike other terns, these birds frequently fly over land areas as they hawk for insects. Black Terns also eat small fish and crustaceans, which they pick from the water.

FAMILY ALCIDAE
Auks, Murres, and Puffins

22 species: Seacoasts of the Northern Hemisphere. Twenty species breed in North America. The alcids are chunky, penguin-like seabirds, chiefly dark above and white below, with short wings and large webbed feet located far back on the body. They live along rocky coasts where they breed mainly on precipitous cliffs and lay their pointed eggs on bare ledges, in crevices, or in burrows. They spend the winter at sea, diving for their food—primarily small fish and squid—which they pursue by using their wings for propulsion.

88, 90 Common Murre
Uria aalge

Description: 17″ (43 cm). Crow-sized. Head and upperparts brownish black, white below; long pointed bill. Winter birds have extensive white on the face, with a dark line behind the eye. See Thick-billed Murre.

Voice: Purring or murmuring, hence the name "murre." Also a guttural croak and higher-pitched bleat.

Habitat: Rocky coasts.

Nesting: 1 blue-green egg, with black marks, on a bare rock ledge.

Range: Breeds along Arctic and subarctic coasts south to central California and Gulf of Saint Lawrence. Winters south to southern California and Massachusetts. Also in Eurasia.

When half grown, young murres jump 30 to 50 feet (9 to 15 meters) into the sea, and accompany their parents, first swimming, then flying, often for hundreds of miles to their wintering areas. Apart from having their nests plundered for the eggs, murres of the Pacific Coast have long been safe from

human intrusion, but oil spills now
pose a threat to whole colonies.

89 Thick-billed Murre
Uria lomvia

Description: 18″ (46 cm). Similar to Common Murre,
but blacker above, with shorter, thicker
bill. In winter, face is mainly black,
with white only on cheeks and throat.

Voice: Similar to Common Murre.

Habitat: Rocky coasts.

Nesting: 1 large bluish-green egg, scrawled with
brown, on a narrow ledge. Nests in
dense colonies.

Range: Breeds on Arctic and subarctic coasts
south to southern Alaska and Gulf of
Saint Lawrence. Winters on coasts south
to southern Alaska and New Jersey.
Also in Eurasia.

Murres are so conservative that
photographs of nesting cliffs taken
decades apart show the same number
of nesters on each ledge, and where
the two species of murres mix, even
the proportion of the two seems to
remain similar—usually a sign of keen
competition for nest sites. They fly
with fast wingbeats on a steady course
but alight with a "stall" and an
ungraceful splash. They take off by
plunging from a cliff or, on water,
by pattering over the surface like
heavy ducks.

87 Black Guillemot
Cepphus grylle

Description: 13″ (33 cm). Similar to Pigeon
Guillemot, but white wing patch not
crossed by 2 bars, underwings white.

Voice: Shrill mouse-like squeaks.

Habitat: Rocky coasts, even in winter.

Nesting: 2 whitish eggs, with dark brown

blotches, placed under rocks either on a
bare surface or on loose pebbles.

Range: Breeds from Arctic Alaska and Canada
south along Atlantic Coast to Maine.
Winters south to Bering Sea and Long
Island (rarely). Also in northern Europe,
Scandinavia, and Alaska.

This species breeds mainly in the
Atlantic and Arctic oceans, entering our
area only in northern Alaska. Here its
range overlaps that of the Pigeon
Guillemot only in the Bering Sea. Its
habits are similar to those of the
Pigeon Guillemot.

85, 86 Pigeon Guillemot
Cepphus columba

Description: 12–14″ (30–36 cm). Pigeon-sized. In
breeding plumage, *black with large white
wing patch* interrupted by 2 black
stripes. In winter, head and upperparts
lighten slightly, giving dusky mottled
effect; underparts are white with buff-
colored barring on flanks and dusky
wing linings. In all seasons, feet and
bill lining brilliant red.

Voice: High thin whistles and squeaks.

Habitat: Rocky coasts.

Nesting: 1 or 2 whitish or greenish, dark-spotted
eggs in a crevice or burrow.

Range: Breeds on coasts and islands from
southern Alaska south to southern
California. Winters far offshore.

Pigeon Guillemots appear to be the
least social of all the alcids. Where
coastal cliffs allow only one nesting
cavity, only one pair will occupy it.
Elsewhere, territories are laid out like
beads on a string. These birds feed by
diving, taking mostly small fish.

93 Marbled Murrelet
Brachyramphus marmoratus

Description: 9½–10″ (24–25 cm). A chubby, robin-sized seabird, with very short neck and tail. In summer, *brown above, marbled with light brown and gray below.* In winter, *black above, white below,* with white wing patch and incomplete white collar.

Voice: A plaintive *keer, keer, keer.*

Habitat: Breeds in coastal rain forests; inshore waters at other times.

Nesting: 1 olive or yellowish egg, spotted with brown, black, and lavender, in a platform of moss placed high in a forest tree.

Range: Breeds from Aleutians Islands south to central California. A few winter along breeding coasts, but main wintering area unknown. Also in Asia.

The nest of this bird was discovered fairly recently. Most alcids use burrows or ledges on coastal cliffs, but Marbled Murrelets, burdened with fish, have been observed taking off from the sea at twilight and disappearing inland. Some weeks later feathered young appear, bobbing on the water. The first clues to their nesting habits were found in Siberia in 1963 by an ornithologist who reported a nest in a huge tree. In 1974 a nest was discovered in a Douglas fir in the Santa Cruz Mountains of California, about 135 feet (41 meters) above the ground. It is now assumed that these birds nest high up in trees, sometimes several miles from the sea. On the water Marbled Murrelets move about in small groups; they dive for fish and other aquatic animals.

92 Kittlitz's Murrelet
Brachyramphus brevirostris

Description: 7½–9″ (19–23 cm). A small chubby seabird. *In summer, dusky above with buff marbling, foreparts buff with dark barring,* belly whitish. *In winter, white below, slate-gray above* and on top of head, white face. White patch on dark wings sometimes visible on swimming birds and always visible in flight. Bill short and stubby.

Voice: Undescribed.

Habitat: Nests on talus slopes of high mountains; winters on ocean waters and glacier bays.

Nesting: Little known; 1 olive egg with heavy markings placed on a mountain slope among rocks.

Range: Breeds on coasts of Bering Sea, Aleutians, and southeastern Alaska. Rarely farther south in winter. Also in Asia.

Kittlitz's Murrelet is among the most mysterious of American birds. Fewer than 20 nests have ever been found. It is not known whether both sexes incubate the single egg, how long the incubation period is, or how long it takes the young bird to fledge.

Xantus' Murrelet
Synthliboramphus hypoleucus

Description: 9½–10½" (24–27 cm). Robin-sized but slender, resembling a tiny murre. *Black above,* with no distinctive pattern; *white cheeks,* throat, and underparts. Underwing coverts white. Bill thin and narrow. No seasonal change in plumage.

Voice: High thin whistles, usually in a quick series.

Habitat: Ocean; nests in colonies on rocky sea islands.

Nesting: 1 or 2 buff-colored eggs, with brown markings, among boulders or in crevices off island beaches.

Range: Breeds on offshore islands of Baja California and southern California; occasionally wanders north to Vancouver Island.

Murrelets are so called because they resemble tiny murres. At sea they are

often seen in pairs. This species was named for its discoverer, the Hungarian explorer John Xantus, who was a pioneer ornithologist on the West Coast in the 1860s.

Craveri's Murrelet
Synthliboramphus craveri

Description: 8½–10″ (22–25 cm). *Black above, white below,* with black extending down neck to form partial collar. Underwing grayish. Black of face extends below bill on Craveri's but not on Xantus'.

Voice: In breeding season, a trilling whistle heard near the colony at sea.

Habitat: Rocky cliffs and offshore waters.

Nesting: 2 white eggs in a rock crevice or under a boulder.

Range: Breeds on islands in Gulf of California and off Baja California north to San Benito Islands. After breeding, wanders to southern California coast, occasionally farther north.

As with many other species that nest in the Gulf of California, Craveri's Murrelet wanders northward in fall to feeding grounds in the California Current. Its habits are similar to those of Xantus' Murrelet.

91 Ancient Murrelet
Synthliboramphus antiquus

Description: 9½–10½″ (24–27 cm). A quail-sized seabird. Black head, gray back, white below, *white plume over eye,* small white-barred area at side of neck. *White bill.* In winter, wide white area on throat and face, back solid slate-gray; similar Marbled Murrelet has white patch on flanks, dark bill.

Voice: Low, shrill whistling notes.

Habitat: Open ocean; nests on oceanic islets with

enough soil for a burrow, often under heavy timber.

Nesting: 2 brown to green eggs, spotted with brown and lavender, in a burrow dug by the adults.

Range: Breeds on offshore islets of North Pacific and mainland shores south to central British Columbia. Winters south to southern California. Also in Asia.

The German ornithologist who first described this bird thought its white plumes similar to an old man's white locks; hence its Latin name *antiquus,* from which its English name is derived. By moving to and from land at twilight, these birds avoid most predators, with the exception of Peregrine Falcons. Ancient Murrelets are not strong flyers, and after heavy storms, which may carry them as far inland as the Great Lakes, masses of dead bodies sometimes wash ashore on the Pacific Coast.

100 Cassin's Auklet
Ptychoramphus aleuticus

Description: 8–9″ (20–23 cm). A dark, stocky, robin-sized seabird. *Slate-gray above,* lighter gray below, white belly. Eyes dark brown during first year, lightening to white in breeding adults. Stubby *bill has white spot* at base of each side of lower mandible. No seasonal change in plumage.

Voice: Weak croaking calls given at night.

Habitat: Open ocean. Nests on sea cliffs and isolated headlands.

Nesting: 1 white egg, usually placed in a burrow but also in a cavity among rocks. Nests in colonies.

Range: Breeds from Aleutians to central Baja California. Winters in waters off southern part of breeding range.

Adult Cassin's Auklets take 24-hour watches while incubating the chick. During the nesting season they grow a

pouch under the tongue and fill it with food. These island birds fly to sea long before dawn to avoid being pursued and devoured by Western Gulls. They feed on shrimp by day and approach the colony only after dark. Most seabirds abandon the nest site as soon as the young fledge, but on California's Farallon Islands, Cassin's Auklets remain longer. From December to March birds occupy the island so densely that vacated burrows are immediately taken over by others. It is believed that this "housing shortage" compels the auklets to defend their burrows year round.

97 Parakeet Auklet
Cyclorrhynchus psittacula

Description: 10″ (25 cm). A robin-sized auklet whose short tail and *chubby body* make it look larger. *Sooty black above, white below.* In summer, *white, mustache-like plume* extends from below eye to lower neck. *Stubby upturned red bill.* In winter, white plume lacking, throat and underparts white, bill duskier.

Voice: Generally silent, clear whistles in breeding colonies.

Habitat: Open ocean; nests on coastal or island cliffs.

Nesting: 1 white oval egg in a cliff crevice or among boulders.

Range: Breeds on Bering Sea islands and nearby coasts. Winters offshore, very rarely south to California.

This auklet, common on its Alaskan home grounds, does not form large colonies but mainly nests scattered among the puffins and Pigeon Guillemots that prefer the same habitat. Adults sit high up on the cliffs, each on watch near its nesting cavity while its mate is incubating or tending the young. In the morning or afternoon it leaves the cliff to feed, diving for krill (a kind of crustacean), which it captures near the sea bottom.

99 Least Auklet
Aethia pusilla

Description: 6" (15 cm). *Sparrow-sized. Black above, white below.* In summer, white plume behind eye; *dark markings on sides and breast (often forming breast band) set off white throat;* bill orange with yellow tip. In winter, plume smaller; unmarked white below; bill dark; white patch on wing.

Voice: Various twittering notes around breeding colonies.

Habitat: Rocky coasts and open ocean.

Nesting: 1 white egg in a small crevice. Nests in huge colonies on rocky slopes.

Range: Breeds on Aleutians and islands of Bering Sea. Winters offshore near breeding range.

In winter vast numbers of Least Auklets leave their Arctic breeding islands before the sea freezes and return in June when the slopes are still snow-clad. One study noted that in June certain birds came back daily from their diving and feeding and sat on the snow in a certain pattern. Photos made from a blind showed that the "snow sitters" sat on their nest site and took possession as soon as the snow melted. Perhaps oriented by a few large boulders, they were apparently able to locate the nest site they had used the previous season.

Whiskered Auklet
Aethia pygmaea

Description: 7–7½" (18–19 cm). Sparrow-sized. In all plumages, *dusky gray* above, lighter gray below. Adults have forward-curling, quail-like gray topknot and *3 white ornamental plumes* projecting

backward from face like long mustaches;
short bill red during summer, brown in
winter. Immatures dark with traces of
3 white head stripes.

Voice: A whining *me-ow.*

Habitat: Nests on rock slides and cliffs; inshore
waters for feeding.

Nesting: 1 white egg in rock crevices; nests in
colonies.

Range: Breeds and winters in Aleutian Islands.
Also in Asia.

The most restricted and rarest of the
four auklets in Alaska, the Whiskered
resembles the larger Crested Auklet in
appearance and habits.

---

98 Crested Auklet
Aethia cristatella

Description: 9½–10½" (24–27 cm). A chubby
seabird without much visible tail.
Slate-black above, brownish gray below.
In breeding season, *white plume* behind
white eye and prominent *forward-curving
black crest; red bill,* with an extra red
plate on side of face. In winter, crest
shorter, bill brown. Juveniles lack crest.

Voice: A variety of loud honking and grunting
notes on breeding grounds; otherwise
silent.

Habitat: Nests on island coasts where sliding
rocks form a talus slope, with the largest
boulders at the bottom and bare cliff at
the top, near sea for feeding.

Nesting: 1 white egg among boulders in coastal
and island cliff areas. Nests in colonies.

Range: Breeds in Aleutians and other islands
and coasts around Bering Sea. Winters
in nearby ocean waters.

Like other auklets, the Crested feeds on
planktonic crustaceans, filling a special
pouch under its tongue with food for its
single chick.

101 Rhinoceros Auklet
Cerorhinca monocerata

Description: 14½–15½" (37–39 cm). A pigeon-sized
seabird. Dark above with lighter gray
throat and breast, white underparts.
Slender pale yellow bill, white eye. In
breeding plumage, short upright *"horn"
at base of bill,* with white drooping
"whiskers" at either side; white plume
above eye. Immatures dark gray above,
light below with duller, smaller bill
and dark eye.

Voice: Low growling notes.

Habitat: Feeds on fish offshore; digs deep burrows
in grassy or timbered headlands.

Nesting: 1 white egg, often spotted, in a burrow.
Nests in colonies, sometimes in large
numbers.

Range: Breeds from Aleutians south to central
California. Winters off breeding
grounds and south to southern
California. Also in Asia.

"Auklet" is a misnomer, since this bird
is not a close relative of the small,
plankton-feeding alcids called auklets
but is actually related to the more
brightly colored, parrot-billed puffins.
Rhinoceros Auklets feed on the open
sea during the day but may be seen at
sunset in summer among inlets and
islands. They swim and bob with a beak
full of fish, waiting for nightfall before
venturing ashore to feed their young.

95, 96 Tufted Puffin
Fratercula cirrhata

Description: 14½–15½" (37–39 cm). A pigeon-sized
puffin, mostly seen sitting upright on
a sea cliff. In breeding plumage, *stubby
body black, face white, down-curved
yellowish tufts hang behind eyes, and parrot-
like bill enlarged, bright orange-red.* In
winter, colored bill plates molt and bill
is smaller and duller, face turns dusky,

and tufts disappear. Immatures dusky
above, light gray below, with small bill.
In flight, the large, webbed red feet
are conspicuous.

Voice: Silent except for occasional growling
notes uttered around the nest site.

Habitat: Nests on vertical sea cliffs, in colonies or
singly. Feeds at sea.

Nesting: 1 white egg, often spotted, in a burrow
on an island or coastal cliff. Nests in
colonies.

Range: Breeds from northern Alaska south to
northern California. Winters at sea off
breeding grounds. Also in Asia.

In most mixed seabird colonies a strict
social order prevails within and between
species. Each seems to have adapted
to a specific niche, which includes
occupying the terrain in a manner most
suited to it. This reduces competition
between species but sharpens it within
each species. The Tufted Puffin has
adapted a burrowing strategy for
nesting. It typically digs a tunnel from
2 to 9 feet (.5 to 3 meters) into a turf-
covered slope, then lays its single egg
at the end of the burrow. Many other
alcids place their eggs on cliff ledges.

94 Horned Puffin
Fratercula corniculata

Description: 14½" (37 cm). Pigeon-sized. Chunky
tailless body. *Black above, white below.
White face* makes head appear big; *large,
parrot-like bill bright yellow with red tip.*
Red eyelids and small black upturned
"horn" above eye visible at close range.
In winter, face darker, feathers
brownish, bill smaller with dusky base.
Young birds have darker face, narrow,
sooty-brown bills.

Voice: Usually silent but utters harsh notes from
its burrow.

Habitat: Cold ocean waters, sea cliffs, and rocky
or grass-covered islets and rocks.

Nesting: 1 whitish egg, with small dark spots, in a crevice or in a deep hole among boulders. Nests in colonies.

Range: Breeds from northern Alaska south to British Columbia border. Winters at sea south to Washington, rarely to California. Also in Asia.

The Horned Puffin's relatively huge bill is useful in catching and holding small fish, enabling parents to bring three or four fish at a time to their young. It is also used to signal to a mate or neighbor, especially during breeding time in crowded colonies. The colonies may contain thousands of these birds, yet in the Aleutians and on other islands where they nest among Tufted Puffins, Horned Puffins are lost among the throngs of the other species.

FAMILY COLUMBIDAE
Pigeons and Doves

310 species: Worldwide. Only 11 species, three of them introduced and well established, breed in North America. Members of this family are stocky, short-legged birds with short necks and small heads; some have long tails. They walk with a mincing gait and, unlike most birds, can drink without raising their heads after each sip. There is no firm distinction between pigeons and doves, although species called pigeons tend to be larger. North American species are clad in soft browns and grays.

360 Rock Dove
Columba livia

Description: 13½″ (34 cm). The common pigeon of towns and cities. Chunky, with short rounded tail. Typically bluish-gray with 2 narrow black wing bands and broad black terminal tail band; *white rump.* There are many color variants, ranging from all white through rusty to all black.

Voice: Soft guttural cooing.

Habitat: City parks, suburban gardens, and farmlands.

Nesting: 2 white eggs in a crude nest lined with sticks and debris, placed on a window ledge, building, bridge, or cliff.

Range: Native to Old World. Introduced and established in most of North America from central Canada southward.

Everyone knows Rock Doves, or domestic pigeons, as city birds that subsist on handouts or country birds that nest in pigeon cotes on farms. Few have seen them nesting in their ancestral home—cliff ledges or high among rocks. Over the centuries, many strains and color varieties have been developed in captivity through selective breeding. Since pigeons have been accused of carrying human diseases, there have been several attempts to eradicate them from our cities, but they are so prolific that little progress has been made in this endeavor.

358 Band-tailed Pigeon
Columba fasciata

Description: 14–15½″ (36–39 cm). Larger than Rock Dove. Dark gray above; pale gray terminal band on tail. Head and underparts purplish plum, whitening toward extreme lower belly. Adults have *narrow white semi-collar on nape.* Yellow bill tipped with black; yellow legs.

Voice: A deep owl-like *whoo-hoo.*

Habitat: Coniferous forests along northwestern Pacific Coast; in southwestern part of range it prefers oak or pine-oak woodlands, where it can feed on acorns.

Nesting: 1 white egg in a loosely constructed platform nest of twigs in a tree.

Range: Breeds from southeastern Alaska south along coast through California, and from Utah and Colorado south into Mexico. Winters north to California, New Mexico, and western Texas.

This shy forest pigeon is adapting to parks and gardens, where it feeds on lawns and ornamental berries, especially holly. Already a city bird in the Northwest, it has spread from natural redwood pockets to conifer plantings in suburbs of Santa Barbara and other California towns. In fall these birds gorge themselves on acorns.

357 Ringed Turtle-Dove
Streptopelia risoria

Description: 12" (30 cm). Slender, pale sandy dove; narrow black collar on hindneck; rounded, not pointed, tail. Mourning Dove similar but darker, with pointed tail, no collar.

Voice: Soft mellow *kooo-krooo,* rising and then falling in pitch.

Habitat: City parks and suburban areas, usually where trees are present.

Nesting: 2 white eggs in a flimsy saucer of twigs and grass on a window ledge or in a dovecote.

Range: Introduced and established in southern California, Arizona, Alabama, and southern Florida. May be encountered elsewhere.

This dove has been domesticated for so long that no one is sure which wild dove was its ancestor, although it is thought to have been an African species. During its centuries in captivity it has become adapted to living with humans and is unsuccessful in rural areas. Its pleasing call makes it a favorite cage bird; such individuals frequently escape into the wild.

359 Spotted Dove
Streptopelia chinensis

Description: 13″ (33 cm). Larger and stockier than Mourning Dove. Dark cinnamon-gray above, buffy below. Light gray head; *wide black collar; white spots on hindneck. In flight, long blunt tail looks black with flashy white corners.* Juveniles lack collar on hindneck.

Voice: A 3-syllable rolling *coo-coo-cooooo.*

Habitat: Suburban areas and gardens.

Nesting: 2 white eggs in a flimsy stick platform in a tree.

Range: Asia native introduced in coastal southern California.

This dove seems to be a harmless addition to the southern California garden avifauna, feeding on seeds and nesting quite secretively. The courting male may be observed bowing rhythmically, then flying up with tail spread wide.

361 White-winged Dove
Zenaida asiatica

Description: 12″ (30 cm). A brownish-gray dove with blackish wings that have a *broad diagonal white bar;* rounded tail has *whitish corners* noticeable in flight.

Voice: Drawn out *hooo-hooo-ho-hooo* or *who-cooks-for-you.*

Habitat: Open country with dense thickets of shrubs and low trees; also in suburban and agricultural areas.

Nesting: 2 cream-buff eggs in a frail platform of loose twigs in low bushes.

Range: Breeds in southwestern United States and southern Texas. Winters south of United States; rarely in southern Florida. Also in American tropics.

Many northern species of pigeons and doves are seed eaters, but tropical species feed primarily on fruit. The White-winged Dove enjoys both: In the desert its main seasonal food is the fruit of cacti; elsewhere it supplements its seed diet with berries. These fast-flying doves are game birds.

355 Mourning Dove
Zenaida macroura

Description: 12" (30 cm). Soft, sandy buff with a long pointed tail bordered with white. Black spots on wings.

Voice: Low mournful (hence its name) *coo-ah, coo, coo, coo.*

Habitat: Open fields, parks, and lawns with many trees and shrubs.

Nesting: 2 white eggs in a loosely made nest of sticks and twigs placed in low bushes and tall trees, more rarely on the ground.

Range: Breeds from southeastern Alaska, Saskatchewan, Ontario, Quebec, and New Brunswick southward to Mexico and Panama. Winters north to northern United States.

This abundant bird has increased with the cutting of forests and burning off of grass. The Mourning Dove is common in rural areas in all parts of the United States, as well as city parks and, in winter, suburban feeders. In some states it is hunted as a game bird while in others it is protected as a songbird. Its species name, *macroura,* is Greek for "long-tailed." The young are fed regurgitated, partially digested food known as pigeon milk.

354 Inca Dove
Columbina inca

Description: 8" (20 cm). A tiny *long-tailed* dove with a *scaly gray body* and contrasting *rufous in the wings*.

Voice: A soft *coo-coo* or *no-hope*, often repeated.

Habitat: Mesquite thickets or cacti in semiarid country; also parks, yards, and ranches.

Nesting: 2 white eggs in a frail nest, usually of small twigs, placed low in a tree or bush.

Range: Resident in southeastern California, Arizona, New Mexico, and southern Texas. Also in tropics.

This tiny bird is shaped much like a Common Ground-Dove except for its long pointed tail. Perhaps because both of these species are too small to be considered game, they show little fear of humans; the Inca Dove is so tame it nests in city parks and gardens.

356 Common Ground-Dove
Columbina passerina

Description: 6½" (17 cm). A sparrow-sized, short-tailed brown dove with much *rufous in the wings*. Tail dark with white corners.

Voice: Soft cooing notes, *coo-oo, coo-oo, coo-oo*, each with rising inflection.

Habitat: Open areas such as fields, gardens, farmlands, and roadsides.

Nesting: 2 white eggs in a nest on or close to the ground, often hidden in a tuft of grass or among weeds.

Range: Resident in southern parts of California, Arizona, and Texas, and east to southern North Carolina.

The Common Ground-Dove flies fast, with its short wings beating rapidly, almost like those of a quail. When it walks, it nods like a pigeon. It searches for seeds on the ground but requires low brush for nesting and roosting. Most courtship behavior takes place on the

ground, with the male pursuing the
female, bobbing his expanded neck in
rhythm with his monotonous cooing.

FAMILY PSITTACIDAE
Parrots

358 species: Widespread in tropical
regions. Of all parrot species, only the
now-extinct Carolina Parakeet
(*Conuropsis carolinensis*) originally nested
within the United States, but several
others have been introduced and are
now well established. Many additional
species can be found in the United
States; however, these are mainly birds
that have escaped from captivity.
Members of this well-known family are
characterized by their strong hooked
beaks and usually green plumage. They
often have pointed tails.

598 Rose-ringed Parakeet
Psittacula krameri

Description: 15–17″ (38–43 cm). A slender green
parakeet with long pointed tail, red bill.
Male has *narrow red and black necklace.*
Voice: A loud screeching *eee-ak, eee-ak.*
Habitat: Suburban areas, parks, and gardens.
Nesting: 2–6 white eggs in a natural cavity,
usually with no lining, or on a layer of
sawdust or wood fragments.
Range: Native to Africa and Asia. Introduced
in southern California and southern
Florida.

A graceful and attractive bird, the Rose-
ringed Parakeet has adapted well to life
in warmer, settled parts of North
America. It visits bird feeders and can
even be seen scavenging in garbage cans.

599 Canary-winged Parakeet
Brotogeris versicolurus

Description: 9″ (23 cm). A small, stocky green parakeet with pointed tail and *flash of yellow and white in wing.*

Voice: A rapid series of shrill metallic notes.

Habitat: Suburban areas, parks, and gardens.

Nesting: 5 white eggs placed in a natural cavity or in a dense cluster of dead palm fronds.

Range: Native to tropical America. Introduced and established in southern California and southern Florida.

This boldly marked parakeet is a frequent escape, and can be seen occasionally in the heart of large cities like New York and San Francisco. But it nests successfully in the wild only in California and Florida.

FAMILY CUCULIDAE
Cuckoos, Roadrunners, and Anis

143 species: Nearly worldwide. Six species breed in North America. Although some Old World species of this family are parasitic in their nesting habits, American cuckoos lay eggs in their own nests. Besides the familiar but secretive cuckoos, this mostly tropical family includes the comical, ground-inhabiting Greater Roadrunner of the Southwest and two all-black anis.

---

481 Black-billed Cuckoo
Coccyzus erythopthalmus

Description: 12″ (30 cm). Very similar to Yellow-billed Cuckoo; brown above, white below, but *bill entirely black,* wings brown, much less white at tips of tail feathers. Narrow red eye ring.

Voice: A series of soft mellow *cu-cu-cu-cu* notes in groups of 2–5, all on the same pitch.

Habitat: Moist thickets in low overgrown pastures and orchards; also occurs in thicker undergrowth and sparse woodlands.

Nesting: 2–4 blue-green eggs in a flimsy shallow nest of twigs lined with grass and plant down, placed within a few feet of the ground in a dense thicket.

Range: Breeds from Alberta and Montana east to Maritime Provinces, and south to northern Texas, Arkansas, and South Carolina. Winters in South America.

Both widespread cuckoos—the Black-billed and the Yellow-billed—are adept at hiding and skulking in dense vegetation and are more often heard than seen. Their distinctive notes, repeated over and over, are reminiscent of those of grebes and doves, but deeper in tone and more repetitive. When tracked down, the birds slip away to another location and repeat the call. Cuckoos are extremely beneficial to the farmer and horticulturist, consuming enormous quantities of destructive hairy caterpillars, especially gypsy moth and tent caterpillars. They are most numerous in years of tent caterpillar infestations.

480 Yellow-billed Cuckoo
Coccyzus americanus

Description: 10½–12½" (27–32 cm). Jay-sized. A slender, long-tailed bird, brown above and white below, with *large white spots on underside of tail and a flash of rufous in wings.* Bill slightly curved, with yellow lower mandible. Black-billed Cuckoo similar, but has very little rufous in wings and smaller white spots on tail.

Voice: A rapid, harsh, rattling *ka-ka-ka-ka-ka-ka-kow-kow-kowp, kowp, kowp, kowp,* slowing down at the end.

Habitat: Moist thickets, willows, overgrown pastures, and orchards.

Nesting: 2–4 pale blue-green eggs in a flimsy saucer of twigs placed in a bush or small sapling.

Range: Breeds from central California, Minnesota, and southern New Brunswick southward. Winters in South America.

This bird's tendency to utter its distinctive call at the approach of a storm has earned it the name "Rain Crow." Both the Yellow-billed and Black-billed cuckoos are fond of hairy caterpillars, and during outbreaks of tent caterpillars are valuable in helping to keep these creatures in check. Usually shy and elusive, these birds are easy to overlook.

285 Greater Roadrunner
Geococcyx californianus

Description: 24" (61 cm). Bigger than a crow. A long-legged, *long-tailed,* streaked, gray-brown ground bird with a *bushy crest.* Bright yellow eyes.

Voice: Clucks, crows, dove-like coos, dog-like whines, and hoarse guttural notes.

Habitat: Open arid country with scattered thickets.

Nesting: 3–5 ivory-colored eggs in a flat stick nest lined with grass, usually in a thick shrub or cactus not far above ground.

Range: Resident from northern California, Nevada, Utah, Colorado, Kansas, Oklahoma, Arkansas, and Louisiana southward into Mexico.

The Greater Roadrunner is famous for its rather distinctive behavior. It is a reticent bird that when surprised on a road runs rapidly away (hence its name), vanishing into cover. It feeds on a wide variety of desert life including insects, scorpions, lizards, and snakes; it also takes rodents and young of ground-nesting birds.

FAMILY TYTONIDAE
Barn Owls

17 species: Worldwide. Only one species, the Barn Owl, occurs in North America. These long-legged, densely plumaged owls have conspicuous heart-shaped facial disks and dark eyes. They are found mostly in forests, but several species in the Old World tropics are adapted to open grasslands.

316 Barn Owl
Tyto alba

Description: 18" (46 cm). W. 3'8" (1.1 m). Crow-sized. Buff-brown above and white below, with *heart-shaped face* and numerous fine dark dots on white underparts; *dark eyes,* long legs.

Voice: Hissing notes, screams, guttural grunts, and bill snapping. Young give rapid grackle-like clicks.

Habitat: Open country, forest edges and clearings, cultivated areas, and cities.

Nesting: 5–10 white eggs on bare wood or stone in buildings, hollow trees, caves, or even in burrows.

Range: Resident from southern British Columbia, Dakotas, Michigan, and southern New England southward. Also in South America and Old World.

In the glare of auto headlights, a flying Barn Owl looks snow white and so is often mistaken for a Snowy Owl. Barn Owls are effective mousers and take many rats. Owls do not digest fur and bone but periodically rid themselves of these in the form of regurgitated pellets. Barn Owl pellets are easily collected from roosts and can be a useful source of information about the small mammals in an area.

FAMILY STRIGIDAE
True Owls

161 species: Worldwide. Eighteen species breed in North America. Members of this well-known family range from the huge Great Horned and Great Gray owls to the diminutive Elf Owl of the arid Southwest. Nearly all of the species are nocturnal, but some, such as the beautiful Snowy Owl of the Arctic, also hunt in the daytime. Owls do not build their own nests but use abandoned nests of other birds, such as stick nests in trees. They also nest in hollow trees and, more rarely, on cliffs or on the ground. All species lay white eggs. During the cold months, many of these birds roost in dense evergreens. Although like hawks they have sharp talons and hooked beaks for killing their prey, they are not related to hawks.

312   Flammulated Owl
Otus flammeolus

Description: 6–7" (15–18 cm). Slightly larger than a sparrow; similar to but smaller than a Western Screech-Owl, with small indistinct *ear tufts, rufous edges on the facial disks, and dark eyes,* rather than yellow. Grayish above, light below, with white and rust-colored markings. Sexes look similar, but female larger than male.

Voice: A monotonous low hoot, single or double, repeated almost endlessly.

Habitat: Coniferous woodlands and forest edges in the Northwest; dry ponderosa pine woods in the Southwest.

Nesting: 3 or 4 white eggs in a tree hollow or deserted woodpecker hole.

Range: Breeds in southern British Columbia south to southern California, Arizona, New Mexico, and western Texas. Winters south of United States.

As with other owls, during the breeding season the male Flammulated supplies food and protection, while the female is the chief nest-tender. Mice and similar prey are usually decapitated, the male feeding on the head, the female and young getting the softer body. Later the female leaves the nestlings and shares hunting duties with her mate.

319 Western Screech-Owl
Otus kennicottii

Description: 7–10″ (18–25 cm). A small, mottled gray owl with *ear tufts.* Eastern Screech-Owl (*Otus asio*) of East overlaps with Western in small part of western Texas; gray phase of Eastern almost identical to Western but has different call: a tremulous descending wail. See also Whiskered Screech-Owl.

Voice: An accelerating "bouncing ball" series of 6–8 low whistles, often dropping in pitch toward the end. Also a quick series on 1 pitch.

Habitat: Woodlands, orchards, yards with many trees.

Nesting: 4 or 5 white eggs in a natural cavity, a woodpecker's hole, or even a man-made nest box.

Range: Resident from southeastern Alaska and British Columbia southward into Mexico and east throughout U.S. Rockies.

This common owl incubates each egg as it is laid. Thus the eggs hatch in sequence and the young within a brood vary widely in size and age. This allows the parents to raise all their young if food is plentiful, or only the first few if food is scarce. This pattern is widespread among owls and birds of prey that feed on mice and meadow moles, whose populations fluctuate widely.

320 Whiskered Screech-Owl
"Whiskered Owl"
Otus trichopsis

Description: 6½–8″ (17–20 cm). Almost identical to Western Screech-Owl, but with longer bristles at base of bill, larger *white spots on upperparts,* and heavier streaking on breast. Best identified by voice.

Voice: A series of low whistles in a distinctive Morse code–like pattern: *hoo-hoo hooo hoo, hoo-hoo hooo hoo,* and so on. Also a rapid *hoohoohoohoo.*

Habitat: Pine-oak woods, oaks, and sycamores.

Nesting: 3 or 4 white spherical eggs in a deep tree cavity or a flicker hole.

Range: Resident in southern Arizona and southwestern New Mexico. Also in Central America.

This common owl of the oak canyons of southeastern Arizona is virtually indistinguishable from the Western Screech-Owl, except at night when its distinctive voice identifies it. Birders in the Tucson area make night trips to find this and many other species of owls in the nearby canyons and mountains. The owls respond readily to imitations or recordings of their calls, often coming close enough to be seen with a spotlight.

303 Great Horned Owl
Bubo virginianus

Description: 25″ (64 cm). W. 4′7″ (1.4 m). A large owl, varying in color from nearly white (in Arctic) to dark brown and gray. Mottled and streaked below, setting off the *white throat;* prominent, *widely spaced ear tufts;* yellow eyes.

Voice: Series of low, sonorous, far-carrying hoots, *hoo, hoo-hoo, hoo, hoo,* with second and third notes shorter than the others.

Habitat: Forests, deserts, open country, swamps, and even city parks.

Nesting: 2 or 3 white eggs on the bare surface

of a cliff or cave or even on the ground; in the East it most often appropriates the unused stick nest of a heron, hawk, or crow.

Range: Resident throughout North America south of tree line.

This owl hunts rabbits, rodents, and birds, including crows, ducks, and other owls. On occasion, it even captures skunks. It is the largest and best known of the common owls. Since owls can see in the dark, they were believed to possess supernatural powers; because of their solemn appearance they have become symbols of wisdom or occult knowledge.

---

314 Snowy Owl
Nyctea scandiaca

Description: 24″ (61 cm). W. 4′7″ (1.4 m). A big, round-headed owl, ranging in color from *pure white* to white with dark spotting or barring. Female is larger and more heavily marked than male.

Voice: Usually silent; hoarse croak and shrill whistle on breeding grounds.

Habitat: Open country: tundra, dunes, marshes, fields, plains, and airports in winter.

Nesting: 5–8 white eggs with a lining of feathers, mosses, and lichens placed on open tundra.

Range: Breeds in northern Alaska and in northernmost Canada. Winters south throughout Canada into northern United States, irregularly farther. Also in Eurasia.

Snowy Owls depend on lemmings for their major food. The population of lemmings fluctuates from year to year, and when the supply gets too low, the owls migrate southward in great numbers. At such times observers south of the normal range note an irruption of Snowy Owls.

306 Northern Hawk Owl
Surnia ulula

Description: 15–17″ (38–43 cm). W. 33″ (84 cm).
Smaller than a crow. A *long-tailed, day-flying owl* that behaves more like a hawk.
Barred breast; facial disks have bold
black borders.

Voice: Whistling *ki-ki-ki-ki-ki-ki,* similar to
call of a kestrel.

Habitat: Clearings in boreal coniferous forest
and muskeg.

Nesting: 3–7 white eggs in a tree cavity, in an
abandoned bird's nest, or (rarely) on
a cliff.

Range: Resident from Alaska east to Labrador
and south to British Columbia,
Newfoundland, and Gaspé Peninsula.
May wander farther south in winter.
Also in Eurasia.

In the northern domain of this owl the
sun seldom sets during the summer half
of the year. Adapted to these conditions,
this is the most diurnal of all North
American owls. It feeds on rodents,
including mice and lemmings, that are
active throughout the 24-hour day. In
winter, when rodent runways are deep
beneath the snow, it eats more birds,
including grouse, than mammals. Like
many northern birds that have rarely
seen humans, the Northern Hawk Owl
can be exceedingly tame.

317 Northern Pygmy-Owl
"Pygmy Owl"
Glaucidium gnoma

Description: 7–7½″ (18–19 cm). A sparrow-sized
owl. Small round head and *long, finely
barred tail* that is often cocked at an
angle. Varying shades of brown with
fine buff spotting above; buff-white
with bolder brown streaks below.
2 white-edged black spots at back of
neck suggest eyes.

Voice: A series of mellow whistles on 1 pitch. Also a thin rattle around the nest.

Habitat: Open coniferous forests or mixed aspen and oak woods; dense canyon growth.

Nesting: 3–6 white eggs in an abandoned woodpecker hole.

Range: Resident from southeastern Alaska southward throughout most of West.

This small owl sometimes hunts by day, attacking birds even larger than itself. In spring the male is conspicuous, uttering a staccato whistle every few seconds while flicking his long tail upward and sideways. In response, the small forest birds sound an excited alarm, scolding and mobbing this tiny owl, just as they would any larger owl.

318 Ferruginous Pygmy-Owl
"Ferruginous Owl"
Glaucidium brasilianum

Description: 6½–7″ (17–18 cm). Resembles Northern Pygmy-Owl, but more rust-colored, with *rusty, faintly cross-barred tail* and streaked flanks. Crown streaked with white, underparts streaked with red-brown. White-bordered black patch on each side of nape.

Voice: Monotonous, repeated, harsh *poip;* also whistles.

Habitat: Saguaro desert; mesquite or dense streamside growth.

Nesting: 3 or 4 white eggs in a hole in a saguaro cactus or a tree.

Range: Resident in southern Arizona and along lower Rio Grande Valley of Texas. Also in American tropics.

The male Ferruginous calls incessantly in spring, at a rate of 90 to 150 times a minute. One is reported to have called for three solid hours. This tiny tropical owl is rare and local in the United States, and the small population around

Tucson, Arizona, is a great attraction
to bird-watchers.

307   Elf Owl
Microthene whitneyi

Description: 5½" (14 cm). A tiny owl with a short
tail, no ear tufts, yellow eyes; buff with
indistinct dark streaks.

Voice: Rapid series of high-pitched notes,
higher in the middle.

Habitat: Deserts, dry open woodlands, and
streamside thickets with trees.

Nesting: 3 white eggs in a deserted woodpecker
hole in a cactus or an oak, pine, or
other tree.

Range: Breeds in southeastern California,
southern Arizona, southwestern New
Mexico, and Rio Grande Valley of Texas.
Winters in Mexico.

When captured, this tiny owl feigns
death until sure that all danger has
passed. It feeds almost exclusively
on insects, catching them in the air
or on the ground, but also takes mice
and lizards.

310   Burrowing Owl
Speotyto cunicularia

Description: 9" (23 cm). A robin-sized terrestrial
owl, short-tailed and long-legged.
Yellow eyes; no ear tufts; *face framed
in white, with blackish collar.*

Voice: Liquid cackling; also a mellow *coo-coooo,*
repeated twice.

Habitat: Plains, deserts, fields, and airports.

Nesting: 5–7 white eggs in a long underground
burrow lined with grasses, roots,
and dung.

Range: Breeds from Canada's southern prairie
provinces south throughout western
United States to southern California and
Texas. Winters in southwestern states.

Resident in central and southern Florida. Also in tropical America.

This comical little bird is one of the most diurnal of all owls. It often perches near its hole; when approached too closely, it will bob up and down and finally dive into its burrow rather than take flight. It usually claims burrows that have been abandoned by prairie dogs or pocket gophers but is quite capable of digging its own.

---

311 Spotted Owl
Strix occidentalis

Description: 16½–19″ (42–48 cm). A medium-sized owl without ear tufts. *Upperparts dark brown with white spots;* underparts white, heavily barred with brown; eyes dark. Barred Owl is paler and grayer, with streaks (not bars) on breast and belly.

Voice: 2 or 3 short barking hoots followed by a louder, more prolonged *hooo-ah.*

Habitat: Old-growth coniferous forests, densely wooded canyons.

Nesting: 2 or 3 white eggs, usually laid in a natural tree or canyon wall cavity or an abandoned hawk's nest.

Range: Resident from southwestern British Columbia to southern California; also in mountains of Utah and Colorado south to Arizona, New Mexico, and western Texas.

This large and secretive rodent eater, rather rare in much of the West, lives in dense stands of mature forests. The cutting of old-growth forest has been followed by the disappearance of the Spotted Owl, and the conflict between the owl and the timber industry has become a political one. Another threat comes from competition with the Barred Owl, which is slowly encroaching from the East.

313   **Barred Owl**
Strix varia

Description: 20″ (51 cm). W. 3′8″ (1.1 m). A large,
stocky, dark-eyed owl. Gray-brown,
with crossbarring on neck and breast
and streaks on belly; *no ear tufts.* See
Spotted Owl.

Voice: A loud barking *hoo, hoo, hoo-hoo; hoo,
hoo; hoo, hooo-aw!* and a variety of other
barking calls and screams.

Habitat: Low, wet woods and swampy forests.

Nesting: 2–4 white eggs in an unlined cavity
in a hollow tree or (rarely) an
abandoned building; sometimes in
an old crow's nest.

Range: Breeds from British Columbia, Alberta,
Quebec, and Nova Scotia south to
northern California and throughout
East to Texas and Florida.

This owl is most often seen by those
who seek it out in its dark retreat,
usually a thick grove of trees in lowland
forest. There it rests quietly during the
day. It sometimes calls in the daytime
and if disturbed will fly easily from one
grove of trees to another. It emerges at
night to feed on rodents, birds, frogs,
and crayfish. In recent years, this owl
has been expanding its range in
Washington, Oregon, and California.

305   **Great Gray Owl**
Strix nebulosa

Description: 24–33″ (61–84 cm). W. 5′ (1.5 m).
A huge, dusky gray, earless owl of the
North Woods, with yellow eyes, large
facial disks, and distinctive black
chin spot bordered by white patches,
resembling a bow tie. Barred and
Spotted owls are smaller, stockier, and
browner, with dark eyes.

Voice: Very deep, booming *whoo,* repeated
10 times or more, and gradually
descending the scale.

Habitat: Coniferous forests and muskeg.
Nesting: 2–5 white eggs in a bulky nest of sticks in a dense conifer.
Range: Resident from Alaska and across interior Canada south to northern California, northern Wyoming, Minnesota, and Quebec. In winter wanders rarely southward into northern New England and Great Lakes region. Also in Eurasia.

Like other owls of the Far North, this species hunts during the day, often watching for prey from a low perch. Because it spends much of its time in dense conifers, it is often overlooked. One of the most elusive of birds, the Great Gray was discovered in America by Europeans before they realized that the species also occurs in Europe.

304 Long-eared Owl
Asio otus

Description: 15" (38 cm). W. 3'3" (1 m). A nearly crow-sized owl with *long ear tufts set close together.* Heavily mottled brown; *chestnut facial disks.*
Voice: Soft low hoots; also whistles, whines, shrieks, and cat-like meows. Seldom heard except during breeding time.
Habitat: Deciduous and coniferous forests.
Nesting: 4 or 5 white eggs in a deserted crow, hawk, or squirrel nest.
Range: Breeds from central British Columbia, southern Mackenzie, and Quebec south to California, Arkansas, and Virginia. Winters in southern part of breeding range and in southern tier of states. Also in Eurasia.

Although these woodland owls are gregarious in winter, they are so quiet during the day that up to a dozen may inhabit a dense evergreen grove without being detected. They have a tendency to roost near the trunk of a tree, and since they elongate themselves by compressing their feathers, they resemble part of the trunk itself. Only by peering intently upward can one detect the round face and telltale long ear tufts. A good way to locate an owl roost is to search in pine woods for groups of pellets on the ground. These regurgitated bundles of undigested fur and bones provide an excellent indication of the bird's food habits.

315   Short-eared Owl
Asio flammeus

Description: 16″ (41 cm). A crow-sized, long-winged owl of open country. Tawny brown with rather heavy streaks below; blackish patch around each eye. Very short ear tufts are rarely visible.

Voice: Usually silent; on nesting grounds, a variety of barks, hisses, and squeals.

Habitat: Freshwater and salt marshes; open grasslands, prairies, dunes; open country generally during migration.

Nesting: 5–7 white eggs in a grass-lined depression on the ground, often concealed in weeds or beneath a bush.

Range: Breeds from Alaska across Canada south locally to California, Kansas, and New Jersey. Winters in southern part of breeding range and south throughout United States to Central America. Also in South America and most of Old World.

This owl is most commonly seen late in the afternoon as it begins to move about in preparation for a night of hunting. It can often be identified at a great distance by its habit of hovering; its flight is erratic and bounding. Occasionally several birds may be seen at once, an indication that small rodents are especially numerous.

308 Boreal Owl
Aegolius funereus

Description: 9–12″ (23–30 cm). W. 24″ (61 cm). A rare, robin-sized owl without ear tufts. Brown with white spots above, rust-streaked below. Similar to Northern Saw-whet Owl but larger, with dark borders on facial disks, *more spotting on upperparts, spotted (not streaked) forehead, and yellow (not dark) bill.*

Voice: Rapid series of whistled notes.

Habitat: Boreal coniferous forests and muskeg.

Nesting: 4–6 white eggs placed in a woodpecker hole or other tree cavity or in the abandoned nest of another bird.

Range: Breeds in Alaska, Yukon, Saskatchewan, Manitoba, Quebec, Labrador, and Newfoundland south to northern British Columbia, Colorado (in Rocky Mountains), southern Manitoba, Ontario, and New Brunswick. In winter wanders rarely south to northern tier of states. Also in Eurasia.

This small, secretive owl is considered one of the rarest winter visitors from the North. Its retiring habits cause it to be overlooked, and it is easily confused with its more common relative the Northern Saw-whet Owl. It is entirely nocturnal, spending the day concealed in dense spruce or a hollow tree. It preys mainly on rodents.

309 Northern Saw-whet Owl
Aegolius acadicus

Description: 7″ (18 cm). A very small, earless, yellow-eyed owl; brown above, with white streaks on forehead, dark bill, and short tail. Juveniles are chocolate-brown above, buff below, with white triangle on forehead extending between eyes. See Boreal Owl.

Voice: Usually silent; in late winter and

spring utters monotonous series of tooting whistles.

Habitat: Coniferous woodlands; in winter also in evergreen thickets in parks, gardens, and estates; also isolated pines.

Nesting: 5 or 6 white eggs placed without a nest lining in a deserted woodpecker hole or natural cavity.

Range: Breeds from southeastern Alaska, Manitoba, and Nova Scotia south to southern California, Arizona, Illinois, North Carolina (in mountains), and Connecticut. Winters in breeding range and south to Arkansas and North Carolina.

A nocturnal hunter of rodents and large insects, the Northern Saw-whet is tame and approachable during the day while resting. Though widespread in Canada and all of the northern and western United States, its distribution is spotty. This pattern may be attributable to uneven or inadequate food supplies in areas with severe winter conditions.

FAMILY CAPRIMULGIDAE
Nightjars

83 species: Worldwide. Eight species breed in North America. These mottled, cryptically colored birds spend most of their time resting on the ground, but feed on flying insects at dusk or at night. They have long wings and short bills, with wide-opening mouths for catching insects. Some American species, such as the Whip-poor-will, have loud rhythmic calls, but others have nasal or buzzy notes.

300 Lesser Nighthawk
Chordeiles acutipennis

Description: 8–9″ (20–23 cm). Similar to Common Nighthawk but smaller, with white wing patch (buff in female) nearer tip of wing (visible in flight). Both sexes have buffy cast to underparts. Male's throat white; female's buffy. Whereas Common Nighthawk hunts and calls from high up, Lesser Nighthawk flies low and utters no loud aerial calls.

Voice: A soft, sustained, tremolo whirring; very difficult to locate.

Habitat: Open dry scrublands; desert valleys; prairies and pastures.

Nesting: 2 spotted, light gray eggs on open ground.

Range: Breeds from central California, Arizona, and parts of Nevada, Utah, New Mexico, and Texas southward. Winters in tropics.

The Lesser is more nocturnal than the Common Nighthawk and hunts its insect prey by flying low above the canopy of trees or the brush and grass of open plains. During courtship flight display, the male pursues the female close to the ground, flashing his white throat as he calls.

299 Common Nighthawk
Chordeiles minor

Description: 10″ (25 cm). A jay-sized bird, mottled brownish-black above and below, perfectly matching the ground. Long notched or square-tipped tail and long pointed wings *with broad white wing bar*. Male has white throat patch and white subterminal tail bar. Female has buffy throat patch and no tail bar. Flight high and fluttery.

Voice: A loud nasal call, *peent* or *pee-yah,* heard primarily at dusk.

Habitat: Open woodlands, clearings, or fields; towns with roosting trees or fence posts.

Nesting: 2 creamy or olive-gray, finely and densely speckled eggs laid on the ground or a roof.

Range: Breeds from central Canada southward to Nova Scotia and through most of United States. Winters in tropics.

This bird has moved into towns and cities, where flat roofs provide abundant nest sites, and railroad yards, vacant lots, and sports fields offer good feeding opportunities. Pioneer settlers mistook this bird for a hawk because of its swift flight and long wings. It flies in daylight as well as at night but is most evident in early evening.

301 Common Poorwill
Phalaenoptilus nuttallii

Description: 7–8½″ (18–22 cm). Our smallest nightjar. Mottled gray-brown with *no white mark on wings;* whitish collar separates black throat from mottled underparts. Dark outer tail feathers are tipped with white, more conspicuously in male; *tail is rounded.*

Voice: A mellow *poor-will.*

Habitat: Desert, chaparral, sagebrush, and other arid uplands.

Nesting: 2 pinkish-white eggs on bare ground.

Range: Breeds from southeastern British Columbia, Alberta, and Montana south throughout western United States. Winters in southwestern states and Mexico.

The Common Poorwill has been discovered hibernating in the desert in California, surviving long cold spells in a torpid condition, without food and with its body temperature lowered almost to that of its surroundings. This adaptation is unique among birds.

These nightjars are seen most often
sitting on roads at night.

Buff-collared Nightjar
Caprimulgus ridgwayi

Description: 9″ (23 cm). Mottled gray-brown with
buff collar. Male has white patches at
corners of tail.
Voice: A staccato *cu-cu-cu-cuc-cuc-cuc-uh-chee-ah,*
heard at night.
Habitat: Dry canyons and rocky streambeds.
Nesting: Nesting habits unknown.
Range: Resident in southeastern Arizona and
southwestern New Mexico.

This little-known nightjar is a rare
summer visitor to the Southwest.
It is much more common south of
U.S.–Mexico border.

302 Whip-poor-will
Caprimulgus vociferus

Description: 10″ (25 cm). Robin-sized. A leaf-brown,
strictly nocturnal bird with black
throat. Male has *broad white tips on outer
tail feathers,* visible in flight. Female has
all-brown tail.
Voice: A loud, rhythmic *whip-poor-will,*
repeated over and over, at night.
Habitat: Dry, open woodlands and canyons.
Nesting: 2 white eggs, scrawled with gray and
brown, placed on the ground among
dead leaves.
Range: Breeds from Saskatchewan and
Maritime Provinces south to Kansas,
northern Louisiana, and northern
Georgia, and in Arizona, New Mexico,
and western Texas. Winters from Florida
and Gulf Coast southward.

Whip-poor-wills, like other night-
flying birds, were once suspected of
witchery. They fly around livestock at

dusk to feed on insects swarming over the animals. It was believed that they sucked milk from goats' udders and caused them to dry up; hence their family name, Caprimulgidae, from the Latin *capri* and *mulgus,* meaning "goat-milker." Until recently they were inaccurately called "goatsuckers," but now the name "nightjar" is preferred.

FAMILY APODIDAE
Swifts

99 species: Worldwide. Four species breed in North America. Members of this well-known family are aerial feeders, catching insects on the wing. They have long wings, short tails, and wide-opening mouths. Swifts never perch but cling to vertical surfaces such as the walls of caves, buildings, and trees. These birds get their name from the fact that they are among the speediest of all birds. The sexes are alike, and colors run from drab grays and browns to black and white. The eggs are pure white, laid in clutches of one to six.

370 Black Swift
Cypseloides niger

Description: 7–7½″ (18–19 cm). Size of a large swallow but with longer, sickle-shaped wings. *All black,* except whitish forehead, apparent at close range. Longish tail, slightly forked, often fanned. Feathers of immature edged with white.

Voice: Less vocal than other swifts. Gives soft, high-pitched twitter: *twit-twit-twit-twit.*

Habitat: Mountains and coastal cliffs; most frequently seen in the open sky.

Nesting: 1 white egg in a moss, grass, and algae nest well hidden under a waterfall, on a protected sea cliff ledge, or on a canyon wall. Nests in colonies.

Range: Breeds from southern Alaska south to southern California, Montana, and Colorado. Winters in tropics.

Swifts, in general the most aerial of all land birds, feed on tiny airborne insects. On sunny days they fly high above the forest, but when the weather worsens they stay at lower altitudes, following the insects. During a summer storm of three or four days' chilling rain, flocks leave the nesting grounds and may fly hundreds of miles until they encounter favorable weather. After the storm they return in small groups to the nests. In their absence, the young survive without food, becoming torpid: cold, motionless, and barely breathing. Lower metabolism prevents starvation, thus allowing the young to be raised through alternating periods of plenty and shortage.

362 Chimney Swift
Chaetura pelagica

Description: 4¾–5½" (12–14 cm). Similar to Vaux's Swift but slightly larger, more uniform gray-brown, with darker throat and breast.

Voice: Loud, chattering twitters.

Habitat: Breeds and roosts in chimneys; feeds entirely on the wing over forests, open country, and towns.

Nesting: 4 or 5 white eggs in a nest made of twigs cemented together with saliva and fastened to the inner wall of a chimney or, rarely, in a cave or hollow tree.

Range: Breeds from southeastern Saskatchewan, southern Manitoba, central Ontario, southern Quebec, and Nova Scotia south to Gulf Coast states. Has also bred in California. Winters in tropics.

The Chimney Swift, the eastern version of Vaux's, may be observed in the western Great Plains states during migration. It is slowly expanding its range westward.

372 Vaux's Swift
Chaetura vauxi

Description: 4–4½" (10–11 cm). A *tiny* swift. Dark overall, with *dingy lighter underparts, especially pale on throat and upper breast.* Wings long, stiff, and gently curved; tail slightly rounded. See Chimney Swift.

Voice: A bat-like chipping. Usually silent on migration.

Habitat: Forests and woodlands.

Nesting: 3–5 white eggs in a nest of small sticks cemented together with saliva and attached to the inside surface of a hollow tree.

Range: Breeds from southeastern Alaska and Montana to central California. Winters in tropics.

The better-known eastern Chimney Swift now uses chimneys for nesting, whereas the Vaux's is still mainly a forest dweller. These swifts have stubby tails, each feather ending in a naked shaft with a hard spine that helps to support the bird as it clings to vertical surfaces, such as its nesting cavity walls. Its fast flight is characterized by sailing glides between spurts of rapid flapping.

371 White-throated Swift
Aeronautes saxatalis

Description: 6–7" (15–18 cm). The size of a Barn Swallow, but with the typical *stiff, fast wingbeats* of a swift. Striking *piebald* appearance in the air; seen from below, wings, flanks, and tail *black,* the rest *white.*

Voice: A prolonged series of grating notes, *jee-jee-jee-jee-jee.*

Habitat: Arid mountains or other rocky areas.
Nesting: 3–6 white eggs in a nest of feathers glued together with saliva built in a cleft of a sea or mountain cliff. Nests in colonies.
Range: Breeds from British Columbia through Rocky Mountains and in Southwest, including California. Winters from central California and Southwest to Central America.

These common swifts are often seen in the vicinity of steep cliffs, where they may fly in small groups, chattering constantly. Like some other swifts, they mate in flight, gyrating earthward in a free fall, separating only when about to hit the ground.

FAMILY TROCHILIDAE
Hummingbirds

320 species: This strictly American family is most numerous in South America, especially in the Andes. Only 14 species breed regularly in North America. These are among the most colorful of birds, with glittering, iridescent plumage. They are the only birds known to fly backward and, like the related swifts, they do not perch while feeding. They hover in front of a flower and sip nectar and pick off insects while on the wing. They lay two white eggs in a soft, very compact nest made of down.

417, 419 Broad-billed Hummingbird
Cynanthus latirostris

Description: 3¼–4″ (8–10 cm). Male dark green above and below, with bright *metallic-blue gorget* (throat patch). Bright red-orange bill with black tip. Female's *unmarked gray throat and underparts* and *red-orange bill* distinguish her from other female hummers of same size.

Voice: A rapid, scratching *chi-dit,* like the note of a Ruby-crowned Kinglet.

Habitat: Desert canyons; mesquite and other thickets in arid country.

Nesting: 2 white eggs in a rough, loosely woven cup nest on a vertical branch of a streamside tree.

Range: Breeds in southern Arizona, southwestern New Mexico, and western Texas. Winters south of U.S.–Mexico border.

The Broad-billed Hummingbird is said to be quieter and less active than most hummers, often sitting on a high perch for long periods. However, its flight is more irregular and jerky than that of others in the same habitat.

403 White-eared Hummingbird
Hylocharis leucotis

Description: 3½" (9 cm). A small hummingbird. Both sexes have *long, broad white stripe behind eye and red bill with dark tip.* Male green above and below, with purple crown and iridescent blue-green chin; female lacks bright crown and chin and is whitish below with *green spotting and barring on throat and sides.*

Voice: Breeding male utters a long, monotonous clinking sound: *tink-tink-tink.*

Habitat: Mountain woodlands.

Nesting: 2 white eggs in a moss nest interwoven with needles, lichens, and twigs, placed in a small tree.

Range: Irregular summer visitor to extreme southeastern Arizona; rare in New Mexico and Texas.

Early in the year male White-eared Hummingbirds establish individual feeding territories. As the breeding season approaches, several males gather in an area where they court vigorously. Females with a nest visit these groups and return to their nesting area with a male.

421 Violet-crowned Hummingbird
Amazilia violiceps

Description: 3¾–4½″ (10–11 cm). *Bronze above, white below, including throat;* no gorget. *Crown violet-blue;* bill red with dark tip. Sexes similar.
Voice: A loud chatter.
Habitat: Canyons, streamside growth.
Nesting: 2 white eggs in a downy, lichen-covered nest on a horizontal branch.
Range: Breeds in southeastern Arizona and southwestern New Mexico. Winters in Mexico.

Although rare in its very limited range in southeastern Arizona, the Violet-crowned Hummingbird is common in Mexico. It is a conspicuous bird and behaves aggressively toward other hummers.

407, 408 Blue-throated Hummingbird
Lampornis clemenciae

Description: 4½–5″ (11–13 cm). A very large hummingbird. Male green above, dusky gray below, with *bright blue gorget.* Blue-black tail with *broad white corners* on outer tail feathers. Female closely resembles female Magnificent Hummingbird, but has much larger white margins on tail feathers. Both sexes have thin white stripes above and below eyes.
Voice: A loud *seep,* often repeated, uttered in flight as well as when perching.
Habitat: Streamside growth in canyons.
Nesting: 2 white eggs in a large cup nest with green mosses woven into the outside

wall, fastened to a vertical plant stalk, occasionally in the shelter of cabins or on electrical wires; usually over or near water.

Range: Breeds in southeastern Arizona and southwestern New Mexico, and western Texas. Winters in Mexico.

Blue-throated Hummingbirds are rapid fliers whose wings make an audible humming sound. They take both nectar and insects. Studies in Mexico show that their nests are always sheltered from rain and sun and located near water, where flowering vegetation abounds. The Blue-throated returns to such a site year after year.

418, 420   **Magnificent Hummingbird**
"Rivoli's Hummingbird"
Eugenes fulgens

Description: 4½–5½" (11–14 cm). A large, long-tailed hummingbird. Male *deep green above, black below, with iridescent purple forehead and crown and metallic-green gorget.* Female olive green above, gray below, with lightly streaked throat and pearly gray tips on outer tail feathers. Immature male heavily flecked with iridescent green below.

Voice: A high-pitched *teek,* not as drawn out as call of Blue-throated Hummingbird.

Habitat: Canyons, deciduous and pine-clad slopes, and streamsides.

Nesting: 2 white eggs in a tiny nest of lichen and plant down placed on a horizontal limb.

Range: Breeds in mountains of southeastern Arizona, southwestern New Mexico, and western Texas. Winters in Mexico.

The Magnificent Hummingbird flies more slowly than the smaller hummers, sometimes sailing on set wings. It is more of an insect gleaner than the other species, though it takes its share of nectar from flowers and feeders.

402 Lucifer Hummingbird
Calothorax lucifer

Description: 3¾" (10 cm). A small hummingbird.
Male iridescent green, with *green crown*
and *long purple gorget;* white below, with
buff on flanks. Forked tail is usually
closed, looking pointed. Female buff
below; has decurved bill; lacks forked
tail. Costa's Hummingbird has similar
gorget but also has purple on forehead
and lacks buff on sides.

Voice: A shrill shriek.

Habitat: Open arid country; desert vegetation,
especially agaves.

Nesting: 2 white eggs in a small cup nest of
downy plant fibers, cobwebs, and
lichens, usually near the ground in
agave and other vegetation.

Range: Breeds in Chisos Mountains of western
Texas. Accidental summer visitor to
extreme southeastern Arizona.

In Latin, *lucifer* means "light-bearing"
and was applied in Old English to the
morning star. Thus, when William
Swainson named this bird in 1827 he
might have been thinking of the
luminous glow of its colors. The male
Lucifer's outer tail feathers are hard and
narrow, and hum loudly during aerial
displays. He performs a zigzagging
dance to attract females and repel
other males.

406, 409 Black-chinned Hummingbird
Archilochus alexandri

Description: 3¼–3¾" (8–10 cm). A small
hummingbird. Male green above
with black chin and *violet-purple throat.*
Female green above with white throat
and breast, buff sides, and white-
tipped outer tail feathers. See
Costa's Hummingbird.

Voice: A low *tup*.

Habitat: Mountain and alpine meadows,

woodlands, canyons with thickets, chaparral, and orchards.

Nesting: 2 white eggs in a nest of fluffy plant wool and lichens woven together with spider webs, placed in a shrub or low tree.

Range: Breeds from British Columbia south throughout West to Mexico and central Texas. Winters in Mexico.

The male Black-chinned, like all hummingbirds, maintains a mating and feeding territory in spring. He courts his female with a dazzling aerial display involving a pendulum-like flight pattern. When mating interest wanes, the male often takes up residence elsewhere, near a good food supply. Later, when plant blooming and insect swarming subside, the birds move south.

401, 404   Anna's Hummingbird
Calypte anna

Description: 3½–4″ (9–10 cm). A medium-sized hummingbird. Both sexes metallic green above; male has *dark rose-red crown and gorget* and grayish chest. Female has spotted throat with central patch of red spots, grayish-white underparts, and white-tipped outer tail feathers. Throat of juveniles frequently unmarked.

Voice: A sharp *chip* and a rapid *chee-chee-chee-chee-chee.*

Habitat: Chaparral, brushy oak woodlands, and gardens.

Nesting: 2 white eggs in a tiny woven cup of small twigs and lichen fastened onto a sheltered horizontal limb.

Range: Resident from northern California southward. Winters regularly from British Columbia south to Arizona.

Anna's and other hummingbirds vigorously defend their feeding territories which, although often as small as a few clumps of fuchsias, provide adequate nectar and small nectar-feeding insects. From July to late fall, however, transient and juvenile birds disregard territorial claims, and competition at feeders increases greatly.

405, 416 Costa's Hummingbird
Calypte costae

Description: 3–3½″ (8–9 cm). A tiny hummingbird. Male's *violet-purple crown and gorget,* which is *flanked with very long, conspicuous side feathers,* distinguish it from Black-chinned Hummingbird. Female is practically indistinguishable from female Black-chinned. Costa's preference for more arid terrain and its habit of soaring between flower clusters are helpful in identifying it.

Voice: A light *chip* and high tinkling notes.

Habitat: Low desert; in California, chaparral.

Nesting: 2 white eggs in a delicately woven cup, with leaves or lichens fastened to the outside, built low on a protected branch of a bush or small tree.

Range: Breeds from central California, southern Nevada, and southwestern Utah southward. Winters in southern California and Mexico.

Hummingbirds feed on both insects and nectar. Although species in North America encounter many nectar-bearing flowers on their migrations, they have a decided preference for red flowers. In southern and central California, Costa's feeds extensively on the red penstemon. Since this plant is found mainly in habitats where Costa's is the only resident hummingbird, it is probably the plant's chief pollinator.

413, 422   Calliope Hummingbird
Stellula calliope

Description:
2¾–3¼" (7–8 cm). The smallest North American hummingbird. Male *metallic green above; has white gorget with purple-violet rays,* which can be raised to give a whiskered effect. (All other North American hummers have solid-colored gorgets.) Female *green above, white below,* with dark streaks on throat, buffy flanks, and white-tipped tail corners. Resembles the female Rufous Hummingbird, but smaller, with smaller bill, paler flanks, and less rufous at base of tail.

Voice:
A high-pitched *tsew.*

Habitat:
Montane and subalpine forest clearings, brushy edges, and alpine meadows.

Nesting:
2 bean-sized white eggs, surprisingly large for such a tiny bird, in a small lichen-and-moss nest covered with cobwebs, placed on a limb of a bush or well-protected small tree.

Range:
Breeds in mountains from interior and southern coastal British Columbia south through Pacific states and east to Colorado. Winters in Mexico.

When defending their feeding flowers or courting a female, male hummers put on a striking spectacle, rising out of sight and then swooping down to buzz their opponent or the female. Each species has its own flight pattern.

415, 423   Broad-tailed Hummingbird
Selasphorus platycercus

Description:
4–4½" (10–11 cm). Male metallic green, with rose-red gorget; green crown; broad tail with little rufous. Female similar to female Rufous and Allen's hummingbirds, but has green central tail feathers; outer tail feathers are rust-colored at base, black in middle, and white on outer tips.

Voice: Call is a sharp *chick*.

Habitat: Mountain meadows, piñon-juniper woodlands, dry ponderosa pines, fir or mixed forests, and canyon vegetation.

Nesting: 2 white eggs in a woven cup nest of lichen and plant down.

Range: Breeds in mountains from eastern California and northern Wyoming south through Great Basin and Rocky Mountain states to southern Arizona and western Texas. Winters in Mexico.

Accounts of this species mention that it nests in the same tree or bush year after year, a phenomenon known as philopatry—faithfulness to the previous home area. It will return to the same branch and even build a new nest atop an old one.

411, 414 Rufous Hummingbird
Selasphorus rufus

Description: 3½–4″ (9–10 cm). Male has *bright rufous upperparts* and flanks and iridescent orange-red throat. Female green above, with rufous tinge on rump and flanks, and much rufous in tail. Adult male Allen's Hummingbird has green crown and back; female and immature Allen's not safely separable from Rufous in field, but have narrower outer tail feathers. See Calliope and Broad-tailed hummingbirds.

Voice: An abrupt, high-pitched *zeee;* various thin squealing notes.

Habitat: Mountain meadows, forest edges; on migration and in winter frequents gardens with hummingbird feeding stations.

Nesting: 2 white eggs in a lichen-covered cup of plant down and spiderweb attached to a horizontal branch.

Range: Breeds from southeastern Alaska, British Columbia, southwestern Alberta, and western Montana south to Washington, Oregon, Idaho, and

northern California. Winters mainly in Mexico. Occurs in small numbers along Gulf Coast during migration and in winter, and casually in Carolinas.

Hummingbirds share certain traits. The first bird to discover a source of food defends it. Even when satiated, it will perch nearby and intercept intruders in the air with angry buzzing. If a female is disturbed when feeding, she gives a "no trespassing" signal by fanning and waving her tail. Females, therefore, have developed distinct tail patterns, whereas males, facing the opponent, signal with their brilliant throat patches, called gorgets. The sexes have separate territories; the female visits the male at mating time, the male ignores the female's territory and moves away after the mating season.

410, 412   Allen's Hummingbird
Selasphorus sasin

Description: 3–3½" (8–9 cm). A very small hummingbird. Male has iridescent green crown and back; rufous rump and tail. *Bright, iridescent copper-red gorget* (appears dark when not in direct sunlight), white breast, rufous sides. Female bronze-green above, including central tail feathers, with white-tipped rufous outer tail feathers, flecked throat, white underparts with rust tinge on flanks. See Rufous Hummingbird.

Voice: A low *chup,* and an excited *zeeee chuppity-chup.*

Habitat: Coastal chaparral, brushland, and edges of redwood forests.

Nesting: 2 white eggs in a tiny, tightly woven cup placed on a sheltered branch.

Range: Breeds along coast from southern Oregon to southern California. Resident in southern California. Also winters in Mexico.

This coastal hummingbird often nests in loose colonies and is quite aggressive in defending its nesting territory from other hummers. Territorial battles are most common in early morning, when intruders are more likely to appear. At this time of day, the birds tend to feed around the edges of their territories.

FAMILY TROGONIDAE
Trogons

39 species: Tropical areas of America, Asia, and Africa. One species breeds in the southwestern United States, and a second is a very rare visitor there. Trogons are long-tailed, slim birds with round heads, large mouths, short hooked bills, short legs, and an upright perching stance. They are forest birds that glean insects and fruit.

518 **Elegant Trogon**
"Coppery-tailed Trogon"
Trogon elegans

Description: 11–12" (28–30 cm). Unmistakable. A jay-sized bird with a stout, hooked yellow bill, *upright posture,* and *long, square-cut tail.* Male has glossy, dark *emerald-green upperparts,* head, and upper breast; white breast band; *crimson belly and undertail coverts.* Copper-red tail has black terminal band, but viewed from below it is gray with broad white bars. Female plain brown where male is green, with white patch on cheek; pink where male is crimson, with white and light coffee-colored bands on breast. Eared Trogon (*Euptilotis neoxenus*), a rare visitor to Southwest, similar but has black bill, no white band on breast, more white on underside of blue (not coppery) tail.

Voice: A loud but hard to locate *ko-ah ko-ah ko-ah* or *kum! kum! kum!*

Habitat: Thick deciduous mountain growth; sycamore canyons.

Nesting: 3 or 4 white eggs in an unlined woodpecker hole, termite nest, or other cavity.

Range: Breeds in southeastern Arizona. A few winter there, but most cross into Mexico.

This beautiful trogon is related to the bird of the Maya emperor-gods, the Quetzal (*Pharomachrus mocinno*). Finding the Elegant Trojan is a prime objective of birders, since its range barely extends into the United States. Trogons are insectivorous, but their diet also includes small fruits.

FAMILY ALCEDINIDAE
Kingfishers

94 species: Chiefly tropical regions in the Old World. Three species breed in North America. Most kingfishers have large, powerful bills, and many are brilliantly colored. Those in our range are relatively plain, although conspicuously crested. These birds dig tunnels into earthen banks where they lay their white eggs. As their name suggests, they feed on fish, but many tropical species also catch insects and lizards on land.

601 **Belted Kingfisher**
Ceryle alcyon

Description: 13″ (33 cm). A pigeon-sized bird, blue-gray above, white below, with *bushy crest, dagger-like bill.* Male has blue-gray breast band; female similar, but also has *chestnut belly band.*

Voice: Loud, penetrating rattle, given on the wing and when perched.

Habitat: Rivers, lakes, and saltwater estuaries.
Nesting: 5–8 white eggs in an unlined
chamber at the end of a tunnel up
to 8′(2.5 m) long, dug in a sand or
gravel bank.
Range: Breeds from Alaska eastward across
southern Canada and south throughout
most of United States. Winters on
Pacific Coast north to southeastern
Alaska, and throughout South north to
Great Lakes and along Atlantic Coast
to New England.

While searching for fish, the familiar
Belted Kingfisher perches conspicuously
on a limb over a river or lake. On
sighting a fish it flies from its post
and hovers like a tern over the water
before plunging after its prey. When
flying from one perch to another, often
a good distance apart, it utters its
loud rattling call.

600 Green Kingfisher
Chloroceryle americana

Description: 8″ (20 cm). Starling-sized. Dark glossy
green above, white below; *male has broad
rufous breast band, female has green breast
band.* Both sexes have white collar.
Voice: An insect-like buzz; also low clicking
notes.
Habitat: Woodland streams and pools.
Nesting: 4–6 white eggs in a cavity at the end of
a burrow in a sandy bank.
Range: Resident from extreme southern Texas
south into tropics. Straggles to southern
Arizona and western Texas.

The Green Kingfisher prefers shaded
rivulets, where pairs can fish on both
sides of the main river and along the
rivulet. Their watching posts are low
above the water.

FAMILY PICIDAE
Woodpeckers

215 species: Widespread, but absent
from Australia, New Guinea, and
Madagascar. Twenty-two species breed
in North America. One North American
species, the Ivory-billed Woodpecker
(*Campephilus principalis*), has recently
become extinct. Woodpeckers have
sharp, chisel-like bills, which they use
for drilling and digging into trees. They
cling to the bark of trees with their
strong claws, using their stiff tails
as props. Most nest in holes in trees.
The flight of most woodpeckers
is undulating.

383 Lewis' Woodpecker
Melanerpes lewis

Description: 10½–11½" (27–29 cm). Smaller than
a flicker. Metallic *greenish black above;
gray collar and breast; pinkish-red belly;*
dark red face framed with greenish
black. Sexes alike. Flight is crow-like,
not undulating.

Voice: Usually silent, but occasionally gives
a low churring note.

Habitat: Open pine-oak woodlands, oak or
cottonwood groves in grasslands,
ponderosa pine country.

Nesting: 6–8 white eggs in a cavity in a
dead stump or tree limb, often at
a considerable height. Nests in
loose colonies.

Range: Breeds from southern British Columbia
and Alberta south to central California,
northern Arizona, and northern New
Mexico. Winters from southern British
Columbia and Oregon to Colorado and
south to northern Mexico; wanders east
to Great Plains.

Unlike most woodpeckers, Lewis' does
not peck at wood for food and is seen
more often on top of a fence post than

clinging to it vertically. As with the Acorn Woodpecker, its main method of getting food is catching flying insects; both species also store acorns and other nuts for winter, and sometimes damage fruit orchards. Lewis' is the common woodpecker of mountain ranchlands, and some ranchers call it the "Crow Woodpecker" because of its dark color, large size, and slow flight.

377 Acorn Woodpecker
Melanerpes formicivorus

Description: 8–9½" (20–24 cm). *Male has yellowish-white forecrown;* red crown; light eyes; black nape, back, wings, and tail. Chin black; throat and sides of head yellowish white; breast and flanks whitish with heavy dark streaking; belly, wing patches, and rump white. *Female has black forecrown,* otherwise identical to male.

Voice: A loud *ja-cob, ja-cob* or *wake-up, wake-up.*

Habitat: Open oak and pine-oak forests.

Nesting: 4 or 5 white eggs in a hole in a tree. Nests in colonies, with all members of colony sharing in excavating holes—mostly in dead oak branches—feeding young, and possibly incubating.

Range: Resident from southern Oregon south through California, and in Arizona, New Mexico, and western Texas. Also in tropics.

This well-named woodpecker harvests acorns and, in agricultural or suburban areas, almonds and walnuts as well. In autumn the birds store their crop of nuts tightly in individual holes so that no squirrel can pry them out. The storage trees are usually mature or dead pines or Douglas firs with thick, soft bark, but dead oak branches and fence posts are also used. The holes made by a colony are used year after year. Acorns seem to be emergency provisions; on mild winter days these birds catch flying insects.

394   Gila Woodpecker
Melanerpes uropygialis

Description: 8–10″ (20–25 cm). Barred with black and white above; buff below and on neck and head. *Male has small red cap.* Female and juvenile similar, but lack red cap. White wing patches are prominent in flight.

Voice: A rolling *churrr.*

Habitat: Low desert scrub with saguaro or mesquite trees for nesting.

Nesting: 3–5 white eggs in a hole in a giant saguaro or a tree.

Range: Resident in southeastern California, southern Nevada, Arizona, and New Mexico.

The Gila Woodpecker is a characteristic bird of the Sonoran Desert. Like the Elf Owl and the "Gilded Flicker," it nests in holes in giant saguaro cacti.

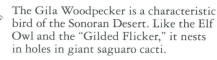

379   Yellow-bellied Sapsucker
Sphyrapicus varius

Description: 8½″ (22 cm). Similar to Red-naped Sapsucker, but male lacks red nape patch, and red throat is enclosed by black; throat of female all white. Hybridizes with Red-naped in Rocky Mountains, where puzzling intermediates can be found.

Voice: Mewing and whining notes.

Habitat: Young, open deciduous or mixed forests with clearings; on migration, visits parks, yards, and gardens.

Nesting: 5 or 6 white eggs in a tree cavity excavated by the birds.

Range: Breeds from central Canada to Newfoundland, south to British Columbia, North Dakota, Missouri, and central New England, and in the mountains to North Carolina. Winters from Missouri east to New Jersey and south to Florida and Texas; also in tropical America.

Sapsuckers feed mainly on insects
extracted from bark, thus keeping
down the number of boring insects
that destroy healthy trees. They also
enjoy sap, drilling holes around a tree
trunk in horizontal lines or a
checkerboard pattern.

376 Red-naped Sapsucker
Sphyrapicus nuchalis

Description: 8–9″ (20–23 cm). A furtive woodpecker
mottled with off-white and black. Male
has *red crown, nape patch, and throat,*
throat patch incompletely enclosed by
black. Female has white chin and red
throat, lacks red nape patch. Both sexes
dull yellowish below. Immatures dull
brown. All plumages have *conspicuous
white wing patch,* visible both at rest and
in flight.

Voice: A soft slurred *whee-ur* or *mew.*

Habitat: Edges of coniferous forests, woodlands,
groves of aspen and alder.

Nesting: 4–6 white eggs in a cavity drilled in
a tree.

Range: Breeds in Rocky Mountains from
British Columbia and Alberta south to
east-central California, central Arizona,
and southern New Mexico. Winters
north to southern California, central
Arizona, and central New Mexico.

The Red-naped Sapsucker is the
common member of the sapsucker
group in the Rocky Mountains. It
interbreeds with the Yellow-bellied at
the eastern edge of its breeding range
and with the Red-breasted to the West.
The resulting hybrids can be difficult to
identify. All three birds were formerly
considered a single species.

381 Red-breasted Sapsucker
Sphyrapicus ruber

Description: 8–9" (20–23 cm). Smaller than a
flicker. A shy woodpecker with *long
white wing patch; barred back; white rump.*
In adults, *entire head, throat, and breast
bright red, belly yellow.* Immature dusky
brown with light spots above, lighter
below, with black and white checkered
wings and tail.

Voice: Like call of Red-naped Sapsucker.

Habitat: Woodlands and their edges, groves of
aspen and alder.

Nesting: 4–6 white eggs in a cavity drilled in
a tree.

Range: Breeds from southeastern Alaska and
British Columbia south to coastal
California. Winters in most of breeding
range except interior British Columbia.

This mainly coastal sapsucker has habits
similar to those of the Red-naped and
Yellow-bellied sapsuckers. It hybridizes
with the Red-naped in California and
British Columbia.

385, 386 Williamson's Sapsucker
Sphyrapicus thyroideus

Description: 9½" (24 cm). Male has *black head, breast,
and back,* white facial stripes, bright
red throat, and large white wing and
rump patches. *Lemon-yellow belly* is
bordered with black and white barred
flanks. Female very different, with
brown head, dark brown and white
zebra stripes above and on flanks, large
dark bib, and smaller, less brilliant
yellow area on belly.

Voice: A soft nasal *churrr,* descending in pitch.

Habitat: Ponderosa pine forests and open
coniferous forests; subalpine forests
in Southwest.

Nesting: 3–7 white eggs, usually in pine or fir
snags; may reuse a nesting tree but it
chisels a new hole each time.

Range: Breeds from southern British Columbia south to southern California, central Arizona, and central New Mexico. Winters in southern part of breeding range and in Southwest.

The distribution of this woodpecker, like that of many birds, is tied to a certain climatic belt. In southern areas the cool climates it likes occur at high elevations, whereas in northern latitudes such conditions occur closer to sea level.

374, 396 Ladder-backed Woodpecker
Picoides scalaris

Description: 7″ (18 cm). Barred black and white back; strong *facial pattern forms triangle on buffy-white cheek.* Male has red cap, female has black cap.
Voice: A sharp *pik,* similar to that of Downy Woodpecker; also a descending whinny.
Habitat: Arid areas with thickets and trees.
Nesting: 4 or 5 white eggs in a hole in a tree, cactus, pole, or post.
Range: Resident in southwestern United States from California, Nevada, Utah, Colorado, Oklahoma, and Texas south into tropics.

Within most of its range, the Ladder-back is the only small woodpecker so marked. The most numerous member of its family in Texas, it replaces the Downy Woodpecker in more arid areas. Familiar and trusting, it frequents ranches, yards in rural areas, and parks. It is closely related to Nuttall's Woodpecker of California.

380 Nuttall's Woodpecker
Picoides nuttallii

Description: 7–7½″ (18–19 cm). Similar to Ladder-backed Woodpecker, but with black

cheeks and wider black bars on back;
black and white areas more sharply
contrasting. Where its range overlaps
that of Ladder-backed, it can be
distinguished by its call.

Voice: A rolling call, *prreep;* a sharp *pit-it.*

Habitat: Canyon scrub oaks, oak woodlands, and
streamside growth.

Nesting: 3–6 white eggs in a hole excavated in a
thin dead branch of an oak or
cottonwood, or even a large, thick-
stemmed elderberry bush.

Range: Resident from northern California to
Baja California.

A small and retiring woodpecker,
Nuttall's is often hidden in foliage
and may be heard before it is seen. It
forages by gleaning the bark, sometimes
tapping and drilling, and occasionally
hawking for insects.

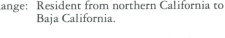

373, 395 Downy Woodpecker
Picoides pubescens

Description: 6″ (15 cm). A sparrow-sized, black
and white woodpecker. Small red patch
on nape in males. Similar to Hairy
Woodpecker, but smaller and with
short, stubby bill.

Voice: A quiet *pik.* Also a descending rattle.

Habitat: Woodlands, parks, and gardens.

Nesting: 4 or 5 white eggs in a hole in a tree.

Range: Resident from Alaska across Canada,
south throughout United States
except Southwest.

The Downy is a familiar bird in the
West, especially in winter, when many
move into the suburbs and feed on suet
at bird feeders. Observers can then learn
to recognize its call and its habit of
tapping on branches hardly thicker than
itself. As with other woodpeckers, the
male is larger than the female and
chisels deep into wood with its longer,
stronger bill, whereas the female pries

under the bark with her shorter bill. Thus a pair is able to share the food resources without competing with one another.

---

375 Hairy Woodpecker
Picoides villosus

Description: 9" (23 cm). A robin-sized woodpecker. Black and white, with *unspotted white back and long bill;* male has red head patch. Like all woodpeckers it has an undulating flight. See Downy Woodpecker.

Voice: A sharp, distinctive *peek,* louder than that of Downy Woodpecker; also a loud rattle on 1 pitch.

Habitat: Deciduous forest; more widespread in winter and on migration.

Nesting: 4 white eggs in a hole in a tree.

Range: Resident from Alaska and across Canada south throughout United States to Gulf of Mexico. Some northern birds migrate south for winter.

Most woodpeckers secure their food by hammering holes through bark and then extracting grubs with their extremely long, flexible tongues. They begin their work with a gentle tapping, which helps them detect the exact location of the food. When drumming to proclaim their territory, they select a dry limb and tap rapidly, building up to a loud drumming that is audible from far off and then fading away.

---

384 Strickland's Woodpecker
"Arizona Woodpecker"
Picoides stricklandi

Description: 7–8" (18–20 cm). An unstreaked, *brown-backed* woodpecker, with brown crown and brown ear patch on white face. Underparts spotted and barred

with brown. Male distinguished by
red nape.

Voice: Call is a sharp *peek!* or a rasping *jee-jee-jee.*
Habitat: Dry live-oak and pine-oak woodlands.
Nesting: 3 or 4 white eggs in a cavity in a dead
branch of a live tree.
Range: Resident in mountains of southeastern
Arizona and locally in southwestern
New Mexico. Also in Mexico.

Strickland's Woodpecker is a shy bird
whose habits are little known. Like
other woodpeckers it lays white eggs in
a cavity, without making a nest. Other
hole-nesters such as chickadees and
some flycatchers, which build nests
and lay patterned eggs, have probably
evolved the hole-breeding habit more
recently and may lose this trait.

382 White-headed Woodpecker
Picoides albolarvatus

Description: 9" (23 cm). Black overall with *white
head, throat,* and *wing patch.* Male has red
patch on nape; female lacks red patch.
Voice: Usually silent. A sharp *pee-dink* and a
more prolonged *pee-dee-dee-dink.*
Habitat: Ponderosa pine belts of the mountains;
also in subalpine belts of firs.
Nesting: 3–5 white eggs in a nest cavity in a
pine stub or snag, often close to the
ground.
Range: Resident from extreme south-central
British Columbia, northeastern
Washington, and Idaho, south to
southern California and western
Nevada. Some birds move down
mountain slopes in winter.

An inconspicuous bird, hard to find due
to its silent habits, the White-headed
Woodpecker rarely taps or drums,
vocalizing only around the nest. It feeds
by scaling bark off trees to reach the
insects underneath. Although its bold
black and white pattern is striking in

flight, it provides excellent camouflage when the bird perches in a shady forest.

388, 390 **Three-toed Woodpecker**
"Northern Three-toed Woodpecker"
Picoides tridactylus

Description: 8½" (22 cm). Starling-sized; similar to Black-backed woodpecker, but smaller; bill shorter; *back barred black and white.* Sexes differ as in that species.

Voice: A soft *pik,* similar to call of Downy Woodpecker.

Habitat: Coniferous forests in the boreal zone, especially where burned, logged, or swampy.

Nesting: 4 white eggs in a tree hole that is beveled on the lower side of the entrance to form a sort of doorstep for the birds.

Range: Resident in Alaska and east across Canada to extreme northern United States and south in West to mountains of Arizona and New Mexico.

In the southern portions of its range, the Three-toed Woodpecker is less numerous than the Black-backed, but its range extends farther south in the Rockies. It is also more sedentary, rarely moving far from its home range.

387, 389 **Black-backed Woodpecker**
"Black-backed Three-toed Woodpecker"
Picoides arcticus

Description: 9" (23 cm). A robin-sized woodpecker. *Solid black back,* barred flanks, white below. Male has *yellow crown;* female has solid *black crown.* See Three-toed Woodpecker.

Voice: A sharp, fast *kyik* and a scolding rattle.

Habitat: Coniferous forests in the boreal zone, especially where burned, logged, or swampy.

Nesting: 4 white eggs in a cavity excavated in a tree, often rather close to ground.

Range: Resident from Alaska east across Canada to the northernmost United States and south to the mountains of California, Wyoming, and South Dakota in West.

Dead conifers with large areas of peeled bark generally indicate the presence of this uncommon woodpecker. When alarmed, it quickly sidles to the far side of the tree and reappears cautiously. If frightened, the bird flies away, often calling sharply. Like the Three-toed Woodpecker, this species has only three toes on each foot.

391, 392, 393 **Northern Flicker**
including "Gilded Flicker,"
"Red-shafted Flicker," and
"Yellow-shafted Flicker"
Colaptes auratus

Description: 12″ (30 cm). A large brownish woodpecker. Brown back with dark bars and spots; *whitish or buff below with black spots; black crescent* on breast; *white rump,* visible in flight. Eastern birds ("Yellow-shafted Flickers") have *red patch on nape and yellow wing linings;* male has black mustache. Western birds ("Red-shafted Flickers") lack nape patch and have *salmon-pink wing linings;* males have red "mustache." Birds in the Southwest ("Gilded Flickers") have *yellow wing linings;* males have red mustache. All three forms interbreed where their ranges come together, and numerous confusing intermediates can be found.

Voice: A loud, repeated *flicker* or *wicka-wicka-wicka;* also a loud *kleeer.*

Habitat: Open country with trees; parks and large gardens.

Nesting: 6–8 white eggs in a tree cavity, utility pole, or birdhouse.

Range: Resident from Alaska east through Manitoba to Newfoundland and

south throughout United States. Northernmost birds are migratory.

Northern Flickers occur in three color forms: the "Red-shafted" in the West, the "Yellow-shafted" east of the Rocky Mountains, and the "Gilded," found in the Sonoran Desert of the Southwest. The ice ages separated the ancestral flickers, keeping them scattered in several refugia for thousands of years. Today those barriers are gone. The "Gilded" has become adapted to the desert, whereas the two northern populations inhabit the same type of woodland habitat, with only the treeless Great Plains keeping them somewhat apart. Flickers are important in the woodland community, providing cavities for many hole-nesting birds. They feed on ants and other ground insects and also, in winter, on berries.

378 Pileated Woodpecker
Dryocopus pileatus

Description: 17″ (43 cm). A crow-sized woodpecker. Black with white neck stripes, conspicuous white wing linings, and prominent *red crest*. Male has red "mustache," female has black.

Voice: A loud, flicker-like *cuk-cuk-cuk-cuk-cuk,* rising and then falling in pitch and volume.

Habitat: Mature forests and borders.

Nesting: 4 white eggs in a tree cavity.

Range: Resident across much of southern Canada, south in mountains of northwestern states and in East to Gulf Coast states.

With the probable extinction of the Ivory-billed Woodpecker (*Campephilus principalis*), this is now the largest woodpecker in North America. Its staple food consists of carpenter ants living in fallen timber, dead roots, and

stumps. The woodpecker excavates
fist-sized rectangular cavities, then uses
its enormously long, sticky tongue to
reach the ant burrows.

FAMILY TYRANNIDAE
Tyrant Flycatchers

416 species: A strictly American family
with the great majority of its species in
South America. No fewer than 35
species breed in North America. These
large-headed birds characteristically sit
on wires and exposed branches waiting
for flying insect prey. The flycatchers
then dart out, grab the insect, and
usually return to the very same spot
before eating the insect. Other species
glean foliage the way warblers or vireos
do, and still others, such as the becards,
are fruit eaters. Species in the genera
Myiarchus and *Empidonax* look much
alike and are best identified by voice.
With few exceptions, the sexes are alike
in all members of the family.

---

631   **Northern Beardless-Tyrannulet
"Beardless Flycatcher"**
Camptostoma imberbe

Description: 4″ (10 cm). A nondescript, dull-colored
bird with a tiny bill. Olive-gray above
with pale buff wing bars; whitish below
with dusky throat and breast.

Voice: A thin *tee-tee-tee-tee-tee,* loudest in the
middle. Also 3 long notes followed
by a trill.

Habitat: Low thorn scrub, especially mesquite
thickets and woodland borders.

Nesting: 2 or 3 brown-speckled white eggs in
a globular nest of plant fibers with a
side entrance.

Range: Breeds in southeastern Arizona and
southernmost Texas. Many birds migrate
to Mexico for the winter. Also in tropics.

This very small bird acts more like a vireo or a Verdin than a typical flycatcher; it moves through the foliage gleaning insects rather than sallying out to capture flying insects. Because it is small, nondescript, and inhabits thickets, it is most often identified by its distinctive calls.

577 Olive-sided Flycatcher
Contopus borealis

Description: 7½" (19 cm). A large-billed and heavy-headed bird, deep olive-brown, with dark sides of breast and flanks separated by *white patch down center of breast.* White feather tufts protrude from lower back at base of tail; tail broad and prominently notched. See Greater Pewee.

Voice: Song a distinctive and emphatic *quick-three-beers;* call a loud *pip-pip-pip.*

Habitat: Boreal spruce and fir forests, usually near openings, burns, ponds, and bogs.

Nesting: 3 brown-spotted buff eggs in a twig nest lined with lichens, mosses, and grasses, placed near the end of a branch among the foliage well up in an evergreen tree.

Range: Breeds in Alaska, east across Canada to northern New England, and south to mountains of California, Arizona, and New Mexico, and in northern New York and New England. Winters in tropics.

This flycatcher almost always perches on dead branches in an exposed position at or very near the tops of the tallest trees. Analysis of stomach contents of these birds has shown that everything it eats is winged; it takes no caterpillars, spiders, or other larvae.

640 Greater Pewee
"Coues' Flycatcher"
Contopus pertinax

Description: 7–7¾" (18–20 cm). *Large-headed flycatcher* with slight crest. Olive-brown above, slightly lighter below. Small light gray throat patch, yellow lower mandible, and indistinct wing bars. Olive-sided Flycatcher is similar, but has olive-brown flanks, giving it a "vested" appearance. Wood-pewees are smaller and lack slight crest.

Voice: Song is a plaintive *Jo-sé-Ma-ri-a.* Call note a repeated *pwit.*

Habitat: Highland coniferous forests, especially pine and pine-oak.

Nesting: 3 or 4 dull-white, spotted eggs in a compact, woven, grass-lined cup nest set high in the prong of a horizontal limb, secured with cobwebs and camouflaged outside.

Range: Breeds from central Arizona and southwestern New Mexico southward. Winters mainly south of U.S.–Mexico border.

Like other flycatchers, Greater Pewees sit upright on prominent posts, watching for insects. When they spot prey, they dart out, catch it in flight, and return in an arc-shaped flight to the same or a nearby perch. This species has a loud and distinctive call that is often heard on the sound tracks of Westerns.

579 Western Wood-Pewee
Contopus sordidulus

Description: 6½" (17 cm). A sparrow-sized flycatcher, dull olive-gray above, slightly paler below, with 2 whitish wing bars. Eastern Wood-Pewee (*Contopus virens*) of eastern United States extremely similar, but generally less dark below; the two species are best distinguished by voice. *Empidonax* flycatchers are smaller and usually have noticeable eye ring.

Voice: A harsh nasal *pee-eeer,* very different from the sweet *peee-ah weee* of the Eastern Wood-Pewee.

Habitat: Open woodland and woodland edges; orchards.

Nesting: 3 or 4 white eggs, spotted with brown, in a shallow saucer of grass fastened to a horizontal branch.

Range: Breeds from eastern Alaska, Mackenzie, and Manitoba south through western United States. Winters in tropics.

This species is generally found in more open, park-like woodlands than the Eastern Wood-Pewee and is thus more readily observed. In a few areas along the western edge of the Great Plains the two pewees occur together without interbreeding—conclusive evidence that despite their great similarity, they are distinct species.

573 Alder Flycatcher
"Traill's Flycatcher"
Empidonax alnorum

Description: 5–6″ (13–15 cm). Slightly smaller than a House Sparrow. Dull gray-green above, whitish below, with 2 dull white wing bars and narrow white eye ring (often not noticeable). Indistinguishable in appearance from Willow Flycatcher, and best identified by voice, breeding habitat, and nest.

Voice: A burry *fee-bee-o,* rather different from the wheezy *fitz-bew* of the Willow Flycatcher.

Habitat: Alder swamps, streamside and lakeside thickets, and second-growth forests.

Nesting: 3 or 4 white eggs, finely speckled with brown, in a loose cup of grass with little or no plant down, placed in a low bush or sapling.

Range: Breeds from Alaska east through

Manitoba to Newfoundland and south to British Columbia, Great Lakes region, and southern New England. Winters in tropics.

These birds hunt in the airspace below the canopy of tall alders in swamps or along creeks. They sit erect on a twig, then dart out after flying insects. The Alder Flycatcher came to be considered distinct from the Willow when studies revealed that the song patterns and breeding habits of these species differed. In the fall, when they do not sing, they are indistinguishable and are called by the former name of both species, "Traill's Flycatcher."

569   Willow Flycatcher
"Traill's Flycatcher"
Empidonax traillii

Description: 6" (15 cm). Distinguishable from Alder Flycatcher only by voice, breeding habitat, and nest. Other western *Empidonax* flycatchers have more conspicuous eye ring or are grayer above.

Voice: A wheezy *fitz-bew* or *pit-speer.* The song of the Alder Flycatcher is a burry *fee-bee-o,* descending more abruptly in pitch.

Habitat: Swampy thickets, upland pastures, and old abandoned orchards; Alder Flycatchers occur along wooded lakeshores and streams.

Nesting: 3 or 4 creamy-white eggs, with fine brown speckling, in a neat, compact cup of plant down and fibers placed in a low bush or sapling.

Range: Breeds from southern British Columbia, Alberta, North Dakota, New York, and Maine south to central California, Nevada, Southwest, Arkansas, and Virginia. Winters in tropics.

The species of the genus *Empidonax* are so similar in appearance that only an expert can tell them apart by sight alone. The Alder and Willow were once considered a single species ("Traill's Flycatcher"). During the breeding season each species lives in its characteristic habitat, but during migration birders may encounter birds of different species in a habitat in which they are not usually found. Thus, the only sure way to identify breeding males is by their voices, which are different in each species. In other seasons when males do not sing, all that can readily be told is that they are *Empidonax* flycatchers.

580 Least Flycatcher
Empidonax minimus

Description: 5¼" (13 cm). Dull olive-gray above, whitish below, with 2 whitish wing bars and conspicuous white eye ring. Distinguished by voice and breeding habitat.

Voice: Dry, insect-like *che-bec,* snapped out and accented on the second syllable, and uttered incessantly through the hottest days of summer.

Habitat: Widely distributed in open country, nesting in shade trees and orchards in villages and city parks, and along rural roadsides and woodland borders.

Nesting: 4 creamy-white eggs in a finely woven, cup-shaped nest made of vegetable fibers and lined with grass and feathers, firmly wedged in the fork or crotch of a tree.

Range: Breeds from southern Yukon east to central Quebec and Maritime Provinces, and south to Wyoming, Indiana, and New Jersey, and south in mountains to North Carolina. Winters in tropics.

Perhaps the most familiar member of the difficult-to-identify *Empidonax* group, the Least Flycatcher is a characteristic bird of large shade trees; its presence is most easily detected by its call. An incubating bird is surprisingly tame and will often allow itself to be touched or even lifted off the nest.

575   Hammond's Flycatcher
Empidonax hammondii

Description: 5–5½" (13–14 cm). *Olive-gray above;* light throat, gray breast, pale yellow belly. Conspicuous white eye ring and white wing bars. Throat not as white as Alder's, breast darker and bill narrower and shorter than Dusky's, but field identification is very difficult. *Flicks wings and tail more vigorously than other similar species.*

Voice: Song is *seweep-tsurp-seep,* the last part rising. Calls are a high *peep* (like the note of a Pygmy Nuthatch) and a soft *wit.*

Habitat: Mature coniferous forests at high altitudes.

Nesting: 3 or 4 white eggs, occasionally spotted, in a well-built cup nest saddled on a branch 15–60′ (4.5–18 m) high in a coniferous tree.

Range: Breeds from eastern Alaska south to northern California and northern New Mexico. Winters in tropics, rarely in Arizona.

Since climatic conditions at sea level in the North are similar to those at higher elevations farther south, this flycatcher is able to nest in boreal forest on the low plains of Alaska as well as in subalpine forest, at around 10,000 feet (3,050 meters), in the southern Rocky Mountains.

566   Dusky Flycatcher
Empidonax oberholseri

Description: 5¼–6" (13–15 cm). Back *gray with slight olive tinge;* breast buffy, with light throat; belly very pale yellow. Narrow white eye ring and white wing bars; long tail.

Voice: Song similar to that of Hammond's Flycatcher: a staccato series of chirps, transcribed as *se-lip, churp, treep.* Call is a sharp *whit.*

Habitat: Woodlands containing tall trees and tall undergrowth, mountain chaparral, and open, brushy coniferous forests.

Nesting: 3–5 white eggs in a neat twiggy cup set low in the crotch of a shrub or small tree.

Range: Breeds from British Columbia and western South Dakota south to southern California, central Arizona, and northern New Mexico. Winters south of U.S.–Mexico border, rarely in southern California.

Hammond's and Dusky flycatchers, very similar in appearance and voice, are closely related and difficult to distinguish. The populations were probably separated when the ice fields of the North advanced and the forests were divided into western and eastern refuges. When the flycatchers returned to the newly forested northern half of the continent, each had developed differing habitat needs, allowing them to coexist without competing for nesting sites and food. The Dusky usually nests in the lower ranges of the forest, preferring chaparral; the Hammond's chooses higher levels of tall fir trees.

571 Gray Flycatcher
Empidonax wrightii

Description: 5½″ (14 cm). Similar to other *Empidonax* flycatchers, but *gray above,* white below. *Lower mandible flesh-colored.* Eye ring not prominent. Slowly bobs its tail.

Voice: Song is in 2 parts, rising in tone: *chiwip* (or *chi-bit*) *cheep.* Call is a soft *whit.*

Habitat: Sagebrush and piñon-juniper woodlands.

Nesting: 3 or 4 white eggs in a grass-woven cup nest placed low in sagebrush or a small tree.

Range: Breeds from southern Washington and southwestern Wyoming south to eastern California, central Arizona, and central New Mexico, Winters in southern California and southern Arizona.

This flycatcher lacks the olive and yellow tinges on the back and underparts that mark the other *Empidonax* flycatchers. Its color blends with the blue-gray hues of sagebrush and helps conceal it from predators.

568   Pacific-slope Flycatcher
"Western Flycatcher"
Empidonax difficilis

Description: 5½–6″ (14–15 cm). Olive-brown above, with *yellow throat* and belly separated by dusky olive breast; elongated white eye ring and light wing bars. Fall birds may be duller. Bill long and wide, lower mandible *bright yellow.* See Cordilleran Flycatcher.

Voice: Quite distinct, rising *pseet-ptsick-seet.* First part alone is often used as a call, or is repeated on a drawn-out, almost sibilant high pitch. Second part is rapid and louder. Call note a sharp *pit-peet.*

Habitat: Moist, shaded coniferous or mixed forests; canyons.

Nesting: 3 or 4 white eggs, spotted with brown, in a moss-lined cup nest of small twigs and rootlets built against a tree trunk where the bark has split, among the roots of a wind-felled tree, in a bank, or under the eaves of a forest cabin.

Range: Breeds from Alaska south along coast to Baja California. Winters south of U.S.–Mexico border.

The Pacific-slope Flycatcher has only recently been recognized as a species

distinct from the Cordilleran. It forages in the shade between the tangled ground cover of huckleberry and salmonberry and the low branches of towering Douglas firs, cedars, or redwoods. It is the most frequently observed *Empidonax* in California.

572 Cordilleran Flycatcher
"Western Flycatcher"
Empidonax occidentalis

Description: 5½–6″ (14–15 cm). Identical in appearance to Pacific-slope Flycatcher; distinguishable only by voice and range.

Voice: Song a thin, high *whee-seet.*

Habitat: Mountain forests and wooded canyons.

Nesting: 3 or 4 white eggs, spotted with brown, in a moss-lined cup nest of small twigs and rootlets. Nest similar to that of Pacific-slope Flycatcher.

Range: Breeds from Alberta south through Nevada and Rocky Mountains to southeastern Arizona, southern New Mexico, and western Texas. Winters south of U.S.–Mexico border.

The Cordilleran Flycatcher is the common, yellow-bellied *Empidonax* flycatcher in the mountains of the western interior. Like the Pacific-slope Flycatcher of the West Coast, it has a large, tear-shaped eye ring.

574 Buff-breasted Flycatcher
Empidonax fulvifrons

Description: 4½–5″ (11–13 cm). Olive above with *rich buffy underparts, lighter on throat and belly;* white eye ring and wing bars.

Voice: Song is a quick *chicky-whew.* Call is a dull *pit.*

Habitat: Open canyon growth and pine-oak forests.

Nesting: 3 or 4 creamy-white eggs in a well-camouflaged nest saddled at the base of a horizontal branch.

Range: Breeds locally in southeastern Arizona. Winters in Mexico.

This bird, the easiest *Empidonax* to identify, characteristically hunts from a low perch, often launching its pursuit from the top of a weed. However, it can also be seen hovering over a pine branch, picking insects from among the needles.

591   Black Phoebe
Sayornis nigricans

Description: 6–7″ (15–18 cm). *Slate-black except for white belly, undertail coverts, and outer tail feathers.* Its *tail-wagging,* erect posture, and insectivorous feeding habits are helpful in field identification.

Voice: Song is a thin, buzzy *pi-tsee,* usually repeated. Call is a sharp, down-slurred *chip.*

Habitat: Shady areas near water, streams, pond and lake banks; in winter, city parks, open chaparral.

Nesting: 3–6 white eggs, with a few faint speckles, in a mud, moss, and grass nest lined with soft material, often feathers or cow hair, built under a bridge, on a sheltered ledge, in a crevice in an old building, or among hanging roots near the top of an embankment close to water.

Range: Resident from northern California south and east to western Texas. Also in tropics.

Black Phoebes are territorial and solitary nesters, often remaining year-round in an established territory. The wanderers found in atypical winter habitats (chaparral or grassland) are thought to be first-year, nonbreeding birds.

592 Eastern Phoebe
Sayornis phoebe

Description: 7″ (18 cm). Dull olive green without an eye ring or wing bars. *Wags its tail.*

Voice: Clear *phoe-be,* repeated many times; the second syllable is alternately higher or lower than the first. Call note a distinctive, short *chip.*

Habitat: Open woodlands near streams; cliffs, bridges, and buildings with ledges.

Nesting: 4 or 5 white eggs in a mud-and-grass nest lined with moss and hair and attached to a ledge of a building, bridge, cliff, or quarry, or among roots of a fallen tree.

Range: Breeds in Canada and United States east of Rockies, south to northern edge of Gulf states. Winters from Virginia, Gulf Coast, and Florida southward.

The Eastern Phoebe arrives early in spring and departs late in fall, sometimes even staying through the winter in the northern states. In the absence of insects, its winter food is berries. Extraordinarily tame at the nest, the Eastern Phoebe was probably the first bird ever banded: Audubon marked one with a silver wire on the leg in 1840 and recorded its return the following year.

590 Say's Phoebe
Sayornis saya

Description: 7–8″ (18–20 cm). Dusky head, breast, and back, with darker wings and *black tail. Light rust-colored belly and undertail coverts.*

Voice: A mellow, whistled *pee-ur* with a plaintive quality.

Habitat: Plains, sparsely vegetated countryside, dry sunny locations, often near ranch houses, barns, and other buildings.

Nesting: 4 or 5 white eggs in a nest of grass and wool in a sheltered, elevated, dry site on a ledge, rock wall, or building.

Range: Breeds from central Alaska, Yukon, and northern Mackenzie south through western mountains to Mexico; not present west of the Cascades and Sierra Nevada except locally in south-central California and western Oregon. Winters in California and Southwest southward.

Although primarily insect eaters (as are all flycatchers), Say's Phoebes will eat other foods, such as berries, during long spells of cold, inclement weather, when insects are unavailable.

521, 570   Vermilion Flycatcher
Pyrocephalus rubinus

Description: 6" (15 cm). Male has *brilliant scarlet crown and underparts,* with dark brown back, wings, and tail; female similar to male above but *white below with dark streaks.* Belly of females and immatures varies from pink to yellow to white.

Voice: Call is *peet-peet* or *peet-a-weet.* Also has a soft, tinkling flight song.

Habitat: Trees and shrubs along rivers and roadsides.

Nesting: 3 creamy-white eggs, with dark brown spots, in a well-made nest of fibers, feathers, and spider web lined with bits of lichen, placed on a horizontal branch.

Range: Breeds from southeastern California east to western Texas and south into tropics. Winters in southern part of breeding range, but wanders as far east as Gulf Coast.

Despite its brilliant color, the Vermilion Flycatcher is hard to detect in cottonwoods, willows, or mesquite, since it hunts from the highest canopy and generally remains well concealed. In sparsely vegetated areas, however, it may descend to the ground after insect prey. The male defends his territory with a prominent aerial display; he flies up singing, his red underparts and cap contrasting with the blue sky. When trying to attract a female he sings even at night.

581 Dusky-capped Flycatcher
"Olivaceous Flycatcher"
Myiarchus tuberculifer

Description: 6½–7″ (17–18 cm). A small *Myiarchus* flycatcher, with much brown, but *no rufous on tail*. Pale olive-brown above, *grayish throat* and breast, pale yellow belly.

Voice: A plaintive *pee-ur,* rising and then falling in pitch, followed by a soft *huit.* Call note a soft *huit.*

Habitat: Scrub oak thickets and canyon growth.

Nesting: 4 or 5 creamy-white, finely marked eggs in a tree cavity.

Range: Breeds in southeastern Arizona and southwestern New Mexico. Winters south of U.S.–Mexico border. Also in tropics.

All flycatchers in the genus *Myiarchus* are similar in appearance. They may be identified by their habitats and, where habitats overlap, by voice. Small groups of Dusky-capped Flycatchers have been observed "sunning" face down, with wings and tails spread wide, on the steep, bare slope of an arroyo, or dry wash. Several other birds, including Common Ground-Doves, also indulge in this activity, which is not yet understood.

578 Ash-throated Flycatcher
Myiarchus cinerascens

Description: 8″ (20 cm). Dull olive above, yellowish below. Like Brown-crested Flycatcher (and Great Crested, *Myiarchus crinitus,* of the East), but smaller and less colorful; back browner, throat and breast grayish white.

Voice: *Purreeeer,* similar to call of Brown-crested Flycatcher but softer. Also a soft *ka-brick.*

Habitat: Deserts with cactus and mesquite thickets; also dry woods.

Nesting: 4 or 5 brown-spotted, creamy-white eggs in a nest lined with vegetable fibers in a tree or a cactus hole.

Range: Breeds from Washington and Wyoming south to southwestern United States, east to Texas. Rare in fall on Atlantic Coast. Winters in southern California and Arizona southward.

The Ash-throated Flycatcher lives in the hottest, driest parts of the West, but is also found farther north in dry, shady, open woodlands. These birds launch their pursuit of insects from the dead upper branches of mature trees at the edges of woods. Trunk rot in these trees creates cavities useful as nesting sites. Open nests would be too exposed in the sparse foliage of this dry habitat, transitional between woodland and open range. Although this flycatcher has become a hole-breeder, it still builds a nest and has streaked, camouflaged eggs like its open-nesting ancestors.

---

576 **Brown-crested Flycatcher**
"Wied's Crested Flycatcher"
Myiarchus tyrannulus

Description: 9½" (24 cm). A large flycatcher, olive above and yellow below, with cinnamon in wings and tail. Larger size, *black bill,* and brighter sulphur-yellow belly distinguish it from Ash-throated Flycatcher.

Voice: A burry *purreeeer,* a sharp *wit!* or *way-burg,*

Habitat: Arid lands in areas with cacti or large trees.

Nesting: 3–5 brown-spotted, creamy-white eggs in a nest lined with feathers, fibers, and hairs, placed in a tree cavity, in cacti, or on fence posts.

Range: Breeds from southern California,

567 Sulphur-bellied Flycatcher
Myiodynastes luteiventris

Description: 7½–8½" (19–22 cm). A large, heavily streaked flycatcher. Upperparts buff-brown with brown streaks; *underparts yellow with blackish streaks. Dark line across eye; dark "mustache." Tail and rump rufous.*

Voice: Loud, shrill *peet-chee* calls, sounding like squeaking wagon wheels, uttered by single bird or pair in duet. Male has soft *tre-le-re-re* song.

Habitat: Wooded canyons; prefers sycamores.

Nesting: 3–5 white or buff eggs, with spots and blotches, in a nest in a tree hole.

Range: Breeds from southeastern Arizona southward. Winters in tropics.

These loud, vividly marked birds are easily detected when they sally forth from treetop perches in pursuit of flying prey, but when sitting still they are well camouflaged. Like the closely related kingbirds, they have a brightly colored crest, but it is hidden among crown feathers.

Tyrannus vociferans

Description: 8–9″ (20–23 cm). Similar to Western Kingbird but darker, *back more olive-gray, black tail lightly white-tipped* but lacking white margins. Darker gray breast makes white throat patch appear smaller and more clearly defined than Western Kingbird's.

Voice: A loud *chi-beer!* and a rapid *chi-beer, ch-beer-beer-beer-r-r.*

Habitat: Savannas, rangelands, piñon-juniper woodlands.

Nesting: 3–5 white, spotted eggs in a bulky nest lined with twigs, grass, or animal hair, placed on a horizontal limb, well hidden.

Range: Breeds in southern California and southern Nevada, central Arizona, a... southern Texas southward. Winters mainly south of U.S.–Mexico border, but a few winter in southern Florida.

Biologists have found that when closely related similar species, like the Brown-crested, Ash-throated, and Dusky-capped flycatchers, occur together, ecological specializations such as differences in size, feeding habits, and vocalizations allow the species to coexist without competing.

from Montana south to southern Utah and Southwest. Winters in southern California.

Cassin's Kingbird is often found high on a tree, where it sits more quietly than a Western Kingbird.

561 Thick-billed Kingbird
Tyrannus crassirostris

Description: 9" (23 cm). *Brownish above,* head darker brown; tail *uniformly gray-brown. Throat and breast whitish,* pale yellow tinge on lower belly. Large thick bill and stocky neck give it a "bull-headed" appearance.
Voice: Loud *kiterreer* and high-pitched *bur-ree.*
Habitat: Streamside growth, sycamore canyons.
Nesting: 3 or 4 white eggs, spotted with brown, in a cup of twigs and weed stems in a sycamore or cottonwood.
Range: Breeds extremely locally in southeastern Arizona and adjacent New Mexico. Winters south of U.S.–Mexico border.

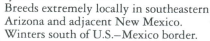

The Thick-billed Kingbird is one of the Mexican species that regularly cross the border and make southeastern Arizona so fascinating for birders. These kingbirds perch high in trees and prey on flying insects. They react to predators with loud cries, calls, and attacks.

560 Western Kingbird
Tyrannus verticalis

Description: 8–9" (20–23 cm). *Olive-brown above, yellow below;* gray head, lighter grayish throat and upper breast. Dusky wings and *blackish tail with white margins.* Red crown feathers not normally visible.
Voice: A loud, sharp *kit.* Various chattering notes.
Habitat: Open country; ranches, roadsides, streams, and ponds with trees.

Nesting: 4 creamy-white eggs in a stick nest lined with plant fibers and placed in a tree or bush.

Range: Breeds throughout West, from southern Canada south to Mexico, east to Great Plains. Regular fall migrant on Atlantic Coast. Winters in tropics.

The Western Kingbird is found on almost every ranch in the West, where alfalfa and livestock pastures provide many of the flying insects that make up the bulk of its diet. After the young fledge it is not uncommon to see half a dozen or more kingbirds sally from the dry upper branches of shade trees to capture insects. When it has a nest full of young to defend, the Western Kingbird will attack crows and other larger birds.

632 Eastern Kingbird
Tyrannus tyrannus

Description: 8–9″ (20–23 cm). Blackish head, blue-black mantle and wings; black tail *with white terminal band;* white below. Red feathers in middle of crown usually concealed. Long crown feathers and upright posture give it a distinctive silhouette.

Voice: A sharp *dzee* or *dzeet.* Also a series of harsh, rapid calls: *kit* and *kitter.*

Habitat: Savannas, rangelands, forest edges, riverside groves, and even city parks and roadsides.

Nesting: 3–5 spotted white eggs in a large bulky nest consisting of heaps of twigs, straw, and twine lined with hair and rootlets; built on horizontal limb of a tree, often near water.

Range: Breeds from British Columbia across interior Canada to Maritime Provinces and south to northern California, central Texas, Gulf Coast, and Florida. Winters in tropics.

The Eastern Kingbird perches on treetops, fences, and utility poles. When another bird flies into its territory—even one much larger than itself—it attacks fiercely, uttering a piercing cry. When one of a pair starts the battle, the other usually joins in. Its aggressive behavior has earned this bird its common name.

655 Scissor-tailed Flycatcher
Tyrannus forficatus

Description: 14" (36 cm). Adult has *bright salmon-pink sides and belly;* pale grayish-white head, upper back, and breast. More than half its length is the very *long and deeply forked black and white tail.* Young birds similar, but have shorter tail and lack bright pink on sides and belly.

Voice: A harsh *kee-kee-kee-kee.* Also chattering notes like those of Eastern Kingbird.

Habitat: Open country along roadsides and on ranches with scattered trees and bushes; also fence wires and posts.

Nesting: 5 creamy, brown-spotted eggs in a bulky stick nest lined with soft fibrous material and placed in an isolated tree.

Range: Breeds from eastern Colorado and Nebraska south to Texas and western Louisiana. Winters south of U.S.–Mexico border; a few in southern Florida.

The Scissor-tail is often seen perching on a telephone wire with its extraordinarily long tail held out in a horizontal position. Like a kingbird, it erects its crest, emits harsh cries, and fiercely attacks hawks, crows, or other large birds that invade its nest area.

595 **Rose-throated Becard**
Pachyramphus aglaiae

Description: 6½″ (17 cm). Sparrow-sized. Male gray above, with black cap and pale rose-red throat; whitish below. Female brown, paler below, with dusky grayish cap.

Voice: A high-pitched whistle, *seeeeooo;* various chattering notes.

Habitat: Thick woodlands along streams and wooded canyons.

Nesting: 4 or 5 white eggs, spotted with brown, in a chamber in a globular nest of grass and plant fibers suspended from the tip of a drooping branch.

Range: Breeds from southeastern Arizona and Rio Grande Valley of Texas southward. Winters south of U.S.–Mexico border.

This quiet, unobtrusive bird spends most of its time foraging in tall trees and is therefore difficult to find. It is adept at catching flying insects like its relatives the flycatchers and also feeds on berries. The northern limit of its range is just within our borders, but it is common nowhere in our area.

FAMILY ALAUDIDAE
Larks

91 species: This almost exclusively Old World family is represented in America by one native species, the Horned Lark, and by the Eurasian Skylark, introduced in British Columbia. Birds of open country, larks feed on seeds and small insects and nest on the ground. The Horned Lark is an exceedingly early breeder, laying its eggs in late winter, even with patches of snow on the ground.

501 Eurasian Skylark
Alauda arvensis

Description: 7–7½" (18–19 cm). *Light earth-brown above,* with heavy, dark streaking; buff below, with lighter streaking. Outer tail feathers and belly white. Elongated crown feathers sometimes raised in small rounded crest.

Voice: Utters a beautiful, trilling song high in the sky that may last for several minutes. Calls *trly* or *prrit.* Also mimics other birds.

Habitat: Grasslands and fields.

Nesting: 3 or 4 brown-spotted whitish eggs in a grass nest in a ground scrape.

Range: Native to Eurasia, northern Africa. Introduced to southern Vancouver Island in British Columbia and San Juan Islands of Washington.

The dense rain-forest habitat of much of the Northwest prevents the Eurasian Skylark from spreading far from Vancouver Island, where a few pairs were introduced early in this century; it has colonized only the grassy slopes of the neighboring San Juan Islands. This bird's most notable feature is its clear, trilling, often Canary-like song. Rising in arcs ever higher until almost out of sight, the songster flutters and sings continuously for three or four minutes, then folds his wings and falls like a stone toward the center of his territory.

495 Horned Lark
Eremophila alpestris

Description: 7–8" (18–20 cm). Larger than a sparrow. Brown, with *black stripe below eye and white or yellowish stripe above, black crescent on breast, and black "horns"* (not always seen). Walks rather than hops. In flight, tail is black with white edges. Similar-looking pipits have brown tails and lack face pattern.

Voice: A soft *ti-ti.* Song delivered in flight is a high-pitched series of tinkling notes.

Habitat: Plains, fields, airports, and beaches.

Nesting: 3–5 brown-spotted gray eggs in a hollow in the ground lined with fine grass.

Range: Breeds in Alaska and Canadian Arctic, coastal Canada, and south throughout all of United States except Southeast. Winters from southern Canada southward. Also in Old World.

The Horned Lark, which walks or runs instead of hopping, moves in an erratic pattern when feeding. On its breeding territory and when in flocks during winter, it feeds on seeds and ground insects. This bird is philopatric, or faithful to its birthplace, where it returns after every migration. Consequently, each local population adapts to the color of its habitat; 15 distinct subspecies have been described in the West.

FAMILY HIRUNDINIDAE
Swallows and Martins

89 species: Worldwide. Eight species breed in North America. Swallows have long pointed wings and are expert flyers and, like swifts, are aerial feeders. Their bills and legs are exceedingly short. Many species use man-made structures, such as buildings, bridges, and culverts, as sites for their nests. They commonly perch on wires. In autumn, large flocks of swallows may be seen on their southward journey.

362 Purple Martin
Progne subis

Description: 7–8½″ (18–22 cm). Our largest swallow. Adult male dark steel-blue. Female and immature male duller above, pale gray below. Overhead, similar in shape to European Starling, but flight more buoyant and gliding.

Voice: Liquid gurgling warble. Also a penetrating *tee-tee-tee.*

Habitat: Open woodlands, residential areas, and agricultural land.

Nesting: 4 or 5 white eggs in a mass of grass and other plant material placed in a cavity—sometimes a hole in a tree or a martin house with many separate compartments, where the birds nest in a colony.

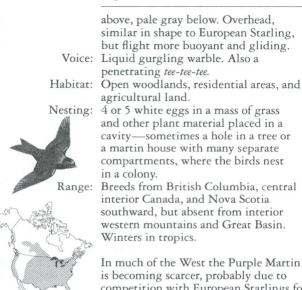

Range: Breeds from British Columbia, central interior Canada, and Nova Scotia southward, but absent from interior western mountains and Great Basin. Winters in tropics.

In much of the West the Purple Martin is becoming scarcer, probably due to competition with European Starlings for nest sites. Unlike martins in the East, it tends not to occupy martin houses placed in gardens, preferring the open countryside or downtown areas.

365 Tree Swallow
Tachycineta bicolor

Description: 5–6¼" (13–16 cm). Sparrow-sized. Metallic blue or blue-green above and clear white below. Young birds are dull brown above but may be distinguished from Bank and Northern Rough-winged swallows by their clearer white underparts. See Violet-green Swallow.

Voice: Cheerful series of liquid twitters.

Habitat: Lakeshores, flooded meadows, marshes, and streams.

Nesting: 4–6 white eggs in a feather-lined cup of grass placed in a hole in a tree or in a nest box.

Range: Breeds from Alaska east through northern Manitoba to Newfoundland and south to California, Colorado, Nebraska, and Maryland. Winters north

to southern California, Gulf Coast, and Carolinas; occasionally farther.

Hole-nesters such as the Tree Swallow often face a housing shortage and must fight to get into, or keep, woodpecker holes or other sought-after nest sites. Man-made breeding boxes may help increase the numbers of these birds. The Tree Swallow almost invariably nests in the immediate vicinity of water.

363   Violet-green Swallow
Tachycineta thalassina

Description: 5–5½″ (13–14 cm). Dark, metallic, *bronze-green* upperparts; iridescent violet rump and tail, the latter slightly forked; *white underparts. White cheek* extending above eye and white on sides of rump distinguish it from Tree Swallow.

Voice: A high *dee-chip* given in flight. Also a series of varying *tweet* notes.

Habitat: Breeds in forests, wooded foothills, mountains, suburban areas.

Nesting: 4 or 5 white eggs in a grass-and-feather nest in a woodpecker hole, a natural cavity, under the eaves of a building, or in a nest box.

Range: Breeds from Alaska east to South Dakota, south to southern California and Texas. Winters mainly south of U.S.–Mexico border, but a few winter in southern California.

Like many other swallows, the Violet-green lives in colonies, basically because of its feeding needs. Where one finds food there is usually enough for all, and when feeding communally these birds can more readily detect and defend themselves from hawks.

367 Northern Rough-winged Swallow
Stelgidopteryx serripennis

Description: 5–5¾" (13–15 cm). Pale brown above,
white below, with *dingy brown throat.*
Bank Swallow is similar, but smaller,
and has white throat and brown
breast band.

Voice: A low, unmusical *br-r-ret,* more drawn
out than the call of the Bank Swallow
and often doubled.

Habitat: Riverbanks. Prefers drier sites than the
Bank Swallow.

Nesting: 4–8 white eggs in a burrow or cavity;
will utilize ready-made cavities in
bridges, culverts, or other streamside
masonry. Not highly colonial; often
nests singly.

Range: Breeds from southeastern Alaska and
southern Canada southward throughout
United States. Winters north to
southern California, Gulf Coast, and
southern Florida.

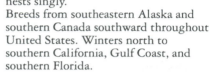

The name "Rough-winged" refers to
tiny hooklets on the outer vane (flat
part of a feather) near the end of the
shaft of the outer primary feathers. The
function of these hooks, visible only
under a magnifying glass and found also
in an unrelated group of African
swallows, is unknown.

369 Bank Swallow
Riparia riparia

Description: 4¾–5½" (12–14 cm). Sparrow-sized;
our smallest swallow. Brown above, dull
white below; *breast crossed by distinct
brown band;* tail notched. Northern
Rough-winged Swallow is warmer
brown, with dusky throat and without
brown breast band.

Voice: Sharp, unmusical *pret* or *trit-trit.*

Habitat: Banks of rivers, creeks, and lakes;
seashores.

Nesting: 4–6 white eggs in a grass and feather

nest in a chamber at the end of a deep tunnel, which it digs near the top of a steep bank. Since it breeds in large colonies, nesting banks may sometimes appear riddled with holes.

Range: Breeds from Alaska across northern Canada south to California, Texas, and Virginia. Winters in tropics. Also in Old World.

The Bank Swallow is a sporadic breeder in the West, perhaps because the soft earth that it needs for nesting is scarce. Since it also forages near the nesting colony, the bank must be near a suitable feeding area.

---

368   Cliff Swallow
Hirundo pyrrhonota

Description: 5–6″ (13–15 cm). Sparrow-sized. A stocky, square-tailed swallow with *pale buff rump.* Upperparts dull steel-blue; underparts buff-white; throat dark chestnut; forehead white. Southwestern birds have chestnut foreheads. Cave Swallow of Texas and Southwest is similar but smaller, with darker rump and pale buff throat.

Voice: Constant squeaky chattering and twittering.

Habitat: Open country near buildings or cliffs; lakeshores and marshes on migration.

Nesting: 4–6 white eggs in a gourd-shaped structure of mud lined with feathers and placed on a sheltered cliff face or under eaves. Nests in colonies.

Range: Breeds from Alaska, Ontario, and Nova Scotia southward through most of United States except Southeast. Winters in tropics.

Cliff Swallows feed on small swarming insects, whose appearance depends on sunny, dry days. In California they often return in early spring to ancestral colonial breeding sites. If it turns

chilly, however, they will abandon
the area until weather and feeding
patterns are more favorable, and
return "on schedule" for their publicized
arrival on March 19 at Mission San
Juan Capistrano.

---

366 Cave Swallow
Hirundo fulva

Description: 5½" (14 cm). A stocky swallow with a
square tail, steel-blue upperparts, *buff
throat and rump,* and chestnut forehead.
The more widespread Cliff Swallow is
similar, but has chestnut throat and
white forehead, or, in Southwest, a
chestnut forehead.

Voice: Series of squeaks, twitters, and warbles.

Habitat: Chiefly open country near caves and cliffs.

Nesting: 4 brown-spotted pinkish eggs in a
mud nest lined with grass, roots,
and feathers, attached to a cliff wall,
cave, or, occasionally, to a bridge or
old building.

Range: Breeds in southern Texas, southeastern
New Mexico, and rarely in southern
Arizona. Winters in tropics.

These birds are extremely local north
of the Mexican border, and relatively
few nest within the United States.
Most nests are in inaccessible places,
plastered to walls far inside remote
caves and crevices. Like all swallows,
Cave Swallows catch their insect prey
on the wing.

---

364 Barn Swallow
Hirundo rustica

Description: 5¾–7¾" (15–20 cm). Sparrow-sized.
Our most familiar swallow, and the only
one with a *deeply forked tail.* Upperparts
dark steel-blue, underparts buff, throat
and forehead rusty.

Voice: Constant liquid twittering and
chattering.

Habitat: Agricultural land, suburban areas,
marshes, lakeshores.

Nesting: 4–6 brown-spotted white eggs in a solid
cup of mud reinforced with grass, lined
with feathers and soft plant material,
and placed on a rafter in a building or
on a sheltered ledge.

Range: Breeds from Alaska east across Canada
to Newfoundland and south through all
of United States except southern Texas,
Gulf Coast, and peninsular Florida.
Winters in tropics. Also in Eurasia.

The great majority of these birds now
nest on or in buildings, but originally
they used rocky ledges over streams and
perhaps attached their nests to tree
trunks in the shelter of branches (as do
related species in Africa). Barn Swallows
perform long migrations; some that
breed in North America winter as far
south as Argentina. Like other swallows,
they migrate by day, often feeding as
they travel. They are swift and graceful
fliers, and it is estimated that they cover
as much as 600 miles (1,000 kilometers)
a day in quest of food for their young.

FAMILY CORVIDAE
Jays, Magpies, and Crows

117 species: Worldwide. Sixteen species
breed in North America. Birds in this
family are among the largest of the
perching birds. The crows and ravens are
black, but the many jays and magpies
are a colorful group. The sexes are either
alike or very similar. Their voices are
mostly harsh and raucous, and can
scarcely be called songs. These birds are
omnivorous in their feeding habits and
eat meat, fruit, insects, and various
vegetable substances.

654 Gray Jay
Perisoreus canadensis

Description: 10–13" (25–33 cm). Gray above, whitish below. Forehead and throat white; nape and stripe through eye dull black. Immatures sooty-gray.

Voice: *Whee-ah, chuck-chuck;* also scolds, screams, and whistles.

Habitat: Coniferous forests.

Nesting: 3–5 gray-green eggs, spotted with dark olive-brown, in a solid bowl of twigs and bark strips lined with feathers and fur and placed near the trunk of a dense conifer.

Range: Resident from Alaska east across Canada to Labrador and south to northern California, New Mexico, northern New York, and northern New England.

Anyone who has camped in the mountains or the northern forests is familiar with this bird, formerly called "Canada Jay" and popularly known as the "Whiskey Jack" or "Camp Robber." This bird is attracted to campsites, where it appropriates as much food as possible. It stores scraps of frozen meat, suet, or hide, gluing them into balls with its saliva and hiding them among pine needles.

613 Steller's Jay
Cyanocitta stelleri

Description: 12–13½" (30–34 cm). *The only western jay with a crest.* Front half of bird sooty black, rear dark blue-gray, with tight black crossbarring on secondaries and tail. Lightly streaked eyebrow, chin, and forehead markings vary considerably.

Voice: A harsh *shack-shack-shack-shack* or *chook-chook-chook* call reveals its presence. May also mimic the screams of hawks.

Habitat: Coniferous forests: pine and oak woods in southern part of range, small groves and stands of mixed oak and redwood in northern California.

Nesting: 3–5 spotted greenish eggs in a neat twiggy bowl lined with small roots and fibers, well hidden in a shady conifer.

Range: Largely resident from coastal southern Alaska east to Rocky Mountains and southward into Central America.

Somewhat more reticent than the Gray Jay, Steller's nevertheless quickly becomes accustomed to campsites and human providers. It is often seen sitting quietly in treetops, surveying the surroundings. Near its nest site, it is silent and shy.

---

610 Blue Jay
Cyanocitta cristata

Description: 12″ (30 cm). *Bright blue* above with much white and black in the wings and tail; dingy white below; black facial markings; *prominent crest.*

Voice: A raucous *jay-jay,* harsh cries, and a rich variety of other calls. One is almost identical to the scream of the Red-shouldered Hawk. Also a musical *queedle-queedle.*

Habitat: Chiefly oak forest, but now also city parks and suburban yards, especially where oak trees predominate.

Nesting: 4–6 brown-spotted greenish eggs in a coarsely built nest of sticks, lined with grass and well concealed in a crotch or forked branch of a tree, often a conifer.

Range: Resident east of Rockies, from southern Canada to Gulf of Mexico. Slowly encroaching westward.

Although sometimes disliked because they chase smaller birds away from feeders, Blue Jays are among the handsomest of birds. They often bury seeds and acorns, and since many are never retrieved they are, in effect, tree planters. They regularly mob predators, and their raucous screaming makes it easy to locate a hawk or a roosting owl. Although seen all year, they are migratory and travel in large loose flocks in spring and fall. Birds from farther north replace local populations in winter.

---

611 **Scrub Jay**
Aphelocoma coerulescens

Description: 11–13″ (28–33 cm). Robin-sized, but large strong bill and long tail make it appear larger. *Head, wings,* and *tail blue* (conspicuous when it glides in a long, undulating flight); *back dull brown;* underparts light gray. No crest; dusky face mask. *White throat* offset by incomplete blue necklace. See Gray-breasted Jay.

Voice: Call is loud, throaty *jayy?* or *jree?* In flight, a long series of *check-check-check* notes.

Habitat: Scrub oak, woodlands, and chaparral, but does not breed in low scrub because it needs watch posts; also inhabits suburban gardens.

Nesting: 3–6 eggs, spotted on darker, greenish or reddish base, in a twiggy nest well hidden in a tree or dense shrub.

Range: Resident from Washington, Wyoming, and Colorado south to Texas, with an isolated population in central Florida; also in Mexico.

Like all jays, this species may be secretive and silent around its nest or while perching in a treetop in early morning but is frequently noisy and conspicuous. Many condemn it as a nest robber, although in summer it is mainly insectivorous. These birds also eat acorns and have been described as "uphill planters," counterbalancing the tendency of acorns to bounce or roll downhill. The jays bury many more acorns than they consume and help regenerate oak forests that have been destroyed by fire or drought.

614 Gray-breasted Jay
"Mexican Jay"
Aphelocoma ultramarina

Description: 11½–13" (29–33 cm). Similar to Scrub
Jay but larger and more muted, without
white markings on throat or above eyes.
Dull blue head, rump, wings, and tail;
gray back and dusky ear patch.

Voice: A loud *shrink?* or *wenk?* often repeated.

Habitat: Oak forests and wooded canyons.

Nesting: 4 or 5 green eggs in a twig bowl lined
with horsehair and placed low in a tree.

Range: Resident from southern Arizona, New
Mexico, and western Texas southward.

Nesting territories of Gray-breasted Jays
are small and adjacent; when a predator
approaches, an entire colony moves to
the defense, scolding loudly from a safe
distance. Acorns are their staple diet,
but they also glean insects and rob eggs
and young from nests.

---

612 Pinyon Jay
Gymnorhinus cyanocephalus

Description: 9–11¾" (23–30 cm). A stocky, short-
tailed jay. Long slender bill gives it a
resemblance to Clark's Nutcracker.
Gray-blue, darkest on head, with white
streaking on throat. Crow-like flight
and flocking habits.

Voice: A high-pitched *caaa,* often quavering
at the end and resembling a laughing
haa-a-a-a.

Habitat: Ponderosa pine, piñon-juniper, and
forests of mixed pine and oak.

Nesting: 3 or 4 speckled, greenish-white eggs in a
twiggy cup nest. Nests in loose colonies.

Range: Resident from central Oregon and
Montana southward to central Arizona,
New Mexico, and extreme northwestern
Oklahoma.

Although they sometimes pull up
earthworms from lawns in the fashion

of robins, Pinyon Jays feed principally on pine nuts, which they store in fall and consume during winter and spring. The birds' local population varies from year to year with the success of the nut crop. They nest early after a good harvest; in poor years they delay breeding until August.

652 Clark's Nutcracker
Nucifraga columbiana

Description:	12–13" (30–33 cm). Pigeon-sized, with flashing black, white, and gray pattern. *Light gray,* with dark eye and long, sharply pointed bill. Black wing with large white wing patch at trailing edge; black tail with white outer tail feathers. Face white from forehead to chin; belly white. Crow-like flight.
Voice:	A guttural *kraaaa.*
Habitat:	Stands of juniper and ponderosa pine or of whitebark pine and larch on high mountain ranges, near the tree line.
Nesting:	2–6 spotted green eggs in a deep bowl nest of sticks in a coniferous tree. Nests very early.
Range:	Resident in southern British Columbia and Alberta south throughout pine-clad western mountains to California and Colorado.

The periodic irruptions of Clark's Nutcrackers, which may bring the birds all the way to the Pacific Coast, are related to failures of the pine nut crop. Near camps and picnic sites this erratic winter wanderer begs and steals food scraps. It can hold several nuts in a special cheek pouch under the tongue in addition to those it holds in the beak.

657   **Black-billed Magpie**
Pica pica

Description: 17½–22″ (44–56 cm). Large *black and white bird with long tail and dark bill.* Bill, head, breast, and underparts black, with green iridescence on wings and tail. White belly and shoulders; white primaries conspicuous as white wing patches in flight. See Yellow-billed Magpie.

Voice: A rapid, nasal *mag? mag? mag?* or *yak yak yak.*

Habitat: Open woodlands, savannas, brush-covered country, streamside growth.

Nesting: 6–9 blotched greenish eggs in a neat cup nest within a large, bulky, domed structure of strong, often thorny twigs, with a double entrance, in a tree or bush.

Range: Resident from Alaska and western Canada south to east-central California and east to Great Plains. Also in Eurasia.

Magpies generally nest individually but can sometimes be found in loose colonies; they are social when feeding or after the breeding season. Those living in western rangeland appear shy of humans, but their behavior in the Old World is very different. In northern Finland magpies live in the middle of settlements and place their nests low. In Hungary a bounty is placed on them because they damage the broods of partridges and other game birds; as a result, they nest out of reach in the tallest trees.

660   **Yellow-billed Magpie**
Pica nuttalli

Description: 16–18″ (41–46 cm). A slightly smaller version of Black-billed Magpie, but with *yellow bill and bare yellow area of skin behind eye.* Large white wing patches and long, wedge-shaped, iridescent greenish-black tail. Juvenile has blackish beak and lacks bare face patch. Ranges of two magpies do not overlap.

Voice: A raucous *qua-qua-qua* and a querulous quack.

Habitat: Oak savannas, oak woods, riverside growth, ranches, and suburbs.

Nesting: 5–8 blotched, olive green eggs in a large, domed stick nest; breeds in colonies in tall trees usually so overgrown with mistletoe that it is often hard to detect the nests.

Range: Resident in California's Central Valley and adjacent foothills.

A colony of Yellow-billed Magpies lives communally year round, feeding, socializing, and collectively mobbing predators. This magpie has found in vacant city lots and weedy storage yards a substitute for habitats it lost to intensive agriculture. It has become a city bird but keeps away from places where people gather.

---

673 American Crow
"Common Crow"
Corvus brachyrhynchos

Description: 17–21″ (43–53 cm). Stocky black bird with stout bill and fan-shaped tail. Smaller Northwestern Crow has hoarser voice; larger Common Raven has wedge-shaped tail.

Voice: Familiar *caw-caw* or *caa-caa*.

Habitat: Deciduous growth along rivers and streams; orchards and city parks. Also mixed and coniferous woods, but avoids closed coniferous forests and desert expanses.

Nesting: 4–6 dull green eggs, spotted with dark brown, in a large mass of twigs and sticks lined with feathers, grass, and rootlets, and placed in a tree.

Range: Breeds from British Columbia, central interior Canada, and Newfoundland south to southern California, Gulf

Coast, and Florida. Winters north to southern Canada.

An opportunist in its feeding, the American Crow consumes a great variety of plant and animal food: seeds, garbage, insects, mice. Its nest-plundering is decried, but in orchards and fields it destroys many injurious insects. However, the labeling of birds as either "harmful" or "useful" is misleading and antiquated. Crows do destroy many eggs and nestlings of woodland and meadow birds, but they also weed out the weak and feeble, and they alert the animals in a neighborhood when danger approaches.

674 Northwestern Crow
Corvus caurinus

Description: 16–17″ (41–43 cm). Black with a slight purplish gloss; smaller and more slender than American Crow.

Voice: Calls resemble those of the American Crow, but are somewhat hoarse.

Habitat: Shorelines, tidewater areas, edges of coastal forest.

Nesting: 4–6 brown-spotted greenish eggs in a bowl-shaped stick nest in a tree, bush, or rarely on the ground.

Range: Resident from coastal southern Alaska to Puget Sound in Washington.

In tidal marshes Red-winged Blackbirds attack these crows, just as inland blackbirds harass the American Crow. This mobbing behavior distracts the crows from their habitual plundering and prevents them from discovering nests; thus broods of marsh birds remain largely unmolested. At cormorant or gull colonies, however, crows walk all day among incubating and brooding birds and quickly snatch any egg or hatchling accidentally exposed and left unprotected.

675 Chihuahuan Raven
"White-necked Raven"
Corvus cryptoleucus

Description: 19–21" (48–53 cm). Similar to
Common Raven, but somewhat smaller.
White bases on feathers of neck seldom
seen. Best told by voice.

Voice: Harsh *kraak*, higher pitched than
Common Raven's.

Habitat: Arid grasslands and mesquite; plains
and deserts.

Nesting: 5–7 dull green eggs, spotted and
streaked with brown and purple, laid in
a loose mass of thorny sticks lined with
grass, moss, and bark strips, placed in
an exposed tree or on a telephone pole.

Range: Breeds from southern Arizona,
southeastern Colorado, and western
Kansas southward into Mexico. Winters
in southern part of breeding range.

The Chihuahuan Raven replaces the
Common Raven at lower elevations,
and in the United States portion of its
range is the only raven likely to be
seen. More gregarious than its larger
northern relative, it gathers in noisy
and conspicuous roosts, soaring high in
the air in group displays. During the
breeding season, however, these birds
are not social, with pairs nesting in
widely spaced territories. A scarcity of
trees may have originally led to this
bird's habit of using the same nest year
after year. Chihuahuan Ravens feed in
groups on grasshoppers or other insects
as well as carrion, and often frequent
garbage dumps.

676 Common Raven
Corvus corax

Description: 21–27" (53–69 cm). Similar to the
American Crow but larger, with heavier
bill and wedge-shaped tail. At rest,
throat appears shaggy because of long,

lance-shaped feathers. Often soars like a hawk. See Chihuahuan Raven.

Voice: Deep, varied, guttural croaking; a hollow *wonk-wonk*.

Habitat: Coniferous forests and rocky coasts; in West also in deserts and arid mountains.

Nesting: 4–7 dull green eggs, spotted with brown, in a large mass of sticks containing a cup lined with fur, moss, and lichens, and placed on a cliff or in the top of a conifer.

Range: Resident from Aleutians, northern Alaska and northern Canada south throughout western United States and to Minnesota, Great Lakes, and northern New England; in Appalachians to northwestern Georgia. Also in Eurasia and North Africa.

A very intelligent bird, the Common Raven seems to apply reasoning in situations entirely new to it. Its "insight" behavior is comparable to that of a dog. It is a general predator and opportunistic feeder, like other members of the crow family, and often feeds at garbage dumps.

FAMILY PARIDAE
Titmice

51 species: North America, Eurasia, and Africa. Eleven species breed in North America. These familiar birds include the tame and trusting chickadees, which not only come to feeders but even take food from the hand. They are small, large-headed, sometimes crested birds that usually travel in small flocks or family groups. They mostly nest in holes or cavities and will utilize birdhouses. The sexes are alike.

644 Black-capped Chickadee
Parus atricapillus

Description: 4¾–5¾″ (12–15 cm). Black cap and throat, white cheeks, gray back, dull white underparts. Wing feathers narrowly and indistinctly edged with white.

Voice: A buzzy *chick-a-dee-dee-dee* or a clear, whistled *fee-bee,* the second note lower and often doubled.

Habitat: Deciduous and mixed forests and open woodlands; suburban areas in winter.

Nesting: 6–8 brown-speckled white eggs in a cup of grass, fur, plant down, feathers, and moss, placed in a hole in a rotten tree stub excavated by the birds, or in a natural cavity or bird box.

Range: Largely resident from Alaska east across Canada to Newfoundland, south to northern California, northern New Mexico, Missouri, and northern New Jersey. Winters south to Maryland and Texas.

These birds are constantly active—hopping, clinging, and hanging from twigs and branches, often near the ground. Black-capped Chickadees usually prepare their own nesting hole in soft, rotting tree stumps. Enticing them into breeding boxes is difficult unless the boxes are filled with sawdust, which deceives the chickadees; they carry the sawdust out bit by bit and accept the box for nesting.

647 Mexican Chickadee
Parus sclateri

Description: 5″ (13 cm). A gray chickadee, with black cap, black bib extending onto upper breast, and gray flanks.

Voice: A husky *chick-a-dee-dee-dee,* huskier and lazier than that of the Mountain Chickadee.

Habitat: Coniferous or pine-oak forests at high altitudes.

Nesting: 5–8 whitish eggs, frequently with reddish-brown spotting, in a fiber nest lined with grass, feathers, or fur placed in an excavated hole in a dead branch.

Range: Resident in extreme southeastern Arizona and southwestern New Mexico. Also in Mexico.

This bird feeds along the outer tree canopy, often hanging upside down to pluck small insects from conifer needles. Like other chickadees, it has an ingenious arrangement of leg tendons that enables it to pull close to a branch while upside down. Vireos, warblers, and kinglets must hover above branches, and are unable to reach the undersides, so the chickadees can exploit this feeding opportunity without competition.

646 Mountain Chickadee
Parus gambeli

Description: 5–5¾" (13–15 cm). Similar to Black-capped Chickadee, but with *white eyebrow* and pale gray flanks.

Voice: A hoarse *chick-a-zee-zee, zee*. Spring song is similar to that of the Black-capped Chickadee, but 3-noted: *fee-bee-bee,* the *bees* at a lower pitch.

Habitat: High-altitude coniferous forests.

Nesting: 7–9 white, sometimes spotted eggs in a hair- or fur-lined natural cavity or woodpecker hole; like other chickadees, it sometimes excavates a hole in soft, rotten wood.

Range: Resident from interior British Columbia south through Rocky Mountain and Cascade-Sierra chains to southern California and western Texas.

A fearless, constantly active insect-gleaner of the mountain forest, the Mountain Chickadee frequently

descends into the lowlands in winter. In November an occasional flock can be found near sea level in desert oases containing planted conifers, while other flocks forage at 8,500 feet (2,600 meters) in the subalpine forests of nearby mountains.

Siberian Tit
"Gray-headed Chickadee"
Parus cinctus

Description: 5–5½" (13–14 cm). Plumper than Black-capped Chickadee, with longer tail than Boreal Chickadee. *Gray-brown cap and mantle; black triangular throat patch;* light underparts with *pale buff flanks.*
Voice: Hoarser, shorter *chick-a-dee-dee* than the call of the Black-capped; often only the *dee-dee* is heard.
Habitat: Aspen, spruce, willow, and sometimes coniferous thickets, near the northern or altitudinal tree line.
Nesting: 6–9 white, finely spotted eggs in a nest of moss and hair, in a tree hole or rotten stump.
Range: Resident in northern Alaska and adjacent Canada. Also in northern Eurasia.

This species and the Boreal Chickadee probably evolved into separate species during the later stages of the Ice Age, the former remaining in northern Eurasia, the latter in the boreal forests of North America. Then, quite recently, the Siberian Tit seems to have crossed the Bering Strait and is now found in the western North American Arctic.

645   Boreal Chickadee
Parus hudsonicus

Description: 5–5½″ (13–14 cm). Similar to Black-capped Chickadee, but crown and back brown, flanks rufous.

Voice: A husky *chick-a-dee-dee,* lazier and more nasal than call of Black-capped.

Habitat: Coniferous forests.

Nesting: 5–7 white eggs, lightly speckled with red-brown, in a cup of plant down, feathers, and moss in a natural cavity, often only a few feet from the ground.

Range: Breeds from northern Alaska east to Labrador and Newfoundland, south to northern edge of United States. Occasionally wanders southward in winter.

During late summer and early fall, when there is an abundance of caterpillars and seeds, Boreal Chickadees store food for winter among needles or under the bark of branches at a height that will be above the winter snow cover.

456   Chestnut-backed Chickadee
Parus rufescens

Description: 4½–5″ (11–13 cm). Dusky, black-capped, and black-bibbed chickadee, with *chestnut flanks and back.*

Voice: A squeaky *chick-a-dee,* somewhat shriller and faster than that of other chickadees. Often simply utters a thin *tsee-deee* and thin lisping notes.

Habitat: Pacific rain forest; moist areas containing conifers.

Nesting: 5–8 creamy-white, lightly spotted eggs in a natural cavity or woodpecker hole; much like the Black-capped Chickadee, it often excavates rotten stumps and then builds a nest of moss and hair.

Range: Resident from coastal Alaska south to central California; also in western ranges of Rocky Mountains in southern British

Columbia, southern Alberta, and
western Montana.

In the coastal forests of the Northwest,
where the Chestnut-backed and Black-
capped chickadees overlap, the former
prefers the top half of conifers, while the
latter feeds in the lower half of trees,
very frequently oaks. Thus they do not
compete for space or food even within
the same area.

641 Bridled Titmouse
Parus wollweberi

Description: 4½–5″ (11–13 cm). Warbler-sized. Gray
above, whitish below, with *gray crest
bordered with black and a "bridle" joining
eye line and throat patch.*

Voice: Vocalizations are similar to calls of other
chickadees and titmice, but more rapid
and on a somewhat higher pitch. The
song is a 2-syllable phrase, resembling
that of the Plain Titmouse, repeated
several times. One of its common calls
is a variant of the familiar *chick-a-dee.*

Habitat: Deciduous and mixed woods in the
mountains.

Nesting: 5–7 white eggs in a tree hole.

Range: Resident from central Arizona and
southwestern New Mexico southward.

The range of the Bridled Titmouse
overlaps that of the Mountain
Chickadee, but the unique face pattern
and crest distinguish this species. It
accepts nesting holes made or used
by other species and even settles in
breeding boxes.

630   Plain Titmouse
Parus inornatus

Description: 5–5½″ (13–14 cm). Sparrow-sized. *Plain gray with paler underparts; small crest,* usually erect.

Voice: A harsh, fussy *see-dee-dee* or *chick-a-dee-dee.*

Habitat: Live oaks and deciduous growth of all kinds: oak woodlands, streamside cottonwoods, forest edges, and oak-juniper woodlands.

Nesting: 5–8 white eggs, with brown spotting, in tree cavities, fence-post holes, or crevices of old buildings. The cavity nest is composed of grasses, fur, and some feathers.

Range: Resident from southern Oregon, northern Nevada, Utah, and southwestern Wyoming, east to Oklahoma and south to southern California, Arizona, southern New Mexico, and western Texas.

Whereas chickadees gather in winter flocks, the related Plain Titmouse is usually found singly or in pairs. This bird is conspicuous, for it calls often as it feeds among juniper and elderberry bushes or high in the spring growth of freshly sprouted oaks. It also frequents gardens in suburbs of towns adjacent to its native habitat.

FAMILY REMIZIDAE
Verdins

10 species: North America, Eurasia, and Africa. One species breeds in North America. Verdins are very small birds with short wings, relatively long tails, and sharply pointed bills. A few species undertake short migrations, but most are nonmigratory. All make large, elaborate nests.

536 Verdin
Auriparus flaviceps

Description: 4–4½" (10–11 cm). Smaller than
a chickadee, a little larger than a
Bushtit. *Gray with yellow head and
throat;* chestnut patch at bend of wing;
white underparts. Juveniles lack both
yellow and chestnut coloration of adults
and are distinguishable from Bushtit
by shorter tail.

Voice: A sharp *seep!* Its infrequent song is a
3-note *kleep-er-zee!* with the final note
highest in pitch.

Habitat: Low desert, containing brush and taller
shrubs.

Nesting: 3–5 spotted greenish eggs in a hanging
nest with an entrance hole in the side,
built among the prickliest branches of
a cholla cactus or in a crotch of a
mesquite tree.

Range: Resident from California, Utah, and
south-central Texas southward to
northern Mexico.

Verdins feed on insects, seeds, and
berries. The small clutch size may be an
adaptation to assure sufficient food in an
area of climatic extremes. The thorny
protection around most nests probably
discourages predators.

FAMILY AEGITHALIDAE
Bushtits

8 species: North America, Eurasia, and
the East Indies. Only one species is
found in North America. These are tiny,
active, mainly insectivorous birds with
small, somewhat conical bills, short
rounded wings, and long tails. They are
social birds, noted for their pendant,
bag-shaped nests.

638 Bushtit
Psaltriparus minimus

Description: 3¾–4" (10 cm). Gray above with light
underparts; small bill; and relatively
long tail. Pacific Coast birds have brown
crown, pale ear patch; Rocky Mountain
birds have gray crown, brown ear patch.
Birds in mountains near Mexican border
have black ear patch; they were formerly
considered a separate species, the
"Black-eared Bushtit."

Voice: Contact calls are light *tsip* and *pit* notes,
constantly uttered. Alarm call is a
high trill.

Habitat: Varied. Deciduous growth, usually
streamside. In the coastal forest, it lives
in second-growth alder thickets or in
edges of coniferous forests composed of
maple, dogwood, and birch; also in oak
woodland, chaparral, and juniper brush.

Nesting: 5–15 white eggs in a hanging gourd-
shaped nest with a side entrance near
the top. Made of soft plant wool and
lichens, the nest is suspended in a bush
or tree.

Range: Resident from extreme southwestern
British Columbia, southern Idaho,
southwestern Wyoming, and Oklahoma
panhandle southward.

Bushtits flock in small bands, flitting
nervously through trees and bushes,
hanging, prying, picking, and gleaning,
and keeping contact through a constant
banter of soft chirps. They pervade a
small area, then vanish, and reappear a
couple of hundred yards away.

FAMILY SITTIDAE
Nuthatches

25 species: North America and Eurasia.
Four species breed in North America.
Like the titmice, these stocky little
birds are cavity-nesters. Their chief
peculiarity is a habit of crawling on tree

trunks head downward. With their stout toes and claws, they can progress in any direction, but their short, soft tails are not used as props like those of woodpeckers and creepers.

399 Red-breasted Nuthatch
Sitta canadensis

Description: 4½–4¾" (11–12 cm). Smaller than a sparrow. Male has blue-gray upperparts, pale rust-colored underparts, *black crown and line through eye, and white eyebrow.* Female similar, but crown is gray.

Voice: A tinny *yank-yank,* higher pitched and more nasal than the call of the White-breasted Nuthatch.

Habitat: Coniferous forests; more widespread during migration and in winter.

Nesting: 5 or 6 white eggs, spotted with red-brown, in a cup of twigs and grass lined with softer material and placed in a tree cavity. The entrance is usually smeared with pitch, presumably to discourage predators; the pitch often gets on the bird's feathers giving them a messy appearance.

Range: Breeds across Canada from southeastern Alaska, Manitoba, and Newfoundland south to southern California, Arizona, Great Lakes region, and northern New England, and south in Appalachians to North Carolina. Winters in breeding range and irregularly south to Gulf Coast and northern Florida.

Nuthatches hoard excess food and will transport seed from a tree heavily laden with mature cones to their distant larders. In years of bad harvest, they migrate in large numbers to more southerly forests. They also feed on bark insects, maneuvering with agility around the tips of small, outer branches or in treetops.

398 White-breasted Nuthatch
Sitta carolinensis

Description: 5–6" (13–15 cm). Sparrow-sized. Blue-gray above, white underparts and face, black crown. Usually seen creeping on tree trunks, head downward.

Voice: A nasal *yank-yank*. Song a series of low whistled notes.

Habitat: Deciduous and mixed forests.

Nesting: 5 or 6 white eggs, lightly speckled with red-brown, in a cup of twigs and grass lined with feathers and hair in a natural cavity, bird box, or hole excavated by the birds.

Range: Largely resident from British Columbia, Ontario, and Nova Scotia south to southern California, Arizona, Gulf Coast, and central Florida. Absent from most of Great Plains.

The habit of creeping headfirst down a tree trunk, then stopping and looking around with head held out at a 90-degree angle, is characteristic of nuthatches. The White-breasted is an inquisitive, acrobatic bird, pausing occasionally to hang and hammer at a crack. Essentially nonmigratory, during the fall it stores food for winter in crevices behind loose tree bark.

400 Pygmy Nuthatch
Sitta pygmaea

Description: 3¾–4½" (10–11 cm). A *small* nuthatch. Bluish gray above, with *gray-brown cap* terminated by indistinct black eye line. Faint white smudge at base of nape. Creamy white below. Usually occurs in flocks.

Voice: A monotonous *peep, peep-peep.*

Habitat: Primarily ponderosa pine forests with undergrowth of bunchgrass. Less common in stands of other pines, Douglas fir, and western larch.

Nesting: 5–9 white eggs, with reddish-brown

speckles, in a nest made of a quantity of soft material, often vegetable down, amassed in the cavity of a dead pine or stump approximately 15′ (5 m) from the ground.

Range: Resident locally from southern British Columbia, eastward to Black Hills of South Dakota (rare), and southward into Mexico.

The three nuthatch species in the West live in separate wooded habitats. The White-breasted is found mainly in the lowland oaks and riparian forests through the foothills into mixed woods, though it also extends into the mountaintop pine forests. The Pygmy Nuthatch keeps mostly to pine woodlands. The Red-breasted Nuthatch is found in the firs of the subalpine forests. All feed on bark and twig insects, as well as stored nuts, seeds, eggs, and hibernating larvae in winter.

FAMILY CERTHIIDAE
Creepers

7 species: Eurasia, North America, and Africa. Only the Brown Creeper is found in North America. Creepers are dull-colored birds that creep up tree trunks and probe for spiders and soft-bodied insects in the crevices of the bark. Their curved bills are well suited to this. Like woodpeckers, they have stiff tail feathers that serve as a prop.

397 Brown Creeper
Certhia americana

Description: 5–5¾″ (13–15 cm). Smaller than a sparrow. A slender, streaked, brown bird, tinged with buff on flanks, usually seen creeping up tree trunks, using long, stiff tail for support.

Voice: A high-pitched, lisping *tsee;* song a
tinkling, descending warble.

Habitat: Deciduous and mixed woodlands.

Nesting: 6 or 7 white eggs, lightly speckled
with brown, in a cup of bark shreds,
feathers, sticks, and moss, usually placed
against a tree trunk behind a peeling
slab of bark.

Range: Breeds from Alaska, Ontario, and
Newfoundland southward throughout
western mountains, Great Lakes region,
North Carolina, and New England.
Winters in breeding range and south to
Gulf Coast and Florida.

As it searches for bark insects, the
inconspicuous Brown Creeper always
moves in an upward direction, circling
tree trunks in spirals, then dropping
down to the base of the next tree.

FAMILY TROGLODYTIDAE
Wrens

75 species: The Western Hemisphere;
one wide-ranging species, the Winter
Wren, also occurs in Eurasia. Nine
species breed in North America. These
mostly small, stocky, short-tailed birds
are clad in browns, grays, and buffs.
They are mainly secretive in their
habits, although the familiar House
Wren builds its nest in man-made
birdhouses. While some wrens nest
near human dwellings, others, like the
Marsh Wren, which lives in cattails,
construct their homes in wet places.

484 Cactus Wren
Campylorhynchus brunneicapillus

Description: 7–8¼″ (18–21 cm). A starling-sized
wren with spotted underparts, white
eyebrows, rusty crown, and white spots
on outer tail feathers.

Voice: Rapid, mechanical *chug-chug-chug-chug-chug*.

Habitat: Desert thickets and cacti.

Nesting: 4 or 5 buff eggs, heavily speckled with brown. The nest, a mass of fine grass and straw with a side entrance, is lined with feathers and hair and placed in the top of a thorny desert shrub or spiny cactus.

Range: Resident from southern California, southern Nevada, Utah, and western Texas southward.

Cactus Wrens forage for food very methodically, searching under leaves and other ground litter. Like other wrens, they build roosting nests and even use them for shelter in rainy weather. They are late sleepers and an early bird-watcher may surprise them still dozing in the snug nest.

486 Rock Wren
Salpinctes obsoletus

Description: 5–6½" (13–17 cm). A sparrow-sized wren, pale grayish brown with a finely streaked breast. Outer tail feathers have whitish or pale buff tips.

Voice: A dry trill; a rhythmic series of musical notes; *chewee, chewee, chewee, chewee*.

Habitat: Rock-strewn slopes, canyons, cliffs, and dams in arid country.

Nesting: 4–6 white eggs, lightly speckled with pale brown, in a shallow nest of plant fibers and roots, lined with feathers and placed in a crevice among rocks or in a hollow stump.

Range: Breeds from interior British Columbia, Saskatchewan, and North Dakota southward in mountains. Winters north to California and Texas.

This species is found in much the same habitat as its relative the Canyon Wren but is more partial to rocky slopes, while the Canyon Wren favors sheer cliffs. The Rock Wren has the unusual habit of laying down a path of small pebbles in front of its nest; this little "pavement" often simplifies an observer's effort to locate nests.

487 Canyon Wren
Catherpes mexicanus

Description: 5½–6″ (14–15 cm). Sparrow-sized. Dark rusty above and below, with conspicuous *white throat and upper breast.*

Voice: A high, clear series of descending notes; *tee-tee-tee-tee-tew-tew-tew-tew.*

Habitat: Rocky canyons and cliffs; old stone buildings.

Nesting: 4–6 white eggs, lightly speckled with reddish brown, in a shallow cup of feathers, plant down, and moss placed in a crevice among rocks or, occasionally, on a building.

Range: Resident from British Columbia, Montana, and western South Dakota southward.

This wren is found in remote, steep-walled canyons and on rocky mountainsides but has also adapted to man-made structures such as stone buildings and rock walls.

485 Bewick's Wren
Thryomanes bewickii

Description: 5½″ (14 cm). Gray-brown above, white below, with white eyebrow and long fan-shaped tail tipped with white.

Voice: Loud, melodious song with the usual bubbly wren-like warble, also reminiscent of a Song Sparrow.

Habitat: Thickets, brush piles, and hedgerows in farming country; also open woodlands and scrubby areas, often near streams.

Nesting: 5–7 brown-spotted white eggs in a stick nest lined with leaves, grass, and feathers, and placed in almost any

available cavity, including woo[...]
holes, tin cans, coat pockets or slee[...]
baskets, tool sheds, and brush piles.

Range: Resident locally from southern British Columbia, Nebraska, southern Ontario, and southwestern Pennsylvania south to Mexico, Arkansas, and northern Gulf States. Eastern birds winter south to Gulf Coast.

Bewick's Wren uses its long, narrow, slightly down-curved bill for scavenging on the ground and picking in crevices for insects and spiders. Searching for food, it may venture into hollow trunks, rock crevices, or barns.

489 House Wren
Troglodytes aedon

Description: 4½–5¼″ (11–13 cm). A tiny bird with a short tail, often held cocked over the back. Dusky brown above, paler below, with no distinctive markings. Winter Wren is similar but smaller and darker, with shorter tail and pale eyebrow.

Voice: A gurgling, bubbling, exuberant song, first rising, then falling.

Habitat: Residential areas, city parks, farmlands, and woodland edges.

Nesting: 5–8 white eggs, thickly speckled with brown, in a cup lined with feathers and other soft material contained within a mass of sticks and grass, placed in a natural cavity or bird box.

Range: Breeds from British Columbia east across Canada to New Brunswick, and south to southeastern Arizona, northern Texas, Tennessee, and northern Georgia. Winters north to southern California, Gulf Coast states, and Virginia. Also in tropical America.

When competing for a nest site, the House Wren may throw out the nest, eggs, and even the young of other hole-breeding birds. In the process this bird may kill its competitors, or if they are more powerful, it harasses them by filling the hole with its own nest material.

488 Winter Wren
Troglodytes troglodytes

Description: 4–4½" (10 cm). A tiny, dark brown bird with a very short tail, narrow pale eyebrow, and heavily banded flanks. See House Wren.

Voice: A high-pitched, varied, and rapid series of musical trills and chatters; call note an explosive *kit!* or *kit-kit!*

Habitat: Dense tangles and thickets in coniferous and mixed forests.

Nesting: 5–7 brown-speckled white eggs in a bulky mass of twigs and moss, with an entrance on the side, lined with softer material and often concealed among the upturned roots of a fallen tree.

Range: Breeds from Alaska and British Columbia east through southern Canada to Newfoundland, and south to California, northern Idaho, Great Lakes region, and southern New England; also in mountains to Georgia. Winters across much of southern United States south to southern California, Gulf Coast, and Florida. Also in Eurasia.

This wren moves like a mouse, creeping through the low, dense tangle of branches covering the forest floor. Its nest is among the hardest to find; even when an observer has narrowed the search to a few square feet, he must sometimes give up, so cleverly is the nest concealed. The Winter Wren's song, when recorded and played back at half- or quarter-speed, reveals a remarkable blend of halftones and overtones all sung at the same time.

490 Marsh Wren
"Long-billed Marsh Wren"
Cistothorus palustris

Description: 4–5½" (10–14 cm). Smaller than a sparrow. Brown above, pale buff below, with *bold white eyebrow and white-streaked back.*

Voice: Liquid gurgling song ending in a mechanical chatter that sounds like a sewing machine.

Habitat: Freshwater and brackish marshes with cattails, reeds, bulrushes, or sedges.

Nesting: 5 or 6 pale brown eggs, speckled with dark brown, in a globular nest of reeds and cattails with a side entrance. Nest is lined with feathers and cattail down and anchored to reeds.

Range: Breeds from British Columbia, central interior Canada, Manitoba, and Nova Scotia south to Mexico, Gulf Coast, and Florida. Winters across southern tier of states, north to Washington on West Coast and in East to New Jersey.

This wren feeds entirely on insects it takes from plants as well as the surface of water. It is a secretive bird; even the singing territorial male remains well hidden, briefly climbing a cattail for a look at an intruder.

FAMILY CINCLIDAE
Dippers

5 species: In temperate zones of the Old World and the Americas. One species breeds in North America, where it is largely nonmigratory. These birds are stocky, short-tailed, and wren-like in appearance. They have dense, waterproof plumage and are well adapted to diving and feeding on aquatic animal life around and at the bottom of fast-running mountain streams.

624 American Dipper
Cinclus mexicanus

Description: 7–8½″ (18–22 cm). A uniformly *slate-gray, wren-shaped* bird with stubby tail; yellowish feet. Always found near rushing water.

Voice: A loud, bubbling song that carries over the noise of rapids. Call is a sharp *zeet.*

Habitat: Near clear, fast mountain streams with rapids.

Nesting: 3–6 white eggs in a relatively large, insulated nest of moss, with a side entrance. Nest is built under roots, in a rock crevice, or on the bank of a stream.

Range: Resident from northern Alaska south throughout mountains of West. May move to lowlands in winter.

The "Water Ouzel" feeds on insect life of streams. Where water is shallow and runs over gravel, the dipper appears to water ski on the surface. At deeper points it dives into the water and runs along the bottom with half-open wings.

FAMILY MUSCICAPIDAE
SUBFAMILY SYLVIINAE
Old World Warblers, Kinglets, and Gnatcatchers

383 species: Worldwide. Six species breed in North America. The American species include some of the smallest birds in the world. They live entirely on insects and spiders.

---

628 Arctic Warbler
Phylloscopus borealis

Description: 4¾″ (12 cm). *Olive green* above, with dark line through eye and *light greenish-yellow eyebrow.* Whitish throat and belly; olive-gray sides; indistinct single wing bar. Pale legs.

Voice: A quick trill, introduced by *zick* or *zick-zick-zick*. The call is also *zick* or *zirrup*.

Habitat: Birch woods, willow thickets.

Nesting: 5–7 pink-speckled white eggs in a domed cup nest placed in grass on the ground.

Range: Breeds in western and northern Alaska. Also in northern Eurasia.

This bird is the only North American pioneer from a large genus of similarly colored Old World warblers. It most resembles the Tennessee Warbler, whose range it does not overlap.

---

594 Golden-crowned Kinglet
Regulus satrapa

Description: 3½–4″ (9–10 cm). Tiny. Olive green above, paler below, with 2 dull-white wing bars. Eyebrow white, crown orange bordered with yellow (adult males) or solid yellow (females and young birds); *narrow black line separates crown patch from white eyebrow.* Ruby-crowned Kinglet lacks the conspicuous face pattern.

Voice: Thin, wiry, ascending *ti-ti-ti,* followed by tumbling chatter.

Habitat: Dense, old conifer stands; also deciduous forests and thickets in winter.

Nesting: 8 or 9 cream-colored eggs, speckled with brown, in a large mass of moss, lichens, and plant down, with a small feather-lined cup at the top. Nest is suspended between several twigs in a densely needled conifer, less than 60′ (18 m) above the ground.

Range: Breeds from Alaska to Alberta and from Manitoba to Newfoundland, and south to southern California and Southwest, and to Michigan, Massachusetts, and in mountains to North Carolina. Winters from southern Canada south to southern California, Arizona, Gulf Coast, and northern Florida.

Outside the breeding season, these tiny, energetic birds are frequently seen in the company of Ruby-crowned Kinglets, creepers, nuthatches, and chickadees. These feeding flocks move as a group through the trees, searching out the greatest abundance of insects and larvae.

593   Ruby-crowned Kinglet
Regulus calendula

Description: 3¾–4½" (10–11 cm). Tiny. Similar to Golden-crowned Kinglet, but greener, with no face pattern except for narrow white eye ring. 2 white wing bars with dark area beyond second. Males have tuft of red feathers on crown, kept concealed unless bird is aroused. Hutton's Vireo is larger, with thicker bill, larger head, and no dark area beyond second wing bar.

Voice: Song an excited musical chattering.

Habitat: Coniferous forests in summer; also deciduous forests and thickets in winter.

Nesting: 6–9 cream-colored eggs, lightly speckled with brown, in a large mass of moss, lichens, and plant down with a small feather-lined cup at the top.

Range: Breeds from Alaska east across Canada to Newfoundland, south to southern California and New Mexico in West, and to Great Lakes region and northern New England in East. Winters south from southern British Columbia and California across southern tier of states to southern New England.

Because kinglets weigh little, they are able to feed on the tips of conifer branches. The Ruby-crowned feeds lower in the canopy than the Golden-crowned and characteristically hovers above a twig looking for caterpillars, aphids, and other insects. The Ruby-crowned is not as social in its winter range as the Golden-crowned and occurs singly more often than in flocks.

637 Blue-gray Gnatcatcher
Polioptila caerulea

Description: 4½–5″ (11–13 cm). Smaller than a
sparrow. Tiny, slender, long-tailed bird,
blue-gray above and white below, with
white eye ring and broad white borders
on black tail. Looks like a miniature
mockingbird.

Voice: Song is a thin, musical warble. Call note
a distinctive, whining *pzzzz,* with a
nasal quality.

Habitat: Deciduous woodlands, streamside
thickets, live oaks, piñon-juniper,
chaparral.

Nesting: 4 or 5 brown-spotted pale blue eggs in
a small, beautifully made cup of plant
down and spider webs, decorated with
flakes of lichen and fastened to a
horizontal branch at almost any height
above ground.

Range: Breeds from northern California,
Colorado, southern Great Lakes region,
southern Ontario, and New Hampshire
southward. Winters north to southern
California, Gulf Coast, and Carolinas.

These gnatcatchers are lively birds,
constantly flicking their conspicuous
long tails upward while gathering
insects from the branches of trees or
bushes. Gnatcatchers and kinglets are
the North American representatives of
the Old World Warbler family.

649 Black-tailed Gnatcatcher
Polioptila melanura

Description: 4½–5″ (11–13 cm). A tiny bird similar
to Blue-gray Gnatcatcher. Gray above,
whitish below. Male has *black crown*
during summer that extends to eyes.
*Long black tail, with narrow white edges and
white tips on outermost feathers.* Winter
male, female, and juveniles duller.

Voice: The common call is a harsh 2- or 3-note
wren-like scold: *chee chee chee.*

Habitat: Deserts and arid country; dry washes in the low desert.

Nesting: 3 or 4 pale blue, spotted eggs in a small, smooth cup nest placed in mesquite or other desert bush or a low tree.

Range: Resident in southeastern California, Nevada, Arizona, New Mexico, and Texas, southward into Mexico.

Identification of gnatcatchers can be difficult, particularly in the Southwest, where there are four species: the Blue-gray, Black-tailed, California, and Black-capped. The amount of white in the tail, the range, and small differences in the voice offer the best means of separating them.

California Gnatcatcher
Polioptila californica

Description: 4½–5″ (11–13 cm). Similar to Black-tailed Gnatcatcher but underparts grayer, and much less white in tail. Best identified by voice and range.

Voice: Similar to calls of the Blue-gray Gnatcatcher (not the Black-tailed), but more prolonged and cat-like.

Habitat: Deserts and arid country; dry washes in the low desert.

Nesting: 3 or 4 pale blue, spotted eggs in a small, smooth cup nest placed in mesquite or other desert bush or a low tree.

Range: Resident in extreme southwestern California.

This newly recognized species is similar to the Black-tailed Gnatcatcher, but the ranges of the two do not overlap. Not long after it was realized that the two were not the same species, the California Gnatcatcher was placed on the endangered list.

Black-capped Gnatcatcher
Polioptila nigriceps

Description: 4½–5" (11–13 cm). Similar to Black-
tailed Gnatcatcher, but black cap of
adult male more extensive; 2 outer tail
feathers wholly white.
Voice: Buzzy and whining calls like those of
Blue-gray Gnatcatcher.
Habitat: Streamside thickets.
Nesting: 3 or 4 pale blue, spotted eggs in a small,
smooth cup nest placed in mesquite or
other desert bush or a low tree.
Range: In the United States found only in
southeastern Arizona (Sonoita Creek).

This is a Mexican species that barely
crosses the border into southern
Arizona. It prefers moister environments
than the Black-tailed Gnatcatcher.

FAMILY MUSCICAPIDAE
SUBFAMILY TURDINAE
Thrushes

310 species: Worldwide except
Australia. Thirteen species breed in
North America. Many members of this
family are excellent singers. The best-
known species in North America are
the American Robin and the Eastern
Bluebird. The last named, a member of
a group of three species, is a hole-nester,
but most others build open, cup-shaped
nests. The family also includes the
brown-backed, spot-breasted thrushes
of the genus *Catharus,* the wheatears,
and the solitaires. Young of all species
have spotted breasts.

609 **Bluethroat**
Luscinia svecica

Description: 4¾" (12 cm). Brown above, white below.
Male has *striking blue throat and breast*

with rusty red "star" in the middle; black, white, and red bands across breast; white neck stripe and eyebrow. Females and juveniles have light buff throat bordered with dark brown feathers. All plumages have *rusty red patch at base of brown tail* (similar to that of American Redstart) displayed during nervous tail-flicking.

Voice: Song loud, varied, and introduced by repeated *dip, dip, dip.* Sometimes mimics the song of other birds. Alarm call is *huyt-tock.*

Habitat: Shrubby tundra in the breeding season.

Nesting: 4–7 brown-dotted green eggs in a cup nest well hidden on the ground.

Range: Breeds in northwestern Alaska. Also in Eurasia.

One of the most recent arrivals among North American birds. As Siberian populations of this handsome songster have increased with the recent warming trend, the species has been able to spread across the Bering Strait into Alaska.

491   Northern Wheatear
Oenanthe oenanthe

Description: 5½–6" (14–15 cm). A very rare, sparrow-sized bird of open ground. Warm brown above, buff-pink below; *bold white rump and sides of tail* contrast with black center and tip of tail, which form an inverted T.

Voice: Harsh *chak-chak!* Song is a jumble of warbling notes.

Habitat: Nests in rocky tundra; barren pastures and beaches in winter.

Nesting: 5–7 pale green eggs in a fur-lined cup of grass concealed under a rock, in a rabbit burrow, or in a crevice in a wall.

Range: Breeds in Alaska and extreme northern Canada, appearing very rarely in northern United States in fall. Winters in Eurasia and North Africa; very rare in North America in winter.

Two geographically separate populations of Northern Wheatears breed in North America. In fall the western population migrates southwestward to southern Asia. The eastern population migrates southeastward to winter in the Middle East. Thus the New World has been colonized by Northern Wheatears from both East and West; they maintain their ancestral distinction by continuing to follow separate migratory routes.

608 Eastern Bluebird
Sialia sialis

Description: 7″ (17 cm). Bright blue above and on wings and tail; rusty throat and breast; white belly and undertail coverts. Female similar, but duller.

Voice: Call a liquid and musical *turee* or *queedle.* Song a soft melodious warble.

Habitat: Open woodlands and farmlands with scattered trees.

Nesting: 4–6 pale blue eggs in a loose cup of grasses and plant stems in natural tree cavities, old woodpecker holes, fence posts, and bird boxes.

Range: Breeds east of Rockies from southeastern Canada to Gulf of Mexico; also in mountains of southeastern Arizona and southwestern New Mexico. Winters in southern part of breeding range. Also in Mexico.

This primarily eastern species breeds along the fringes of our area and also in the mountains of the Southwest, where it lives in open woodlands.

607 Western Bluebird
Sialia mexicana

Description: 6–7″ (15–18 cm). A long-winged, rather short-tailed bird. Male has *deep blue hood and upperparts; rusty red breast and crescent mark across upper back;* white belly. Female sooty gray above, with dull blue wings and tail. Juveniles like female but grayer, with speckled underparts. Female Eastern Bluebird similar to female Western, but usually has pale rusty, not grayish, throat.

Voice: Soft calls sound like *phew* and *chuck.* Song is a short, subdued *cheer, cheer-lee, churr.*

Habitat: Open woodlands and pastures where old trees provide nest sites.

Nesting: 4–6 pale blue eggs in a grass nest placed in a tree cavity or woodpecker hole.

Range: Breeds from southern British Columbia and western Alberta south to Baja and east throughout the mountains of the West to eastern New Mexico and extreme western Texas. Winters throughout most of breeding range, although northernmost populations usually withdraw slightly southward.

Females are attracted by the vivid blue of the male and by the availability of nesting holes, which are often in short supply. Once the male secures a nesting hole he entices the female with a colorful display that also serves to repel rivals. His rusty breast, like that of the American Robin, is used to signal aggression toward other males.

499, 606   Mountain Bluebird
Sialia currucoides

Description: 7″ (18 cm). Male pure sky-blue above, paler blue below, with a white abdomen; female similar, but duller and grayer.

Voice: Soft warbling notes.

Habitat: Breeds in high mountain meadows with scattered trees and bushes; in winter descends to lower elevations, where it occurs on plains and grasslands.

Nesting: 5 or 6 pale blue eggs in a nest of grass and plant fibers built in a natural cavity or bird box.

Range: Breeds from southern Alaska, Mackenzie, and Manitoba south to western Nebraska, New Mexico, Arizona, and southern California. Winters from British Columbia and Montana south through western United States.

Mountain Bluebirds frequently hover low over the ground and drop down to catch insects, or dart out from a branch, flycatcher fashion, and then return to another perch.

625 Townsend's Solitaire
Myadestes townsendi

Description: 8–9½″ (20–24 cm). A slender bird, resembling a mockingbird. *Gray overall,* unstreaked, slightly darker above, with thin *white eye ring and white outer tail feathers; pale rusty wing patch.* Juveniles are mottled gray and white. Sits upright, usually high on a branch.

Voice: Song made up of loud, melodious, fluty rising and falling phrases. Call is a squeaky *eeek.*

Habitat: Open coniferous forests, edges, or burns with single standing trees in the mountains.

Nesting: 3 or 4 grayish-white eggs, with light brown spots concentrated at the large end, in a large, loosely built nest of weeds, lined with rootlets, placed on the ground, in a hole, among roots, in a road cut, in an old mine shaft, or among rocks on talus slopes.

Range: Breeds from central Alaska, western Alberta, and Black Hills of South Dakota south to central California and central New Mexico. Winters throughout western United States north to British Columbia and Black Hills.

This is the northernmost of a number of mountain-forest thrushes (the solitaires) of the New World and the only species north of Mexico. Like other thrushes, it forages on the ground for berries and insects; in winter it descends to lower elevations and may even occur in desert oases.

492 Veery
Catharus fuscescens

Description: 6½–7¼" (17–18 cm). Smaller than a robin. Uniform cinnamon-brown or rufous-olive above, with faint spotting on upper breast. Other thrushes in the genus *Catharus* are more heavily spotted below.

Voice: Song a rich downward spiral with an ethereal quality; call note a descending *whew.*

Habitat: Moist deciduous woodlands; willow thickets along streams in the West.

Nesting: 4 blue-green eggs in a bulky cup of moss, plant fibers, and leaves, placed on the ground in a clump of grass or ferns or a few feet off the ground in a shrub.

Range: Breeds from southern British Columbia east to Newfoundland and south to Arizona, South Dakota, Minnesota, New Jersey, and in mountains to Georgia. Winters in tropics.

The Veery, a secretive bird, lives in dense shade. It migrates at night, the flock keeping together in dark skies by means of a "contact call" characteristic of the species. Experiments on other thrushes show that their vision in shade or twilight is better than that of most other birds.

470 Gray-cheeked Thrush
Catharus minimus

Description: 6½–8" (17–20 cm). Dull olive-brown, with pale, spotted underparts and *no rust color in plumage; sides of face tinged with gray; no eye ring.* Swainson's Thrush similar, but has buff eye ring and buff, not gray, cheeks. Other spotted thrushes show rust color on upperparts or tail.

Voice: Series of thin reedy notes inflected downward at the end.

Habitat: Nests in coniferous forests, especially in dense stands of stunted spruce and balsam; widespread on migration.

Nesting: 3–5 pale blue-green eggs, finely speckled with brown, in a solidly built cup of grass reinforced with mud and placed in a low conifer.

Range: Breeds from northern Alaska across northern Canada to Newfoundland, south to northern British Columbia, New York, and northern New England. Winters in tropics.

A reticent bird, the Gray-cheeked Thrush keeps mostly under cover, searching for food on the ground. This thrush is one of the few American birds that have spread to northeastern Siberia in the scrub tundra but migrate back through North America to the American tropics.

---

471 Swainson's Thrush
Catharus ustulatus

Description: 6½–7¾″ (17–20 cm). Uniformly dull olive-brown or olive-russet above, spotted below, with *buff eye ring and cheek.* The Gray-cheeked Thrush is similar, but has grayish cheeks and lacks conspicuous eye ring.

Voice: Song a series of reedy spiraling notes inflected upward.

Habitat: Coniferous forests and willow thickets.

Nesting: 3 or 4 pale green-blue eggs, finely spotted with light brown, in a well-built cup of moss and lichen lined and strengthened with twigs, leaves, and grass. The nest is generally concealed in a small forest shrub or tree.

Range: Breeds from Alaska east across Canada

to Newfoundland, south to British Columbia, Michigan, and northern New England, and in mountains to southern California, Colorado, and West Virginia. Winters in tropics.

Because each bird's territory is small and the species is abundant, one may hear a chorus of male Swainson's Thrushes sing briefly every morning and evening. This species sings, feeds, and breeds in shady thickets; migrants fly at night, feeding and resting during the day.

473 Hermit Thrush
Catharus guttatus

Description: 6½–7½" (17–19 cm). Smaller than a robin. The only one of our brown, spotted thrushes with dull brown upperparts and a rusty tail. Frequently flicks its tail.

Voice: Series of clear, musical phrases, each on a different pitch, consisting of a piping introductory note and a reedy tremolo. Call note a low *tuck*.

Habitat: Coniferous and mixed forests; deciduous woodlands and thickets on migration and in winter.

Nesting: 4 blue-green eggs in a well-made cup of moss, leaves, and rootlets concealed on the ground or in a low bush in the forest.

Range: Breeds from central Alaska east to Newfoundland and south to southern California, northern New Mexico, Wisconsin, and Virginia. Winters from Washington and southern New England southward.

Hermit Thrushes forage on the ground, most of the time under dense cover, hopping around and then watching in an upright position like a robin.

426 American Robin
Turdus migratorius

Description: 9–11″ (23–28 cm). Gray above, brick
red below. Head and tail black in males,
dull gray in females. Young birds are
spotted below.

Voice: Song is a series of rich caroling notes,
rising and falling in pitch: *cheer-up,
cheerily, cheer-up, cheerily.*

Habitat: Towns, gardens, open woodlands, and
agricultural land.

Nesting: 3–5 blue-green eggs in a well-made cup
of mud reinforced with grass and twigs,
lined with softer grasses, and placed in a
tree or on a ledge or windowsill. Robins
usually have 2 broods a season.

Range: Breeds from Alaska east across continent
to Newfoundland and south to
California, Texas, Arkansas, and South
Carolina. Winters north to British
Columbia and Newfoundland.

The mainstay of the American Robin
is earthworms. It hunts on lawns,
standing stock-still with head cocked
to one side as though listening for its
prey but actually discovering it by
sight. Formerly called simply the
"Robin."

528 Varied Thrush
Ixoreus naevius

Description: 9–10″ (23–25 cm). Superficially similar
to American Robin. *Slate gray upperparts;
rusty orange throat and breast* interrupted
by broad *slate-colored or black breast band;*
2 orange wing bars; off-white belly.
Female is similar, but paler; breast band
gray or absent. Young bird's breast
band incomplete, frequently with
orange and dusky speckles. Flight more
undulating than American Robin's.

Voice: Song 2 or 3 buzzy whistles, each drawn
out until it fades away, followed by a
short silence. Call a low *took.*

Habitat: Dense coniferous or deciduous forests with abundant water.

Nesting: 3–5 pale blue, spotted eggs in a moss-lined twig cup built in a small tree, sapling, or bush.

Range: Breeds from Alaska and Yukon south to Oregon, California, Idaho, and Montana. Winters from coastal Alaska southward.

This thrush lives on the shaded floor of coniferous forests. Like the American Robin, it feeds on earthworms and insects in open, bare areas. In winter it migrates to lowlands or flies south to California parks, habitats it shares with robins.

FAMILY MUSCICAPIDAE
SUBFAMILY TIMALIINAE
Babblers and Wrentits

264 species: Old World, plus one in western North America. The Wrentit is an inconspicuous, sparrow-sized bird confined to the chaparral habitat where it nests and finds its insect food.

639 **Wrentit**
Chamaea fasciata

Description: 6–6½" (15–17 cm). *Uniformly brown,* with faintly streaked breast and *conspicuous white eyes.* Its name is apt, for its head, beak, and eyes resemble those of a tit, whereas the long cocked tail and secretive habits are reminiscent of a wren.

Voice: An accelerating series of musical notes running together into a trill and dropping slightly in pitch toward the end: *peep peep peep-pee-pee-peepeepepeprrrr.* Call is a prolonged dry "growling" note. This species is far more often heard than seen.

Habitat:	Chaparral, shrubs, and brush.
Nesting:	3–5 greenish-blue eggs in a neat cup nest of bark fiber, held together by cobwebs and hidden in a low bush.
Range:	Resident from Columbia River on northern border of Oregon southward along coastal chaparral into Baja California and in Sierra Nevada foothills of California.

The Wrentit spends all of its adult life within the territory chosen in its first year. Individuals hesitate to cross open spaces of even 30 to 40 feet (9 to 12 meters), and it is believed that the wide Columbia River effectively stops the species from entering Washington, even though that side of the river offers a suitable habitat.

FAMILY MIMIDAE
Mockingbirds and Thrashers

34 species: New World. Ten species breed in North America. This family includes such well-known birds as the Gray Catbird, the Northern Mockingbird, and several thrashers. They are good to excellent singers, and the familiar Northern Mockingbird is a mimic of other birds. These birds are long-tailed and short-winged and have slender, slightly to strongly curved bills.

---

626 Gray Catbird
Dumetella carolinensis

Description:	8–9¼″ (20–23 cm). Smaller than a robin. A slender, long-tailed, *dark gray* bird with *black cap* and rusty undertail coverts.
Voice:	A long, irregular succession of musical and mechanical notes and phrases; a cat-like mewing. Sometimes seems to mimic other birds.

Habitat: Thickets and brush, residential areas and gardens.

Nesting: 4 or 5 glossy blue-green eggs in a bulky mass of twigs, stems, and leaves, lined with finer plant material and concealed in a dense bush or in a tangle of vines.

Range: Breeds from British Columbia, Manitoba, and Nova Scotia south to Washington, Texas, and Georgia. Winters from Carolinas and Gulf Coast southward.

This bird is often seen in suburban gardens. It forages mainly on the ground, gleaning insects from litter and low bushes and eats fallen berries during late summer and fall. It does not uncover litter with its feet like a sparrow but pokes with its bill, turning leaves and twigs to find the food underneath. It was formerly known simply as the "Catbird."

623   Northern Mockingbird
Mimus polyglottos

Description: 9–11″ (23–28 cm). Robin-sized. A slender, long-tailed gray bird with white patches on wings and tail.

Voice: A long series of musical and grating phrases, each repeated 3 or more times; often imitates other birds and regularly sings at night. Call a harsh *chack*.

Habitat: Residential areas, city parks, farmlands, open country with thickets, and desert brush.

Nesting: 3–5 blue-green eggs, spotted with brown, in a bulky cup of sticks and weed stems in a bush or low tree.

Range: Breeds from northern California, eastern Nebraska, southern Ontario, and Maritime Canada southward. Winters in southern part of range.

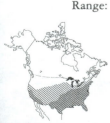

At mating time, the male Northern Mockingbird becomes increasingly exuberant, flashing his wings as he flies up in an aerial display, or singing while flying from one song post to another. After breeding, each parent establishes and vigorously defends its own winter territory. Mockingbirds require open grassy areas for their feeding; thick, thorny, or coniferous shrubs for hiding the nest; and high perches where the male can sing and defend his territory. Suburban gardens provide ideal habitats.

477 Sage Thrasher
Oreoscoptes montanus

Description: 8½" (22 cm). Brown-gray above, buff below with conspicuous black streaks; bill strongly curved; tail relatively short with white patches in corners; 2 white wing bars (often worn away by spring).

Voice: Continuous sweet warble without the broken-up phrases of the more familiar Brown Thrasher. The common call note is a deep *chuck*.

Habitat: Dry sagebrush plains and arid areas such as the floors of rocky canyons; winters in dense thickets and lowland scrub.

Nesting: 4 or 5 brown-blotched, blue-green eggs in a stick nest lined with rootlets and grass, and often with fur or feathers, and placed in a bush, usually with thorns.

Range: Breeds from southern interior British Columbia, central Idaho, and southern Montana south to southern inland California, southern Nevada, New Mexico, and western Oklahoma; also in an isolated area in southwestern Saskatchewan. Winters chiefly in southwestern states and southern Texas.

A good songster from a conspicuous perch or in flight, the Sage Thrasher is a less repetitious mimic than the Northern Mockingbird. It feasts on fruits and vegetables in gardens of desert towns, but also eats many damaging insects in alfalfa fields near its sagebrush nesting area.

476　**Bendire's Thrasher**
Toxostoma bendirei

Description:　9–11″ (23–28 cm). Robin-sized. A grayish-brown, short-billed thrasher of desert thickets. Similar to a young Curve-billed Thrasher with a short bill, but smaller, with a shorter tail and more triangular spots on breast. Eyes yellow.

Voice:　A clear, melodious warble with some repetition, and continuing at length. Call is a low *chuck.*

Habitat:　Desert scrub.

Nesting:　3 or 4 pale greenish eggs, with buff spots, in a stick nest lined with fine, soft material and hidden in a bush or cactus.

Range:　Breeds in southeastern California, southern Nevada, Arizona, and western New Mexico. Winters from southern Arizona southward.

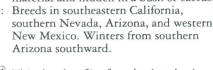

This thrasher flies from bush to bush, whereas other desert thrashers almost never fly. However, it does most of its feeding on the ground.

475　**Curve-billed Thrasher**
Toxostoma curvirostre

Description:　9½–11½″ (24–29 cm). Pale gray-brown with long tail and *strongly down-curved bill.* Breast faintly spotted; eyes yellow to orange. See Bendire's Thrasher.

Voice:　Song a rapid series of musical notes and phrases; call a sharp, whistled *whit-wheet!*

Habitat:　Desert brush and cactus.

Nesting:　4 pale blue-green eggs, finely speckled with brown, in a bulky cup of twigs and rootlets placed in a dense thorny desert shrub or in a branching clump of cactus.

Range:　Resident from northwestern and central Arizona, southeastern Colorado, and western Oklahoma southward.

The Curve-billed Thrasher forages on the ground, tossing aside litter in

search of insects with its prominently down-curved bill.

474 California Thrasher
Toxostoma redivivum

Description: 11–13" (28–33 cm). A large slender thrasher with a *long, deeply curved bill.* Dark brown above, with lighter gray-brown breast; *buff-brown undertail coverts.* Dark brown eyes; indistinct light brown eyebrow and dark "mustache."

Voice: Song recalls that of a Northern Mockingbird, but harsher, more halting, and less repetitious. An expert mimic. Call a low harsh *chuck* and a throaty *quip.*

Habitat: Chaparral, foothills, dense shrubs in parks or gardens.

Nesting: 2–4 pale blue-green, speckled eggs in a bowl-shaped nest of sticks and roots lined with finer materials and placed in a shrub.

Range: Resident in California west of Sierra Nevada.

The California Thrasher feeds on the ground under the shelter of bushes, using its heavy curved bill to turn over leaf litter in search of food. Its wings are shorter than those of the desert thrashers and it often escapes by scurrying rather than flying.

478 Crissal Thrasher
Toxostoma crissale

Description: 10½–12½" (27–32 cm). A large dark thrasher with a deeply curved bill. Brown above, with *lighter gray-brown, unstreaked underparts; dark "mustache" line;* yellowish eyes. Undertail coverts are *chestnut brown.*

Voice: Call is a rolling *chorilee, chorilee.* Song consists of loud repeated phrases.

Habitat: Dense underbrush near desert streams;

edge of canyon chaparral in the hot, low desert.

Nesting: 2–4 pale blue-green eggs in a rather large twiggy nest well hidden in dense mesquite or other thick desert vegetation.

Range: Resident in southeastern California, southern Nevada, southwestern Utah, and western Texas southward.

The Crissal Thrasher seldom flies in the open, but moves furtively among streamside mesquite thickets, willows, and other tangles. This bird resembles the California Thrasher in its habit of gathering food by hacking the ground with its heavy curved bill, but their ranges do not overlap. Except during the hottest months and briefly after molting, it delivers its loud melodious song year-round.

479 Le Conte's Thrasher
Toxostoma lecontei

Description: 10–11" (25–28 cm). The palest of the thrashers. *Light sand color,* with lighter, unstreaked underparts and darker tail. Dark bill, *dark eyes,* and dark eye line. Freshly molted (fall) birds have deep buff undertail coverts.

Voice: Song is a loud, rich melody recalling that of a California Thrasher, but less harsh and with infrequent repetition of phrases. Calls are a rising *whit* and *tu-weep.*

Habitat: Deserts with scant vegetation (mostly cholla and creosote bush), where the bird blends with the light-colored sandy soil.

Nesting: 2–4 light blue-green eggs, speckled with brown, in a bulky twig nest covered with coarser grasses and lined with fine stems and feathers, placed in a cholla cactus or low thorny bush.

Range: Resident in southeastern California, southern Nevada, southwestern Utah, and western and central Arizona.

This thrasher is a permanent resident in the Southwest. Like most other desert thrashers, it prefers to escape by scurrying away through the sparse vegetation, but will fly if pressed. It feeds mostly in early morning or just before dark, when insects are most active, and seeks shade in the midday heat.

FAMILY MOTACILLIDAE
Pipits and Wagtails

65 species: Primarily an Old World family; only two species breed in North America south of Alaska. These two are the widespread American Pipit and the localized Sprague's Pipit of the Great Plains. As with the similar larks, the pipits are birds of open country, inhabiting short-grass fields. Like larks they feed and nest on the ground, walking rather than hopping. These birds are plain brown and streaked. Many bob their tails.

Yellow Wagtail
Motacilla flava

Description: 6½" (17 cm). Small and dainty; tail makes up half its total length. Adult olive-gray above, *bright yellow below. White eye stripe,* wing bars, and outer tail feathers, which flash in flight. Immatures are olive-gray above, with buff underparts and eye stripe; dusky throat collar. Bobs its tail constantly.

Voice: Rarely sings, but often utters a call: *tsweep.* Alarm note sounds like *ple-ple-ple.*

Habitat: Willow tundra.

Nesting: 4–7 buff or greenish eggs, heavily mottled and spotted, usually hidden in a sheltered place on the ground.

Range: Breeds in northern and western Alaska and Aleutians. Winters in Old World. Also in Eurasia.

Although its range in North America is limited, the Yellow Wagtail is easy to locate during its short Arctic breeding season. When a ground predator or a human appears, several males gather, fly up, and circle the intruder.

653 White Wagtail
Motacilla alba

Description: 7″ (18 cm). A slim, small-bodied bird with a *long slender tail* that *wags constantly* and is half its total length. In summer, *black crown, nape, and extensive bib;* white face and underparts; black back, wings, and tail, with large white wing patch and white outer tail feathers. In fall, adult's black areas mute to grays. Immatures have olive-gray head and back, with dark throat band and white eye stripe, underparts, wing bars, and outer tail feathers.

Voice: Call constantly uttered in flight is a 2-tone *tschizzik* or *tzilip*. Warning call is *zipp*.

Habitat: Open country with short vegetation; frequently near water: streamsides, riverbanks, seacoasts. Also seen about towns and villages.

Nesting: 5 or 6 grayish-white eggs, finely speckled with blackish-brown, especially around the larger end, in a nest of grasses, rootlets, and leaves. Nest placed near or on the ground in an earthen bank, rock crevice, stone wall, or niche of an old building.

Range: Breeds in western Alaska and on neighboring islands. Winters in Old World. Also in Eurasia.

A lively ground bird that bobs its head in dove-like fashion and walks rather than hops; the White Wagtail flies in uneven arcs, calling as it flies. Except when breeding, it is very social.

461 **Red-throated Pipit**
Anthus cervinus

Description: 6″ (15 cm). Sparrow-sized; slim, long-legged ground bird; erect stance. *Light brown above, with dark streaking on mantle;* indistinct white wing bars. In winter, buff-white below, *heavily streaked on sides of neck and breast,* extending to flanks. In summer, face, throat, and breast washed with *wine-red or pink.*

Voice: Call a sharp *seeep,* or *see-eep.*

Habitat: Shrubby tundra or open areas of forest tundra; in winter, fallow agricultural fields, meadows, or beaches.

Nesting: 5–7 bluish eggs, spotted with brown, in a grass nest lined with fine material, on the ground sheltered by a tussock.

Range: Breeds in western Alaska. Winters in Old World, but a few turn up along Pacific Coast in fall and winter. Also in Eurasia.

A ground feeder in its territory, this pipit sings from the top of shrubs or, more often, in the air, as it rises slowly and then silently falls with wings and tail spread.

460 **American Pipit**
"Water Pipit"
Anthus rubescens

Description: 6–7″ (15–18 cm). A sparrow-sized, slender brown bird of open country. Crown and upperparts uniform brown; underparts buff with streaks; outer tail feathers white; legs usually black. Often bobs its tail and usually walks rather than hops. Sprague's Pipit has a streaked back and yellow legs, seldom bobs its tail.

Voice: Flight song a weak and tinkling trill; call a paired, high-pitched *pip-pip.*

Habitat: Arctic and alpine tundra; during migration and winter, beaches, barren fields, agricultural land, and golf courses.

Nesting: 4 or 5 gray eggs, thickly spotted with
brown and streaked with black, in a cup
of grass and twigs built on the ground
in the shelter of a rock or tussock.

Range: Breeds from northern Alaska,
Mackenzie, Canadian Arctic islands, and
Newfoundland, south in mountains to
California, New Mexico, and northern
New Hampshire. Winters across
southern states and north to British
Columbia and southern New England.

In the North the American Pipit feeds
on the countless insects on the edges
of tundra puddles, whereas in alpine
meadows it visits unmelted snowbanks.
Warm air rising from valleys below
transports many insects to high
altitudes; most of these die and are
frozen in snowbanks, providing food
for the pipits.

462   **Sprague's Pipit**
Anthus spragueii

Description: 6¼–7″ (16–18 cm). Sparrow-sized. A
slender-billed, streaked bird with white
outer tail feathers, *yellow legs*. Rarely
bobs its tail. American Pipit is similar,
but has darker legs and unstreaked
back; constantly bobs its tail.

Voice: Flight song, performed high in the air, is
a descending series of tinkling double
notes. Call a series of sharp *pips.*

Habitat: Short-grass plains and plowed fields.

Nesting: 4 or 5 gray eggs, spotted with purple
and brown, placed in a cup of grass,
concealed in a tussock on the ground,
and usually covered by an arch of bent
grass stems.

Range: Breeds from Alberta and Manitoba
south to Minnesota and Montana.
Winters from southern Great Plains east
to Mississippi and in Southwest.

More secretive and solitary than the
American Pipit, Sprague's does not

run in the open when disturbed but tries to hide in dense grass. When flushed, it flies low for a short distance and then drops down. Since it has not adapted to grasslands converted to cultivation, its range and numbers are now much reduced.

FAMILY BOMBYCILLIDAE
Waxwings

3 species: Temperate portions of the Northern Hemisphere. Two species breed in North America. These handsome, sleek, crested birds are named for the unique red, wax-like tips on the wing feathers of the adults. Waxwings are among the tamest of birds, often permitting a very close approach. They are very gregarious and often form large flocks, except in the nesting season, which is usually in late summer. They feed on both insects and berries.

482 Bohemian Waxwing
Bombycilla garrulus

Description: 7½–8½″ (19–22 cm). A sleek, gray-brown, crested bird. Similar to Cedar Waxwing but larger, grayer, and with conspicuous white wing patches and rusty (not white) undertail coverts.

Voice: High-pitched, lisping *seeee,* harsher and more grating than call of Cedar Waxwing.

Habitat: Open coniferous forests.

Nesting: 4–6 pale blue eggs, heavily spotted and scrawled with black, placed in a loose, flat saucer of twigs, lichens, and grass in a conifer.

Range: Breeds from Alaska, Yukon, Mackenzie, Saskatchewan, and Manitoba south to central Washington, northern Idaho, and northwestern Montana. Wanders

irregularly farther south and east during winter. Also in Eurasia.

This species forms large winter flocks in the northern United States only about once a decade. Its occasional erratic movements southward in winter are thought to be caused by food shortages in the North.

483 Cedar Waxwing
Bombycilla cedrorum

Description: 6½–8″ (17–20 cm). Smaller than a robin. A *sleek, crested, brown* bird with black mask, yellow tips on tail feathers, and hard red wax-like tips on secondary wing feathers. Almost always seen in flocks.

Voice: A thin lisp, *tseee.*

Habitat: Open woodlands, orchards, and residential areas.

Nesting: 4–6 blue-gray eggs, spotted with dark brown and black, in a bulky cup of twigs and grass placed in a tree in the open.

Range: Breeds from southeastern Alaska east to Newfoundland and south to California, Illinois, and Virginia. Winters from British Columbia, Great Lakes region, and New England southward.

In summer Cedar Waxwings are rather inconspicuous but in winter they travel in flocks of 40 or more, incessantly calling, turning, and twisting in flight, and frequently alighting in the same tree. Berries are their main food source in winter, but they revert to fly-catching in milder seasons.

FAMILY PTILOGONATIDAE
Silky Flycatchers

4 species: Central America; one species reaches the southwestern United States.

Silky flycatchers are slender, crested, short-winged, towhee-sized birds. They feed by catching flies or gleaning insects; they also take berries.

671, 672 **Phainopepla**
Phainopepla nitens

Description: 7–7¾" (18–20 cm). Larger than a sparrow. A slender, elegant bird with a *conspicuous crest,* longish tail, and *upright posture.* Male *glossy black,* with 2 white wing patches that show only in flight. Females and juveniles plain gray with pale wing patches.

Voice: Common calls include an up-slurred whistled *hoooeet* and a low *quirk.* The short warbled song is rarely heard.

Habitat: Desert scrub, but does not have strong preference for desert; it favors hot country with single, tall trees, preferably with mistletoe or other berries available when flying insects are scarce.

Nesting: 2–4 pale greenish, speckled eggs in a simple shallow nest placed in a mistletoe-bearing desert tree, such as the mesquite along washes, or in a tall tree bordering a river.

Range: Breeds in northern interior California, southern Nevada, southern Utah, and southern New Mexico southward into Mexico. Winters in southern part of breeding range.

The Phainopepla is the northernmost of a group of tropical birds that feed on mistletoe. In the Southwest the berries are seasonal, so it supplements them with insects, which it takes from the air in long sallies, like a typical flycatcher.

FAMILY LANIIDAE
Shrikes

74 species: Mainly Old World. Only two species live in North America, both of them migratory. These are sparrow- to robin-sized perching birds with hooked bills. They are territorial, living in open, brushy, or wooded habitats, and pursue insects or small reptiles, mammals, and birds from lookouts. They are known for impaling their prey on a thorn or pressing it into a tree crotch, often as a food cache.

643 Northern Shrike
Lanius excubitor

Description: 9–10½" (23–27 cm). Robin-sized. Pale gray above, white below, with faint barring on underparts, and *bold black mask ending at bill.* Black tail with white edges. Stout, hooked bill. Immature is browner. Usually seen perched atop a tree in the open. Loggerhead Shrike is shorter-billed, with black mask that crosses forehead.

Voice: Mixture of warbles and harsh tones with a robin-like quality.

Habitat: Open woodlands and brushy swamps in summer; open grasslands with fence posts and scattered trees in winter.

Nesting: 4–6 pale gray eggs, spotted with dark gray and brown. Nest a large mass of twigs, lichens, moss, and feathers, usually in a dense conifer.

Range: Breeds from Alaska across northern Canada to Labrador, south to northern British Columbia. Winters irregularly across northern tier of states south to northern California, Kansas, and Pennsylvania. Also in Old World.

The Northern Shrike sits quietly, often in the top of a tree, before swooping down after insects, mice, and small birds. It kills more than it can eat,

impaling the prey on a thorn or
wedging it in a forked twig. On lean
days it feeds from its larder.

642 Loggerhead Shrike
Lanius ludovicianus

Description: 8–10" (20–25 cm). Slightly smaller
than Northern Shrike, and slightly
darker gray above, white below, with
black face mask extending over bill.

Voice: A variety of harsh and musical notes and
trills; a thrasher-like series of double
phrases.

Habitat: Grasslands, orchards, and open areas
with scattered trees; open grassy
woodlands; deserts in the West.

Nesting: 4–6 white eggs, spotted with gray and
brown, in a bulky mass of twigs and
grass lined with plant down and feathers
and set in a thorny shrub or tree.

Range: Breeds from southern British Columbia,
central Alberta, central Saskatchewan,
southern Manitoba, southern Ontario
and southern Quebec, south throughout
United States. Winters in southern half
of breeding range.

The Loggerhead feeds mainly on large
insects such as locusts. In cold weather,
when insects are hard to find, it will
hunt small birds or mice. When
hunting is good, it stores excess food by
impaling it on thorns, barbed wire, or
the like, which explains its old name,
"Butcher Bird."

FAMILY STURNIDAE
Starlings

114 species. Tropical and temperate
regions of the Old World. Two species
have been introduced into North
America. Members of this family are
medium-sized songbirds with large feet

and strong bills, often with brilliantly glossy, black plumage. They are mainly birds of open country, although a few are adapted for living in forests. Most species are gregarious, and some form huge flocks outside the breeding season.

622, 670 European Starling
Sturnus vulgaris

Description: 7½–8½" (19–22 cm). Smaller than a robin. A short-tailed, chunky, iridescent black bird; long pointed bill, yellow in summer and dark in fall and early winter. Plumage flecked with white in winter. Juvenile is uniform dull gray with dark bill.

Voice: A series of discordant, musical, squeaky, and rasping notes; often imitates other birds. Call a descending *whee-ee.*

Habitat: Cities, suburban areas, farmlands, and ranches.

Nesting: 4–6 pale blue eggs in a mass of twigs, grass, and trash lined with finer plant material and feathers, and placed in a tree or building cavity.

Range: Occurs from Alaska and Quebec south throughout continent to Gulf Coast and northern Mexico. Native to Eurasia and widely introduced around the world.

Hordes of these birds damage vegetable or fruit crops and do considerable damage around orchards and feedlots, consuming and fouling the feed of domestic cattle. They join blackbirds to feed on locusts, ground beetles, and the like. Starlings compete with native hole-nesters for woodpecker holes and natural cavities.

656 Crested Myna
Acridotheres cristatellus

Description: 10½" (27 cm). A chunky, robin-sized bird. *All black with prominent bushy crest.* In flight, shows large *white patch on each wing and white tail tip.* Eyes, bill, feet yellow.

Voice: Song a variety of rich or harsh phrases with much repetition. An excellent mimic.

Habitat: Cities, suburbs, farms.

Nesting: 4 or 5 greenish-blue eggs in a large nest of grass, string, and so on, in a hole or cavity in a tree, building, or box.

Range: Introduced from southeastern Asia to Vancouver, British Columbia, in 1897, whence it spread through lower Fraser River Valley; it is seen sporadically in neighboring Washington.

Crested Mynas roost in colonies, but the flocks are small compared with those of European Starlings. Bold and fearless, these birds waddle on streets amid traffic and pick food from lawns, roadsides, and gardens.

FAMILY VIREONIDAE
Vireos

51 species: New World, mostly tropical and subtropical. Twelve species breed in North America, all in the genus *Vireo*. These birds are small, mostly plainly colored, and inhabit woodlands and forest edges. They are usually sluggish in movement and live on insects found among foliage and small branches. Vireos are persistent and tireless singers. They lay from three to five eggs in nests usually suspended from branches.

583 Bell's Vireo
Vireo bellii

Description: 4¾–5" (12–13 cm). Smaller than a
sparrow. Dull olive-gray above, whitish
below, with faint white eye ring and
fainter wing bars.

Voice: Fast, warbled *tweedle-deedle-dum?
tweedle-deedle-dee!* First phrase up,
second phrase down.

Habitat: Dense bottomland thickets, willow
scrub, and mesquite.

Nesting: 3–5 white eggs, sparsely marked with
brown, in a well-made pendant cup of
plant down and bark strips, placed in a
dense tree or shrub.

Range: Breeds from southern California,
Colorado, Dakotas, and Indiana
southward. Absent from eastern third of
United States. Winters in tropics.

Incubating Bell's Vireos, like other
vireos, are so fearless around their well-
camouflaged nests that an observer
may photograph them from a few feet
away. The strong, somewhat curved
beak, with a slight hook at the end,
like a miniature of a shrike's beak,
reminds us that these birds, however
gentle they seem, are determined
predators. They feed on caterpillars,
aphids, various larvae, and spiders. The
birds in southern California, known
as "Least Bell's Vireos," have been so
disturbed by cowbirds that they are
now nearly extinct.

Gray Vireo
Vireo vicinior

Description: 5–5¾" (13–15 cm). *Gray above, whitish
below, with faint white eye ring and lores;*
single, indistinct wing bar. The *sideways
twitching of its tail* is unique among
vireos and is reminiscent of that of
gnatcatchers.

Voice: Song is a series of 4–6 phrases with a

pause between each phrase and a much longer pause between stanzas: *cheerio . . . che-whew . . . chireep? . . . cheerio.*

Habitat: Dry brush, especially juniper in the piñon- and juniper-covered slopes of the southwestern mountains; scrub oak and other types of chaparral.

Nesting: 3 or 4 white eggs, lightly spotted with brown, in a nest hung from a forked branch in a bush.

Range: Breeds from southern California east to Utah, south to western Texas and Baja California. Winters south of U.S.–Mexico border.

This bird's overall gray blends with the blue-gray of the junipers. Even the bunchgrass and sagebrush have the same pale grayish color, a feature of the vegetation widespread on the arid mesas, slopes, and plateaus of the West. The Gray Vireo needs this camouflage when it searches for food near the top of the low cover it prefers.

584, 585 Solitary Vireo
Vireo solitarius

Description: 5–6″ (13–15 cm). Gray hood; olive green back; *white throat and underparts; 2 broad white wing bars and large white "spectacles."* The olive-backed birds of the Pacific states have yellowish flanks; those in the Rocky Mountains ("Plumbeus Vireos") are gray-backed with no yellowish tinge below.

Voice: Song a rather slow series of sweet, slurred phrases like that of Red-eyed Vireo, but slower and more musical. Call a husky chatter.

Habitat: Coniferous and mixed forests.

Nesting: 3–5 white eggs, lightly spotted with brown, in a pendant cup of bark strips and down, placed in a forked twig of a small forest tree.

Range: Breeds from British Columbia, central interior Canada, and Newfoundland

south through western mountains and to Great Lakes region, southern New England, and in Appalachians to North Carolina. Winters from South Carolina and Gulf Coast southward.

The Solitary Vireo is extraordinarily tame and seems to ignore humans near its nest; frequently, an incubating bird will allow itself to be touched. Like other vireos it moves slowly and deliberately through the trees, peering with head cocked to one side in search of insects.

587   Hutton's Vireo
Vireo huttoni

Description: 4¼–4¾" (11–12 cm). A small, grayish-olive vireo with a *partial white eye ring below, incomplete "spectacle,"* and 2 white wing bars separated by blackish. See Ruby-crowned Kinglet.

Voice: Loud short whistles and chatter. A monotonous 2-part phrase, either up-slurred or down-slurred: *chu-whe, chu-wee* or *che-eer, che-eer.* Call is a harsh *chit-chit.*

Habitat: Deciduous and mixed forests, primarily oak woodlands; also, live-oak tangles in canyons of the Southwest.

Nesting: 3 or 4 white eggs, with scattered brown spots, in a hanging cup nest lined with feathers and moss suspended from a shrub branch or young tree.

Range: Resident in southwestern British Columbia south to southern California, central Arizona, southwestern New Mexico, and western Texas.

This bird moves slowly, almost sluggishly through the canopy, halting after every move to forage for insects among the foliage. During winter, Hutton's Vireo may join a mixed flock, where it is easily confused with the smaller Ruby-crowned Kinglet.

586 Warbling Vireo
Vireo gilvus

Description: 5–6″ (13–15 cm). Sparrow-sized.
Similar to Red-eyed Vireo—olive green
above, whitish below, with no wing
bars—but lacks bold face pattern,
having only a narrow white eyebrow. The
Philadelphia Vireo (*Vireo philadelphicus*)
is also similar, but has yellow tinge to
underparts and dark spot between eye
and base of bill.

Voice: Drowsy, rambling warble, like song
of Purple Finch but slower; ends on
rising note.

Habitat: Deciduous woodlands, especially near
streams; in isolated groves and shade
trees.

Nesting: 3 or 4 brown-spotted white eggs in a
well-made pendant cup of bark strips
and plant down fastened to a forked
twig, usually near the top of a tall tree.

Range: Breeds from British Columbia,
southern Mackenzie, Manitoba, and
New Brunswick south to northern
Mexico, Louisiana, and Virginia.
Winters in tropics.

The best place to look for this modestly
plumaged vireo is in trees on the bank
of a stream. Here, in the breeding
season, one may hear its rambling song
and, after a careful search, spot it
moving deliberately through the foliage
in pursuit of insects. Although still
common in many areas, the Warbling
Vireo has decreased considerably
because of extensive spraying of
pesticides on shade trees.

582 Red-eyed Vireo
Vireo olivaceus

Description: 5½–6½″ (14–17 cm). Sparrow-sized.
Olive green above, whitish below, with
a *narrow white eyebrow bordered above with
black. Gray crown; red eye* (eye dark in

immature); no wing bars. Warbling
Vireo similar, but lacks gray crown and
black border over bold white eyebrow.

Voice: A series of short, musical, robin-like
phrases endlessly repeated; like that of
Solitary Vireo but faster and not so
musical.

Habitat: Broad-leaved forests; shade trees in
residential areas.

Nesting: 3 or 4 white eggs, sparsely marked with
dark brown, in a thin-walled pendant
cup of bark strips and plant fibers,
decorated with lichen and attached to a
forked twig.

Range: Breeds from British Columbia, Ontario,
and Gulf of Saint Lawrence south to
Oregon, Colorado, Gulf Coast, and
Florida. Winters in tropics.

The Red-eyed Vireo is a fierce fighter
around its nest and can intimidate even
the large Pileated Woodpecker. Its
horizontal posture and slow movement
through the understory of broad-leaved
woods make it an easy bird to study.

FAMILY EMBERIZIDAE
SUBFAMILY PARULINAE
Wood Warblers

115 species: New World. Fifty-two
species breed in North America. Most
members of this group are brightly
colored, active insect eaters. These
birds are misnamed, however, as the
vast majority produce nothing more
than buzzy, insect-like songs, hardly
what could be called a warble. In
spring warblers are the delight of bird-
watchers, with their distinctive patterns
and bright colors. In autumn, however,
when many of them are in dull plumage
and difficult to identify, they are
sometimes referred to as the "confusing
fall warblers." Several eastern species are
very rare visitors to the West Coast.

555 Tennessee Warbler
Vermivora peregrina

Description: 5" (13 cm). In spring, male greenish above, white below, with gray cap, white line over eye, dusky line through eye. In fall, olive above, yellowish below.

Voice: A sharp, staccato *di-dit-di-dit-di-dit-di-dit-dit-dit-dit,* fastest at the end; song often comprised of 3 distinct parts.

Habitat: Open mixed woodlands in the breeding season; in trees and bushes during migration.

Nesting: 5 or 6 brown-spotted white eggs in a nest lined with fine grasses, placed on the ground, and usually well hidden under a shrub or in a moss clump under a tussock.

Range: Breeds from Yukon, Manitoba, and Labrador south to British Columbia, Wisconsin, southern Ontario, and Maine. Winters in tropics.

This warbler was discovered in 1811 by the noted ornithologist Alexander Wilson, who chose its common name because he first saw it in Tennessee. Its numbers fluctuate greatly from year to year; at times it is very numerous, and a dozen or more may be observed in a single tree, while in other years very few are seen.

554 Orange-crowned Warbler
Vermivora celata

Description: 4½–5½" (11–14 cm). *Olive green above* with orange crown feathers, which usually remain hidden. Olive-yellow underparts with very faint breast streaking. *No eye ring or wing bars.*

Voice: Song is a simple trill going up or down the scale toward the end. Call a sharp *stik.*

Habitat: Forest edges, especially in low deciduous growth, burns, clearings, and thickets. On migration, often seen in riverside willows and in scrub oak chaparral.

Nesting: 4–6 white eggs, with reddish or
lavender spots often concentrated
around the large end, in a rather large
nest of grass and other plant fibers that
is lined with fur or feathers. Nest is
usually placed on the ground or in a
low shrub.

Range: Breeds from Alaska east to Quebec and
Labrador and south to California,
Arizona, and New Mexico. Winters from
southern United States into tropics.

The Orange-crowned Warbler is one of
the most common western warblers. Its
very lack of conspicuous field marks is
an aid to its identification. Like other
birds with concealed crown patches, this
warbler displays the crown only during
courtship or when alarmed.

---

551 Nashville Warbler
Vermivora ruficapilla

Description: 4–5″ (10–13 cm). Olive green above,
bright yellow below, with *top and sides
of head gray, narrow white eye ring,* and
inconspicuous patch of rust on crown.
Differs from Mourning Warbler
(*Oporornis philadelphia*) and
MacGillivray's Warbler in having
yellow throat, not gray or black, and
complete white eye ring.

Voice: A loud, ringing *teebit-teebit-teebit,
chipper-chipper-chipper-chipper;* usually
has 2 distinct segments.

Habitat: Woodland edges; thickets in open mixed
forests or brushy borders of swamps.

Nesting: 4 or 5 white eggs, speckled with brown,
in a cup of grasses, leaves, and roots,
lined with pine needles and fine grass
and concealed on the ground in the base
of a bush or a tussock of grass.

Range: Breeds from British Columbia and
northwestern Montana south to central
California and central Idaho; and from
Manitoba, Quebec, and Nova Scotia,
south to Minnesota, northern West

Virginia, and western Maryland.
Winters south of U.S.–Mexico border.

The Rocky Mountains and the prairies
form a barrier between the western and
eastern forms of this species. The two
populations show minor differences in
color but have similar habits. The
western bird was once called the
"Calaveras Warbler."

633 Virginia's Warbler
Vermivora virginiae

Description: 4–4¼" (10–11 cm). Male *gray above,*
with *yellow breast, rump, and undertail
coverts.* Throat and belly white. Chestnut
crown patch and white eye ring visible
at close range. Female is duller.

Voice: Song a musical *seedle-seedle-seedle, sweet,
sweet.* Call is a sharp *plink.*

Habitat: Scrub oak and other chaparral, piñon-
juniper brushland, pine and oak
woodlands.

Nesting: 3–5 white, finely speckled eggs in a
loosely built cup nest on the ground.

Range: Breeds from southeastern California,
southern Idaho, and northern Colorado
south to Arizona, New Mexico, and
western Texas. Winters south of
U.S.–Mexico border.

This warbler forages for insects and
spiders in scrub oaks near the ground.
Though males occasionally use a song
post such as the top of a juniper, they
also sing while feeding in the middle
of the chaparral. Virginia's closely
resembles three other warblers:
Nashville, Lucy's, and the rare Colima.

629 Colima Warbler
Vermivora crissalis

Description: 5″ (13 cm). Larger than Virginia's Warbler; lacks yellow on breast. *Gray above,* with chestnut crown patch and *olive-yellow rump. Whitish below,* with yellow undertail patch. Narrow eye ring, no wing bars.

Voice: Song like that of Virginia's Warbler. Call a sharp *plisk.*

Habitat: Deciduous and mixed montane forests.

Nesting: 4 creamy-white, spotted and splashed eggs in a cup nest built on the ground.

Range: Breeds in Chisos Mountains of western Texas and adjacent Mexico. Winters in Mexico.

This bird has one of the most restricted ranges of any American bird, comparable to that of the similarly local Kirtland's Warbler (*Dendroica kirtlandii*), which breeds only in central Michigan. However, because of its high mountain home, this warbler is not as well known. It is a rather slow-moving warbler that feeds in the low canopy of bushes or scrub oaks, although the male sings his territorial song from a high perch.

634 Lucy's Warbler
Vermivora luciae

Description: 4″ (10 cm). A small, plain warbler with white eye ring. Both sexes gray above, creamy white below, with *bright chestnut rump.* Chestnut crown feathers usually concealed, except in display. In fall, underside buff but undertail coverts white. Immatures have buff rump.

Voice: Song reminiscent of that of Yellow Warbler: *chit chit chit chit sweeta che-che-che.* Call is a soft *plenk,* often run into a series.

Habitat: Southwestern deserts, especially among cottonwoods and streamside trees and mesquite in washes or canyons.

Nesting: 4 or 5 white, speckled eggs in a well-lined cup nest in a tree, placed under loose bark or in a hole—a rare nest site among warblers.

Range: Breeds from California, Nevada and Utah south to southern Arizona and New Mexico. Winters south of U.S.–Mexico border.

The only desert warbler, Lucy's is characterized by a flicking tail, rapid motions, and a rich song.

549 Northern Parula
Parula americana

Description: 4½″ (11 cm). A small warbler; blue above with yellow-green "saddle" on its back, yellow throat and breast, and white belly; 2 white wing bars. Male has orange-brown chest band.

Voice: 1 or more rising buzzy notes dropping abruptly at the end, *bzzzzz-zip* or *bz-bz-bz-zip*.

Habitat: Breeds in wet, chiefly coniferous woods, in swamps, and along lakes and ponds; more widespread during migration.

Nesting: 4 or 5 brown-spotted white eggs in a woven basket-shaped nest of grass, bark, and vegetable fibers—neatly hidden in Spanish moss in the South, in "beard moss" or *Usnea* lichen in the North.

Range: Breeds from southeastern Canada to Gulf Coast. Winters from southern Florida southward into tropics.

This species is almost entirely dependent upon either Spanish moss or "beard moss" for nest sites. Although they breed mostly in coniferous forests in the North, during migration these birds also frequent deciduous trees and shrubs. In spring they are seen in large numbers along roadsides and in parks, yards, orchards, and gardens as well as woods.

542 **Yellow Warbler**
Dendroica petechia

Description: 4½–5″ (11–13 cm). Bright yellow with a light olive green tinge on back. Male has fine rusty streaks on breast. The only largely yellow warbler with *yellow spots in the tail* (not white).

Voice: Song a bright, musical *sweet-sweet-sweet, sweeter-than-sweet.* Call a sharp *chip.*

Habitat: Moist thickets, especially along streams and in swampy areas; gardens.

Nesting: 4 or 5 pale blue eggs, thickly spotted with brown, in a well-made cup of bark, plant fibers, and down, placed in an upright fork in a small sapling.

Range: Breeds from Alaska east across Canada to Newfoundland and south to southern California, northern Oklahoma, and northern Georgia; local in southern Florida. Winters in tropics.

Warblers are favorite hosts of cowbirds, and some warbler populations are in danger from such pressure. A cowbird lays only one egg per foster nest, but she may lay eggs in four or five nests in a short time, thus jeopardizing many broods. If the female Yellow Warbler discovers a cowbird parasitizing her nest, she quickly covers the alien egg with a new foundation and lays another clutch.

547 **Magnolia Warbler**
Dendroica magnolia

Description: 5″ (13 cm). Male bright yellow below with heavy black streaks, black facial patch, large white wing patch, and yellow rump. Female and immature birds similar, but duller. Broad white patches on sides of tail in all plumages.

Voice: *Weeta-weeta-weeteo.* Call note a *tslip.*

Habitat: Breeds in open stands of young spruce and fir. On migration, almost any place with shrubbery or trees.

Nesting: 4 brown-spotted white eggs in a shallow twig-and-grass nest lined with rootlets.
Range: Breeds from British Columbia across central Canada to northeastern United States, and in Appalachian mountains south to Virginia. A rare visitor to West Coast. Winters in tropics.

This attractive warbler received its name when it was discovered in the early 1800s in a magnolia tree in Mississippi during the spring migration to its northern breeding grounds.

494, 545 **Yellow-rumped Warbler including "Myrtle Warbler" and "Audubon's Warbler"**
Dendroica coronata

Description: 5–6″ (13–15 cm). Breeding male dull bluish above, streaked with black; breast and flanks blackish. *Rump, crown, and small area at sides of breast yellow.* Western male ("Audubon's Warbler") has yellow throat, large white patch in folded wing. Eastern male ("Myrtle Warbler") has white throat, 2 white wing bars. Females, fall males, and young are streaked gray-brown but always have yellow rump and white spots in tail.
Voice: A colorless buzzy warble; a sharp *chek!*
Habitat: Coniferous and mixed forests; widespread during migration and in winter.
Nesting: 4 or 5 white eggs, spotted and blotched with brown, in a bulky nest of twigs, rootlets, and grass, lined with hair and feathers and placed in a conifer.
Range: Breeds from northern Alaska, northern Manitoba, central Quebec, and Newfoundland south in West to northern Mexico and in East to Michigan, northern New York, Massachusetts, and Maine. Winters from southern part of breeding range southward into tropics.

Yellow-rumped Warblers are vivid and conspicuous birds that search for food both high and low in Douglas firs or pines. They most often sing from the high canopy of trees. During winter they disperse in loose flocks, and usually two or three birds at most are observed at a time. The birds constantly chirp a "contact call" that keeps the flock together.

546   Black-throated Gray Warbler
Dendroica nigrescens

Description: 4½–5″ (11–13 cm). *Head striped black and white; black bib on throat; white below,* with black stripes on sides; *gray back,* with black striping; 2 white wing bars and white outer tail feathers. Yellow spot between bill and eyes. Winter male, female, and juvenile lack black bib.

Voice: Song a series of buzzes, rising in pitch and intensity, then falling: *zee zee zee zee bzz bzz.* Call is a dull *tup.*

Habitat: Shrubby openings in coniferous forest or mixed woods, dry scrub oak, piñon and juniper, chaparral, and other low brushy areas; also in forests.

Nesting: 3–5 creamy white eggs, splashed with brown, in a tightly woven plant-fiber cup in a bush or tree, usually not higher than 10′ (3 m).

Range: Breeds from southern British Columbia (except Vancouver Island), Washington, Idaho, and Colorado southward. Winters in Southwest and in Mexico.

This bird resembles Townsend's Warbler in every respect except that it lacks the green and yellow colors of the latter. Whereas the bright plumage of Townsend's blends well with the bright green of the spruces and pines of the coastal forest, the drab appearance of the Black-throated Gray is a good adaptation to the bluish gray-green of western junipers.

544 Townsend's Warbler
Dendroica townsendi

Description: 4¼–5" (11–13 cm). Adult male has black crown, nape, ear patch, throat, and bib, and olive green back. *Face and breast bright yellow;* sides heavily streaked with black; white belly. Wings and tail dusky, with 2 white wing bars and white outer tail feathers. In winter, in male, female, and immature, black bib is replaced by dark streaking and black elsewhere becomes dusky olive.

Voice: A rising series of notes, usually with 2 phrases, the first repeated 3 or 4 times, the second once or twice: *weazy weazy weazy weazy twea* or *dee dee dee-de de.* Call is a soft *chip.*

Habitat: Coniferous forests; in old stands of Douglas firs, where it forages in the upper canopy.

Nesting: 3–5 white eggs, wreathed and speckled with brownish markings, in a well-concealed shallow cup in a conifer.

Range: Breeds from Alaska and British Columbia to northern Washington; Idaho, Montana, and Wyoming. Winters from southwestern California southward.

This warbler is a darker counterpart of the Black-throated Green Warbler (*Dendroica virens*), which breeds east of the Rocky Mountains. The pattern of Townsend's plumage is similar to that of the Hermit, Black-throated Gray, and Golden-cheeked (*Dendroica chrysoparia*) warblers; all these warblers are believed to have developed from one ancestral stock.

548 Hermit Warbler
Dendroica occidentalis

Description: 4½" (11 cm). *Yellow head; black chin and throat; gray back;* white underparts with black-streaked flanks. Gray wings and

tail, with white wing bars and outer tail
feathers. Female and immature have
little or no dark on throat; gray of back
extends to top of crown. No other
western warbler is as white underneath.

Voice: A series of high notes, somewhat less
buzzy than the song of a Townsend's
Warbler; recalls Yellow Warbler song
in pattern but less emphatic. Call is a
soft *chup.*

Habitat: Mature coniferous forests.

Nesting: 3–5 creamy-white eggs, speckled and
wreathed with light brown markings, in
a neat shallow cup nest of rootlets, bark,
and pine needles, "saddled" on a conifer
branch, usually 20–40′ (6–12 m) high,
but occasionally near the ground.

Range: Breeds from Washington to northern
California and Sierra Nevada. Winters
south of U.S.–Mexico border.

This species lives high in the canopy of
the tallest redwoods and Douglas firs
and is therefore difficult to observe.
Occasionally it has been found to
hybridize with Townsend's Warbler.
The similarity in their songs indicates
that the two species are close relatives.

552   Grace's Warbler
Dendroica graciae

Description: 4½–5″ (11–13 cm). Bright *yellow eye
stripe, chin, throat, and breast;* upperparts
gray streaked with black; underparts
white with black striping on sides;
wings and tail dark, with 2 white wing
bars and whitish outer tail feathers.
Sexes similar, though female and
juveniles may be paler.

Voice: Song is a short musical trill, faster
toward the end: *che che che che che-che-che-
che.* Call is a soft *chip.*

Habitat: Forests of pine or mixed pine and oak.

Nesting: 3 or 4 white or creamy eggs, finely
spotted with reddish brown, in a small
cup nest of rootlets and bark shreds

lined with hair or feathers, well concealed in a conifer, some 20–60′ (6–18 m) above the ground.

Range: Breeds from southern Nevada, Utah, and Colorado southward along mountains of Southwest. Winters south of U.S.–Mexico border.

Because this small bird lives high up in pine trees and is difficult to observe, little is known of its life history. It moves from treetop to treetop with a quick erratic flight, darting out of the canopy to catch prey in midair. During migration it prefers mountain forests similar to those in which it breeds, but in winter, in Central America, it also frequents lowland pine savannas and stands of tall pines.

553, 648 Blackpoll Warbler
Dendroica striata

Description: 5½″ (14 cm). Breeding male gray streaked above, with *black cap,* white cheeks and underparts, blackish streaks on sides. Female and nonbreeding male greenish above with vague streaking, yellowish green below. *Feet usually pinkish.*

Voice: Rapid series of high lisping notes all on 1 pitch, increasing and then decreasing in volume; *seet-seet-seet-seet-seet-seet-seet-seet.*

Habitat: Breeds in coniferous forests. During migration is found chiefly in tall trees.

Nesting: 4 or 5 brown-spotted white eggs in a twig-and-grass nest, often lined with feathers and usually placed in a small evergreen tree.

Range: Breeds from Alaska and northern Canada to southern Canada and northern New England. Winters in tropics.

The Blackpoll Warbler breeds in the Far North. In August it takes off toward the

Southeast, across the Atlantic states, through Florida, then on to South America. It returns by the same route in April and May, but is rarely seen west of the Rockies in spring; however, in fall small numbers of mostly young birds occur regularly along the Pacific Coast.

541, 661 American Redstart
Setophaga ruticilla

Description: 4½–5½" (11–14 cm). Male black with bright orange patches on wings and tail; white belly. Females and young birds dull olive-brown above, white below, with yellow wing and tail patches.

Voice: 5 or 6 high-pitched notes or 2-note phrases, ending with an upward or downward inflection: *chewy-chewy-chewy, chew-chew-chew.*

Habitat: Second-growth woodlands; thickets with saplings.

Nesting: 4 dull-white eggs, speckled with brown, in a neat, well-made cup of grass, bark shreds, plant fibers, and spiderweb lined with fine grass and hair, and placed in a fork in a sapling or next to the trunk of a tree.

Range: Breeds from southeastern Alaska east to central Manitoba, Quebec, and Newfoundland, and south to northern California, Colorado, Oklahoma, northern Louisiana, and South Carolina. Winters in California, Texas, and Florida, and in tropics.

The American Redstart's flashy color and constant movement—it frequently droops its wings and fans its tail to expose its bright signal patches—make this fly-catching warbler unmistakable.

472 Northern Waterthrush
Seiurus noveboracensis

Description: 6″ (15 cm). A terrestrial, thrush-like warbler. Olive-brown above; pale yellowish below with black streaks; *narrow, yellowish-white eyebrow; streaked yellowish throat. Frequently bobs tail.*

Voice: Song *chee-chee-chee, chip-chip-chip-chew-chew-chew,* loud and ringing, speeding up at the end. Call a sharp *chink.*

Habitat: Lakeshores, wooded swamps, and cool bogs, in the breeding season; almost any wooded habitat during migration.

Nesting: 4 or 5 creamy-white eggs, with brown blotches, in a nest of moss set in a bank, at the base of a trunk, or among the roots of an overturned tree.

Range: Breeds from Alaska and much of Canada south to northern United States. Winters in tropics.

Ornithologist E. H. Forbush's observation about the Northern Waterthrush, made more than half a century ago, still applies: "It is a large wood warbler disguised as a thrush and exhibiting an extreme fondness for water."

550 MacGillivray's Warbler
Oporornis tolmiei

Description: 4¾–5½″ (12–14 cm). *Slate gray hood extending to upper breast,* where it darkens to black. *Olive green above, yellow below;* female slightly paler. Both sexes have *broken white eye ring.* In fall, hood lighter, broken eye ring less distinct.

Voice: Song a chanting *tree tree tree tree sweet sweet!* Call a loud *tik,* sharper than the calls of most other western warblers.

Habitat: Coniferous forest edges, burns, brushy cuts, or second-growth alder thickets and streamside growth.

Nesting: 3–5 white eggs, with brown spotting, in a grassy cup nest close to the ground in a bush or tall weeds.

Range: Breeds from Alaska and Yukon south to
California and central New Mexico.
Winters in tropics.

MacGillivray's is a common western
warbler. Two similarly hooded warblers
occur east of the Rockies, the
Connecticut Warbler (*Oporornis agilis*)
and the Mourning Warbler (*Oporornis
philadelphia*). No doubt these all
originated from a common "hooded
warbler" forebear during the vicissitudes
of the past Ice Age, when during warm
interglacial periods the forests
expanded, only to be split again when
the cold grip of the glaciers returned.

563, 564 Common Yellowthroat
Geothlypis trichas

Description: 4½–6" (11–15 cm). Olive-brown above,
bright yellow on throat and upper breast.
Male has *bold black mask,* bordered
above with white. Females and young
males lack face mask, but may be
recognized by bright yellow throat and
wren-like behavior.

Voice: Loud, fast *witchity-witchity-witchity-
witchity-wit* or *which-is-it, which-is-it,
which-is-it.* Call a sharp *chip.*

Habitat: Moist thickets and grassy marshes.

Nesting: 3–5 white eggs, with brown and black
spots, in a loose mass of grass, sedge,
and bark, lined with rootlets, hair, and
fine grass, and concealed on or near
the ground in a dense clump of weeds
or grass.

Range: Breeds from Alaska, Ontario, and
Newfoundland south throughout
United States. Winters in southern
states and in tropics.

This warbler of moist thickets is
common throughout North America,
but we get a glimpse of it only when the
male climbs the tallest stalk and utters
his abrupt song. To foil predators,

parents drop down into the thick of the grasses or weeds, secretly approach their well-hidden nest, deliver the food, and depart by another route.

543 Wilson's Warbler
Wilsonia pusilla

Description: 4½–5″ (11–13 cm). Adult male olive green above and yellow below, with *black crown patch.* Most females and all young birds lack black crown and may be distinguished from other olive green warblers with yellow underparts by lack of wing bars, streaks, tail spots, or other markings.

Voice: A rapid, staccato series of *chips,* which drop in pitch at the end.

Habitat: Moist thickets in woodlands and along streams; alder and willow thickets and bogs.

Nesting: 4 or 5 brown-spotted white eggs in a bulky mass of leaves, rootlets, and moss, lined with hair and fine plant materials, concealed on the ground in a dense clump of weeds or sedge.

Range: Breeds from Alaska eastward to Newfoundland and south to southern California, New Mexico, central Ontario, and Nova Scotia. Winters in tropics.

It is easy to observe this common warbler, which has little fear of humans, because it searches the outsides of leafy branches, often catching flying insects on the wing. During early summer, the foraging male utters long bursts of vivid song.

519 Red-faced Warbler
Cardellina rubrifrons

Description: 5¼″ (13 cm). Gray above, white below, with bright *red forehead, throat, and breast;* black crown and ear patch; white nape patch and rump.

Voice: Song is a series of rich notes: *sweet-sweet-sweet-weeta-see-see-see,* similar to that of the Yellow Warbler. Call is a loud *chup.*

Habitat: Montane coniferous forests.

Nesting: 3 or 4 white, marked eggs in a loosely assembled ground nest of rootlets and grasses, sheltered by a log, rock, or patch of weeds.

Range: Breeds in southeastern Arizona and southwestern New Mexico. Winters in tropics.

Active and energetic like most warblers, the Red-faced keeps to the outside canopy of tall trees. This warbler has the characteristic habit of flicking its tail sideways.

514 Painted Redstart
Myioborus pictus

Description: 5″ (13 cm). *Black* hood and *upperparts* accentuated by large white wing patch and outer tail feathers. Bright *red breast* and *white belly.* Sexes are alike.

Voice: Song is a rich, chanting *cheery cheery cheery chew.* Call is a *cheereo,* different from calls of other warblers.

Habitat: Pine or pine-oak woods, oak canyons, piñon- and juniper-covered high slopes.

Nesting: 3 or 4 creamy-white, finely speckled eggs in a grass nest, with fine grass or hair lining, placed in a ground hollow.

Range: Breeds in southern Arizona, New Mexico, and western Texas. Winters south of U.S.–Mexico border.

This bird flits energetically, drooping its wings and fanning its tail in typical redstart fashion. It catches flying insects, much as the American Redstart does. The two birds are not closely related but have evolved in a similar way and fill the same ecological niche in the forest.

540 Yellow-breasted Chat
Icteria virens

Description: 6½–7½" (17–19 cm). The size of a large
sparrow. Olive green above, with bright
yellow breast and white abdomen. *Stout
black bill;* black face mask bordered
above and below with white; *white
"spectacles."* Tail long.

Voice: Series of widely spaced croaks, whistles,
and short repeated phrases, very unlike
a typical warbler's song. Often sings at
night. At times it performs a musical
display flight, flopping awkwardly up
and down with legs dangling, while
singing.

Habitat: Dense thickets and brush, often with
thorns; streamside tangles and dry
brushy hillsides.

Nesting: 4 or 5 brown-spotted white eggs in a
bulky mass of bark, grass, and leaves,
lined with finer grass and concealed in
a dense bush.

Range: Breeds from British Columbia, Ontario,
and (rarely) Massachusetts south to
California, Gulf Coast, and Florida.
Winters in tropics.

The Yellow-breasted Chat is an atypical
wood warbler. Its large size and stout
bill, long tail, and distinctive display
flight, hovering with slow, deep-
flapping wings and dangling feet,
make it seem more like one of the
mockingbirds or thrashers. Since it
prefers brushy tangles and is relatively
shy, it is more often heard than seen.

529 Olive Warbler
Peucedramus taeniatus

Description: 4½–5" (11–13 cm). *Tawny orange head,
nape, and breast;* broad *black mask* extends
from bill to behind ear. Gray above,
white below, with dark wings and tail,
and broad white wing bars. Female has
olive-gray crown, nape, and ear patch;

upperparts gray; eye stripe, throat, and upper breast have dingy yellowish wash; belly white. Plumage duller in fall; young males resemble females.

Voice: Song a whistled, titmouse-like series of phrases: *peter-peter-peter.* Call a down-slurred *kew.*

Habitat: High-altitude pine and subalpine fir belts in mountains.

Nesting: 3 or 4 grayish-white or bluish eggs, heavily speckled with black, in a neat cup of fine rootlets, grass, moss, and lichens, placed high in a conifer near the end of a horizontal branch.

Range: Breeds in central and southeastern Arizona and southwestern New Mexico. Winters mainly south of U.S.–Mexico border.

The Olive Warbler has no close allies among the warblers, and indeed may not really be a warbler at all. Its habits are not well known since it lives in tall trees, often in inaccessible mountains.

FAMILY EMBERIZIDAE
SUBFAMILY THRAUPINAE
Tanagers

241 species: Chiefly tropical America; only five species—one of them introduced—breed in North America north of Mexico. These brightly colored, usually stout-billed birds are mainly forest inhabitants and are chiefly insectivorous but also eat small fruits. They occur in our area in the warmer months and spend the winter well within the tropics.

522, 589 Hepatic Tanager
Piranga flava

Description: 7–8″ (18–20 cm). Male is a subdued *orange-brick color,* darker than Summer

Tanager. Both sexes have *dark bill* and *ear patch.* Female olive green above, deep yellow below, with more orange tint to throat than other female tanagers.

Voice: Strong short phrases, whistled vireo-fashion at even intervals; each phrase may rise, fall, or remain on the same tone. Call notes are a low *chup* and an inquisitive *wheet?*

Habitat: Coniferous mountain forests; live oaks.

Nesting: 3–5 bluish eggs, with fairly heavy overall blotches, in a shallow nest of rootlets and weeds on a low horizontal branch.

Range: Breeds from northwestern Arizona, New Mexico, southern Nevada, southeastern California, and Texas, south to Mexico; also from Costa Rica to South America. Winters south of U.S.–Mexico border.

Though insect feeders during the nesting period, these tanagers eat figs, ripe guavas, and other fruits on their winter grounds in Central America.

523, 530 Summer Tanager
Piranga rubra

Description: 7–8″ (18–20 cm). Male solid rose-red with *pale bill.* Female pale olive green above, dull yellow below. Male Northern Cardinal has black face, conical red bill, and crest. See Hepatic Tanager.

Voice: Song like an American Robin's, but softer and sweeter. Distinctive rattling *chick-tucky-tuck.*

Habitat: Open woodlands and shade trees.

Nesting: 3 or 4 blue-green eggs, spotted with brown, in a shallow, flimsy cup near the end of a horizontal branch, 10–20′ (3–6 m) above the ground.

Range: Breeds from southern California, Nevada, Nebraska, and New Jersey, south to Gulf Coast and northern Mexico. Winters in tropics.

Tanagers eat insects and small fruits obtained from the canopy of trees, where they spend most of their time. In this species the adult males remain red all year.

531, 565   **Western Tanager**
Piranga ludoviciana

Description: 6–7½" (15–19 cm). Adult male has *brilliant red head, bright yellow body, with black back, wings, and tail.* 2 wing bars; smaller uppermost bar yellow, lower one white. Female is yellow-green above, yellow below; wing bars similar to male's.

Voice: Song is robin-like in its short fluty phrases, rendered with a pause in between. The quality is much hoarser, however. Call is a dry *pit-r-ick.*

Habitat: Open coniferous forests.

Nesting: 3–5 bluish-green, speckled eggs in a frail, shallow saucer nest of woven rootlets, weed stalks, and bark strips, "saddled" in the fork of a horizontal branch of Douglas fir, spruce, pine, or occasionally oak, usually at a low elevation.

Range: Breeds from southern Alaska and Mackenzie southward. Winters in tropics.

In late spring and early summer the Western Tanager, first recorded on the Lewis and Clark expedition (1803–1806), feeds on insects, often like a flycatcher, from the high canopy. Later it feeds on berries and other small fruits.

FAMILY EMBERIZIDAE
SUBFAMILY CARDINALINAE
Cardinals, Grosbeaks, and Allies

39 species: Chiefly tropical America. Ten species occur in North America. These mainly bright-colored birds have

conical bills that are adapted for crushing seeds. Some are nonmigratory and strongly territorial the year round, while others migrate back to the tropics at the end of the breeding season.

520, 616 Northern Cardinal
Cardinalis cardinalis

Description: 8–9″ (20–23 cm). Male bright red with *crest,* black face, *stout red bill.* Female buff-brown tinged with red on crest, wings, and tail.

Voice: Rich *what-cheer, cheer, cheer; purty-purty-purty-purty* or *sweet-sweet-sweet-sweet.* Also a metallic *chip.*

Habitat: Woodland edges, thickets, brushy swamps, and gardens.

Nesting: 3 or 4 pale green eggs, spotted with red-brown, in a deep cup of twigs, leaves, and plant fibers concealed in a thicket.

Range: Resident in eastern United States and southern Canada (locally) south to Gulf Coast, and from southern California, Arizona, and southern Texas southward.

Feeding mainly on the ground in the open and nesting in thickets, the Northern Cardinal is well suited to garden areas. Nonmigratory, it stays around bird feeders even in the snowy winters of southern Canada and the northeastern states, but it does best where winters are milder.

618, 621 Pyrrhuloxia
Cardinalis sinuatus

Description: 7½–8½″ (19–22 cm). Male gray with rose-red breast, crest, wings, and tail. Female similar but paler, and lacks red on the breast. Stubby, parrot-like, *yellow bill.*

Voice: A series of whistled notes, similar to

those of Northern Cardinal, but thinner and shorter.

Habitat: Desert brush, especially along streambeds.

Nesting: 3 or 4 white eggs, lightly speckled with brown, in a loosely built cup of grass, twigs, and bark strips concealed in dense, thorny bush.

Range: Resident from Arizona, southern New Mexico, and southern Texas southward.

Pyrrhuloxias feed on seeds and insects and benefit cotton fields by destroying great numbers of cotton worms and weevils. When an observer approaches, a pair will fly up to a high watch post, erect their crests, and sound a loud alarm. The name Pyrrhuloxia comes from Latin and Greek words meaning "bullfinch with a crooked bill." As has been suggested repeatedly, it would be more appropriate to call it the Gray Cardinal.

Rose-breasted Grosbeak
Pheucticus ludovicianus

Description: 8″ (20 cm). Starling-sized. Heavy pinkish-white bill. Male black and white with conspicuous *rose-red patch on breast and underwings.* Female white above and below with heavy brown streaking; prominent white eyebrow; yellow wing linings.

Voice: Its distinctive call note is a sharp, penetrating, metallic *eek-eek.* Song is like that of an American Robin, but softer and more melodious.

Habitat: Moist woodlands adjacent to open fields with tall shrubs; also old and overgrown orchards.

Nesting: 4 or 5 purple-spotted whitish eggs in a loosely made nest of twigs, grass, and plant fibers set in a low branch of a tree.

Range: Breeds from northeastern British Columbia, southern Manitoba, and Nova Scotia south to southern Alberta,

central North Dakota, central Oklahoma, and New Jersey, and in mountains as far south as northern Georgia. Appears regularly on West Coast. Winters in tropics.

This handsome grosbeak is one of the most conspicuous birds before the foliage comes into full leaf in early May. It is beneficial to farmers, consuming many potato beetles and larvae as well as weed seeds, wild fruits, and buds.

424, 497 Black-headed Grosbeak
Pheucticus melanocephalus

Description: 7½″ (19 cm). Starling-sized. Heavy pinkish-white bill. Male has black head; *tawny-orange breast;* yellow belly; and *tawny back with black streaking;* black wings and tail with conspicuous white patches. Female has white eyebrows and pale buff underparts; breast very finely streaked. Young resemble females.

Voice: Rich warble similar to that of a robin but softer, sweeter, and faster. Call note an emphatic, sharp *tick,* slightly metallic in tone.

Habitat: Open, deciduous woodlands near water, such as river bottoms, lakeshores, and swampy places with a mixture of trees and shrubs.

Nesting: 3 or 4 greenish eggs, spotted with brown, in a loosely built stick nest lined with rootlets, grasses, and leaves, and placed among the dense foliage of an outer tree limb.

Range: Breeds from southwestern Canada east to western North Dakota and Nebraska and south to mountains of Mexico. Winters in Mexico.

The Black-headed Grosbeak hybridizes with its eastern counterpart, the Rose-breasted Grosbeak, along their mutual boundary. This situation arose when the treeless prairies, which once formed a barrier between the two species, became dotted with towns and homesteads, providing suitable habitats for both species. The Black-headed Grosbeak is a rather still and secretive bird throughout the summer.

496, 615   Blue Grosbeak
Guiraca caerulea

Description: 6–7½" (15–19 cm). Slightly larger than a House Sparrow. Male dark blue with *2 chestnut wing bars* and a stout, dark bill. Female dark buff-brown with 2 buff wing bars.

Voice: Sweet, jumbled warble. Also a metallic *klink.*

Habitat: Brushy moist pastures and roadside thickets.

Nesting: 3 or 4 pale blue eggs in a loose cup of grass, weed stems, and leaves concealed in a clump of weeds.

Range: Breeds from California, Colorado, Missouri, Illinois, and New Jersey southward. Winters in tropics.

After breeding, small flocks of Blue Grosbeaks feed together or mix with other seed-eating birds such as sparrows. They also search out insects, especially grasshoppers, that live in the grassy vegetation of open fields.

465, 605   Lazuli Bunting
Passerina amoena

Description: 5–5½" (13–14 cm). Sparrow-sized. Male bright blue with pale cinnamon breast, white belly and wing bars. Female dull brown, lighter below, with 2 pale wing bars.

Voice: A high-pitched, excited series of warbled phrases, the first notes usually repeated, descending the scale and ascending again at the end.

Habitat: Dry, brushy ravines and slopes; cleared areas and weedy pastures.

Nesting: 3 or 4 pale blue eggs in a loose cup of grass and rootlets in a bush.

Range: Breeds from British Columbia, Saskatchewan, and North Dakota south through western United States to southern California, northern New Mexico, western Oklahoma, and eastern Nebraska. Winters south of U.S.–Mexico border.

The Lazuli hybridizes with its eastern counterpart, the Indigo Bunting (*Passerina cyanea*), on the Great Plains, where their ranges overlap. A diligent songster, the male patrols the perimeter of his territory, spending much time on his song perches.

602 Indigo Bunting
Passerina cyanea

Description: 5½" (14 cm). Sparrow-sized. *In bright sunlight male brilliant turquoise blue,* otherwise looks black; wings and tail darker. Female drab brown, paler beneath.

Voice: Rapid, excited warble, each note or phrase given twice.

Habitat: Brushy slopes, abandoned farmland, old pastures and fields grown to scrub, woodland clearings, and forest edges adjacent to fields.

Nesting: 3 or 4 pale blue eggs in a compact woven cup of leaves and grass placed in a sapling or bush in relatively thick vegetation and within a few feet of the ground.

Range: Breeds from southeastern Saskatchewan east to New Brunswick, and south to central Arizona, central Texas, Gulf Coast, and northern Florida. Winters in southern Florida and in tropics.

Indigo Buntings have no blue pigment; they are actually black, but the diffraction of light through the structure of the feathers makes them appear blue. These attractive birds are also found in rural roadside thickets and along the right-of-way of railroads, where woodlands meet open areas. They are beneficial to farmers and fruit growers, consuming many insect pests and weed seeds.

604   Varied Bunting
Passerina versicolor

Description: 4½–5½" (11–14 cm). Sparrow-sized. Male dark purple-blue, with a dull red patch on nape; looks all black at a distance. Female dull gray-brown *without distinctive markings.*

Voice: A series of sweet notes, each note or phrase repeated.

Habitat: Dense desert brush, especially along streambeds.

Nesting: 3 or 4 pale blue eggs in a deep cup of grass, twigs, and bark strips placed in a dense thicket.

Range: Resident in southern Arizona, southern New Mexico, and southern Texas.

As with other, more common and widespread buntings, the singing male Varied Bunting is conspicuous, while the female is secretive and lives hidden in vegetation.

597, 603   Painted Bunting
Passerina ciris

Description: 5½" (14 cm). Sparrow-sized. Perhaps North America's most colorful bird: male has bright red underparts and rump, green back, blue head, and red eye ring; female bright green all over, paler below.

Voice: Loud, clear, and variable song consisting of a series of high-pitched musical notes. Call is a sharp, metallic *tsick.*

Habitat: Brushy tangles, hedgerows, briar patches, woodland edges, and swampy thickets.

Nesting: 3 or 4 white eggs, marked with reddish-brown dots, in a cup of compactly woven grass stems, rootlets, and bark strips, lined with moss and hair, placed near the ground in the fork of a bush or small tree.

Range: Breeds from Missouri and North Carolina south to the southeastern states and west to New Mexico and Oklahoma. Winters from Gulf Coast states southward.

Though the Painted Bunting's song is not particularly musical, males used to be favorite cage birds because of their beautiful coloration; they are still sold in Mexico. Males sing all year round except during late summer, when they molt.

FAMILY EMBERIZIDAE
SUBFAMILY EMBERIZINAE
New World Sparrows and Their Allies

279 species: Worldwide except the Australian region. Fifty-two species breed in North America. They range from the small, streaked sparrows to the larger towhees, and include the juncos, longspurs, and the Snow and McKay's buntings. All have conical bills, which they use to crush seeds. Most species also eat insects, especially during the summer when there are young to be raised.

596 **Green-tailed Towhee**
Pipilo chlorurus

Description: 6¼–7" (16–18 cm). A ground-dwelling species, smaller than the other towhees. *Rufous cap; olive green above;* white throat and belly; gray breast. White lores and dark "mustache" stripe. Yellow wing linings. Sexes similar.

Voice: Song a loud, lively series of slurred notes and short, buzzy trills. Call a short, nasal *mew*.

Habitat: Sagebrush, mountain chaparral, piñon-juniper stands, and thickets bordering alpine meadows.

Nesting: 4 heavily spotted white eggs in a rather loosely built nest on the ground or in low, protected sites such as chaparral, juniper, or yucca.

Range: Breeds from central Oregon south through mountains to southern California and Great Basin to southeastern New Mexico. Winters at lower elevations and south to southern Arizona and central and southern Texas. Also in Mexico.

This shy bird hops and scratches for food under low cover, flicking its tail and raising its rufous cap into a crest. It prefers low scrub and occurs in brushy openings in boreal forests on western mountains, as well as in sagebrush habitats.

425 Rufous-sided Towhee
Pipilo erythrophthalmus

Description: 7–8½″ (18–22 cm). Male has *black hood, back, and wings, with white wing bars and spots.* Tail black with white edging on outer feathers; breast and belly white with *bright rufous sides.* Female has same pattern, but is brown where male is black. Both sexes have red eyes. Eastern birds lack white spots on upperparts.

Voice: The song varies, often with a few introductory notes and usually ending with a long trill, such as *drink-your-teeaaa* or *to-wheeeee.* On the Pacific Coast, the buzzy trill makes up the entire song. Call is an inquisitive *meewww?*

Habitat: Forest edges, thickets, woodlands, gardens, and shrubby park areas.

Nesting: 3–6 white eggs, with reddish-brown and lilac spots, in a loose cup nest built in a dense bush, such as cedar or juniper

hedge, close to or on the ground if sheltered by tall planting.

Range: Breeds from British Columbia east to Maine and south to California, Southwest, and Gulf Coast to Florida. Winters across United States north to British Columbia, Nebraska, and southern New England.

Suburban gardens as well as chaparral perfectly suit this towhee, which is not as secretive as other towhees in the West.

620 California Towhee
Pipilo crissalis

Description: 8–10″ (20–25 cm). Uniform gray-brown above and below, with buff or rust-colored undertail coverts.

Voice: Song is a series of squeaky *chips* on the same pitch, accelerating into a rapid trill. The pattern varies according to the geographical area. The call is a sharp *chink* and thin *tseeee*.

Habitat: Shady underbrush, open woods, piñon-juniper woodlands, and suburban gardens.

Nesting: 3 or 4 bluish-green eggs, lightly spotted or scrawled with blackish-brown markings, in a cup nest placed low in a bush or young tree.

Range: Resident in coastal and foothill chaparral from Oregon to southern Baja California.

The California Towhee is easily overlooked because it often forages quietly among chaparral bushes or garden cover. Although its range in the chaparral overlaps during winter with that of the Rufous-sided Towhee, this bird lives in low scrub, whereas the Rufous-sided keeps to scrub oaks and other taller "forest edge" areas.

617 Canyon Towhee
"Brown Towhee"
Pipilo fuscus

Description: 8–10″ (20–25 cm). Upperparts gray-brown, with paler buff throat, buff undertail coverts, and rusty crown. There is a dark spot in center of breast.

Voice: Song is a musical *chili-chili-chili-chili.* Call a clear *chud-up.*

Habitat: Brushy and rocky hills in arid country.

Nesting: 3 or 4 bluish-green eggs, lightly spotted or scrawled with blackish-brown markings, in a cup nest placed low in a bush or young tree.

Range: Resident from western and central Arizona, northern New Mexico, southeastern Colorado, and west-central Texas southward.

The California and Canyon towhees were long considered the same species, called the "Brown Towhee," although birders knew they had different songs and calls.

619 Abert's Towhee
Pipilo aberti

Description: 8–9″ (20–23 cm). Grayish brown above; slightly paler underparts, with buffy belly and tawny undertail. Black facial patch surrounds pale bill.

Voice: Call is a single bell-like note.

Habitat: Along arroyos in desert thickets; associated with cottonwood, willow, and mesquite, although it is also found around farms, orchards, and urban areas.

Nesting: 3 or 4 pale blue-green, scrawled eggs in a cup nest close to the ground in a bush or tree.

Range: Resident in southern and western Arizona, parts of neighboring Utah, New Mexico, and California, southward into Baja California and Sonora in Mexico.

This bird, while related to and closely resembling the California and Canyon towhees, is paler, more secretive, and has a different song. The three do not interbreed, even though their ranges overlap.

Botteri's Sparrow
Aimophila botterii

Description: 5¼–6¼" (13–16 cm). Similar to Cassin's Sparrow but more slender, browner, and less boldly streaked on upperparts, with a more conspicuous eyebrow and a slightly less conical bill.

Voice: Song consists of several short trills often introduced by a couple of *clips* and *che-licks,* but is variable.

Habitat: Open arid country such as grasslands, savannas, or desert-scrub areas.

Nesting: 2–5 white eggs. Apparently builds nest on the ground, but little else is known about its breeding habits.

Range: Breeds in southeastern Arizona and southern Texas. Winters south of U.S.–Mexico border.

Botteri's Sparrow is an entirely terrestrial bird that lives and feeds on the ground and hides in thick vegetation. It is best distinguished from the similar Cassin's Sparrow by its song and its more limited range.

447 Cassin's Sparrow
Aimophila cassinii

Description: 5¼–5¾" (13–15 cm). Fine brown streaking on *grayish-brown head and back;* dingy buff unstreaked underparts, with faint streaking on lower flanks occasionally visible. Sexes look alike. Young streaked on breast as well. See Botteri's Sparrow.

Voice: 4 loud, melodious, clear whistles, uttered from the tops of tall grass stalks and also in flight. Second note is

prolonged and quavering; third note
is lowest.

Habitat: Semidesert; arid uplands such as those
with yuccas and tall grass.

Nesting: 3 or 4 white eggs in a deep, almost
tunnel-like cup placed on the ground or
at the base of a bush or cactus.

Range: Breeds from southern Arizona and
southwestern Kansas south to southern
New Mexico and western and southern
Texas; also in Mexico. Winters in
southern part of breeding range.

This bird is very secretive except when
the male is on its breeding grounds.
There it steadily proclaims its territory
with its lark-like flight song. Rival
males often hold song duels from atop
grass stalks just 20 feet (6 meters)
apart. The Great Plains population is
believed to migrate southwestward after
breeding into the grassy deserts of
Arizona and Mexico.

---

449 Rufous-winged Sparrow
Aimophila carpalis

Description: 5–5½″ (13–14 cm). Resembles Rufous-
crowned Sparrow, but is lighter, with
finer streaking on back and 2 pronounced
"whisker" marks (instead of 1). Has
rufous crown divided by gray median
stripe; *rufous eye line and shoulder patch.*
Unstreaked whitish below, with light
wing bars and rounded tail. Juveniles
lack rufous markings and wing bars but
display double "whiskers" and finely
streaked, light brown upper breast
and sides.

Voice: Characteristic call is a sharp *seep;* song is
variable but always ends in a trill of
rapid *chips.*

Habitat: Grasslands mixed with thorn bushes,
mesquite trees, or cholla patches.

Nesting: 4 or 5 light bluish-white eggs in a cup
of coarse grass lined with finer grasses,
placed low in a bush, young mesquite,

or cactus, not well hidden. It nests at the end of summer when rains come.

Range: Resident in south-central Arizona.

An important habitat requirement for this very restricted species seems to be tall sacaton grass. Its range was formerly more widespread in Arizona, but areas heavily grazed by cattle have seriously reduced its habitat and it has all but disappeared. It lives in small, scattered populations in isolated areas, and expert guidance is necessary to locate it.

454 Rufous-crowned Sparrow
Aimophila ruficeps

Description: 5–6" (13–15 cm). *Rufous crown with darker rufous eye stripe* on gray head; conspicuous black "whisker" mark. Mantle gray with rufous-brown streaks; underparts unstreaked gray. Juveniles have buff-colored breast with faint streaking and little, if any, rufous marking. See Rufous-winged Sparrow.

Voice: Song is a rapid, pleasing jumble of notes, recalling that of the House Wren, but with "sparrow quality." Distinctive call is a down-slurred *dear dear dear* and a thin, plaintive *tseeee.*

Habitat: Open oak woodlands; treeless dry uplands with grassy vegetation and bushes, often near rocky outcrops.

Nesting: 3–5 white or slightly bluish eggs in a neat nest of plant fiber and grasses on or near the ground.

Range: Mainly resident from California, southern Arizona, and southern New Mexico east to Texas and central Oklahoma.

A secretive bird, the male Rufous-crowned Sparrow sings in the early morning from the tops of boulders in spring, but otherwise it is usually on the ground. If disturbed, it will fly to

a nearby rock for a short survey, then
return to the grass.

452 American Tree Sparrow
Spizella arborea

Description: 5½–6½″ (14–17 cm). Gray head with
rufous crown and ear stripe; streaked
brown above; 2 prominent wing bars;
plain gray below, with *dark spot in center
of breast.* Similar to Field Sparrow, but
larger and without white eye ring or
pink bill.

Voice: 1 or 2 clear notes followed by a sweet,
rapid warble. Winter feeding call a
silvery *tsee-ler.*

Habitat: Arctic willow and birch thickets; fields,
weedy woodland edges, and roadside
thickets in winter.

Nesting: 4 or 5 pale blue eggs, speckled with
brown, in a bulky, well-insulated cup of
bark strips and weed stems lined with
feathers and hair, concealed in low
tundra vegetation.

Range: Breeds from Alaska, northern
Saskatchewan, northern Manitoba, and
northern Quebec south to northern
British Columbia, central Quebec, and
Newfoundland. Winters regularly across
most of United States south to
California, Arkansas, and Carolinas.

These birds can tolerate subzero
temperatures if they get sufficient
calories from their seed diet; thus they
are able to winter in open country where
snow does not entirely cover the weeds
and grasses. They are more commonly
seen in brushy pastures at the edges of
fields and woods.

453 Chipping Sparrow
Spizella passerina

Description: 5–5½″ (13–14 cm). A small sparrow.
Upperparts are brown, streaked with
black; underparts, sides of face, and
rump are gray. Adult has *chestnut crown,
white eyebrow,* with thin black line
through eye. Young birds have streaked
crown, buff eyebrow, and duller
underparts.

Voice: Thin musical trill, all on 1 note like the
whir of a sewing machine.

Habitat: Grassy woodland edges, gardens, city
parks, brushy pastures, and lawns.

Nesting: 3–5 pale blue eggs, lightly spotted with
brown, in a solid cup of grass and stems,
almost always lined with hair, placed in
shrubbery or in a tangle of vines.

Range: Breeds throughout most of continent
from Yukon, Manitoba, and
Newfoundland south to California,
Texas, and northern Florida; also in
Mexico. Winters across southern United
States southward into Mexico.

The Chipping Sparrow's habit of lining
its nest with hair has earned it the
name "Hairbird." Formerly, it utilized
horsehair, but with the decline in the
use of horses it takes any hair available
and will even pluck strands from the
coat of a sleeping dog. Originally
inhabitants of natural clearings and
brushy forest borders, these sparrows
are now found in gardens and suburban
areas and have become familiar
songbirds. During most of the year
they feed on the ground, but in the
breeding season males always sing from
an elevated perch. Their food consists
mainly of seeds, but in summer the
adults and the young feed on insects.

440 Clay-colored Sparrow
Spizella pallida

Description: 5–5½" (13–14 cm). A small sparrow
with streaked crown and buffy
upperparts and *clear gray breast;* similar
to an immature Chipping Sparrow but
brighter, with rump brownish buff
instead of lead gray, sides of neck gray,
and buff cheek patch bordered above
and below with black. Grasshopper
Sparrow has buff underparts. See
Brewer's Sparrow.

Voice: Series of 4 or 5 toneless, insect-like
buzzes.

Habitat: Brushy grasslands and prairies.

Nesting: 3–5 pale blue eggs, spotted with dark
brown, in a bulky cup of hair-lined grass
placed in a bush or clump of weeds up
to 6' (2 m) above the ground.

Range: Breeds from north-central Canada and
Great Lakes region south to Colorado
and Michigan. Winters north to
southern Texas.

The plowing of the prairies reduced the
habitat of the Clay-colored Sparrow, but
with the clearing of forests it has
extended its range northeastward and
has recently been found nesting in
eastern Canada near Ottawa.

450 Brewer's Sparrow
Spizella breweri

Description: 5" (13 cm). Light brown upperparts
with black streaks; unmarked pale
underparts. Resembles Clay-colored
Sparrow, but has *brown crown, finely
streaked with black.* Well-defined darker
ear patch bordered by fine black eye
line and 2 parallel "whisker" marks.
Unstreaked breast; darker, finely
streaked back with buff wing bars.

Voice: Alternating trills, musical or buzzy,
often quite prolonged. Call note a soft
seep, most often given in flight.

Habitat: Sagebrush and alpine meadows.
Nesting: 3–5 brown-spotted bluish eggs in a grass nest on or near the ground.
Range: Breeds in northern Rocky Mountains of Yukon and British Columbia, and in Great Basin south to southern California and New Mexico. Winters in southwestern states. Absent from Pacific Coast.

This sparrow is unusual in having two distinct nesting populations, one in the alpine meadows of the Rocky Mountains of the Yukon and the other in the sagebrush deserts of the western United States.

438 Field Sparrow
Spizella pusilla

Description: 5¼" (13 cm). The combination of *bright pink bill, rufous cap, white eye ring,* and unstreaked buff breast distinguishes this from other sparrows.
Voice: A series of soft, plaintive notes, all on the same pitch, accelerating to a trill at the end.
Habitat: Abandoned fields and pastures overgrown with weeds, scattered bushes, and small saplings.
Nesting: 4 brown-spotted pale green eggs in a woven cup-shaped nest of grass, lined with rootlets or fine grass and set on or near the ground.
Range: Breeds from northern North Dakota, central Minnesota, northern Wisconsin and central New England south to Georgia, Mississippi, Louisiana, central Texas, and western Colorado. . Winters south to Gulf of Mexico and northeastern Mexico.

When farms and pastures become overgrown with weeds and bushes, birds such as Field Sparrows and Indigo Buntings move in and nest. Although

shyer than its close relative the
Chipping Sparrow—and thus more
difficult to observe—the Field Sparrow
may be studied at leisure when it
sings its sweet plaintive song from a
conspicuous perch atop a bush or fence
post. During fall migration it may be
seen among mixed flocks of sparrows.

---

451   **Black-chinned Sparrow**
       Spizella atrogularis

Description: 5–5½″ (13–14 cm). A gray sparrow
with *black chin and eye smudge, pink bill,
chestnut-streaked mantle, white belly.* Thin
white wing bars. Female and juveniles
lack black facial markings.

Voice: The beautiful song is a series of slurred
notes, either *swee? swee?* or *chew chew
chew,* running together into a rapid
canary-like trill.

Habitat: Low, dense chaparral on arid mountain
slopes; sagebrush.

Nesting: 3 or 4 pale blue, plain or spotted eggs
in a grass-lined cup well concealed in a
low bush.

Range: Breeds from central California, southern
Nevada, southern Utah, Arizona,
southern New Mexico, and western
Texas southward. Winters along
Mexican border.

Very little is known about the habits
of this sparrow. Singing males are
conspicuous when they sit on top of
high bushes; their song carries well
through the narrow, brushy canyons
they inhabit, but in general the species
is shy and secretive.

---

444   **Vesper Sparrow**
       Pooecetes gramineus

Description: 5–6½″ (13–17 cm). A grayish, streaked
sparrow with *white outer tail feathers,*

narrow white eye ring, and a small patch of chestnut on bend of wing.

Voice: Song a slow series of 4 clear musical notes, the last 2 higher, ending in a descending series of trills—sometimes rendered as *come-come-where-where-all-together-down-the-hill.*

Habitat: Fields, pastures, and roadsides in farming country.

Nesting: 4–6 white eggs, heavily spotted with brown, in a well-made cup of grass and rootlets concealed in grass on the ground.

Range: Breeds from British Columbia, Ontario, and Nova Scotia south to central California, Texas, Tennessee, and western North Carolina. Winters north to central California, Oklahoma, New Jersey, and Long Island.

The rich, musical song of this sparrow is a most distinctive sound on rolling farmlands. Long known as the "Bay-winged Bunting," the bird was given the pleasing if somewhat inappropriate name Vesper Sparrow by the naturalist John Burroughs, who thought the song sounded more melodious in the evening. The bird is usually found on the ground but often mounts to an exposed perch to deliver its song.

435 Lark Sparrow
Chondestes grammacus

Description: 5½–6½″ (14–17 cm). Head boldly patterned with black, chestnut, and white; streaked above; white below, with black spot in center of breast; tail black with white edges.

Voice: Alternating buzzes and melodious trills.

Habitat: Grasslands with scattered bushes and trees; open country generally in winter.

Nesting: 3–5 white eggs, heavily spotted with dark brown, in a well-made cup of grass and plant stems on the ground or in a bush.

Range: Breeds from British Columbia,

Saskatchewan, and northern Minnesota, south to California, northern Mexico, Louisiana, and Alabama. Winters from southern California to Florida and southward.

A male Lark Sparrow may be monogamous or may have two females with nests close together. He defends his nests but not a large territory. Lark Sparrows are very social, crowding together for feeding even during the nesting season.

---

433 Black-throated Sparrow
Amphispiza bilineata

Description: 5¼" (13 cm). Gray above, white below, with striking black throat and breast; 2 conspicuous white stripes on sides of head, 1 above and 1 below the eye. Sexes alike.

Voice: 2 clear notes followed by a buzzy trill.

Habitat: Deserts with cactus, mesquite, and creosote bush, and also sagebrush; partial to rocky places.

Nesting: 4 white eggs in a loosely built nest of bark strips, grass, and stems, lined with wool, hair, or feathers, and placed in a thorny bush.

Range: Breeds from northeastern California, southwestern Wyoming, and southeastern Colorado southward. Winters north to desert regions of southern United States.

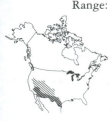

The Black-throated Sparrow is well adapted to the extremes of its habitat. Studies have shown that it has a great tolerance for heat and drought. During the hot months of late summer and early fall it maintains itself on dry seeds and drinks regularly at water holes. After the rains, these sparrows scatter into small flocks and feed on vegetation and insects, from which they derive all the moisture they need. They raise their young in the dry upland desert. This bird is thus known as the "Desert Sparrow" in the Southwest.

---

448 Sage Sparrow
Amphispiza belli

Description: 5–6" (13–15 cm). Gray above; *white belly with small black midbreast spot.* Back and sides striped, wings lighter with buff-colored feather edges that also form 2 wing bars. *Pronounced white eye ring.* Gray cheek, white eyebrow, black "mustache" stripe. Immatures browner and have white throat and fine dark streaking on buff breast and belly.

Voice: Song is a short pattern of finch-like jumbling notes, rising, then falling. Call is a soft tinkling.

Habitat: Sagebrush, chaparral, dry foothills.

Nesting: 3 or 4 bluish-white, speckled eggs in a loose cup built of sagebrush pieces, lined with fur, and well hidden in sagebrush or other scrub.

Range: Breeds from Washington south to Baja California and throughout Great Basin. Winters in small flocks in low desert of southern California, Arizona, New Mexico, and western Texas, south into Mexico.

The Sage Sparrow is secretive, moving under cover rapidly when approached, except during the spring breeding season, when males sing from a sagebrush perch to announce their territory. It has a habit of flicking its tail while hopping around on the ground.

455 Five-striped Sparrow
Amphispiza quinquestriata

Description: 5½″ (14 cm). A very dark sparrow with white stripes above and below eye and at sides and in center of throat. Bold, triangular black "whisker" mark. Rich, dark brownish gray above, rustier on back. Breast dark gray with central black stripe; sides dark gray; belly whitish.

Voice: Song variable, but similar to that of Black-throated Sparrow.

Habitat: Arid rocky hills with dense brush.

Nesting: 2–4 bluish eggs, speckled with brown, in a loose cup of grass and twigs hidden deep in the base of a shrub.

Range: Resident in southeastern Arizona.

This Mexican species was first found in the United States south of Tucson in 1957. Since that time it has been seen north of the border occasionally, sometimes feeding newly fledged young.

463, 659 Lark Bunting
Calamospiza melanocorys

Description: 6–7½″ (15–19 cm). Breeding *male black, with large white wing patch*. Female, immature, and winter male streaked sandy buff above, white below, with white eye line, faint "mustache" stripe, *white wing patch* (not always visible), and rounded, white-tipped tail feathers.

Voice: A canary-like song with loud bubbling sequences and trills interspersed with harsher notes. Call is a 2-note whistle.

Habitat: Dry plains and prairies; open sagebrush.

Nesting: 4 or 5 light blue eggs in a loose grass nest placed in a scrape with rim flush with the ground; often protected by weedy patch.

Range: Breeds on prairies of south-central Canada and central United States. Winters in Southwest and into Mexico.

The spectacular black and white male is one of the most conspicuous birds of the prairies. When giving its flight song it rises almost vertically, then drops back to its original perch.

441 Savannah Sparrow
Passerculus sandwichensis

Description: 4½–6″ (11–15 cm). Pale and streaked, yellowish eyebrow and pinkish legs. Tail notched; other grassland sparrows have shorter, more pointed tails.

Voice: High-pitched, buzzy *tsip-tsip-tsip-se-e-e-srr.*

Habitat: Fields, prairies, salt marshes, and grassy dunes.

Nesting: 4–6 pale blue-green eggs, variably spotted and speckled with dark brown, in a cup of grass lined with finer plant material and hair, placed on the ground.

Range: Breeds from Alaska east to Labrador and south to New Jersey, Missouri, and northern Mexico. Winters regularly north to southeastern Alaska and Massachusetts.

Sixteen subspecies of Savannah Sparrows are recognized, each slightly different in coloration and song. The formation of many subspecies usually indicates that the birds are faithful to their native area.

445 Baird's Sparrow
Ammodramus bairdii

Description: 5–5½″ (13–14 cm). A pale streaked sparrow. Whitish below; breast crossed by a band of narrow black streaks; *bright ocher crown stripe.*

Voice: 3 short notes followed by a musical trill on a lower pitch.

Habitat: Dry upland prairies.

Nesting: 3–5 white eggs, blotched and scrawled with dark brown, in a cup of weed stems and grass, concealed in grass or weeds on the ground.

Range: Breeds from Saskatchewan and Manitoba south to Montana and Minnesota. Winters in Texas, Arizona, and northern Mexico.

Of all grassland sparrows, Baird's is the most reluctant to fly, and when flushed, slips through the grass like a mouse. Its numbers have declined with the plowing of the prairies.

---

446   Grasshopper Sparrow
Ammodramus savannarum

Description: 4½–5" (11–13 cm). A small, chunky grassland sparrow with *clear buff breast* and scaly-looking, dark rufous upperparts. Pale central stripe on crown; short, pointed tail.

Voice: A high-pitched, insect-like *kip-kip-kip, zeeee,* usually uttered from the top of a weed stalk.

Habitat: Open grassy and weedy meadows, pastures, and plains.

Nesting: 4 or 5 white eggs, speckled with red-brown, in a cup of grass, often domed, lined with rootlets and hair and placed on the ground.

Range: Breeds from British Columbia, Manitoba, and New Hampshire south to Florida (rare), West Indies, and Mexico. Winters north to California, Texas, and North Carolina.

When flushed, this sparrow flies a short distance and drops out of sight, into tall grass. Although widespread, it is easily overlooked because of its secretive behavior and grasshopper-like song.

439 Fox Sparrow
Passerella iliaca

Description: 6–7½" (15–19 cm). A chubby, large
sparrow, either dusky brown, fox red, or
slate-colored, often so dark that no back
pattern can be discerned. *Heavy streaking
of underparts* converges at midbreast into
a large brown spot. Heavy bill with
lighter-colored lower mandible, slightly
notched *rust-colored tail,* and rounded
head outline.

Voice: A lively song that opens with 1 or more
clear whistles followed by several short
trills or *churrs.* Call a sharp *chink.*

Habitat: Thickets and edges of coniferous, mixed,
or second-growth forests or chaparral.
On islands off coast of Pacific Northwest
in chaparral-like low shrub cover.

Nesting: 4 or 5 pale green eggs, densely spotted
with red-brown, in a thick-walled cup of
leaves in grass and moss, concealed in
vegetation on or near the ground.

Range: Breeds from Aleutians and mainland
Alaska east to northern Quebec and
Maritimes and south to southern
California and Colorado. Winters south
from British Columbia and across
southern United States, and locally
farther north.

The Fox Sparrow spends much time in
the shade of shrubs and bushes,
scratching in fallen litter for insects
and seeds. It sings from a rather high
but not prominent post and nests near
the ground.

442 Song Sparrow
Melospiza melodia

Description: 5–7" (13–18 cm). Heavy brown
streaking on white underparts, with
prominent *central breast spot* (sometimes
lacking in juveniles). Subspecies show
considerable variations in size and
colors, ranging from pale sandy to dark

brown. Pumps its relatively long, rounded tail in flight.

Voice: Song consists of 3 short notes followed by a varied trill, sometimes interpreted as *Madge-Madge-Madge, put-on-your-tea-kettle-ettle-ettle.*

Habitat: Forest edges, clearings, thickets, and marshes with open grassy feeding areas; low dense scrub for nesting; tall vantage points for singing.

Nesting: 3–6 pale greenish-white, heavily marked eggs in a neat, well-hidden grassy cup nest, placed in a bush or on the ground. Lays up to 3 clutches in a season.

Range: Breeds from Aleutians and mainland Alaska east to Newfoundland and south to California, North Dakota, and Carolinas. Winters from southern Canada throughout United States to Gulf Coast and Mexico.

The Song Sparrow is one of the most widespread, diverse, and geographically variable of North American birds. The 34 recognized subspecies range from very large, dark-colored, large-billed birds on the rocky beaches of the humid Aleutian Islands to small, sandy, short-billed birds in scrub desert areas in the lower Colorado River valley. Other subspecies are found in coastal salt marshes, freshwater marshes, humid coastal belts, and dry, sagebrush-covered regions.

443 Lincoln's Sparrow
Melospiza lincolnii

Description: 5–6" (13–15 cm). Crown has 2 rusty stripes; gray eyebrow. *Buff band, finely streaked with black, across upper breast.* Similar to Song Sparrow, but more finely streaked and *shyer.*

Voice: A rich, gurgling, wren-like song rising in the middle and dropping abruptly at the end.

Habitat: Brushy bogs, willow or alder thickets; winters in woodland thickets and brushy pastures.

Nesting: 4 or 5 pale green eggs, heavily spotted with brown, in a cup of grass well concealed in forest undergrowth.

Range: Breeds from Alaska, northern Quebec, Labrador, and Newfoundland south to California, northern New Mexico, and northern New England. Winters across the southern tier of United States.

When not singing, Lincoln's Sparrow is wary and secretive. In winter a lone bird is often seen amid other sparrows that winter on the Pacific Coast and in bushy areas inland.

430 White-throated Sparrow
Zonotrichia albicollis

Description: 6–7″ (15–18 cm). Upperparts streaked, underparts clear gray. There are 2 color forms, one with black and white head stripes, the other with tan and black head stripes. Both have *sharply defined white throat patch; dark bill.* Females and young birds are duller. Similar White-crowned Sparrow lacks white throat patch, is slimmer, and has a pink bill.

Voice: Song a clear, whistled *Poor Sam Peabody, Peabody, Peabody,* or *Sweet Sweet Canada, Canada, Canada.* The latter rendition is perhaps more appropriate, since most of these birds breed in Canada.

Habitat: Brushy undergrowth in coniferous woodlands. Winters in brush woodlands, pastures, and suburban areas.

Nesting: 4 or 5 pale green eggs, heavily spotted with brown, in a cup of grass, rootlets, and moss on or near the ground in forest undergrowth.

Range: Breeds from Mackenzie, central Quebec, and Newfoundland south to North Dakota, Wisconsin, and Pennsylvania. Winters in much of eastern United

States and in small numbers in southwestern states.

This large-headed sparrow is usually found on the ground near brushy thickets. In winter it may join mixed flocks of White-crowned and Golden-crowned sparrows.

---

436 Golden-crowned Sparrow
Zonotrichia atricapilla

Description: 6–7" (15–18 cm). Similar to White-crowned Sparrow. Male's *gold crown* bordered by *wide black cap.* Dusky bill. Brown above, with unstreaked gray breast, cheek, and collar; 2 white wing bars. Fall immatures have 2 dark brown crown stripes with dusky yellowish central area and a trace of "mustache" stripe.

Voice: Song consists of 3 descending plaintive notes sounding like *oh, dear me.* Calls are *tseet* and *chink.*

Habitat: Alpine meadows and coniferous forest clearings; winters in coastal brushland and chaparral.

Nesting: 4 or 5 bluish, speckled eggs in a neat cup nest well hidden in a dense weed clump or bush.

Range: Breeds from western Alaska south through Yukon Territory to northwestern Washington. Winters from Kodiak Island and coastal Alaska south to Baja California.

One or two of these sparrows often join winter flocks of White-crowned Sparrows. They live with the flock but feed more in the shelter of bushes and visit open lawns less often.

432 White-crowned Sparrow
Zonotrichia leucophrys

Description: 6–7½" (15–19 cm). Similar to White-
throated Sparrow, but more slender,
without white throat, and generally
with a more erect posture. *Crown has
bold black and white stripes.* Upperparts
streaked, underparts clear pearly gray.
Pink bill. Young birds similar, but crown
stripes buff and dark brown, underparts
washed with dull buff.

Voice: Short series of clear whistles followed by
buzzy notes.

Habitat: Nests in dense brush, especially near
open grasslands; winters in open woods
and gardens.

Nesting: 3–5 pale green eggs, thickly spotted
with brown, in a bulky cup of bark
strips, grass, and twigs, lined with grass
and hair, on or near the ground.

Range: Breeds from Alaska and Manitoba east to
Labrador and Newfoundland, and south
in western mountains to northern New
Mexico and central California. Winters
north to southern Alaska, Idaho, Kansas,
Kentucky, and Maryland.

The northern, northwestern, and
mountain subspecies of White-crowned
Sparrows have slightly different head
patterns and songs. Song dialects vary
locally as well. In the Arctic, where the
sun does not set during the breeding
season, these sparrows sing all night
long; however, White-crowns farther
south, in the Pacific Northwest, also
sing frequently during the dark May
nights. This conspicuous and abundant
sparrow is one of the most studied birds
in the West.

429 Harris' Sparrow
Zonotrichia querula

Description: 7½" (19 cm). Adult has *black crown,
throat, and chest;* pink bill; gray face;

brown back, wings, and tail; and *white abdomen with spotted or streaked sides.* Immatures have buff faces and lack solid black crown, throat, and breast.

Voice: Series of clear, high notes followed by another series, each on a different pitch.

Habitat: Breeds in mossy bogs and scrub forests; migrates through the prairie regions; winters in dense riverside thickets, woodland borders, clearings, and brush piles.

Nesting: 3–5 pale green, brown-blotched eggs in a plant-fiber and leaf nest, lined with grass and placed on the ground at the base of a bush or in a stunted spruce tree.

Range: Breeds in northern Canada west of Hudson Bay south to northern Manitoba. Winters in interior from Iowa and Nebraska south to Texas and Louisiana. Stragglers reach Pacific Coast nearly every year.

In winter, Harris' Sparrows mix with and generally dominate flocks of the more numerous White-crowned and Golden-crowned sparrows. When a flock is disturbed it often flies up to the top of a nearby bush. This sparrow is shyer and warier in its northern breeding territory.

428, 636 Dark-eyed Junco
including "Oregon Junco,"
"Slate-colored Junco,"
"White-winged Junco,"
and "Gray-headed Junco"
Junco hyemalis

Description: 5–6¼" (13–16 cm). This species shows much geographic variation in color. Typically, male of western population ("Oregon Junco") has *black hood, chestnut mantle,* white underparts with buff sides. Eastern male ("Slate-colored Junco") is *dark slate-gray on head,* upper breast, *flanks, and upperparts,* with white lower breast and belly. Both forms have pink bill and dark gray tail with *white outer tail feathers.* The pine forests of the Black Hills in western South Dakota and eastern Montana have an isolated population ("White-winged Junco") similar to the eastern form but with 2 white wing bars and extensive white outer tail feathers. Birds of the Southwest ("Gray-headed Juncos") are gray overall, with a reddish-brown back. Female "Oregon Junco" has gray hood; females of all forms less colorful.

Voice: Ringing metallic trill on the same pitch. Members of a flock may spread out widely, keeping in contact by constantly calling *tsick* or *tchet.* Also a soft buzzy *trill* in flight.

Habitat: Openings and edges of coniferous and mixed woods; in winter, roadsides, parks, suburban gardens.

Nesting: 3–6 pale bluish or greenish eggs, with variegated blotches concentrated at the larger end, in a compact nest of rootlets, shreds of bark, twigs, and mosses, lined with grasses and hair, placed on the ground, protected by a rock ledge, a mud bank, tufts of weeds, or a fallen log.

Range: Breeds from Alaska east across Canada to Newfoundland, south to mountains in Mexico and Georgia. Winters south to Gulf Coast and northern Mexico.

This lively territorial bird is a ground dweller and feeds on seeds and small fruits in the open. It also moves through the lower branches of trees and seeks shelter in tangles of shrubs.

635 **Yellow-eyed Junco**
Junco phaeonotus

Description: 5½–6½" (14–17 cm). Unique *bright yellow-orange eye* and black lores. Bill has *dark upper mandible* and *pale lower mandible.* Gray above, with *bright rusty mantle* and white outer tail feathers. Underparts lighter. Walks rather than hops. "Gray-headed" form of Dark-eyed Junco is similar, but has dark eye, all-pink bill, and hops.

Voice: Song is more highly patterned than that of the Dark-eyed Junco. One representation is *chip-chip, seedle-seedle, chee-chee-chee,* although it is variable.

Habitat: Coniferous forests; pine-oak woods.

Nesting: 3 or 4 bluish-white, spotted eggs in a slight cup nest of small rootlets and fine grass lined with horsehair, on the ground under the protection of a log, a stump, or grass tufts, or in a low tree.

Range: Resident in mountains of southeastern Arizona and southwestern New Mexico.

This junco is slower and more deliberate in its movements than the Dark-eyed Junco; it walks, rather than hops, on the forest floor.

---

457 McCown's Longspur
Calcarius mccownii

Description: 5¾–6" (15 cm). Sparrow-sized. Breeding male streaked above, with black crown, whitish face, and black "mustache"; gray below with bold black band across breast. Female and winter male duller and more streaked; best identified by tail pattern, which is largely white, with central pair of tail feathers black and with narrow black band at tip.

Voice: Dry rattle; also a clear sweet warble given during a fluttering flight with wings raised high over back.

Habitat: Arid plains.

Nesting: 3 or 4 pale green eggs, spotted with dark brown and black, in a hollow scrape lined with fine grass and hair, on open ground.

Range: Breeds from Alberta and southwestern Manitoba south to Dakotas, Wyoming, and Colorado. Winters from Nebraska and Colorado southward.

This longspur nests in higher and more arid short-grass plains than does the Chestnut-collared Longspur, and so has been less affected by the plowing of the prairies. These birds so dislike moisture that in wet seasons they may abandon areas where they normally are abundant. In summer they feed chiefly on grasshoppers, but in fall and winter, when they gather in large flocks with other longspurs and with Horned Larks, they prefer seeds. In winter plumage they can be difficult to distinguish from the other longspurs, but close up they are easily identified by their stouter bill.

---

427 Lapland Longspur
Calcarius lapponicus

Description: 6–7″ (15–18 cm). Sparrow-sized. Breeding male has black face, crown, and upper breast; chestnut nape; and is streaked above and white below, with streaked flanks. Female and winter male dull and without bold pattern; best identified by largely black tail with white outermost feathers. Smith's Longspur has a similar tail, but is always buff above and below, and usually shows a small white wing patch.

Voice: Rattling call. Flight song is sweet and bubbling.

Habitat: Arctic tundra; winters in open windswept fields and on grassy coastal dunes.

Nesting: 4 or 5 pale, olive green eggs, heavily spotted with brown and purple, in a grass-lined hollow in the ground, concealed under a clump of grass or a dwarf birch.

Range: Breeds from Aleutians, Alaska, and Arctic islands to northern Quebec. Winters regularly throughout northern states to California, Texas, and New York. Also in northern Eurasia.

Both the Lapland Longspur and the Snow Bunting have a long hind toenail, which may aid them in walking since these birds run or walk rather than hop, as other finches normally do. The most common small bird in the vast expanses of sedgy, moist tundra, the Lapland Longspur is bold in breeding territories, but wintering flocks are wary.

458   Smith's Longspur
Calcarius pictus

Description: 5¾–6½" (15–17 cm). Sparrow-sized. Breeding male streaked dark brown and buff above, clear warm buff below; bold black and white head pattern. Small white wing patch, most evident in flight; tail black, with white outer feathers. Females and winter males duller and without head pattern, but always more buff-colored than other longspurs.

Voice: Dry rattle, like a finger running along the teeth of a comb.

Habitat: Arctic tundra and forest edges; winters on open grassy plains.

Nesting: 3–5 pale brown eggs, spotted with darker brown, in a grass-walled hollow lined with plant down and feathers and concealed under a clump of grass or a dwarf willow.

Range: Breeds from northern Alaska across northern Canada to Hudson Bay. Winters from Nebraska south to Texas.

This beautiful longspur breeds at the tree line. Unlike the Lapland Longspur, which is truly a bird of open tundra, Smith's does not have a flight song but marks its territory by singing from the top of a small tree or hillock.

434 Chestnut-collared Longspur
Calcarius ornatus

Description: 5½–6½″ (14–17 cm). Sparrow-sized.
Similar to Lapland Longspur, but
breeding male has *wholly black underparts*
and some white on its face. Tail of
female and winter male similar to that
of Lapland Longspur but with *more white
at sides.*

Voice: Soft, sweet, and tumbling, somewhat
like that of the Western Meadowlark;
also a hard *ji-jiv* in flight.

Habitat: Dry elevated prairies and short-grass
plains.

Nesting: 3–5 pale green eggs, spotted with
brown and lavender, in a grass-lined
hollow under a clump of grass.

Range: Breeds from Alberta and Manitoba
south to Minnesota and Wyoming.
Winters from Colorado and Kansas
south to Texas and northern Mexico.

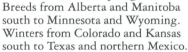

This is the common longspur of the
prairies. In spring males are conspicuous
as they give their flight song and,
descending, perch on a prominent
plant or hillock.

464, 651 Snow Bunting
Plectrophenax nivalis

Description: 6–7¼″ (15–18 cm). Sparrow-sized.
Breeding male has black back with
much white on head, underparts, wings,
and tail. Female similar, but duller.
Winter birds have brown on crown and
upperparts, duller underparts, but still
show much white in wings.

Voice: Clear whistle or low buzzy note. Song is
a sweet warble.

Habitat: Arctic tundra; winters on windswept
grasslands and beaches.

Nesting: 4–6 white eggs, with red-brown spots
in a ring around the larger end, placed
in a cup of grass lined with fur and

feathers and concealed among rocks or in tundra vegetation.

Range: Breeds from Aleutians, northern Alaska and Arctic islands south to northern Quebec. Winters regularly across southern Canada and upper tier of states to Oregon and Pennsylvania. Also in Eurasia.

This circumpolar bird, often called "Snowflake," breeds farther north than almost any other land bird. In severe winters large flocks descend to our northern states, where they favor the most barren places. They occasionally can be found at beach parking lots in the dead of winter searching for weed seeds.

650 McKay's Bunting
Plectrophenax hyperboreus

Description: 7″ (18 cm). Similar to, but whiter than, the widespread Snow Bunting. Breeding male *snow white,* except for *dark bill, black tips of primaries, and tips of central tail feathers.* Female has darkish areas on back but *pure white head.* In winter, both sexes have light brown areas on head and back, more so on female.

Voice: A loud warbling song reminiscent of that of the goldfinch. Call is a musical rattle.

Habitat: Tundra; coastal shores in winter.

Nesting: 3 or 4 light green, brown-dotted eggs in a grass-lined scrape on the ground in a rock crevice.

Range: Breeds on Hall and Saint Matthew islands in Bering Sea. Winters east to coast of western Alaska and Nunivak Island.

McKay's Buntings may represent the last survivors of a population of large white buntings that lived north of the ice sheet of the last ice age. The more common Snow Bunting occupies adjacent breeding territory on all surrounding Arctic mainlands, but McKay's seems to hold its ground on its tiny, remote nesting islands.

FAMILY EMBERIZIDAE
SUBFAMILY ICTERINAE
New World Blackbirds and Their Allies

95 species: This exclusively American family contains such familiar species as the Bobolink, the meadowlarks, orioles, grackles, and cowbirds, as well as the many blackbirds. Twenty-three species breed in North America. Members of this family are diverse in appearance, nesting habits, and habitat. The orioles are master nest builders, weaving bag-like, hanging nests; the Bobolink and meadowlarks are ground-nesters; and the cowbirds are nest parasites.

459, 658 Bobolink
Dolichonyx oryzivorus

Description: 6–8" (15–20 cm). Breeding male largely black, with *white rump* and back, *dull yellow nape.* Female and winter male rich buff-yellow, streaked on back and crown. *Short, finch-like bill.* Female Red-winged Blackbird is darker, less buffy, and has longer bill.

Voice: Flight song is a series of joyous, bubbling, tumbling, gurgling phrases with each note on a different pitch. Call a soft *pink,* often heard on migration.

Habitat: Prairies and meadows; marshes during migration.

Nesting: 4–7 gray eggs, spotted with red-brown and purple, in a poorly made but well-concealed cup of grass, stems, and rootlets, placed on the ground in a field.

Range: Breeds from British Columbia, Manitoba, and Newfoundland south to northern California, Colorado, and

Pennsylvania. Winters in southern South America.

A polygamous bird, the male Bobolink courts with the basic blackbird stance: head down, neck feathers ruffled, tail fanned, and wings arched downward, displaying his prominent white shoulder patches. In fall Bobolinks join with other blackbirds and are often seen in rice fields or other agricultural areas.

466, 662   Red-winged Blackbird
Agelaius phoeniceus

Description: 7–9½" (18–24 cm). Smaller than a robin. Male is black with *bright red shoulder patches.* Female and young are heavily streaked with dusky brown. See Tricolored Blackbird.

Voice: A rich, musical *o-ka-leeee!*

Habitat: Marshes, swamps, and wet and dry meadows; pastures.

Nesting: 3–5 pale blue eggs, spotted and scrawled with dark brown and purple, in a well-made cup of marsh grass or reeds, attached to growing marsh vegetation or built in a bush in a marsh.

Range: Breeds from Alaska east across Canada to Newfoundland and south to northern Baja California, central Mexico, Gulf Coast, and Florida. Winters regularly across United States north to British Columbia, Great Lakes, and Pennsylvania.

Red-wings form the nucleus of the huge flocks of mixed blackbird species that feed in fields, pastures, and marshes from early fall to spring. Although blackbirds are often considered pests because they consume grain in cultivated fields, farmers benefit because the birds consume harmful insects during the nesting season.

663 Tricolored Blackbird
Agelaius tricolor

Description: 7½–9″ (19–23 cm). Similar to Red-winged Blackbird. Male is black but with *dark red "epaulets," very broadly margined with white.* Female much darker than the brownish-dusky female Red-winged Blackbird and lacks streaks on rump and belly.

Voice: Calls rather similar to those of the Red-wing, but song is more nasal, less musical.

Habitat: Cattail marshes, marshy meadows, and rangelands.

Nesting: 3 or 4 greenish eggs, covered with brown scrawls, in a nest woven onto reed stems or blackberry brambles. It is more colonial than the Red-winged Blackbird, and its territories are crowded, with nests often less than 5 or 6′ (1½–2 m) apart. Colonies in California's Central Valley contain thousands of birds.

Range: Breeds from southern Oregon southward throughout most of California. Winters north to northern California.

During the late-summer drought, grasshoppers abound and support the wandering hordes of Tricolored Blackbirds; in winter rice fields and marshes provide food. Until recently, some colonies were estimated to contain one to two million birds; today the total population is down to about 750,000, due to the draining of marshes.

535 Eastern Meadowlark
Sturnella magna

Description: 9–11″ (23–28 cm). Robin-sized. A stocky, brown-streaked bird with *white-edged tail; bright yellow throat and breast, black V crossing breast.* Western Meadowlark is very similar, but paler

above, yellow of throat extends onto
cheeks; best distinguished by voice.

Voice: Clear, mellow whistle, *see-you, see-yeeeer;*
also a loud rattling alarm note.

Habitat: Meadows, pastures, and prairies;
generally in open country during
migration.

Nesting: 3–7 white eggs, spotted with brown
and dull lavender, in a partly domed
structure of grass concealed in a
depression in a meadow.

Range: Breeds from southeastern Canada south
throughout eastern United States, west
to Nebraska, Texas, and Arizona.
Winters in most of breeding range.

The Eastern and Western meadowlarks
are so similar that at a distance only
their songs and calls distinguish them.
Moreover, the two may even learn each
other's song where their ranges overlap.
Meadowlarks are shaped like starlings.
In flight they keep their wings stiff,
typically fluttering them a few times
and then sailing.

534 Western Meadowlark
Sturnella neglecta

Description: 8½–11″ (22–28 cm). Robin-sized.
Streaked brown above, bright yellow
below, with a bold black V on breast.
Very similar to Eastern Meadowlark,
but *upperparts paler, and yellow of throat
extends onto cheeks.* Best identified
by voice.

Voice: Rich flute-like jumble of gurgling
notes, usually descending the scale; very
different from Eastern Meadowlark's
series of simple, plaintive whistles.

Habitat: Meadows, plains, and prairies.

Nesting: 3–7 white eggs, with dark brown and
purple spots, in a domed cup of grass and
weed stems concealed in grass or weeds.

Range: Breeds from British Columbia,
Manitoba, northern Michigan, and
northwestern Ohio south to Missouri,

central Texas, and northern Mexico. Has spread eastward in recent years. Winters in much of breeding range north to southern British Columbia, Utah, and Arkansas.

Its bright colors, fearless behavior, abundance, and above all its loud, cheerful song make the Western Meadowlark one of the best known of western birds.

469, 537 Yellow-headed Blackbird
Xanthocephalus xanthocephalus

Description: 8–11″ (20–28 cm). Robin-sized. Male much larger than female. *Male is bright yellow on head, neck and upper breast, blackish elsewhere,* with conspicuous white markings on wings. Female duller and lighter; yellow on chest, throat, and face; no white wing marks.

Voice: Harsh, incessant *oka-wee-wee* and *kruck* calls, coming from many individuals in a colony, blend into a loud, wavering chorus.

Habitat: Freshwater marshes.

Nesting: 3–5 brown-speckled whitish eggs in a basket woven around several strong stalks. Nests in colonies.

Range: Breeds from central British Columbia, northern Alberta, and Wisconsin south to southern California, northern New Mexico, and Illinois. Winters mainly in Southwest and Mexico.

The surrounding water provides safety for this bird's breeding colonies but it often limits available nesting space and causes crowding. One study found about 25 nests in an area of 15 square feet (1.5 square meters). In a colony, some males are always in display flight, with head lowered, feet and tail dropped, wings beating slowly. Others quarrel with neighbors about boundaries. Approaching predators are mobbed

by clouds of Yellow-heads, with
neighboring Red-wings joining in.

468, 664 Rusty Blackbird
Euphagus carolinus

Description: 9″ (23 cm). In spring males are black,
with a bluish and greenish iridescence;
females are dark gray. In fall they are
much more rust-brown, especially head,
breast, and back. *Conspicuous pale yellow
eyes in both sexes.*

Voice: Like the squeaks of a rusty gate; call
note a sharp *check*.

Habitat: Boreal bogs in the breeding season;
wooded swamps and damp woods with
pools during migration.

Nesting: 4 or 5 blue-green eggs, with brown
blotches, in a bulky stick nest lined
with grass, moss, and lichens set in a
dense shrub or low tree near or over
water.

Range: Breeds from Alaska and across northern
Canada to southern Canada, northern
New York, and northern New England.
Winters in eastern half of United States
south to Gulf Coast.

In the breeding season, the Rusty is the
only blackbird in most of its range and
is easily identified. In autumn, the rusty
tinge to the mantle and light eyes of
both sexes distinguish this species from
the similar Brewer's Blackbird, which is
abundant in most of the West.

467, 665 Brewer's Blackbird
Euphagus cyanocephalus

Description: 8–10″ (20–25 cm). Robin-sized. Male
is solid black with purplish-blue
iridescent head and yellow eyes. Female
is gray with dark eyes. Similar to Rusty
Blackbird, but male Rusty has faint
green reflections on head; female Rusty

has yellow eyes and jerks its head as
it walks.

Voice: Gurgles, squawks, and whistles.

Habitat: Prairies, fields, and farmyards.

Nesting: 3–5 gray eggs, with dark brown spots,
in a nest of coarse grass and twigs
reinforced with mud and lined with fine
grass and hair, placed on the ground or
in a tree. Nests in loose colonies of up
to 30 pairs.

Range: Breeds from British Columbia,
Manitoba, and Ontario south to
southern California, New Mexico, and
Texas. Winters north to British
Columbia and Carolinas.

Following man and his cattle, the
Brewer's first pushed north into
Washington around the turn of the
century. Later it traveled northeastward,
reaching Wisconsin, and it is still
spreading in Ontario, Canada. A very
social species, it mixes not only with its
own kind but with other species such
as the Red-winged Blackbird and the
Brown-headed Cowbird.

511, 669 Great-tailed Grackle
Quiscalus mexicanus

Description: Male, 16–17″ (41–43 cm); female,
12–13″ (30–33 cm). Tail very long and
keel-shaped. Male black, with *iridescent
purple on back and breast.* Female smaller,
brown with a pale breast. *Eyes always
yellow.* Common Grackle is smaller;
female lacks pale breast.

Voice: Variety of whistles, clucks, and hissing
notes.

Habitat: Farmlands with scattered trees and
thickets.

Nesting: 3 or 4 pale blue eggs, spotted and
scrawled with brown and purple, placed
in a bulky nest of sticks, grass, and mud
in a tree. Nests in loose colonies.

Range: Resident from California, Colorado,

Kansas, and western Louisiana southward.

Like magpies, these noisy, opportunistic birds feed on a great variety of food: fruits, grain, insects, garbage, and offal. They are usually bold but become cautious and wary when in danger. The polygamous male is more cunning and shyer than the female; he often remains safe in a treetop until all his females are feeding on the ground. He will then join them.

510, 668   Common Grackle
Quiscalus quiscula

Description: 12″ (30 cm). Jay-sized. *Long, wedge-shaped tail* displaying a longitudinal ridge or keel when in flight. Appears all black at a distance but is actually highly iridescent, with colors varying from blue to purple to green to bronze, depending on the light. Bright yellow eyes. Female duller and somewhat smaller than male.

Voice: Clucks; high-pitched rising screech, like a rusty hinge.

Habitat: Lawns, parks, fields, open woodlands.

Nesting: 5 pale blue eggs, with black scrawls, in a bulky stick nest lined with grass, placed anywhere from low in a bush to high in a tree. Nests partly in colonies, most often in tall evergreens.

Range: Breeds from northern Alberta, central Ontario, and Newfoundland south to Gulf Coast states east of Rockies, but expanding into Idaho and Washington in Northwest. Winters north to Kansas, southern Great Lakes region, and New England.

The Common Grackle is an opportunistic feeder, varying an insect and grain diet with both the eggs and the young of small birds. During courtship, it jerks its body, lowers wing, tail, and head, and squeals. It also exhibits its long, conspicuous tail in display flight. This species is smaller and lacks the strong sex differences of the Great-tailed Grackle.

666, 667 Bronzed Cowbird
Molothrus aeneus

Description: 8½″ (22 cm). Male bronze-black with bluish-black wings and tail. Prominent red eye can be seen at close range. Female similar but duller. Brown-headed Cowbird smaller, with a distinctive brown head.

Voice: Wheezy and guttural whistling notes and various squeaks and squeals.

Habitat: Pastures, roadside thickets, ranches, open country generally; also parks and orchards.

Nesting: 1–3 blue-green eggs laid in other birds' nests, particularly nests of orioles, tanagers, flycatchers, buntings, and grosbeaks, more rarely thrashers and thrushes.

Range: Breeds in southern Arizona, New Mexico, and south-central Texas. Withdraws southward from much of Arizona during winter.

A strongly social bird, the Bronzed Cowbird associates with blackbirds as well as its own species and roosts in huge flocks, often in city parks. During the courtship display, the male raises the ruff on his neck; he also leaves the ground in front of the female and hovers one or two feet in the air.

508, 509 Brown-headed Cowbird
Molothrus ater

Description: 6–8″ (15–20 cm). Male black with glossy brown head; female plain gray-brown. Both have a finch-like bill.

Voice: Squeaky gurgle. Call is *check* or a rattle.
Habitat: Agricultural land, fields, woodland edges, and suburban areas.
Nesting: 4 or 5 white eggs, lightly speckled with brown, laid one at a time in the nests of other songbirds.
Range: Breeds from British Columbia, central Saskatchewan, central Ontario, Quebec, and Newfoundland southward throughout United States except extreme Southeast and Florida. Winters in central and southern part of breeding range as well as in Florida.

Cowbirds are promiscuous; no pair bond exists. In late spring the female cowbird and several suitors move into the woods. The males sit upright on treetops, uttering sharp whistles, while the female searches for nests in which to lay her eggs. Upon choosing a nest, she removes one egg of the host's clutch, and deposits one of her own in its place. The young cowbird is so much larger than the young of the host that it crowds and starves them out.

526 Hooded Oriole
Icterus cucullatus

Description: 7–7¾" (18–20 cm). Male *orange,* with black wings crossed with 2 white bars, black tail, and *black throat and upper breast.* Bill thin and curved; tail long and graduated. Female olive-gray above, olive-yellow below, with 2 white wing bars. Yearling male looks like female, but has black throat.
Voice: Series of whistles, chatters, and warbles.
Habitat: Originally preferred streamside growth, but has adapted to tree plantations, city parks, and suburban areas with palm or eucalyptus trees and shrubbery.
Nesting: 3–5 white eggs, blotched with dark brown and purple, in a basket of plant fibers with the entrance at the top,

hanging from palm fronds or the branches of eucalyptus or other trees.

Range: Breeds from central California, Nevada, central Arizona, southern New Mexico, and southern Texas southward. A few winter in southern California and southern Texas.

This oriole is easy to observe as it moves slowly through the taller trees in search of insects. Its nest is often parasitized by cowbirds, the aggressive young cowbird usually receiving the most food and starving the oriole nestlings.

527, 562 **Northern Oriole**
including "Baltimore Oriole"
and "Bullock's Oriole"
Icterus galbula

Description: 7–8½" (18–22 cm). Eastern male, formerly "Baltimore Oriole," has black head, back, wings, and tail; orange breast, rump, and shoulder patch. Eastern female olive-brown, with dull yellow-orange underparts and 2 dull white wing bars. Western male, formerly "Bullock's Oriole," is similar to eastern male but has orange cheeks and eyebrow and large white wing patch. Western female has whitish underparts.

Voice: Clear and flute-like whistled single or double notes in short, distinct phrases with much individual variation.

Habitat: Deciduous woodlands and shade trees. Before the tree's decline, the American elm was a favorite nesting site for the eastern bird.

Nesting: 4–6 grayish eggs, spotted and scrawled with dark brown and black. Nest a well-woven pendant bag of plant fibers, bark, and string, suspended from the tip of a branch.

Range: Breeds from British Columbia, Saskatchewan, and Nova Scotia south throughout most of United States. Winters in tropics.

For many decades the western population of this bird ("Bullock's Oriole") was thought to be a separate species from the eastern population, which was called the "Baltimore Oriole." When trees were planted on the Great Plains, the two forms extended their ranges and met. Despite the differences in their appearance, it was found that they interbreed; most birds in the central plains are hybrids, so the birds were combined into a single species. Now, it seems that in some places the birds are choosing mates of their own type; some time soon these birds may be considered separate species again.

538, 588 Scott's Oriole
Icterus parisorum

Description: 7½–8¼" (19–21 cm). Male has *black head, mantle, throat, and central breast area; bright lemon-yellow underparts,* rump, and outer tail feathers. Wings, central tail feathers, and wide terminal band are also black. Male has 1 slender white wing bar. Female lime-yellow with dusky streaks on back; 2 wing bars. First-year male resembles female, but with small, faint black throat and bib.

Voice: The song, a series of rising and falling flute-like notes, resembles that of a Western Meadowlark. Call is a harsh *chuck.*

Habitat: Breeds in the piñon-juniper woodlands of semidesert areas; in yucca trees or palms in deserts; or in sycamores or cottonwoods in canyons.

Nesting: 3–5 bluish-white, irregularly spotted eggs in a grassy hanging pouch nest, often skillfully hidden among dry yucca fronds, pines, or live oaks.

Range: Breeds in southern California, southern Nevada, Utah, Arizona, New Mexico, and western Texas. Winters mainly south of U.S.–Mexico border.

Besides gleaning insects, this fine songster feeds on available fruits, including those of cacti, and has been observed taking nectar—a habit practiced by many tropical orioles. Like most orioles, it skillfully climbs drooping branches and twigs as well as delicate yucca flowers.

FAMILY FRINGILLIDAE
Finches

145 species: Worldwide. Sixteen species breed in North America. These are small to medium-sized birds with conical bills and often brightly colored plumage. Some species wear various shades of red, others are yellow. Outside the nesting season they are sociable and often travel in flocks. Many nest in northern areas, entering the United States in large numbers only when their usual food supply fails them.

505 Gray-crowned Rosy-Finch
Leucosticte tephrocotis

Description: 5¾–6¾" (15–17 cm). *Dark brown back and underparts;* black forehead; gray nape and crown; *pink shoulder and rump. Face gray* in *coastal* birds, *brown* in *interior populations.* Female is similar, but less colorful.

Voice: Flying flocks give harsh *cheep, cheep* notes.

Habitat: Alpine tundra and high snowfields; winters in nearby lowlands.

Nesting: 3–5 white eggs in a bulky nest placed in a rock cavity.

Range: Breeds from Alaska to California. Descends to lower elevations near breeding areas in winter.

During breeding, both the male and the female Gray-crowned Rosy-Finch grow a pair of "gular pouches," opening from

the floor of the mouth, which they use to carry food to the young. This species feeds mainly on minute alpine plant seeds and insects wind-borne from lower elevations. The Gray-crowned Rosy-Finch is found farther to the west than the similar Brown-capped Rosy-Finch and Black Rosy-Finch. The ancestors of the rosy-finches came from Asia. The mosaic distribution of forms in the West may result from the splitting of one population during glacial periods, or from multiple invasions from Asia.

---

507   Black Rosy-Finch
Leucosticte atrata

Description: 5½–6½" (14–17 cm). *Male is dark blackish-brown,* with *conspicuous gray cap,* black forehead, and much pink on belly, rump, wings, and tail. Female is browner, showing some pink, and may not have gray cap. Bill yellowish in both sexes.

Voice: A variety of low *cheep* notes are used in various situations: as a contact call in flight and in proclaiming an occupied nesting territory.

Habitat: Alpine tundra and meadows; winters in nearby lowlands.

Nesting: 3–5 white eggs in a cup nest placed in a hole in a vertical cliff.

Range: Breeds in Rocky Mountains of southwestern Montana, Idaho, Wyoming, northeastern Nevada, and northern Utah. Winters south to northern Arizona and New Mexico.

In winter, when mixed flocks of rosy-finches roam the highlands of the Great Basin, Blacks and Gray-crowns are seen roosting together in caves or abandoned mine shafts, in barns, or under bridges.

506 Brown-capped Rosy-Finch
Leucosticte australis

Description: 5¾–6½" (15–17 cm). Mostly *light brown, without gray crown patch* of closely related Gray-crowned Rosy-Finch and Black Rosy-Finch. Rump, wing, and belly pinkish rose. Female chiefly brown. Both sexes have blackish bills.

Voice: A series of low *cheep* notes are uttered to maintain contact in the flock. In the mating season the male gives a similar song during a long, circular, undulating flight.

Habitat: Alpine tundra and meadows; winters in nearby lowlands.

Nesting: 3–5 white eggs in a cup nest in a rock crevice or on a hidden, covered ledge.

Range: Resident in southern Rocky Mountains from southeastern Wyoming to northern New Mexico. Descends to lower elevations near breeding areas in winter.

Winter flocks are noisy with the sound of twittering; upon alighting, these finches hop over the ground looking for seeds. Trusting birds, they let observers come close.

493, 513 Pine Grosbeak
Pinicola enucleator

Description: 8–10" (20–25 cm). A large plump finch. Stubby, strongly curved black bill. *Male has dull rose-red body,* with dark streaking on back, dark wings with 2 white wing bars, and dusky, notched tail. *Juvenile male dull pinkish red* on head and rump, with gray body. *Females* similar to first-year males in pattern, with *dull mustard* head and rump markings.

Voice: A 3-note whistle similar to that of Greater Yellowlegs.

Habitat: Coniferous forests.

Nesting: 2–5 pale blue-green, blotched eggs in a bulky nest of grasses, rootlets, and moss lined with hair; nest placed low in a coniferous tree, usually no more than about 10–12′ (3–4 m) from the ground.

Range: Breeds from Alaska east to Newfoundland and Nova Scotia, and south in western mountains to California and Arizona. Winters south to Dakotas and New York, occasionally farther. Also in Eurasia.

During snowy winters these grosbeaks can be located in scattered open forests by the feeble calls that keep the flock together. They settle in a tree and feed, snapping off buds or seeking the pits in fruit, until sated or disturbed. When food is scarce, they may descend from mountains into woods at sea level.

504, 515   Purple Finch
Carpodacus purpureus

Description: 5½–6½″ (14–17 cm). Larger and stockier than House Finch, but smaller than Cassin's and darker than both. *Dusky rose-red of male* extends from upperparts to *breast and flanks,* brightest at *crown and rump.* Off-white below, mantle streaked with brown, wings and notched tail brown. *Female has pronounced light stripe behind eye, dark stripe on jaw,* and more heavily streaked breast than female House or Cassin's finches.

Voice: Rich musical warble. Call a distinctive *tick* in flight.

Habitat: Mixed and coniferous woodlands; ornamental conifers in gardens.

Nesting: 4 or 5 blue-green eggs, spotted at the larger end with dark brown, in a well-made cup of grasses and twigs, often lined with hair, placed in a conifer.

Range: Breeds from British Columbia east to Newfoundland, southward in western mountains to California and from eastern Minnesota east to West Virginia. Winters south to U.S.–Mexico border.

During the breeding season, pairs are
territorial, the male displaying in front
of the female with his loud warbling
song. After the clutch is raised, they
may be seen in large flocks visiting
orchards, parks, and other woodlands.

502, 516 Cassin's Finch
Carpodacus cassinii

Description: 6–6½" (15–17 cm). Larger than both
House and Purple finches. Male's breast
coloration *paler rose-red* than that of
Purple Finch; brown-streaked nape and
mantle make rosy crown and rump,
especially *crown,* appear more *brilliant.*
Unstreaked flanks and belly pale pink
to whitish. Female resembles female
Purple Finch, but more finely streaked
above and below, with less distinct eye
line and jaw stripe. House Finch smaller
and slimmer; male redder, with brown-
streaked belly.

Voice: Song is a series of warbles, similar to
the Purple Finch's but flutier and more
varied. Call note, a high *pwee-de-lip,*
is diagnostic.

Habitat: Open conifer stands at high elevations.

Nesting: 4 or 5 bluish-green eggs, with dark
brownish spots, in a cup nest of twigs
and rootlets, in a conifer.

Range: Breeds from southwestern Canada south
to southern California, Arizona, and
New Mexico. Visits lowlands during
winter.

The closely related Cassin's, House,
and Purple finches are each found in
different altitudes and habitats; thus
there is no competition among them. In
California the House Finch is common
in arid, hot plains, deserts, and foothills,
nesting widely in chaparral and oak
woodlands. In the montane forest belt,
the Purple Finch is found at the edges of
coniferous stands and the shady oak

growth of canyons. Cassin's is found higher up in firs and yellow pines.

503, 517 House Finch
Carpodacus mexicanus

Description: 5–6″ (13–15 cm). Sparrow-sized. Most adult *males bright red on crown, breast, and rump,* but less extensively so than male Cassin's and Purple finches. Female has plain, unstriped head and heavy streaking on light underside. Immature males less highly colored, often orangish or yellowish on head and breast.

Voice: A *chirp* call like that of a young House Sparrow. The song is an extensive series of warbling notes ending in a *zeee,* canary-like but without the musical trills and rolls. Sings from a high tree, antenna, or similar post for prolonged periods. Call a *chirp.*

Habitat: Chaparral, deserts, and orchards, as well as coastal valleys that were formerly forested with redwood, cedar, or Douglas fir but have now become suburban.

Nesting: 3–5 bluish, lightly streaked or spotted eggs, with each pair breeding 2–4 times a summer; tightly woven, compact nest set anywhere from a bush to a building.

Range: Resident throughout West, from southern Canada to southern Mexico, and east to Nebraska. Introduced and now widespread in eastern North America.

House Finches are omnivorous, gleaning insect pests and, in winter, grass and weed seeds. Garden-bred birds join large field flocks during the fall, often feeding in farmers' fields, and may become agricultural pests.

525 Red Crossbill
Loxia curvirostra

Description:	5¼–6½" (13–17 cm). Sparrow-sized. *Mandibles crossed* at tips. Male dusky brick red. Female gray tinged with dull green, brightest on rump. White-winged Crossbill has 2 white wing bars.
Voice:	Song *chipa-chipa-chipa, chee-chee-chee-chee;* also a sharp *kip-kip-kip.*
Habitat:	Coniferous forests; visits ornamental evergreens in winter.
Nesting:	3 or 4 pale blue-green eggs, lightly spotted with brown, in a shallow saucer of bark strips, grass, and roots lined with moss and plant down, placed near the end of a conifer branch.
Range:	Breeds from southern Alaska, Manitoba, Quebec, and Newfoundland, south in West to northern Nicaragua, in eastern United States to Wisconsin and North Carolina (mountains). Winters irregularly south to Gulf Coast. Also in Eurasia.

The bill of these unusual birds is specialized for opening pine cones. Holding the cone with one foot, the bird inserts its closed bill between the cone and the scales, pries the scales apart by opening its bill, and extracts the seed with its flexible tongue. Because of its dependence on pine seeds, the Red Crossbill is an erratic and nomadic species. When the cone supply fails, these birds gather in flocks and may wander far from their normal haunts. They may breed almost anywhere, and at any season, so long as the food supply is adequate.

524 White-winged Crossbill
Loxia leucoptera

Description:	6–6½" (15–17 cm). Size of a largish sparrow. *Mandibles crossed* at tips. Male

raspberry-pink; females grayer, without pink. Both sexes have 2 white wing bars.

Voice: Call like that of the Red Crossbill, but a softer *chiff-chiff-chiff*. Song a series of sweet canary-like warbles and trills.

Habitat: Coniferous forests.

Nesting: 2–4 pale blue eggs, spotted with dark brown, laid in a shallow saucer of bark strips, grass, and roots lined with moss and plant down, placed near the end of a conifer branch.

Range: Breeds from Alaska and northern Quebec south to Newfoundland and British Columbia. In winter, south to Carolinas and Oregon. Also in Eurasia.

The White-winged Crossbill with its smaller, slimmer bill is more dependent upon spruce cones than pines, but like the Red Crossbill it wanders widely and irregularly in search of cones and may breed at any month of the year. During its wanderings it feeds on a great variety of other seeds or fruits and even insects. At such times it may be seen in association with Red Crossbills.

512 Common Redpoll
Carduelis flammea

Description: 5–5½″ (13–14 cm). Smaller than a sparrow. Pale, brown-streaked, with *bright red cap* and black chin. Male has pink breast.

Voice: Twittering trill; call a soft rattle.

Habitat: Tundra and dwarf arctic birch in summer; brushy pastures, open thickets, and weedy fields in winter.

Nesting: 4–6 pale green eggs, spotted with red-brown, in a well-made cup of grass, moss, and twigs lined with plant down and placed in a low willow or birch.

Range: Breeds from Alaska and northern Quebec south to British Columbia, Newfoundland, and Magdalen Islands. Winters irregularly south to California,

Oklahoma, and Carolinas. Also in Eurasia.

These are lively birds, extremely social and constantly moving; even when resting at night members of the flock fidget and twitter. During the long Arctic night, redpolls sleep in snow tunnels to keep warm. They are able to hang upside down—like chickadees—and pry the birch seed from hanging catkins. They are somewhat nomadic; where the birch supply is good they settle in numbers, but may move away with their fledglings and attempt a second brood elsewhere if they find another area with ample food supply.

Hoary Redpoll
Carduelis hornemanni

Description: 4½–5½″ (11–14 cm). Smaller than a sparrow. Similar to the Common Redpoll but slightly paler, with a smaller bill and an unstreaked rump and undertail coverts.

Voice: Series of metallic *chips* given in flight; soft twittering calls when feeding on ground. Calls are sharper than those of Common Redpoll.

Habitat: Weedy pastures and roadsides in winter, tundra in summer.

Nesting: 5 or 6 pale blue eggs, lightly spotted with brown, in a feather-lined cup of grass and shreds of bark, concealed under a rock or a clump of tundra vegetation.

Range: Breeds along Arctic coasts, wandering southward in winter to much of Canada and northern United States.

The Hoary Redpoll generally breeds and winters farther north than the related Common Redpoll, only occasionally reaching the northern United States. In areas where their ranges overlap, the two birds do not interbreed, although

some experts consider them two forms
of a single species.

500 Pine Siskin
Carduelis pinus

Description: 4½–5″ (11–13 cm). A dark, streaked
finch with notched tail and small
patches of yellow in wings and tail.
Usually seen in flocks, which have a
distinctive flight pattern: the birds
alternately bunch up and then disperse
in undulating flight.

Voice: Distinctive rising, *bzzzzzt*. Song like a
hoarse goldfinch.

Habitat: Coniferous and mixed woodlands, alder
thickets, and brushy pastures.

Nesting: 3 or 4 pale green eggs, lightly speckled
with dark brown and black, in a shallow
saucer of bark, twigs, and moss lined
with plant down and feathers and
placed in a conifer.

Range: Breeds from southern Alaska,
Mackenzie, Quebec, and Newfoundland
south to California, Arizona, New
Mexico, Texas, Great Lakes region,
and northern New England. In winter
wanders southward throughout
United States.

Siskins, redpolls, and goldfinches are a
closely related group of seed specialists.
All have short, conical beaks; short,
slightly forked tails; bright wing
markings; and "nervous" behavior. They
feed in flocks, which, after breeding,
may contain hundreds of birds. They
are all acrobats, often hanging upside
down, like titmice and chickadees,
plucking seeds from hanging seedpods
and cones.

556 Lesser Goldfinch
Carduelis psaltria

Description: 3½–4" (9–10 cm). Two forms of males: *black-backed* and *green-backed;* both have black crown, white markings on black wing and tail, with *bright yellow underparts.* Nonbreeding black-backed male turns greenish, but both races *retain black cap.* Female is similar to American Goldfinch but smaller, with *dark rump.* Immature is similar to female, but with greener underparts.

Voice: Song a rapid medley of twittering notes. Calls include a plaintive *tee-yee?* or *cheeo?*

Habitat: Oak savannas, woodlands, suburban gardens.

Nesting: 4–5 pale blue eggs in a twiggy nest in a bush or low tree.

Range: Resident from Washington, Oregon, and northern Nevada east to northern Colorado and Texas, and south to beyond U.S.–Mexico border. Black-backed males are found from northern Colorado southward through Texas and westward to Utah and Arizona. Green-backed birds occur from Utah westward to Columbia River and southward into Mexico.

Lesser Goldfinches feed on dandelion seeds and raise their young on soft unripe seeds. They adjust the time and place of their breeding to the presence of this staple food. Their Old World cousins, the Siskins, goldfinches, serins, and canaries, have been kept as cage birds for centuries, the males singing incessantly all year except during the molt period.

533, 627 Lawrence's Goldfinch
Carduelis lawrencei

Description: 4–4½" (10–11 cm). Male has *black cap* and face; pale pink bill; *gray nape, cheek, and mantle; yellow* breast, lower back, and rump; white undersides and belly.

Female lacks black facial markings.
Both sexes have dark wings and tail
with bright yellow wing bars. In winter,
the blacks and yellows are paler.
Juveniles are streaked with buff or
light brown on back.

Voice: Song a hurried jumble of melodious and
scratchy notes, often incorporating both
its own call notes and those of other
species. Flight note, often revealing the
bird's presence high overhead, is a high
tinkle, the first note higher.

Habitat: Dry grassy slopes with weed patches,
chaparral, and open woodlands.

Nesting: 4 or 5 bluish-white eggs in a tightly
woven cup nest in a low tree or bush.

Range: Breeds in central and southern
California, west of Sierra Nevada and
south into Baja California. Winters
south and east to extreme western
Texas.

Goldfinches are late nesters, waiting
until plants and weeds have grown,
bloomed, and gone to seed so the soft
fresh seeds can be fed to the young.
Lawrence's nests late in May. It breeds
erratically; one year many may be found
in an area, the next, when the seed crop
fails, few may be seen. After breeding,
they feed in flocks on the abundant
chamise chaparral. They appear even in
the driest washes and slopes, as long as
they have access to water.

532, 557   American Goldfinch
Carduelis tristis

Description: 4½–5″ (11–13 cm). Smaller than a
sparrow. Breeding male *bright yellow*
with a white rump, *black forehead, white
edges on black wings and tail,* and yellow
at bend of wing. Female and winter
male duller and grayer with black
wings, tail, and white wing bars. Travels
in flocks; undulating flight.

Voice: Bright *per-chick-o-ree,* also rendered as

potato-chips, delivered in flight and coinciding with each undulation.

Habitat: Brushy thickets, weedy grasslands, and nearby trees.

Nesting: 4 or 5 pale blue eggs in a well-made cup of grass, bark strips, and plant down, placed in the upright fork of a small sapling or a shrub.

Range: Breeds from southern British Columbia east to Newfoundland and south to California, Utah, southern Colorado, central Oklahoma, Arkansas, and Carolinas. Winters in much of United States.

American Goldfinches migrate in compact flocks with an erratic, "roller coaster" flight. Studies of their winter migrations from Vancouver, British Columbia, and Washington State have shown that these birds hesitate before flying across water. In one instance, some returned to the mainland. One by one, the whole flock followed suit. Ten minutes later they returned to the waterside, chattering noisily. Many birds then continued on. Those remaining repeatedly took wing only to veer off and again return to land. Finally, a sharp drop in temperature forced the birds to complete their migration.

498, 539 Evening Grosbeak
Coccothraustes vespertinus

Description: 7½–8½" (19–22 cm). Starling-sized, stocky finch with a very large, *pale greenish or yellowish conical bill.* Male has brown head shading to *yellow on lower back,* rump, and underparts; bright yellow forehead and eyebrow; *bold white wing patches.* Female similar but grayer.

Voice: Song a series of short, musical whistles. Call note similar to the chirp of the House Sparrow but louder and more ringing.

Habitat: Nests in coniferous forests; visits
deciduous woodlands and suburban
areas in winter.

Nesting: 3 or 4 pale blue-green eggs, lightly
speckled with dark brown, gray, and
olive, in a shallow, loose cup of twigs
lined with rootlets and placed in
a conifer.

Range: Breeds from British Columbia east to
Nova Scotia and south to northern
New England, Minnesota, Mexico (in
mountains), and California. Winters
south to southern California, Texas, and
South Carolina.

This grosbeak formerly bred no farther
east than Minnesota, but more food
available at bird feeders may have
enabled more birds to survive the
winter, and the species now breeds east
to the Atlantic. Like most of the
northern finches, however, these birds
are more numerous in some years than
in others. In winter they feed in flocks
mainly on the seeds of box elder or on
sunflower seeds at feeders. In spring
the outer coating of the bill peels off,
exposing the blue-green color beneath.

FAMILY PASSERIDAE
Old World Sparrows

37 species: Widespread in the Old
World, especially in Africa. Represented
in North America by only two species,
both of them introduced. The Eurasian
Tree Sparrow is confined to the region
around Saint Louis, Missouri, but the
House Sparrow is abundant from coast
to coast. These are finch-like birds, with
stout conical bills and short legs. They
are highly gregarious and often roost in
large flocks.

431, 437 House Sparrow
Passer domesticus

Description: 5–6½" (13–17 cm). Male has *black throat,* white cheeks, and chestnut nape; gray crown and rump. Female and young are streaked dull brown above, dingy white below, with pale eyebrow.

Voice: Shrill, monotonous, noisy chirping.

Habitat: Cities, towns, and agricultural areas.

Nesting: 5 or 6 white eggs, lightly speckled with brown, in a loose mass of grass, feathers, strips of paper, string, and similar debris placed in a man-made or natural cavity. 2 or 3 broods a season. Sometimes builds a globular nest in a tree.

Range: Introduced and resident throughout temperate North America. Native to Eurasia and North Africa, and introduced on all continents and on many islands.

Within a short time after their introduction, these sparrows adapt to the local environment. Thus the sparrows of the rainy climate of Vancouver, British Columbia, are plump, dark birds, whereas those inhabiting Death Valley, California, are slim, pale, sand-colored birds. These changes took less than 60 years, and influence our ideas about the speed of evolutionary change in birds.

Part III
Appendices

LIST OF ACCIDENTAL SPECIES

Accidental species are rare birds that do not breed regularly or occur annually in North America, but whose presence has been accepted by the American Ornithologists' Union. The following list includes only those species that have been either collected or photographed in the area covered by this guide at least once and that have been accepted by the American Ornithologists' Union; species that have been observed but never collected or photographed are not included. The list is broken down into the three following categories, based on the regions the birds come from:

Oceanic: Coming mainly from the southern oceans, and usually but not always driven to our shores by tropical storms.

Asian: Coming mainly from western Europe or eastern Asia, and occurring mainly along the East Coast and in Alaska.

Mexican: Species that wander north from Mexico or Central America and occur mainly in the southwestern states.

Oceanic   Wandering Albatross, *Diomedea exulans*
Short-tailed Albatross, *Diomedea albatrus*
Shy Albatross, *Diomedia cauta*
Streaked Shearwater, *Calonectris leucomelas*
Wedge-tailed Shearwater, *Puffinus pacificus*

Little Shearwater, *Puffinus assimilis*
Mottled Petrel, *Pterodroma inexpectata*
Solander's Petrel, *Pterodroma solandri*
Murphy's Petrel, *Pterodroma ultima*
Cook's Petrel, *Pterodroma cookii*
Stejneger's Petrel, *Pterodroma longirostris*
Band-rumped Storm-Petrel,
Oceanodroma castro
Wedge-rumped Storm-Petrel,
Oceanodroma tethys
Red-tailed Tropicbird, *Phaethon
rubricauda*
White-tailed Tropicbird, *Phaeton
lepturus*

Asian   Chinese Egret, *Egretta eulophotes*
Yellow Bittern, *Ixobrychus sinensis*
Greylag Goose, Anser anser
Whooper Swan, *Cygnus cygnus*
Bean Goose, *Anser fabalis*
Baikal Teal, *Anas formosa*
Falcated Teal, *Anas falcata*
Spot-billed Duck, *Anas poecilorhyncha*
Garganey, *Anas querquedula*
Common Pochard, *Aythya ferina*
Smew, *Mergellus albellus*
White-tailed Eagle, *Haliaeetus albicilla*
Steller's Sea-Eagle, *Haliaeetus pelagicus*
Northern Hobby, *Falco subbuteo*
Eurasian Kestrel, *Falco tinnunculus*
European Coot, *Fulica atra*
Common Crane, *Grus grus*
Little Ringed Plover, *Charadrius dubius*
Mongolian Plover, *Charadrius mongolus*
Black-winged Stilt, *Himantopus
himantopus*
Oriental Pratincole, *Pratincola
maldivarum*
Common Greenshank, *Tringa nebularia*
Marsh Sandpiper, *Tringa stagnatilis*
Spotted Redshank, *Tringa erythropus*
Common Redshank, *Tringa nebulari*a
Wood Sandpiper, *Tringa glareola*
Green Sandpiper, *Tringa ochropus*
Gray-tailed Tattler, *Heteroscelus brevipes*
Common Sandpiper, *Actitis hypoleucos*
Terek Sandpiper, *Xenus cinereus*
Far Eastern Curlew, *Numenius
madagascariensis*

Little Curlew, *Numenius minutus*
Black-tailed Godwit, *Limosa limosa*
Great Knot, *Calidris tenuirostris*
Rufous-necked Stint, *Califris ruficollis*
Little Stint, *Calidris minuta*
Temminck's Stint, *Calidris temminckii*
Long-toed Stint, *Calidris subminuta*
Spoon-billed Sandpiper, *Eurynorhynchus pygmeus*
Broad-billed Sandpiper, *Limicola falcinellus*
Jack Snipe, *Lymnocryptes minimus*
Slaty-backed Gull, *Larus schistisagus*
Black-tailed Gull, *Larus crassirostris*
White-winged Tern, *Chlidonias leucopterus*
Eurasian Collared-Dove, *Streptopelia decaocto*
Oriental Turtle-Dove, *Strepotpelia orientalis*
Common Cuckoo, *Cuculus canorus*
Oriental Cuckoo, *Cuculus saturatus*
Oriental Scops-Owl, *Otus sunia*
Jungle Nightjar, *Caprimulgus indicus*
White-collared Swift, *Streptoprocne zonaris*
White-throated Needle-tail, *Hirundapus caudacutus*
Common Swift, *Apus apus*
Fork-tailed Swift, *Apus pacificus*
Hoopoe, *Upupa epops*
Eurasian Wryneck, *Jynx torquilla*
Great Spotted Woodpecker, *Dendrocopus major*
Common House-Martin, *Delichon urbica*
Eurasian Jackdaw, *Corvus monedula*
Great Tit, *Parus major*
Middendorff's Grasshopper Warbler, *Locustella ochotensis*
Lanceolated Warbler, *Locustella lanceolata*
Wood Warbler, *Phylloscopus sibilatrix*
Dusky Warbler, *Phylloscopus fuscatus*
Mugimaki Flycatcher, *Ficedula mugimaki*
Narcissus Flycatcher, *Ficedula narcissina*
Red-breasted Flycatcher, *Ficedula parva*
Siberian Flycatcher, *Muscicapa siberica*
Gray-spotted Flycatcher, *Muscicapa griseisticta*

Asian Brown Flycatcher, *Muscicapa dauurica*
Siberian Rubythroat, *Luscinia calliope*
Siberian Blue Robin, *Luscinia cyane*
Red-flanked Bluetail, *Tarsiger cyanurus*
Stonechat, *Saxicola torquata*
Eyebrowed Thrush, *Turdus obscurus*
Dusky Thrush, *Turdus naumanni*
Fieldfare, *Turdus pilaris*
Siberian Accentor, *Prunella montanella*
Gray Wagtail, *Motacilla cinerea*
Black-backed Wagtail, *Motacilla lugens*
Brown Tree-Pipit, *Anthus trivialis*
Olive Tree-Pipit, *Anthus hodgsoni*
Pechora Pipit, *Anthus gustavi*
Brown Shrike, *Lanius cristatus*
Little Bunting, *Emberiza pusilla*
Rustic Bunting, *Emberiza rustica*
Yellow-breasted Bunting, *Emberiza aureola*
Gray Bunting, *Emberiza variablis*
Pallas' Reed-Bunting, *Emberiza pallasi*
Common Reed-Bunting, *Emberiza schoeniclus*
Brambling, *Fringilla montifringilla*
Hawfinch, *Coccothraustes coccothraustes*
Eurasian Bullfinch, *Pyrrhula pyrrhula*
Oriental Greenfinch, *Carduelis sinica*
Common Rosefinch, *Carpodacus erythrinus*

Mexican Ruddy Ground-Dove, *Columbia talpacoti*
Thick-billed Parrot, *Rhynchopsitta pachyrhyncha*
Green Violet-ear, *Colibri thalassina*
Berylline Hummingbird, *Amazilia beryllina*
Plain-capped Starthroat, *Heliomaster constantii*
Bumblebee Hummingbird, *Atthis heloisa*
Xantus' Hummingbird, *Hylocharis xantusii*
Nutting's Flycatcher, *Myiarchus nuttingi*
San Blas Jay, *Cissilopha sanblasiana*
Gray Silky-Flycatcher, *Ptilogonys cinereus*
Rufous-backed Robin, *Turdus rufopalliatus*
Aztec Thrush, *Ridgwayia pinicola*

Flame-colored Tanager, *Piranga bidentata*
Yellow Grosbeak, *Pheucticus chrysopeplus*
Crescent-chested Warbler, *Parula superciliosa*
Fan-tailed Warbler, *Euthlypis lachrymosa*
Slate-throated Redstart, *Myioborus miniatus*
Rufous-capped Warbler, *Basileuterus rufifrons*
Scarlet-backed Oriole, *Icterus pustulatus*
Black-vented Oriole, *Icterus wagleri*
Worthen's Sparrow, *Spizella wortheni*

BIRD-WATCHING

Bird-watching, or birding, is a hobby that can be as inexpensive or as costly as one wishes. One can even begin without purchasing anything except a field guide, relying on eyes and on memory. But sooner or later a birder will want to buy that most basic piece of equipment, a pair of binoculars.

In selecting binoculars, a major consideration is weight; a lightweight pair is better for hours of continuous use than a heavier one. Choose a pair with an adjustable right eyepiece and central focusing; this will permit you to adjust the focus quickly from a nearby sparrow to a distant soaring hawk. In general, the best magnification will depend on how steadily you can hold your field glasses. Seven- or eight-power glasses will provide adequate magnification, but after years of experience, and if you are very steady-handed, you may be able to use a pair of ten-power glasses. To ensure adequate light, the objective (front) lens should have a diameter in millimeters of at least five times the magnification. Thus, a seven-power binocular should have an objective lens diameter of not less than 35 millimeters (7×35), an eight-power pair should have an objective diameter of 40 millimeters (8×40), and so on. A pair of binoculars with an objective wider

than this ratio will let in more light.
This may be useful in a dimly lit forest,
but on an open, strongly illuminated
beach there may be too much glare to
allow you to see the birds well. Then,
too, glasses with wider objectives are
generally heavier than those of the same
power with a smaller objective. The best
advice on binoculars is to buy the best
you can afford. Binoculars suitable for
brief use at the opera or racetrack may
cause eyestrain and fatigue when used
for hours at a time under the varying
conditions of an all-day field trip.

Most experienced birders also purchase a
telescope, which, if mounted on a sturdy
tripod or gunstock, is an excellent way
to view and identify distant shorebirds
and water birds. Many of the
considerations that apply to binoculars
apply here. Choose a good telescope,
one that will last for years. A suitable
telescope may have adjustable eyepieces,
offering various magnifications such
as 15-, 20-, 40-, and 60-power. At
higher magnifications—above about
30-power—one may have trouble with
vibrations caused by the wind or with
distortion of the image by shimmering
heat waves.

Another useful piece of equipment is
a pocket notebook. It is wise to jot
down a description of unfamiliar birds
immediately after observing them. Not
only will this enable you to remember
critical field marks, but it will train
you to notice small but important
details that might otherwise be
overlooked. You might also record
other observations, such as numbers
of birds seen, dates of their arrival
and departure, peak numbers of
migrants, and interesting behavioral
or ecological details.

Sooner or later you may want to
preserve these notes in a more
permanent form, using larger, bound
notebooks or a system of file cards.
Notes can be grouped according to date,

locality, or species, or by whatever arrangement best suits your needs and purposes. A gradually increasing store of notes is a valuable record not only of past field trips, but of your own steadily growing knowledge of birds.

GLOSSARY

Accidental A species that has appeared in a given area only a very few times and whose normal range is in another area. Also used as an adjective.

Auriculars Feathers covering the ear opening and the area immediately around it; often distinctively colored. Also called ear coverts.

Boreal forest The belt of coniferous forest stretching from Alaska to Newfoundland and across northern Eurasia; also called the taiga.

Breeding plumage A coat of feathers worn by many birds during the breeding season; often more brightly colored than the winter plumage.

Casual A species that has appeared in a given area somewhat more frequently than an accidental, but whose normal range is in another area. Also used as an adjective.

Cere A fleshy, featherless area surrounding the nostrils of hawks, falcons, pigeons, and a few other groups of birds.

Circumpolar Of or inhabiting the Arctic (or Antarctic) regions in both the Eastern and Western hemispheres.

Clutch A set of eggs laid by one bird.

Colonial Nesting in groups (or colonies) rather than in isolated pairs.

Cosmopolitan Worldwide in distribution, or at least occurring in all continents except Antarctica.

Coverts Small feathers that overlie or cover the bases of the large flight feathers of the wings and tail, or that cover a particular area or structure (e.g., ear coverts).

Crest A tuft of elongated feathers on the crown or nape.

Crown The top of the head.

Cryptic Serving to conceal.

Eclipse plumage A dull-colored coat of feathers acquired immediately after the breeding season by most ducks and worn for a few weeks; it is followed in males by a more brightly colored plumage.

Ecosystem An ecological unit consisting of interrelationships between animals, plants, and the physical environment.

Eyebrow A conspicuous stripe of color above, but not through, the eye.

Eye stripe A stripe that runs horizontally from the base of the bill through the eye; also called eye line.

Field mark A characteristic of color, pattern, or structure useful in distinguishing a species in the field.

Flight feathers The long stiff feathers of the wings and tail, used during flight. The flight feathers of the wings are divided into primaries, secondaries, and tertials. See also Rectrix.

Frontal shield A fleshy, featherless, and often brightly colored area on the forehead of moorhens and a few other birds.

Gorget A patch of brilliantly colored feathers on the chin or throat of certain birds, such as male hummingbirds.

Immature A young bird no longer under parental care but not yet wearing an adult plumage.

Juvenile (*adj.* juvenal) A bird wearing its first coat of feathers, often molted into a first-winter plumage within a few weeks after the bird leaves the nest.

Lek A place where males of some species of birds, such as certain grouse and the European Ruff, gather and perform courtship displays in a group, rather than courting females individually and in isolation from one another; females visit a lek to mate but generally build their nests elsewhere.

Local Occurring in relatively small, restricted areas within the range, rather than commonly and widespread throughout the range. Birds whose occurrence is local usually have highly specialized habitat requirements.

Lore (*pl.* lores) The small area between the eye and the base of the bill, sometimes distinctively colored.

Mandible One of the two parts of a bird's bill, termed the upper mandible and the lower mandible.

Mantle A term used to describe the back of a bird together with the upper surface of the wings when these areas are of one color.

Molt The process of shedding and replacing feathers; usually occurs after breeding but before the autumn migration. In many species there is another molt in spring or late winter.

Morph One or more distinctive plumages seen in certain species; see Phase.

Mustache　A colored streak running from the base of the bill back along the side of the throat.

Naris (*pl.*nares)　The external nostril; in birds located near the base of the upper mandible.

Pelagic　Of or inhabiting the open ocean.

Phase　One or more distinctive plumages seen in certain species, such as the Snow Goose and certain hawks and owls, irrespective of age, sex, or season. Also called a morph.

Plume　A feather that is larger, longer, or of a different color than the feathers around it, generally used in displays.

Primaries　The outermost and longest flight feathers on a bird's wing. Primaries vary in number from 9 to 11 per wing, but always occur in a fixed number in any particular species.

Race　A geographical population of a species that is different in appearance from other populations; a subspecies.

Range　The geographical area or areas normally inhabited by a species.

Raptor　A bird of prey.

Rectrix (*pl.* rectrices)　One of the long flight feathers of the tail.

Resident　Remaining in one place all year; nonmigratory.

Riparian　Of or inhabiting the banks of rivers or streams.

Scapulars　A group of feathers along the side of the back and overlapping the folded wing.

Scrape　A shallow depression on the ground made by a bird to serve as a nest.

Secondaries The large flight feathers located in a series along the rear edge of the wing, immediately inward from the primaries.

Shoulder The point where the wing meets the body, as in the Red-shouldered Hawk. The term is also loosely applied to the bend of the wing when this area is distinctively colored, as it is in the Red-winged Blackbird.

Spatulate Spoon-shaped or shovel-shaped; used to describe the bill of certain birds, such as the Northern Shoveler.

Speculum A distinctively colored area on the wing of a bird, especially the metallic patch on the secondaries of some ducks.

Subalpine Of or pertaining to the stunted forest or other vegetation immediately below the treeless, barren alpine zone on high mountains.

Subspecies A geographical population of a species that is different in appearance from other populations of that species; also called a race.

Taiga The belt of coniferous forest covering the northern part of North America and Eurasia; also called the boreal forest.

Tarsus The lower, usually featherless part of a bird's leg.

Territory An area defended by the male, by both members of a pair, or by an unmated bird.

Tertials The innermost flight feathers on a bird's wing, immediately adjacent to the body. They are often regarded simply as the innermost secondaries. Also called tertiaries.

Tules Certain species of large bulrushes abundant in California.

Window A translucent area in the wing of certain

birds such as the Red-shouldered Hawk, visible from below in flight.

Wing bar A crosswise stripe on the folded wing, formed by the tips of the wing coverts.

Wing stripe A conspicuous stripe running the length of the open wing.

Winter plumage A coat of feathers worn by many birds during the nonbreeding season, and often less brightly colored than the breeding plumage.

CONSERVATION STATUS OF WESTERN BIRDS

Federal laws in the United States and Canada prohibit the taking or molesting of birds or their nests, eggs, or young, other than those species that damage property or agriculture or that are covered by hunting regulations. In addition, rare or endangered species are protected by special measures and by bird management agencies. Increasingly, states are also passing conservation measures and are studying the status of their bird populations with the aim of protecting this precious natural heritage. In our species accounts we have noted those birds that have a special conservation status. But it should be understood that the status of birds changes and that they may be differently categorized by different authorities.

Unprotected Birds Two introduced species, the European Starling and the House Sparrow, have become so numerous and widespread that they are not protected in the United States or Canada. A few other species, including the Rock Dove and members of the blackbird family, may damage crops or other birds and are therefore not fully protected in some areas.

Game Birds   These may be hunted during an open season regulated by the various states and provinces. Information on limitations, licenses and so forth can be secured from local agencies.

Threatened or Endangered Birds   The populations of the following birds are threatened or endangered. Birders should take care not to disturb these birds or their nests or to damage their environments.

Brown Pelican, *Pelecanus occidentalis*
Wood Stork, *Mycteria americana*
California Condor, *Gymnogyps californianus*
Bald Eagle, *Haliaeetus leucocephalus*
Crested Caracara, *Caracara plancus*
Peregrine Falcon, *Falco peregrinus*
Whooping Crane, *Grus americana*
Eskimo Curlew, *Numenius borealis*
Least Tern, *Sterna antillarum*
"Northern" Spotted Owl, *Strix occidentalis*
California Gnatcatcher, *Polioptila californica*

PICTURE CREDITS

The numbers in parentheses are plate numbers. Some photographers have pictures under agency names, which appear in boldface. Photographers hold copyrights to their works.

Robert P. Abrams (73)

Ron Austing (70, 109, 110, 138, 140, 302, 304, 337, 347, 375, 496, 530, 569, 582, 593)

Robert A. Behrstock (318, 366)

Steve Bentsen (292, 350, 352, 435, 601)

Nick Bergkessel (271)

Fred Bruemmer (29, 32, 35, 41, 89, 282)

Gay Bumgarner (313, 504, 557, 615)

Robert Campbell (316, 652)

John Cancalosi (256)

W.S. Clark (346)

Eliot Cohen (269)

Cornell Laboratory of Ornithology
Lang Elliott (369)
J. Hough (235)
Keith Walton (491)
Ken Wilson (173)

Sharon Cummings (62, 121, 267, 310, 608, 662)

Rob Curtis/The Early Birder (33, 48, 49, 145, 209, 260, 331, 333, 367, 397, 399, 442, 444, 473, 486, 519, 522, 564, 579, 594, 595, 655, 675)

Mike Danzenbaker (23, 46, 59, 60, 63, 72, 136, 139, 193, 229, 244, 257, 261, 266, 295, 370, 372, 416, 446, 447, 461, 501, 529, 555, 609, 633, 634, 647, 663)

Susan Day (510)

Dembinsky Photo Associates
Barbara Gerlach (459)
John Gerlach (82, 236, 441)
Doug Locke (644)
Anthony Mercieca (30, 418)
Gary Meszaros (24)

270, 283, 286, 287, 324,
332, 343, 344, 363, 380,
382, 387, 388, 389, 390,
407, 410, 429, 477, 493,
498, 500, 502, 505, 516,
531, 538, 540, 545, 556,
565, 590, 597, 600, 603,
604, 605, 614, 616, 653,
668)

VIREO
Nick and Nora Bowers
(631)
R.K. Bowers (462, 629)
R.J. Chandler (262)
B. Chudleish (214)
H. Clarke (172)
Harry Darrow (36)
J. Hoffman (76)
H.C. Kyllingstad (232)
R.L. Pitman (74)
R. Ridgely (598)
D. Roby (135)
M. Strange (359)
Doug Wechsler (96)
Dale & Marian
Zimmerman (640)

Mark F. Wallner (123,
151, 202, 203, 206, 258,
452, 495)

Larry West (17, 204, 342,
398, 506, 610, 673)

Brian K. Wheeler (330,
349)

Gregory J. Winston (279)

Jim Yuskavitch (400)

Dale & Marian
Zimmerman (21, 143,
210, 218, 234, 326, 335,
402, 403, 413, 414, 443,
511, 566, 572, 574, 575,
576, 577, 588, 589, 602,
625, 667)

Paul Zimmerman (298,
351, 361, 392)

Tim Zurowski (22, 31,
57, 61, 64, 65, 66, 86,
90, 92, 93, 100, 101,
113, 115, 154, 205, 208,
220, 227, 246, 252, 265,
290, 317, 364, 365, 376,
411, 425, 428, 436, 439,
456, 460, 464, 515, 525,
528, 537, 554, 571, 599,
607, 612, 613, 638, 665,
674)

INDEX

Numbers in boldface type refer to plate
numbers. Numbers in italic refer to
page numbers.

NATIONAL AUDUBON SOCIETY
FIELD GUIDE SERIES

Also available in this unique all-color,
all-photographic format:

**African Wildlife • Birds *(Eastern Region)* • Butterflies
• Fishes, Whales, and Dolphins • Fossils • Insects
and Spiders • Mammals • Mushrooms • Night Sky
• Reptiles and Amphibians • Rocks and Minerals •
Seashells • Seashore Creatures • Trees *(Eastern
Region)* • Trees *(Western Region)* • Tropical Marine
Fishes • Weather • Wildflowers *(Eastern Region)* •
Wildflowers *(Western Region)***

Prepared and produced by
Chanticleer Press, Inc.

Founding Publisher: Paul Steiner
Publisher: Andrew Stewart

Staff for this book:

Managing Editor: Edie Locke
Text Editor: Amy K. Hughes
Copyeditor: Kathryn Clark
Editorial Assistant: Peggy Grohskopf
Art Director: Amanda Wilson
Production Manager: Deirdre Duggan Ventry
Photo Editor: Lori J. Hogan
Publishing Assistant: Kelly Beekman
Consultant: Wayne R. Petersen
Drawings and Silhouettes: Paul Singer, Douglas Pratt
Range Maps and Map of North America: Paul Singer

Original series design by Massimo Vignelli

All editorial inquiries should be addressed to:
Chanticleer Press
665 Broadway, Suite 1001
New York, NY 10012
www.eNature.com

To purchase this book or other National Audubon Society
illustrated nature books, please contact:
Alfred A. Knopf
299 Park Avenue
New York, NY 10171
(800) 733-3000
www.randomhouse.com